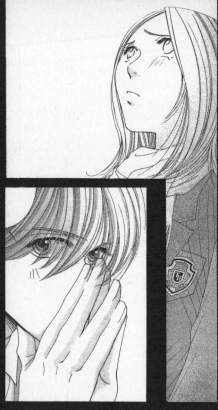
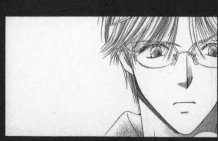

Hot Gimmick

vol.1
MIKI
AIHARA

HOT GIMMICK
CONTENTS

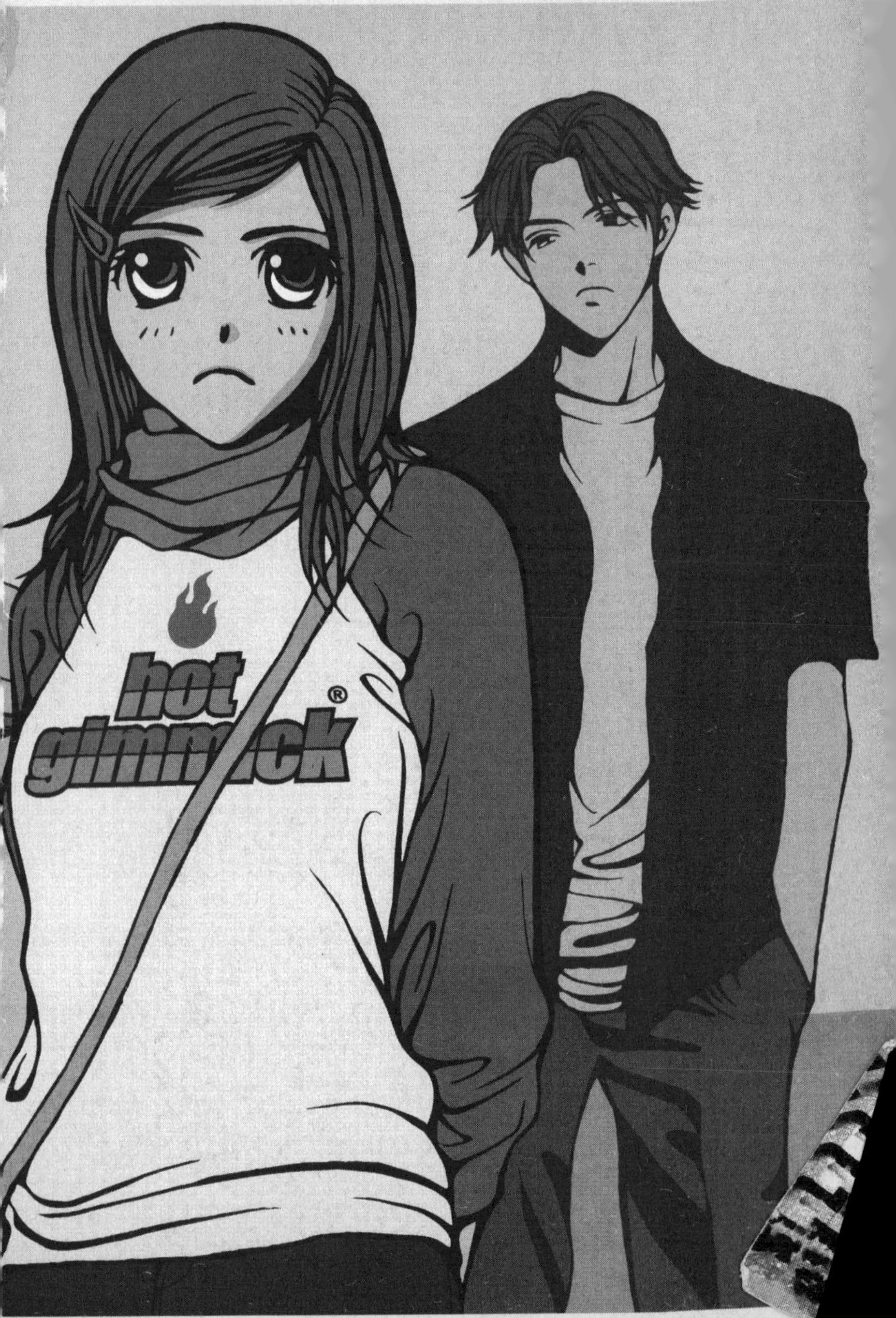
hot

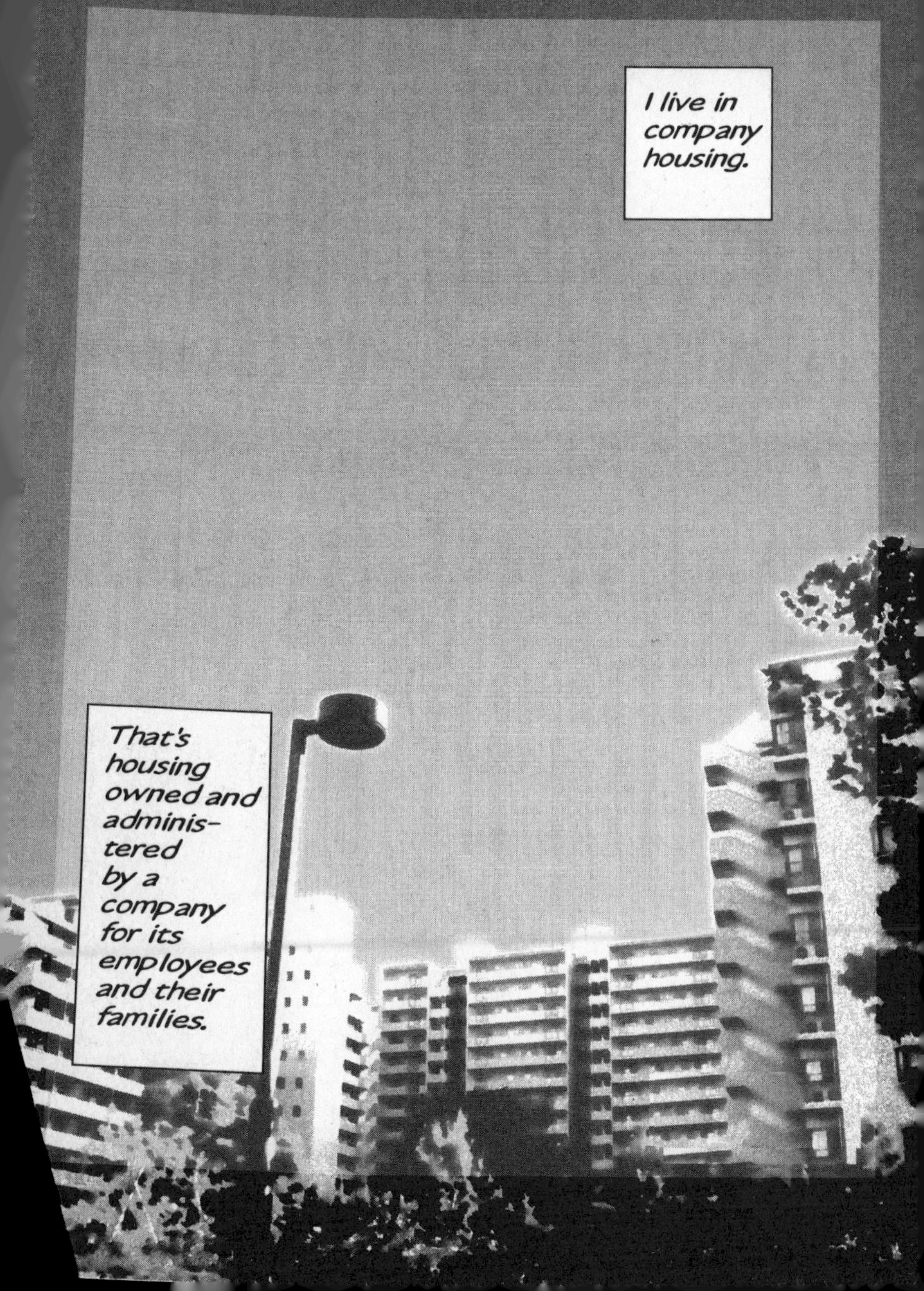
I live in company housing.
That's housing owned and adminis-tered by a company for its employees and their families.

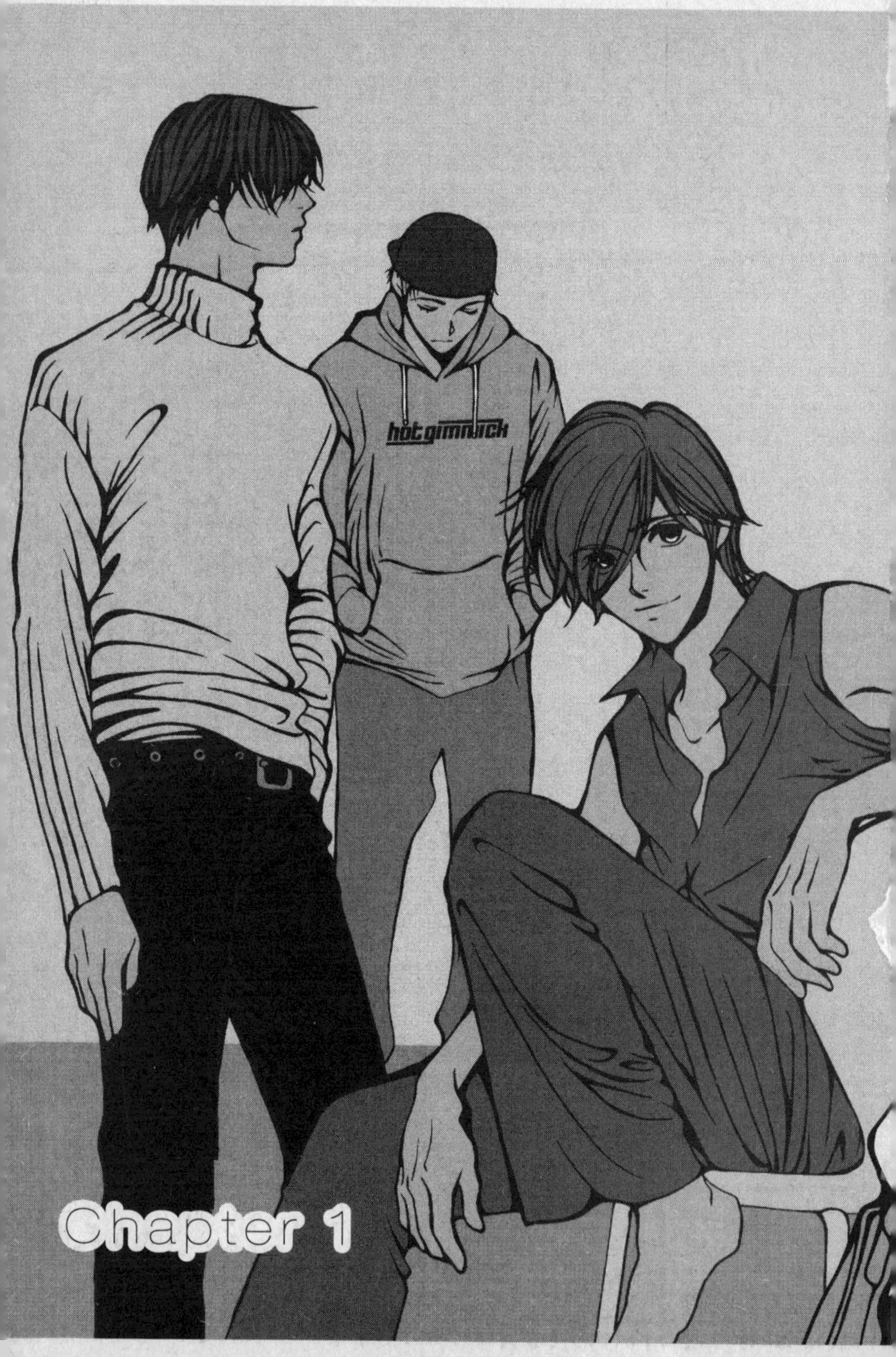
hot gimmick
Chapter 1

hot gimmick

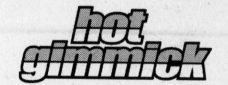

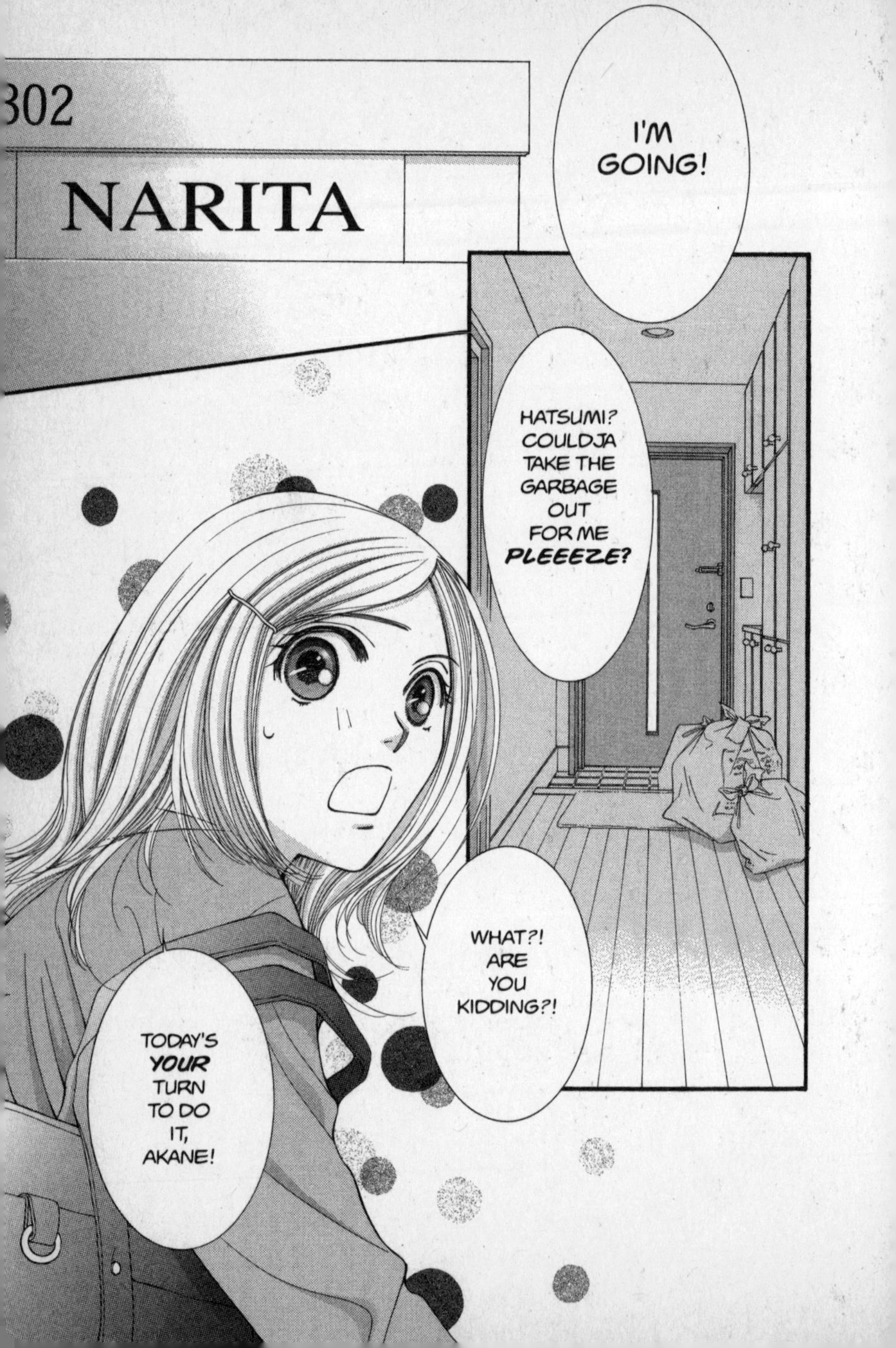
I'M GOING!
302
NARITA
HATSUMI? COULDJA TAKE THE GARBAGE OUT FOR ME PLEEEZE?
WHAT?! ARE YOU KIDDING?!
TODAY'S YOUR TURN TO DO IT, AKANE!

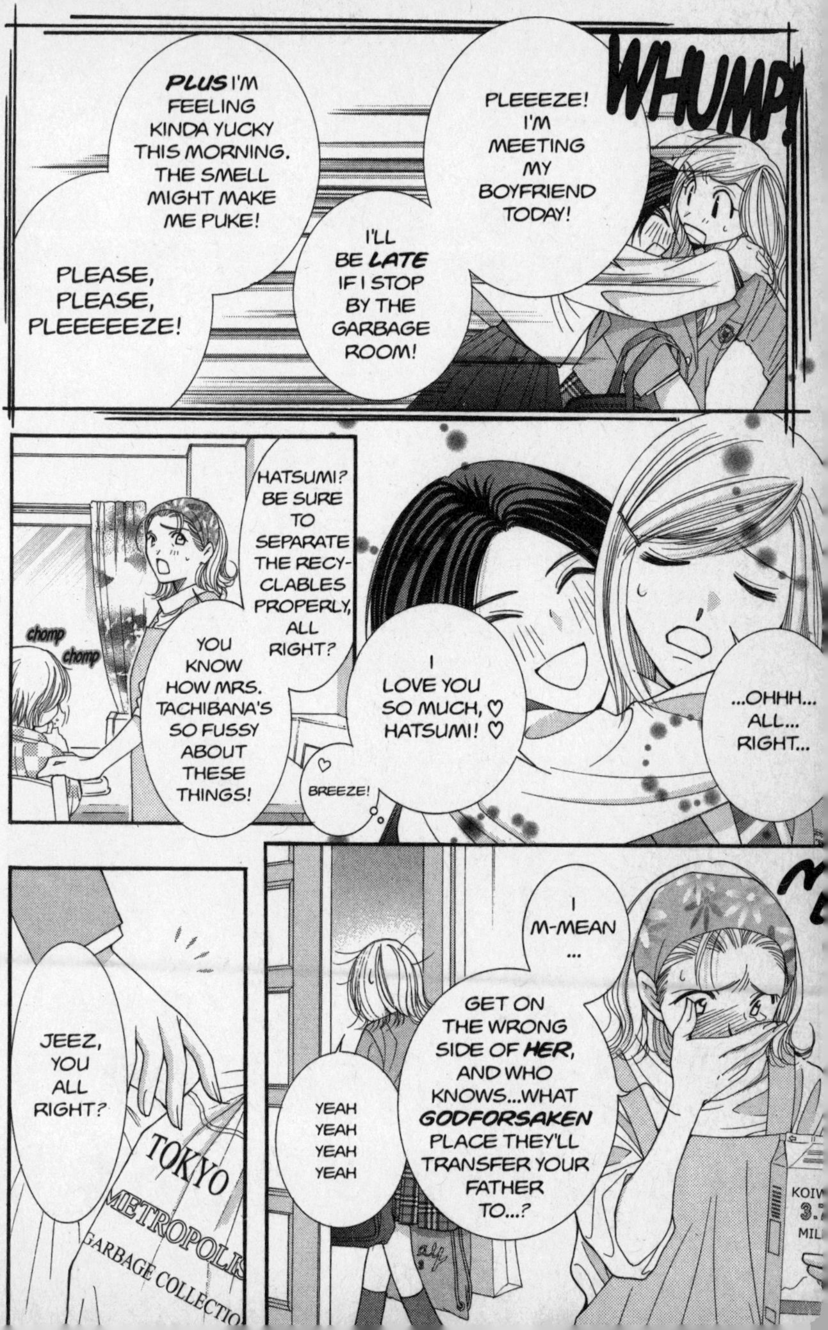
WHUMP!
PLEEEZE! I'M MEETING MY BOYFRIEND TODAY!
I'LL BE LATE IF I STOP BY THE GARBAGE ROOM!
PLUS I'M FEELING KINDA YUCKY THIS MORNING. THE SMELL MIGHT MAKE ME PUKE!
PLEASE, PLEASE, PLEEEEEEZE!
...OHHH... ALL... RIGHT...
I LOVE YOU SO MUCH, ♡ HATSUMI! ♡
♡ BREEZE!
HATSUMI? BE SURE TO SEPARATE THE RECYCLABLES PROPERLY, ALL RIGHT?
YOU KNOW HOW MRS. TACHIBANA'S SO FUSSY ABOUT THESE THINGS!
chomp chomp
I M-MEAN ...
GET ON THE WRONG SIDE OF HER, AND WHO KNOWS...WHAT GODFORSAKEN PLACE THEY'LL TRANSFER YOUR FATHER TO...?
YEAH YEAH YEAH YEAH
JEEZ, YOU ALL RIGHT?
TOKYO METROPOLIS
GARBAGE COLLECTIO

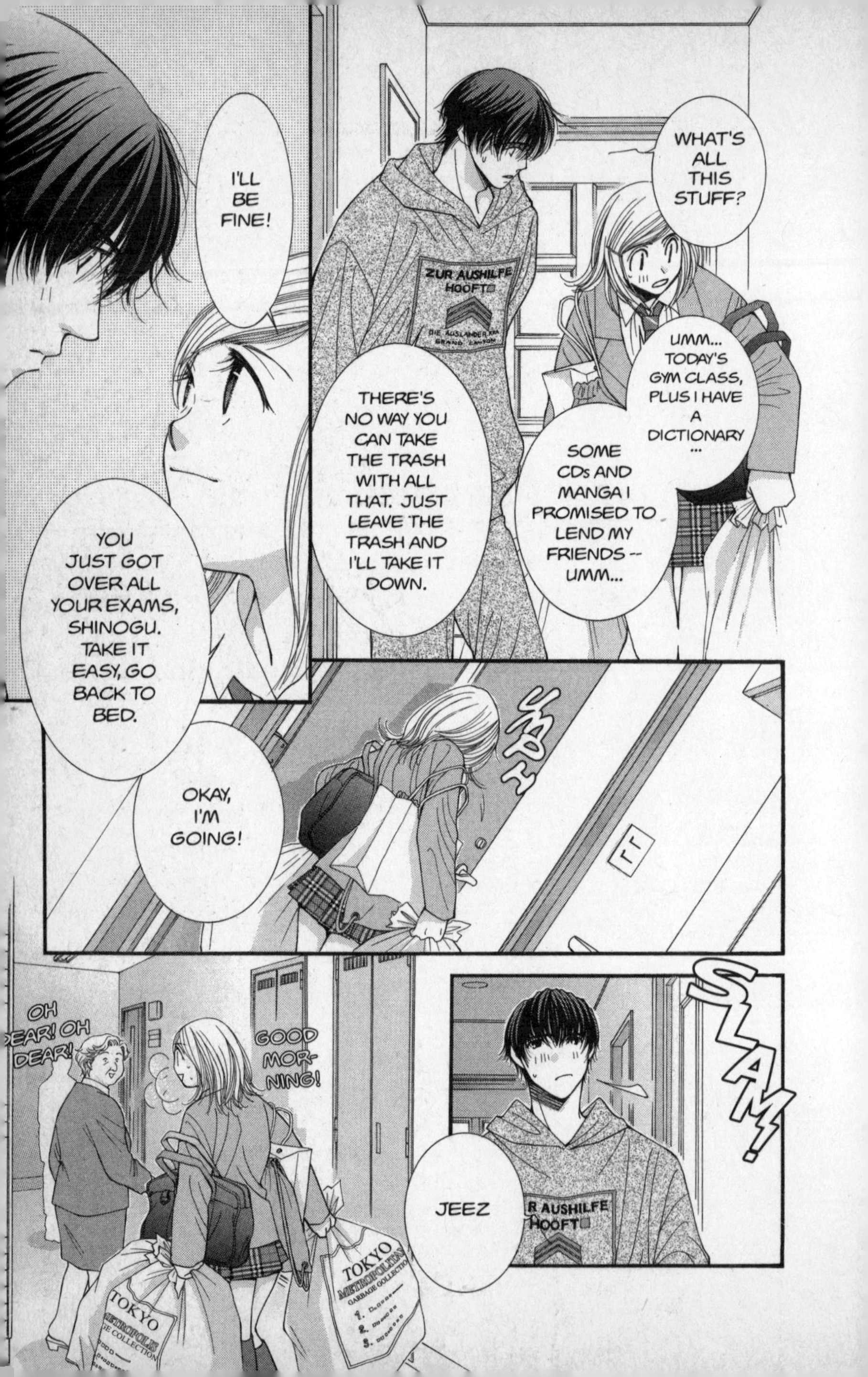
WHAT'S ALL THIS STUFF?
UMM... TODAY'S GYM CLASS, PLUS I HAVE A DICTIONARY ...
SOME CDs AND MANGA I PROMISED TO LEND MY FRIENDS -- UMM...
THERE'S NO WAY YOU CAN TAKE THE TRASH WITH ALL THAT. JUST LEAVE THE TRASH AND I'LL TAKE IT DOWN.
I'LL BE FINE!
YOU JUST GOT OVER ALL YOUR EXAMS, SHINOGU. TAKE IT EASY, GO BACK TO BED.
UMPH
OKAY, I'M GOING!
SLAM!
JEEZ
GOOD MOR-NING!
OH DEAR! OH DEAR!

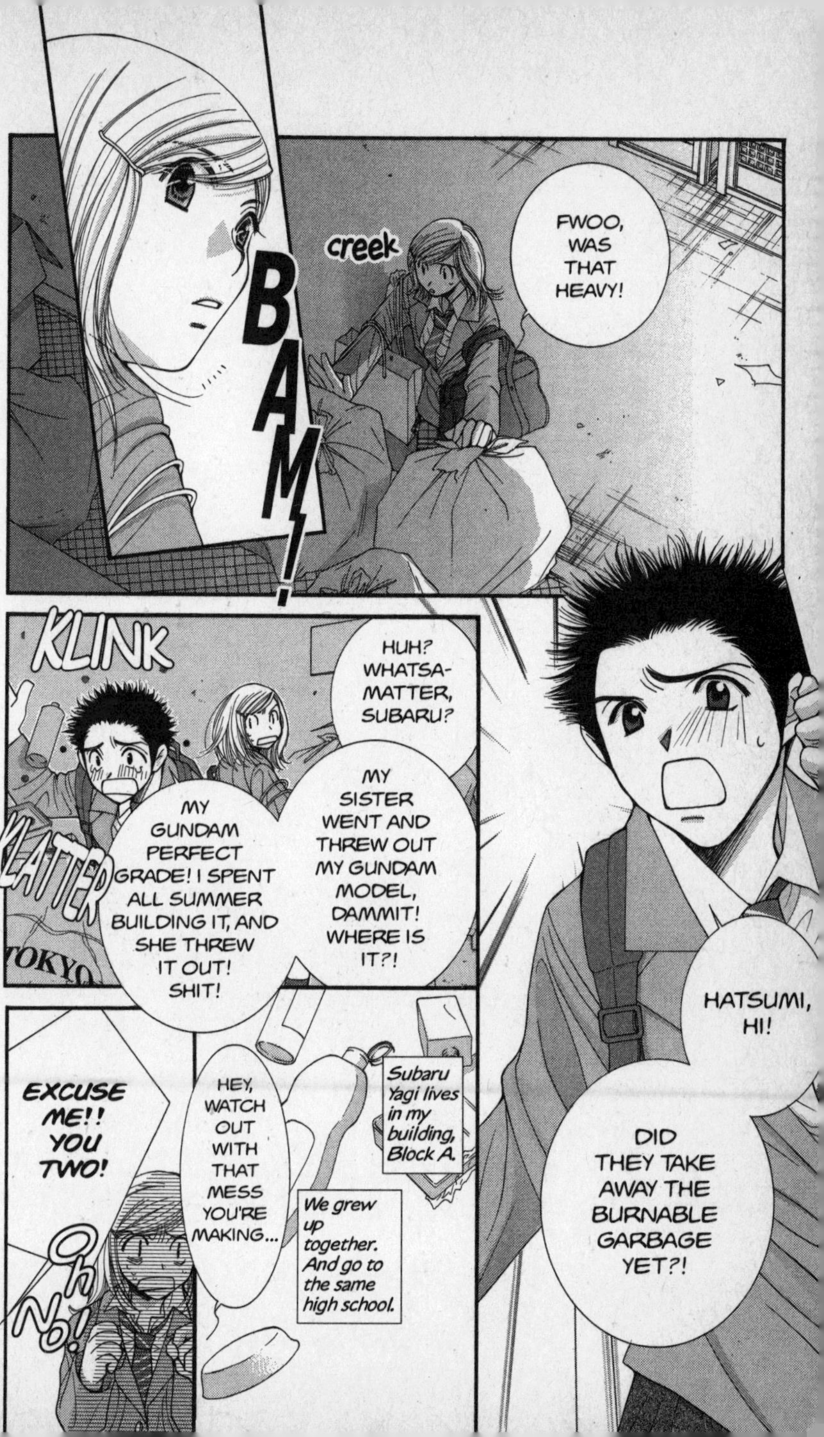
FWOO, WAS THAT HEAVY!
creek
BAM!
HATSUMI, HI!
DID THEY TAKE AWAY THE BURNABLE GARBAGE YET?!
HUH? WHATSA-MATTER, SUBARU?
KLINK
MY SISTER WENT AND THREW OUT MY GUNDAM MODEL, DAMMIT! WHERE IS IT?!
MY GUNDAM PERFECT GRADE! I SPENT ALL SUMMER BUILDING IT, AND SHE THREW IT OUT! SHIT!
KLATTER
TOKYO
Subaru Yagi lives in my building, Block A.
We grew up together. And go to the same high school.
HEY, WATCH OUT WITH THAT MESS YOU'RE MAKING...
EXCUSE ME!! YOU TWO!
Oh No!

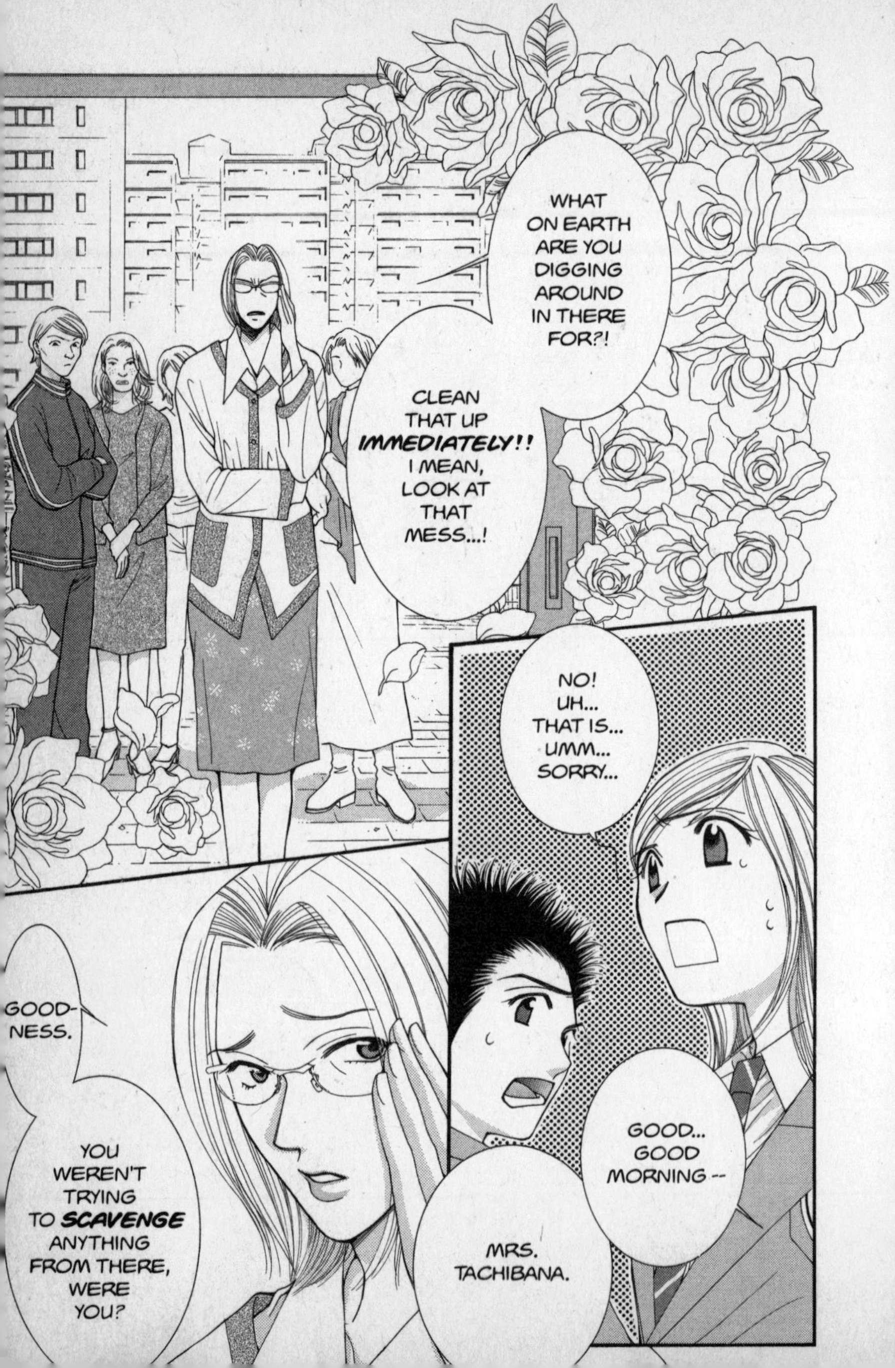
WHAT ON EARTH ARE YOU DIGGING AROUND IN THERE FOR?!
CLEAN THAT UP **IMMEDIATELY!!** I MEAN, LOOK AT THAT MESS...!
NO! UH... THAT IS... UMM... SORRY...
GOOD... GOOD MORNING --
MRS. TACHIBANA.
GOOD-NESS.
YOU WEREN'T TRYING TO **SCAVENGE** ANYTHING FROM THERE, WERE YOU?

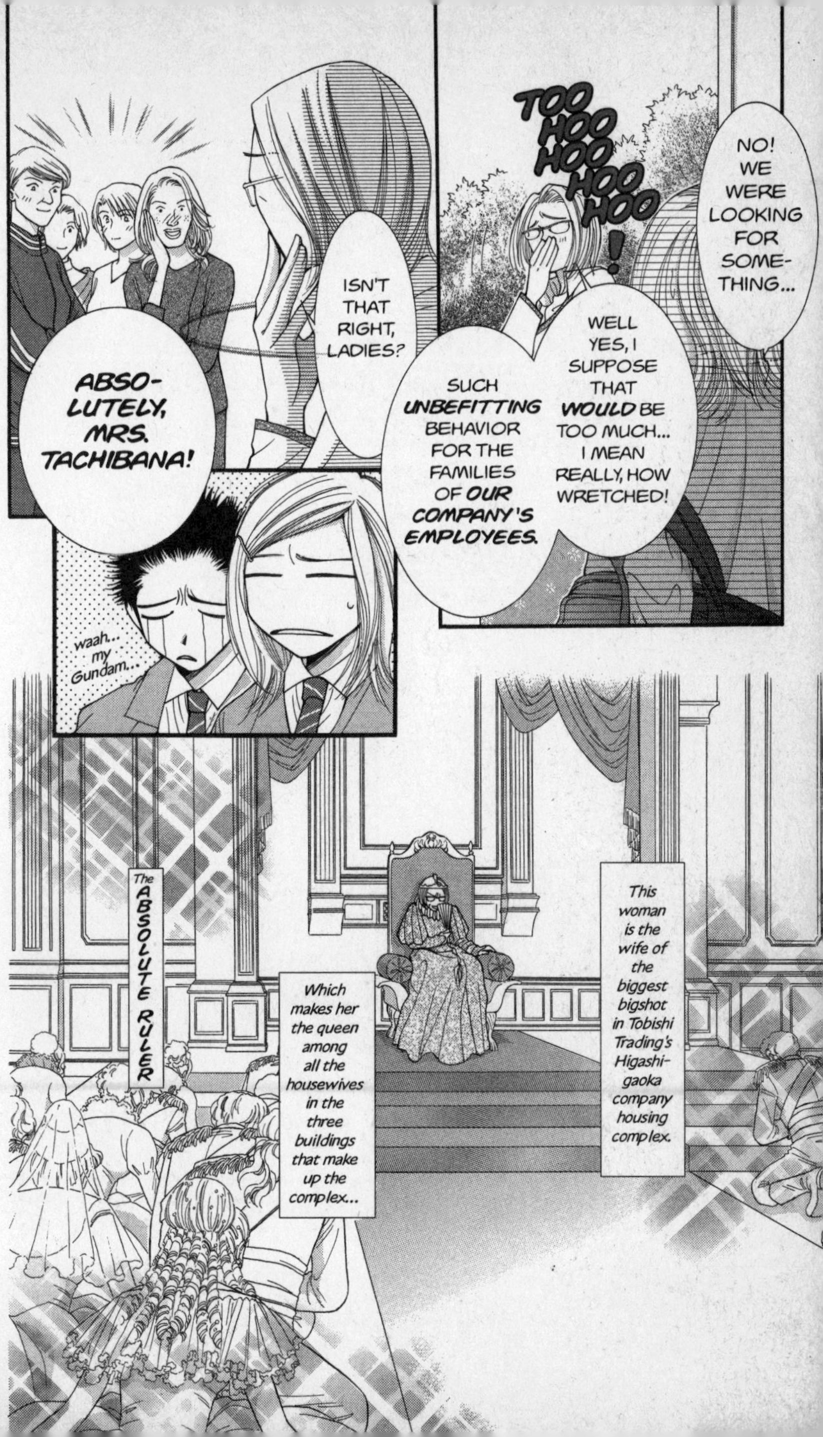
NO! WE WERE LOOKING FOR SOMETHING...
TOO HOO HOO HOO HOO!
WELL YES, I SUPPOSE THAT WOULD BE TOO MUCH... I MEAN REALLY, HOW WRETCHED!
SUCH UNBEFITTING BEHAVIOR FOR THE FAMILIES OF OUR COMPANY'S EMPLOYEES.
ISN'T THAT RIGHT, LADIES?
ABSOLUTELY, MRS. TACHIBANA!
waah... my Gundam...
This woman is the wife of the biggest bigshot in Tobishi Trading's Higashigaoka company housing complex.
Which makes her the queen among all the housewives in the three buildings that make up the complex...
The ABSOLUTE RULER

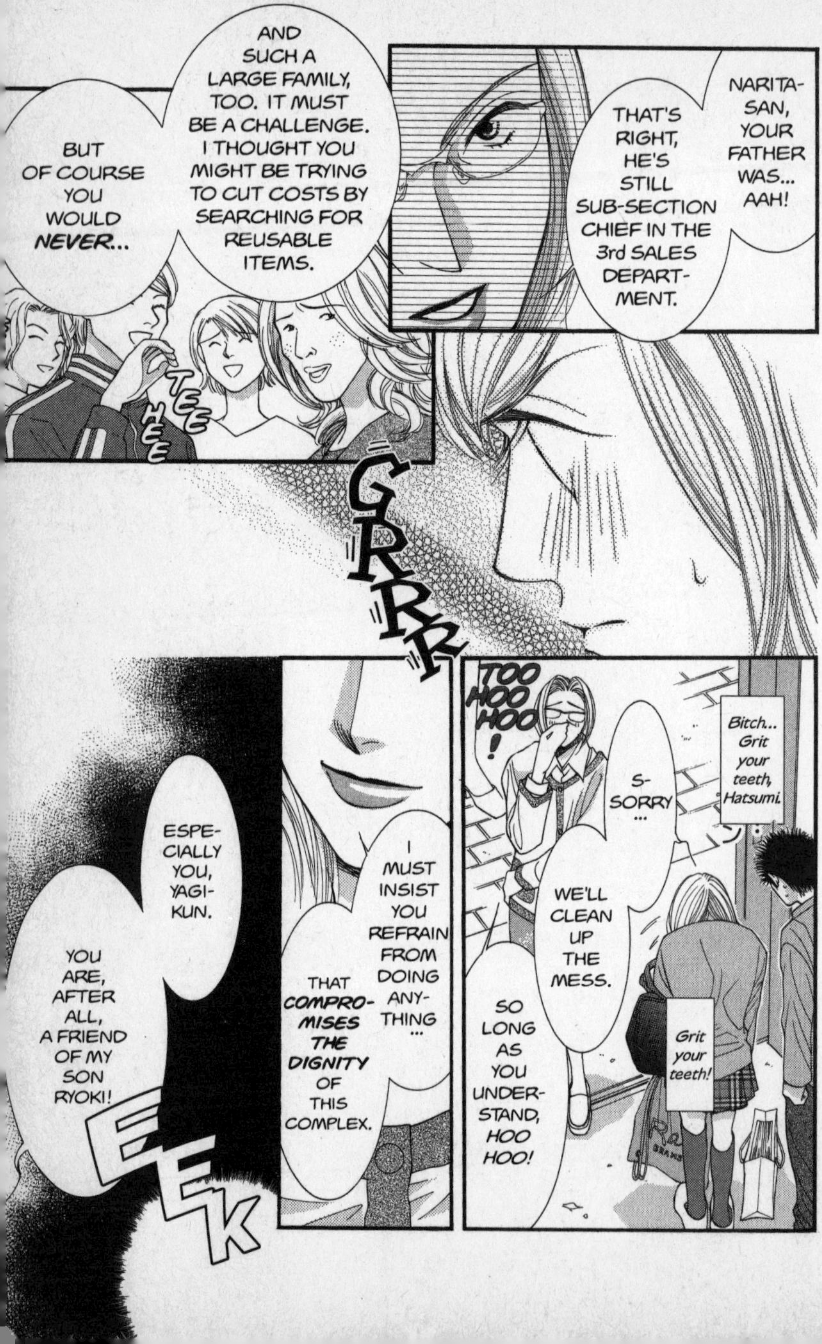
NARITA-SAN, YOUR FATHER WAS... AAH!
THAT'S RIGHT, HE'S STILL SUB-SECTION CHIEF IN THE 3rd SALES DEPARTMENT.
AND SUCH A LARGE FAMILY, TOO. IT MUST BE A CHALLENGE. I THOUGHT YOU MIGHT BE TRYING TO CUT COSTS BY SEARCHING FOR REUSABLE ITEMS.
BUT OF COURSE YOU WOULD NEVER...
TEE HEE
GRRRR
TOO HOO HOO!
Bitch... Grit your teeth, Hatsumi.
S-SORRY...
WE'LL CLEAN UP THE MESS.
SO LONG AS YOU UNDERSTAND, HOO HOO!
Grit your teeth!
I MUST INSIST YOU REFRAIN FROM DOING ANYTHING...
THAT COMPROMISES THE DIGNITY OF THIS COMPLEX.
ESPECIALLY YOU, YAGI-KUN.
YOU ARE, AFTER ALL, A FRIEND OF MY SON RYOKI!
EEEK

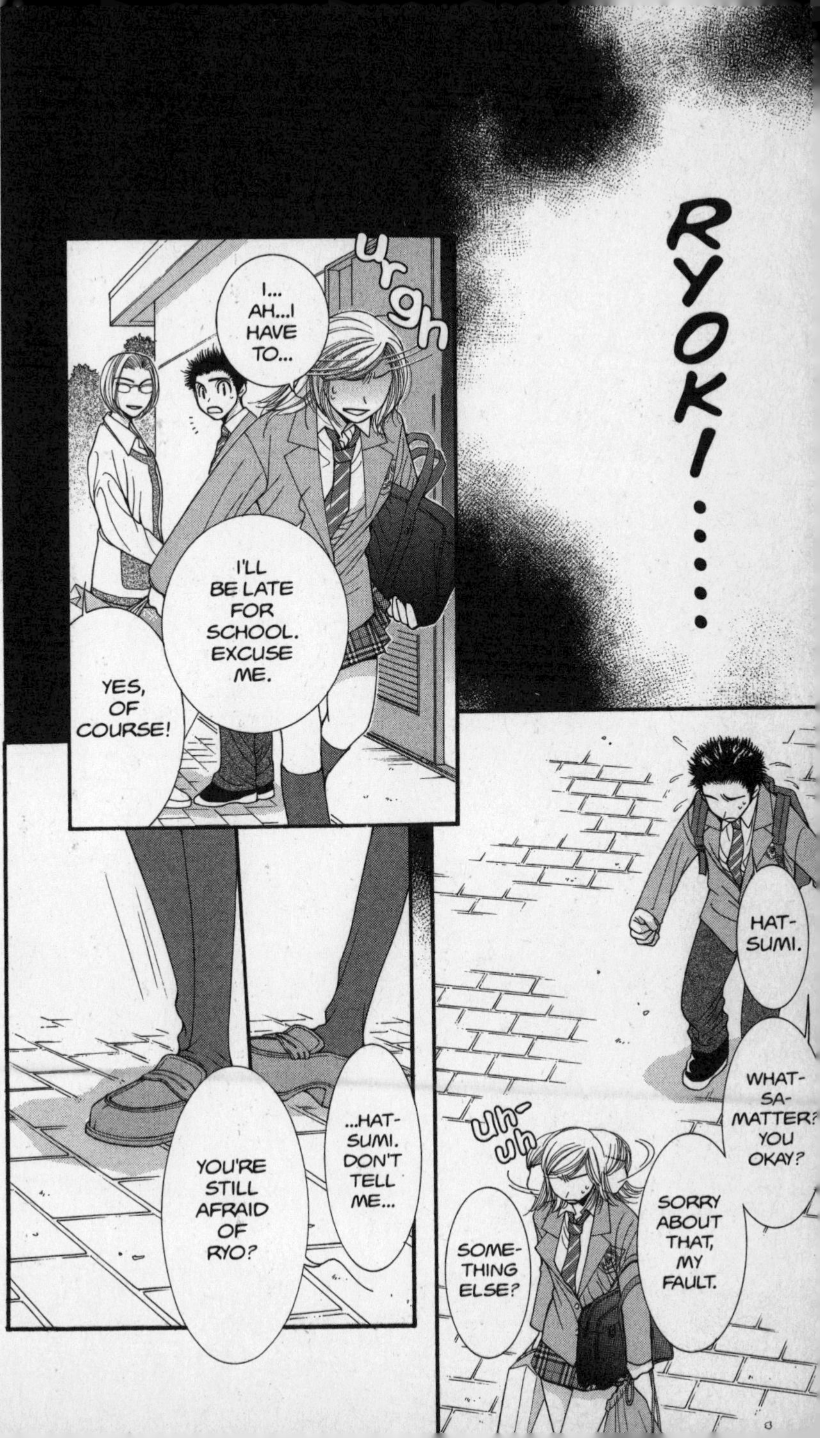
RYOKI....
urgh
I... AH...I HAVE TO...
I'LL BE LATE FOR SCHOOL. EXCUSE ME.
YES, OF COURSE!
HAT-SUMI.
WHAT-SA-MATTER? YOU OKAY?
SORRY ABOUT THAT, MY FAULT.
uh-uh
SOME-THING ELSE?
...HAT-SUMI. DON'T TELL ME...
YOU'RE STILL AFRAID OF RYO?

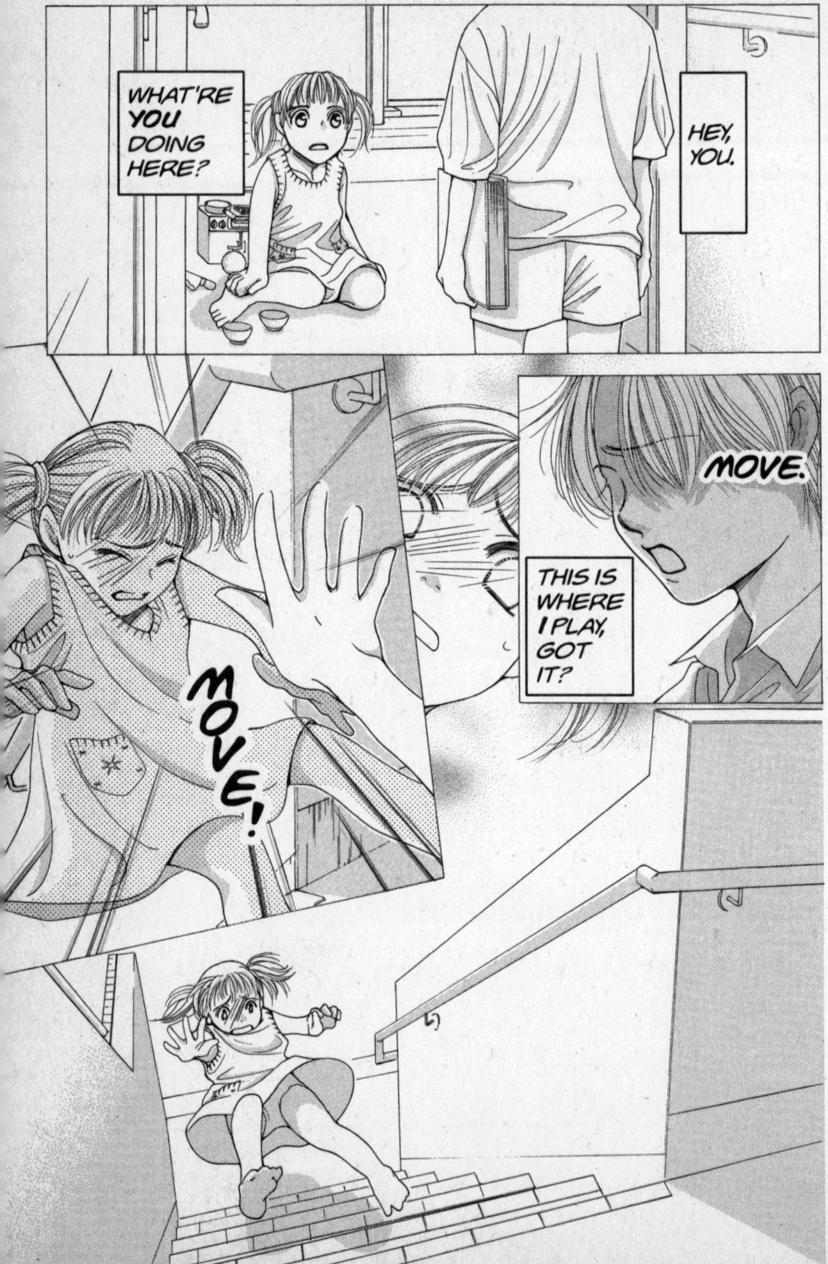
HEY, YOU.
WHAT'RE YOU DOING HERE?
MOVE.
THIS IS WHERE I PLAY, GOT IT?
MOVE!

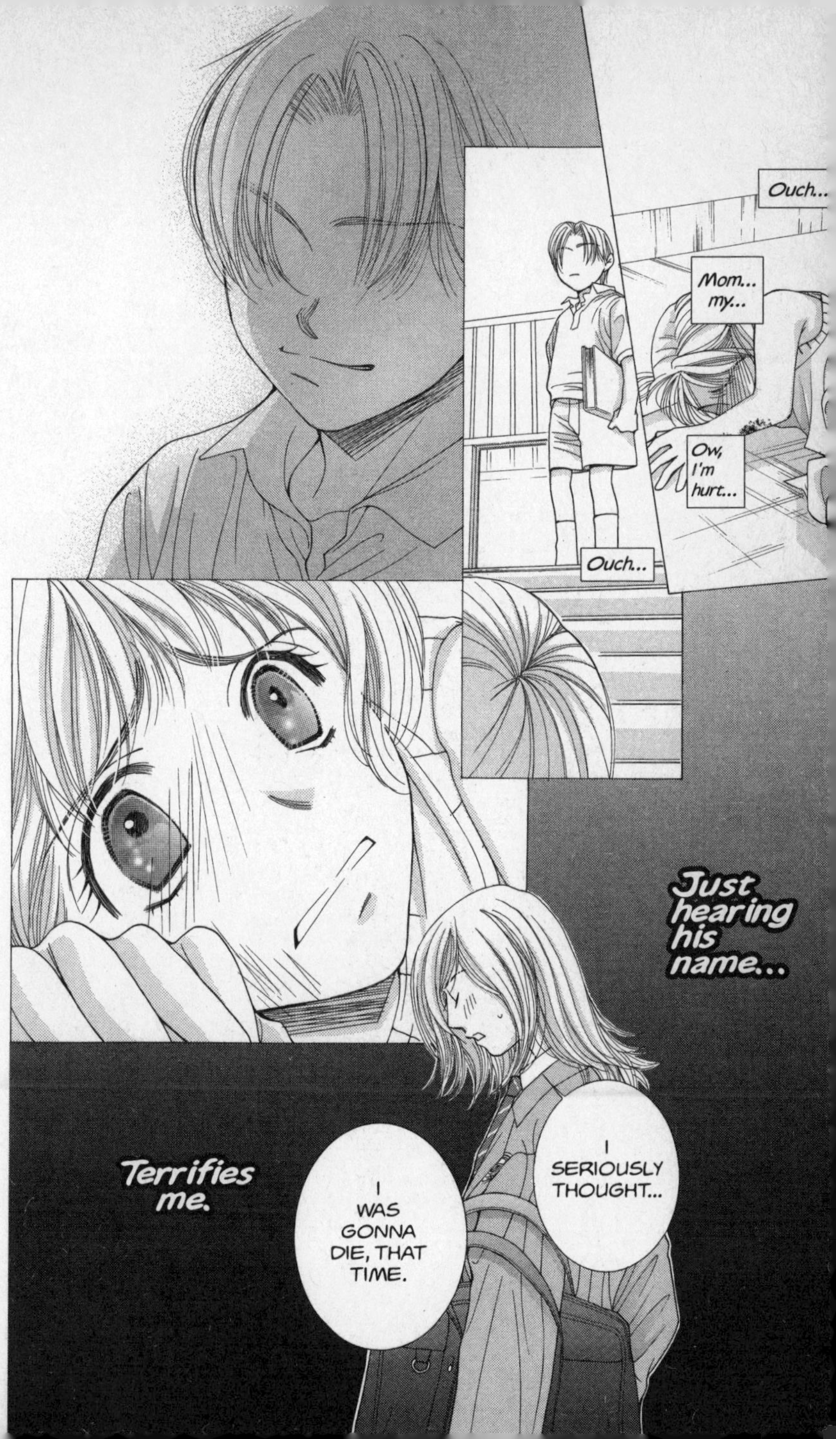
Ouch...
Mom... my...
Ow, I'm hurt...
Ouch...
Just hearing his name...
I SERIOUSLY THOUGHT...
I WAS GONNA DIE, THAT TIME.
Terrifies me.

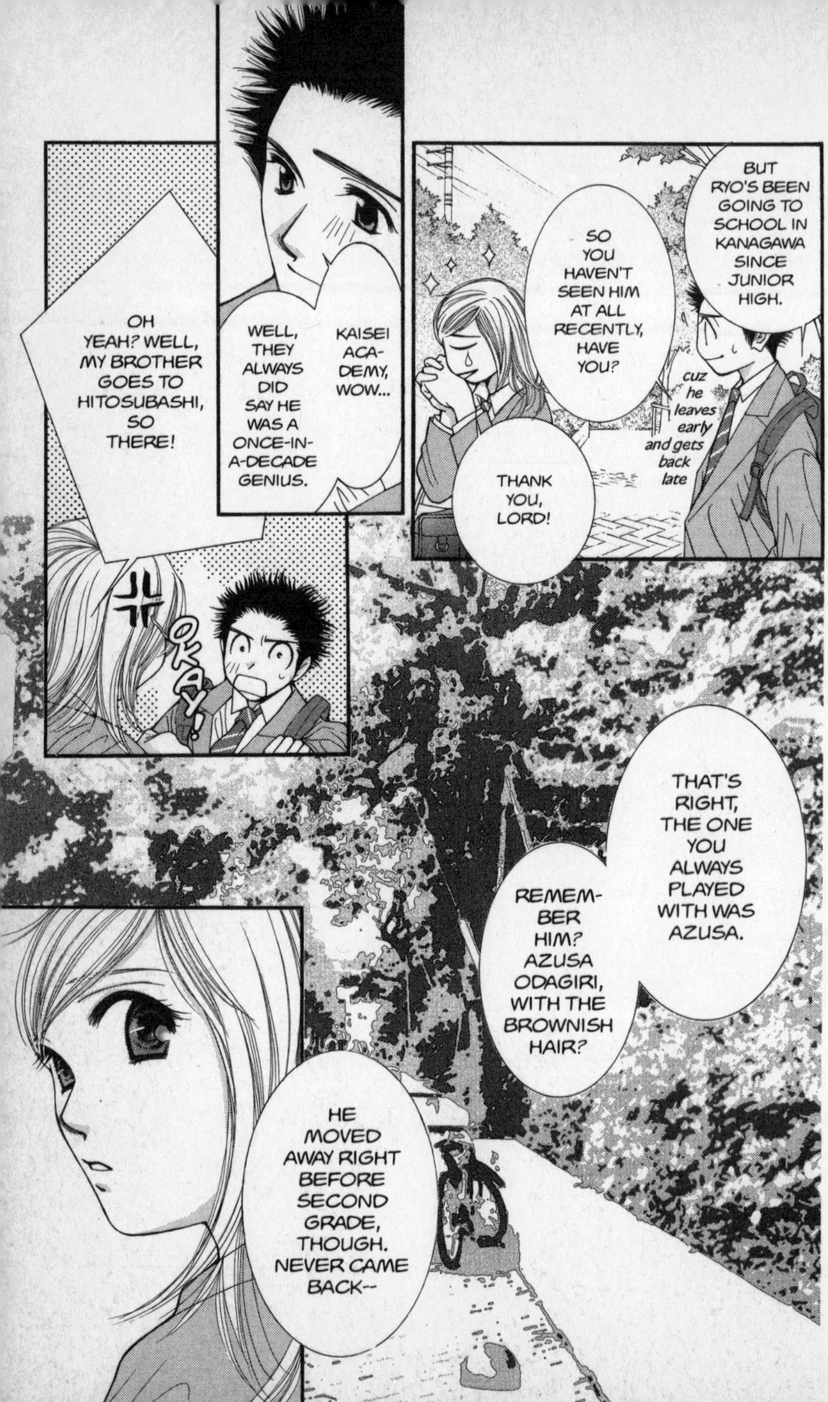
BUT RYO'S BEEN GOING TO SCHOOL IN KANAGAWA SINCE JUNIOR HIGH.
SO YOU HAVEN'T SEEN HIM AT ALL RECENTLY, HAVE YOU?
cuz he leaves early and gets back late
THANK YOU, LORD!
KAISEI ACA-DEMY, WOW...
WELL, THEY ALWAYS DID SAY HE WAS A ONCE-IN-A-DECADE GENIUS.
OH YEAH? WELL, MY BROTHER GOES TO HITOSUBASHI, SO THERE!
OKAY!
THAT'S RIGHT, THE ONE YOU ALWAYS PLAYED WITH WAS AZUSA.
REMEM-BER HIM? AZUSA ODAGIRI, WITH THE BROWNISH HAIR?
HE MOVED AWAY RIGHT BEFORE SECOND GRADE, THOUGH. NEVER CAME BACK--

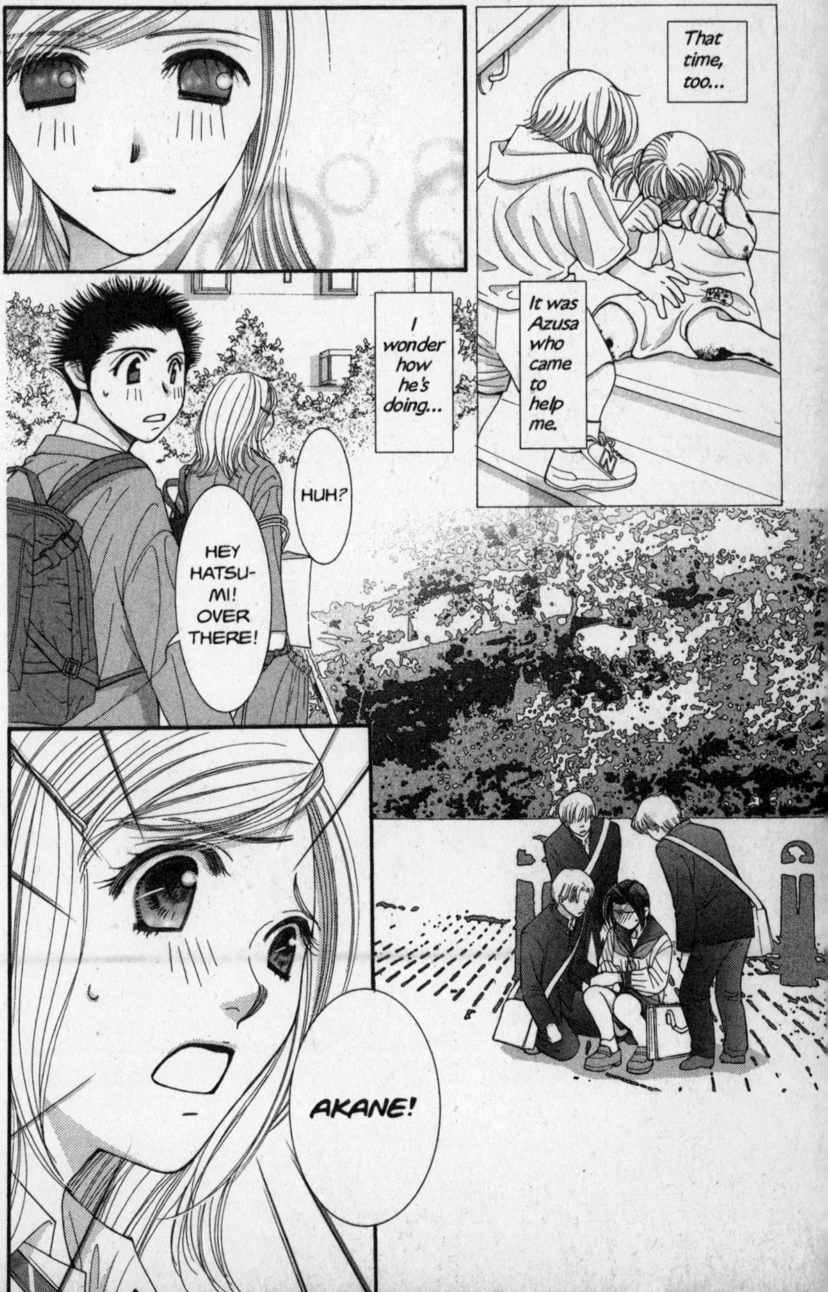
That time, too...
It was Azusa who came to help me.
I wonder how he's doing...
HUH?
HEY HATSUMI! OVER THERE!
AKANE!

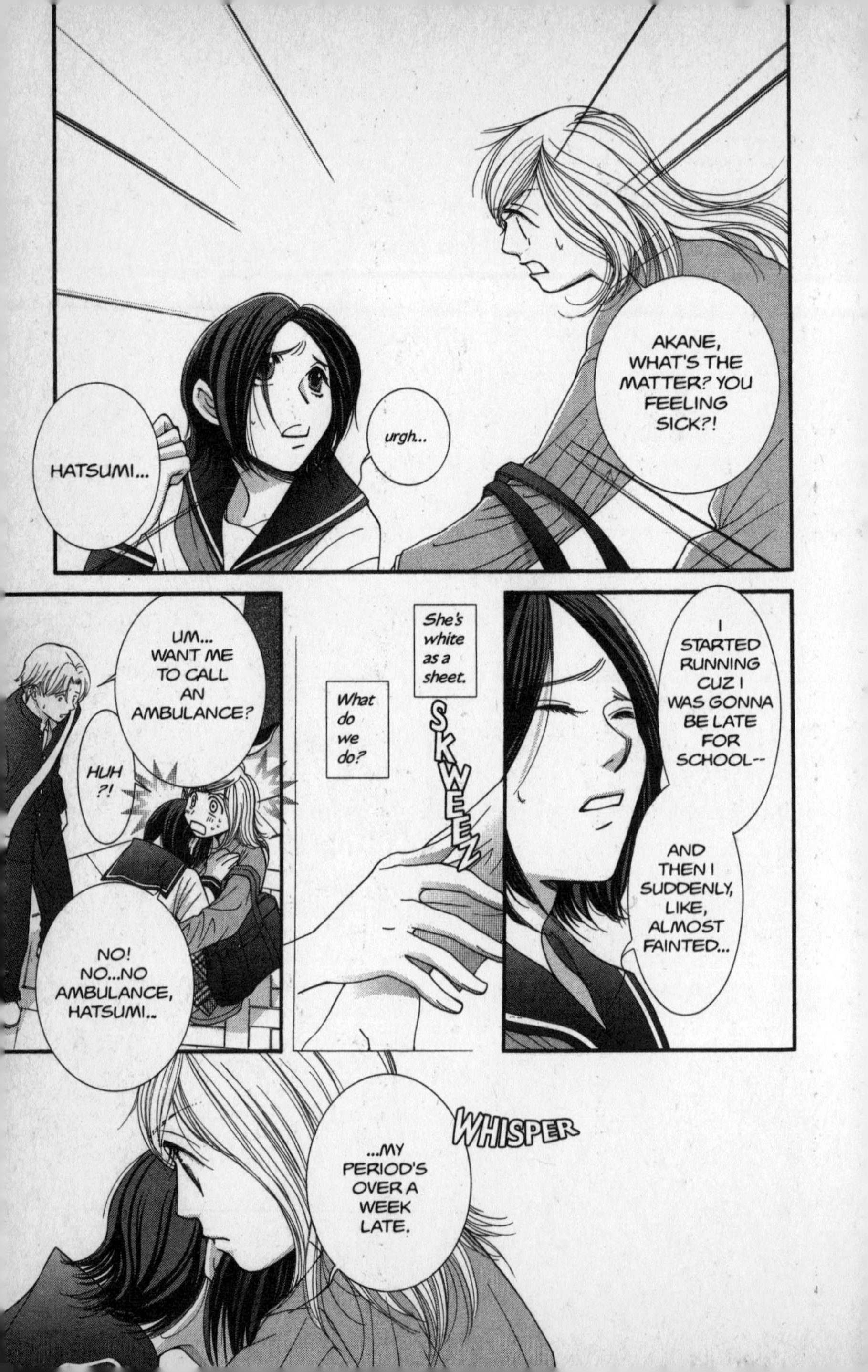
AKANE, WHAT'S THE MATTER? YOU FEELING SICK?!
urgh...
HATSUMI...
I STARTED RUNNING CUZ I WAS GONNA BE LATE FOR SCHOOL--
AND THEN I SUDDENLY, LIKE, ALMOST FAINTED...
She's white as a sheet.
SKWEEZ
What do we do?
UM... WANT ME TO CALL AN AMBULANCE?
HUH?!
NO! NO...NO AMBULANCE, HATSUMI..
WHISPER
...MY PERIOD'S OVER A WEEK LATE.

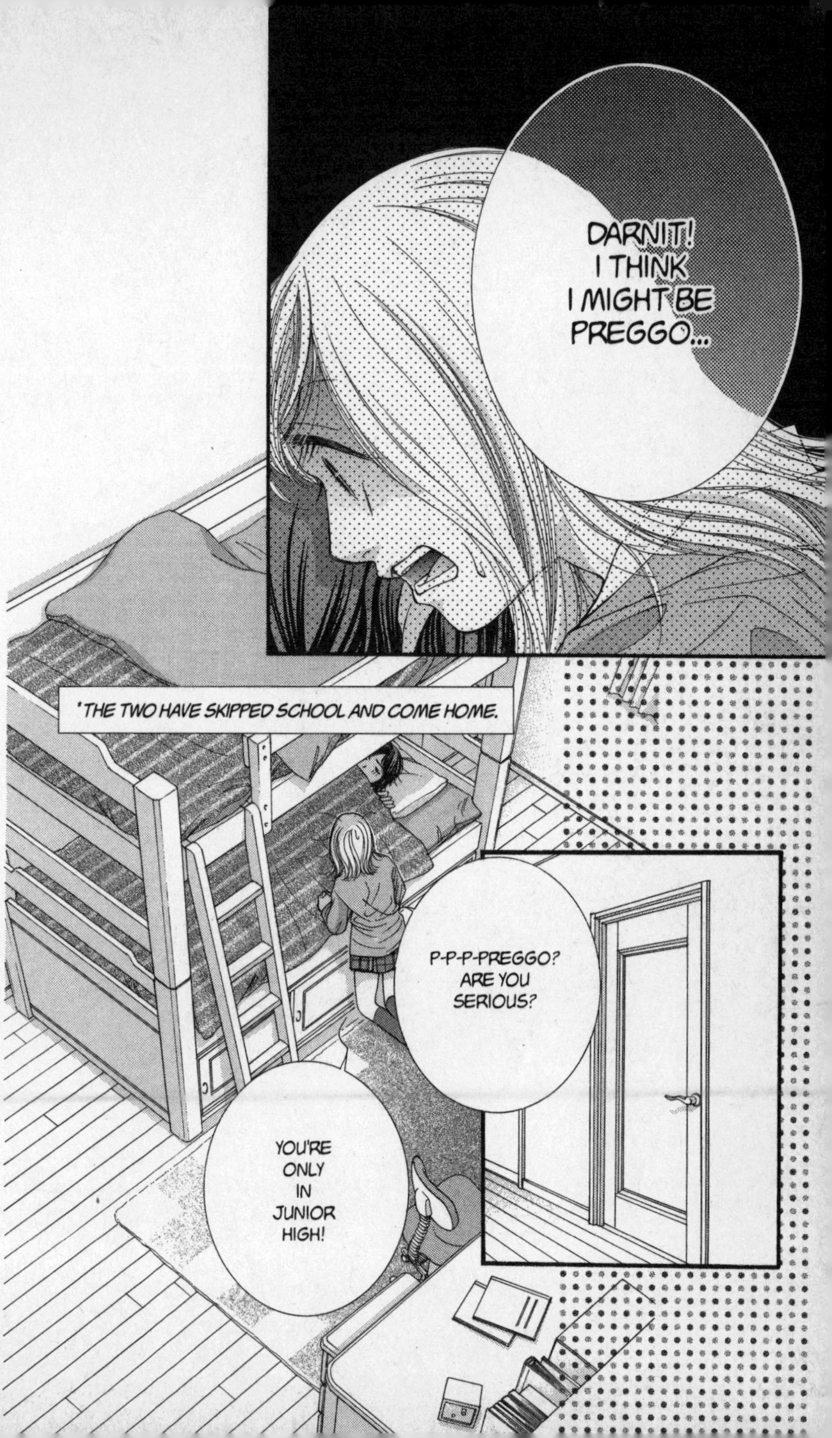
DARNIT! I THINK I MIGHT BE PREGGO...
*THE TWO HAVE SKIPPED SCHOOL AND COME HOME.
P-P-P-PREGGO? ARE YOU SERIOUS?
YOU'RE ONLY IN JUNIOR HIGH!

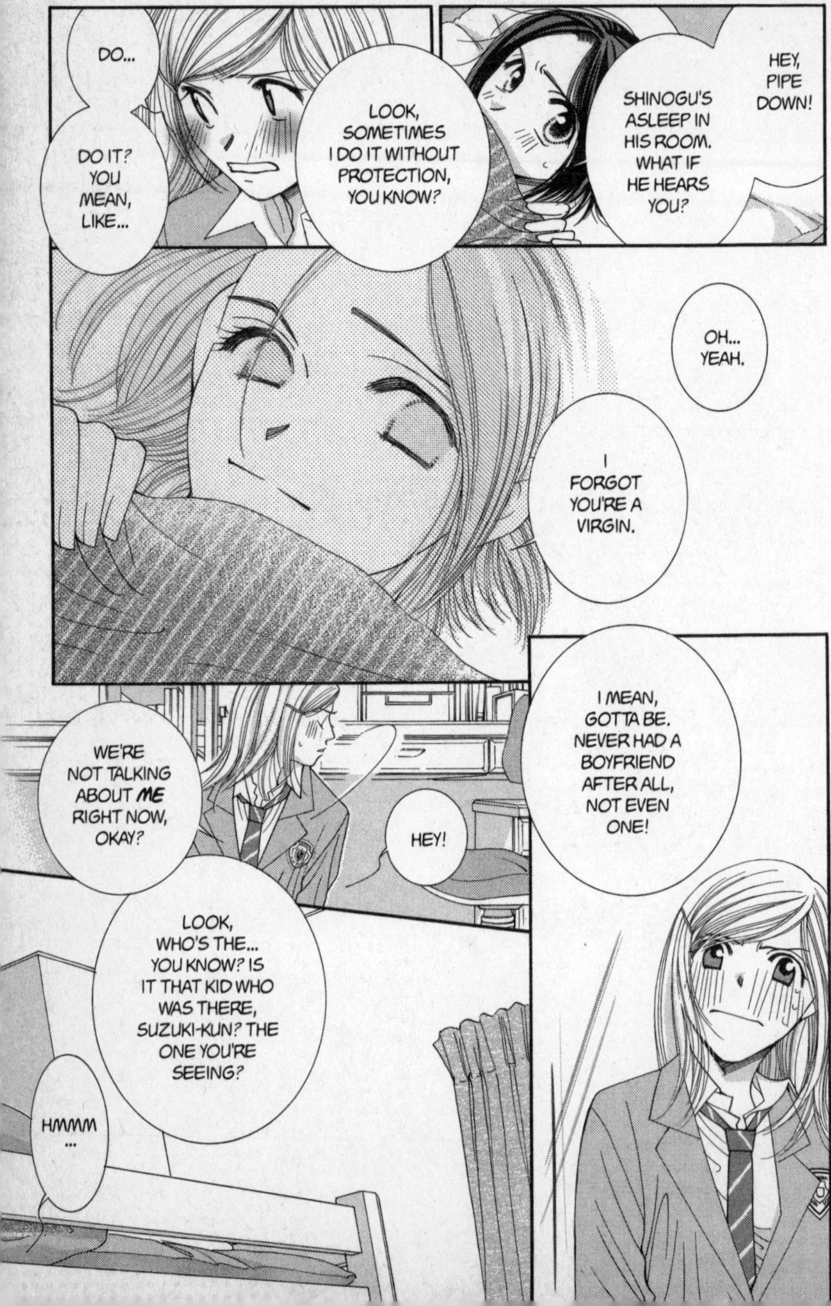
HEY, PIPE DOWN!
SHINOGU'S ASLEEP IN HIS ROOM. WHAT IF HE HEARS YOU?
LOOK, SOMETIMES I DO IT WITHOUT PROTECTION, YOU KNOW?
DO...
DO IT? YOU MEAN, LIKE...
OH... YEAH.
I FORGOT YOU'RE A VIRGIN.
I MEAN, GOTTA BE. NEVER HAD A BOYFRIEND AFTER ALL, NOT EVEN ONE!
HEY!
WE'RE NOT TALKING ABOUT ***ME*** RIGHT NOW, OKAY?
LOOK, WHO'S THE... YOU KNOW? IS IT THAT KID WHO WAS THERE, SUZUKI-KUN? THE ONE YOU'RE SEEING?
HMMM ...

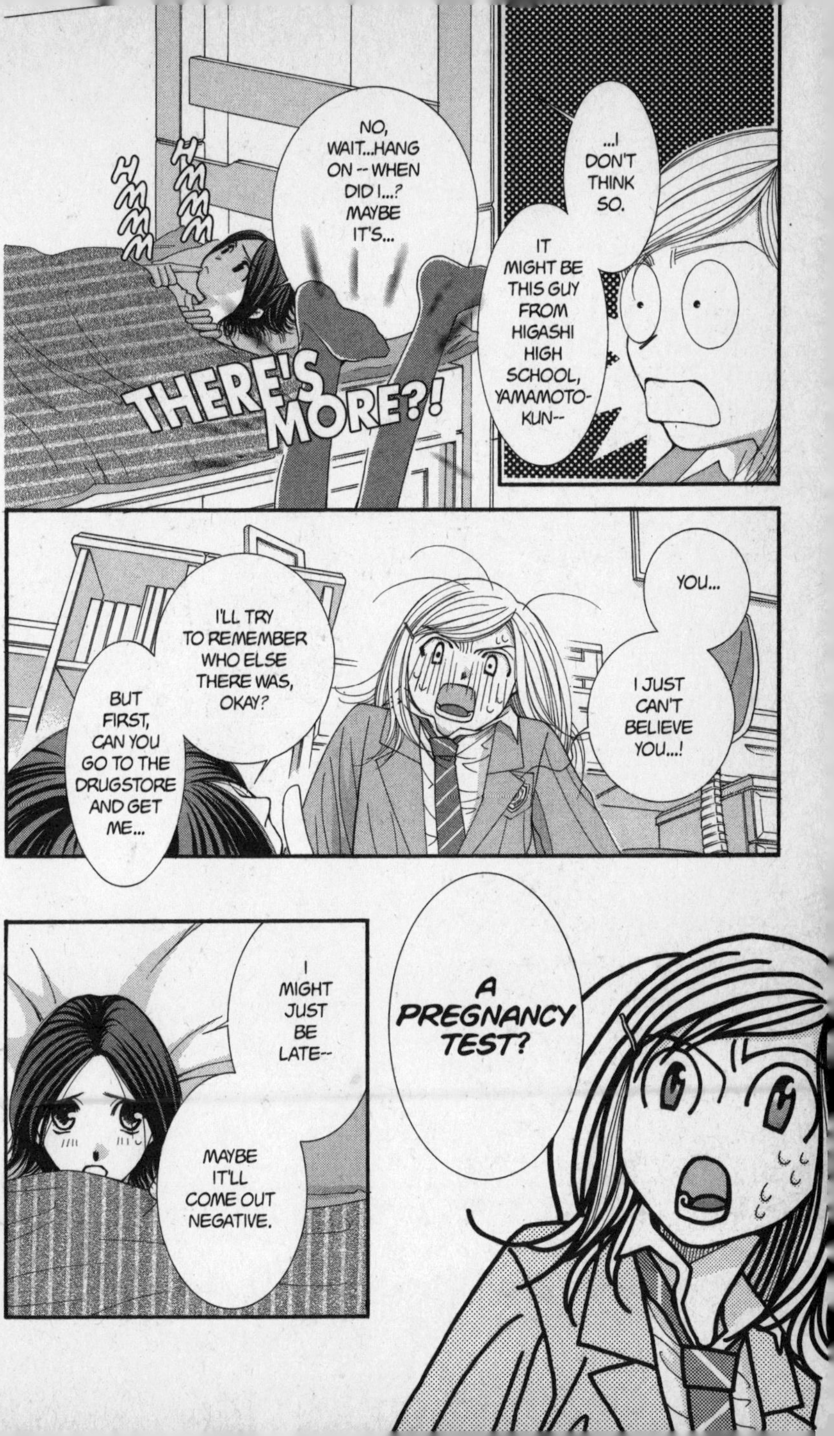
...I DON'T THINK SO.
IT MIGHT BE THIS GUY FROM HIGASHI HIGH SCHOOL, YAMAMOTO-KUN--
THERE'S MORE?!
NO, WAIT...HANG ON -- WHEN DID I...? MAYBE IT'S...
HMMM
HMMM
YOU...
I JUST CAN'T BELIEVE YOU...!
I'LL TRY TO REMEMBER WHO ELSE THERE WAS, OKAY?
BUT FIRST, CAN YOU GO TO THE DRUGSTORE AND GET ME...
A PREGNANCY TEST?
I MIGHT JUST BE LATE--
MAYBE IT'LL COME OUT NEGATIVE.

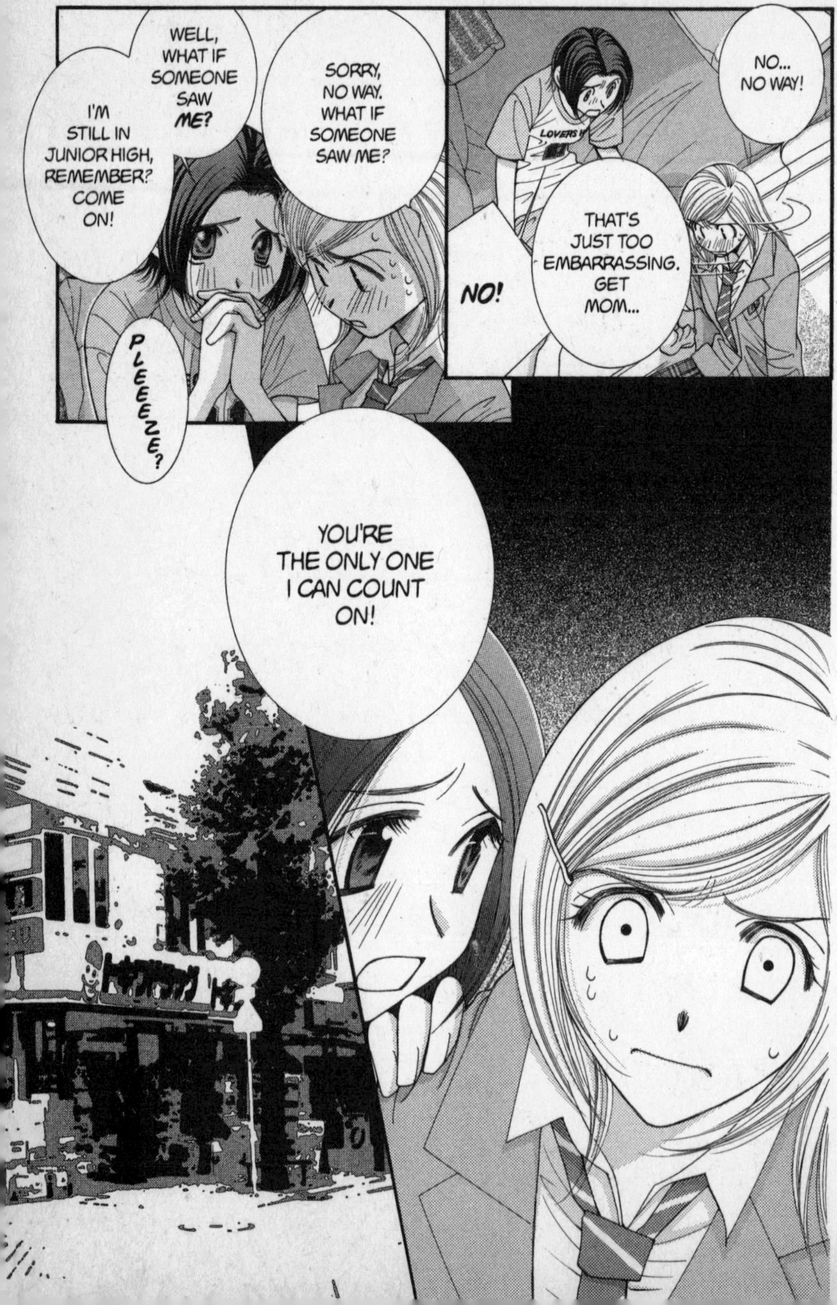
NO... NO WAY!
THAT'S JUST TOO EMBARRASSING. GET MOM...
NO!
SORRY, NO WAY. WHAT IF SOMEONE SAW ME?
WELL, WHAT IF SOMEONE SAW ME?
I'M STILL IN JUNIOR HIGH, REMEMBER? COME ON!
PLEEEZE?
YOU'RE THE ONLY ONE I CAN COUNT ON!

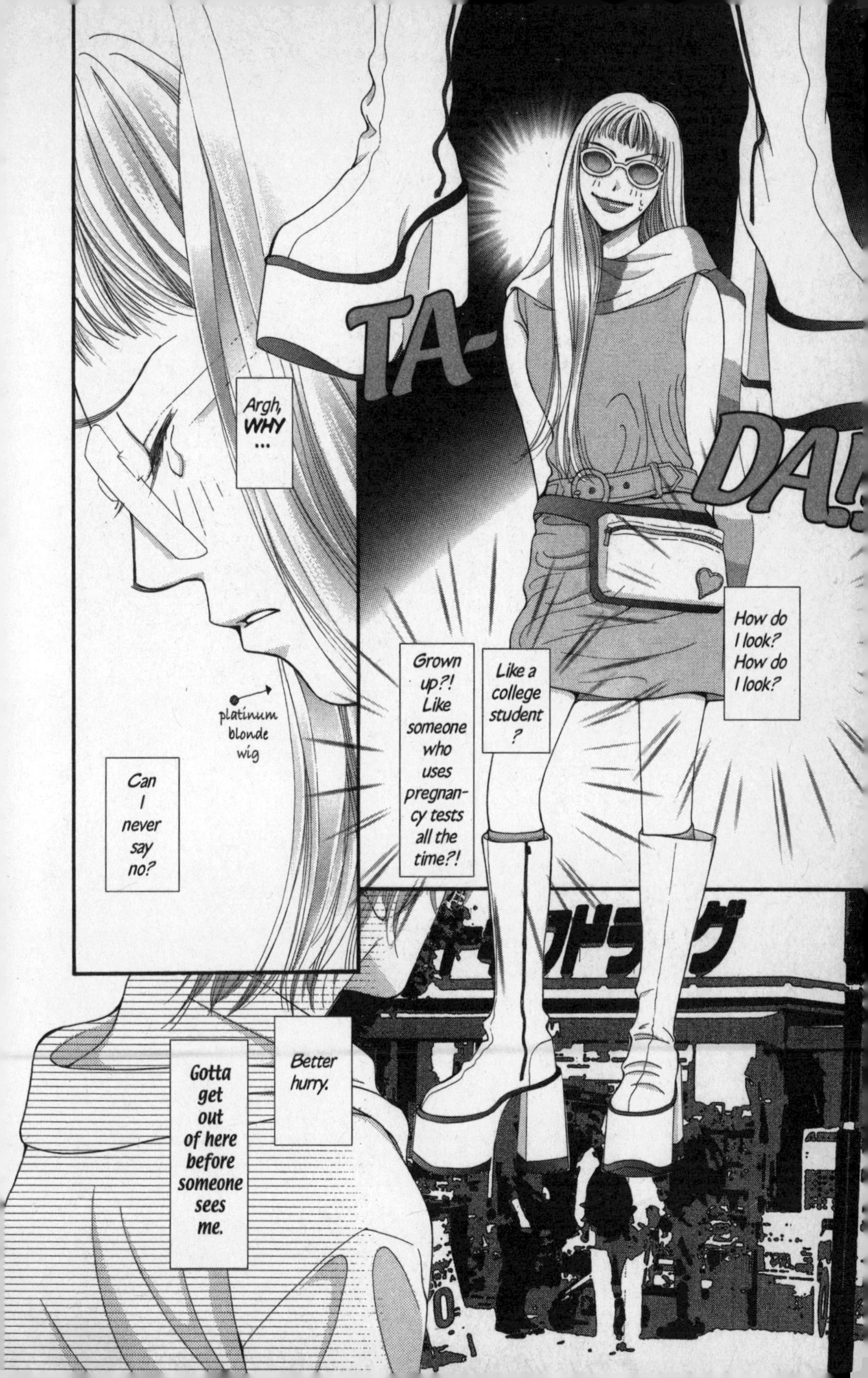
TA-DA!
How do I look? How do I look?
Like a college student?
Grown up?! Like someone who uses pregnancy tests all the time?!
Argh, WHY...
platinum blonde wig
Can I never say no?
Better hurry.
Gotta get out of here before someone sees me.

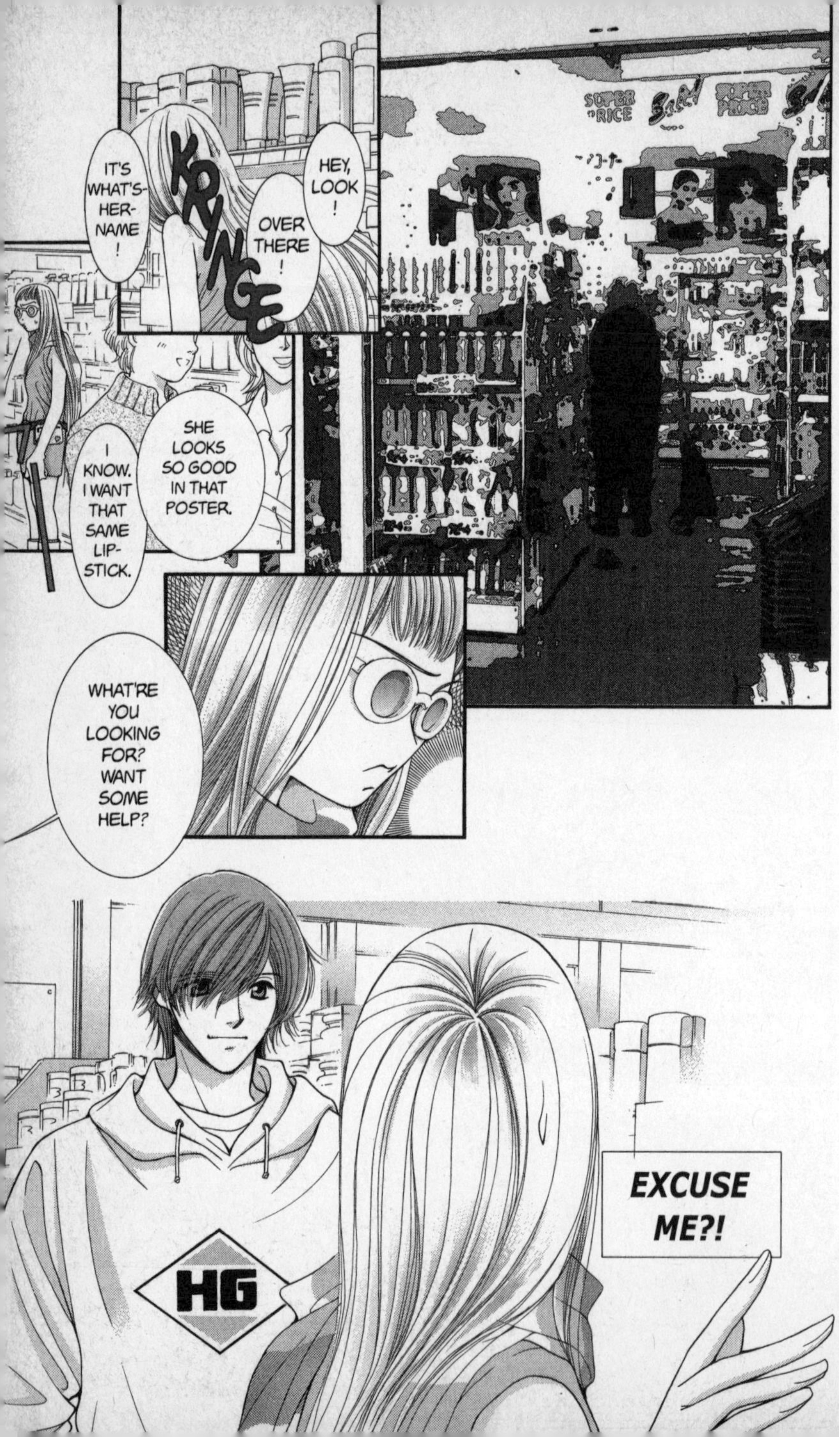
SUPER PRICE
HEY, LOOK!
OVER THERE!
IT'S WHAT'S-HER-NAME!
KRINGE
SHE LOOKS SO GOOD IN THAT POSTER.
I KNOW. I WANT THAT SAME LIPSTICK.
WHAT'RE YOU LOOKING FOR? WANT SOME HELP?
EXCUSE ME?!
HG

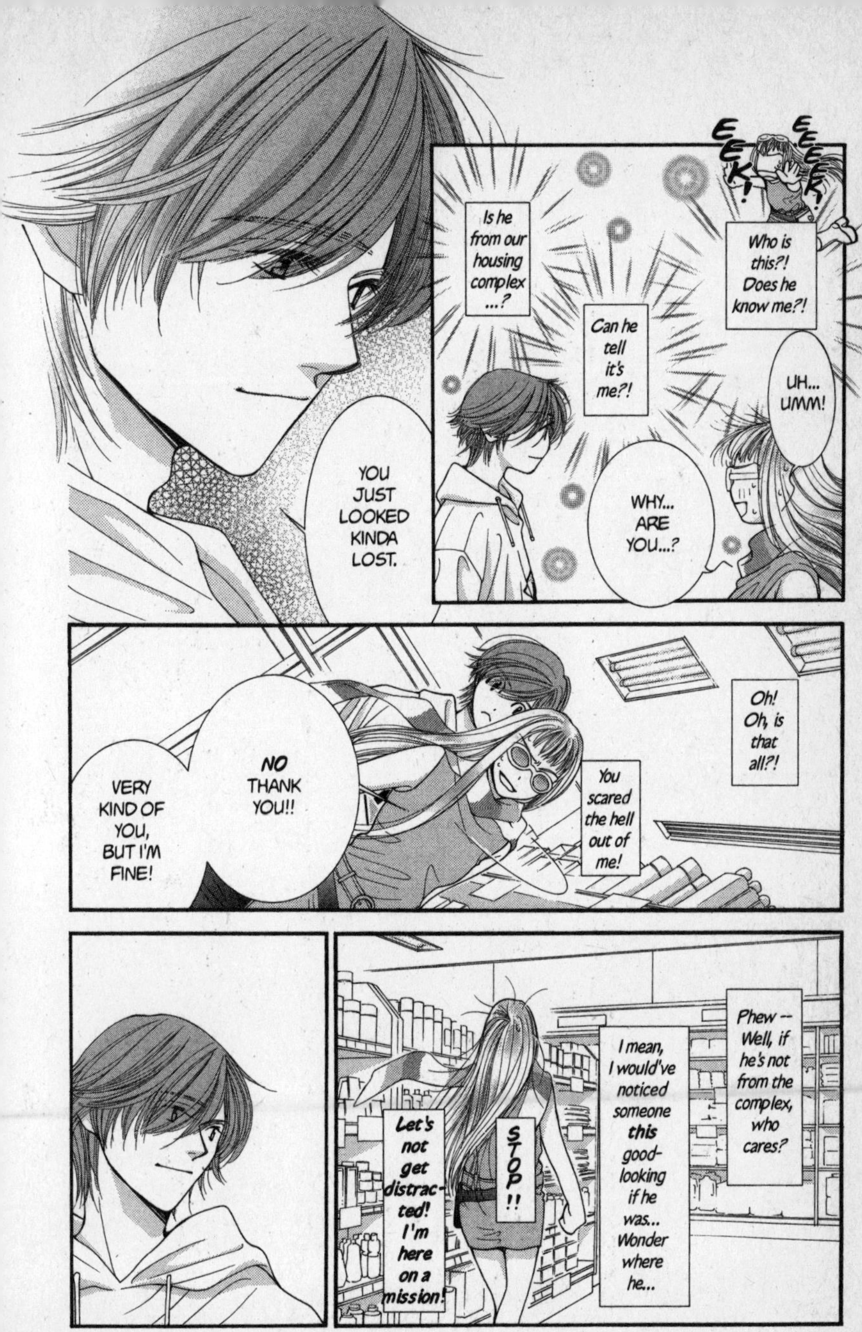

EEK!
EEEEK!
Who is this?! Does he know me?!
Is he from our housing complex ...?
Can he tell it's me?!
UH... UMM!
WHY... ARE YOU...?
YOU JUST LOOKED KINDA LOST.
Oh! Oh, is that all?!
You scared the hell out of me!
NO THANK YOU!!
VERY KIND OF YOU, BUT I'M FINE!
Phew -- Well, if he's not from the complex, who cares?
I mean, I would've noticed someone this good-looking if he was... Wonder where he...
STOP!!
Let's not get distracted! I'm here on a mission!

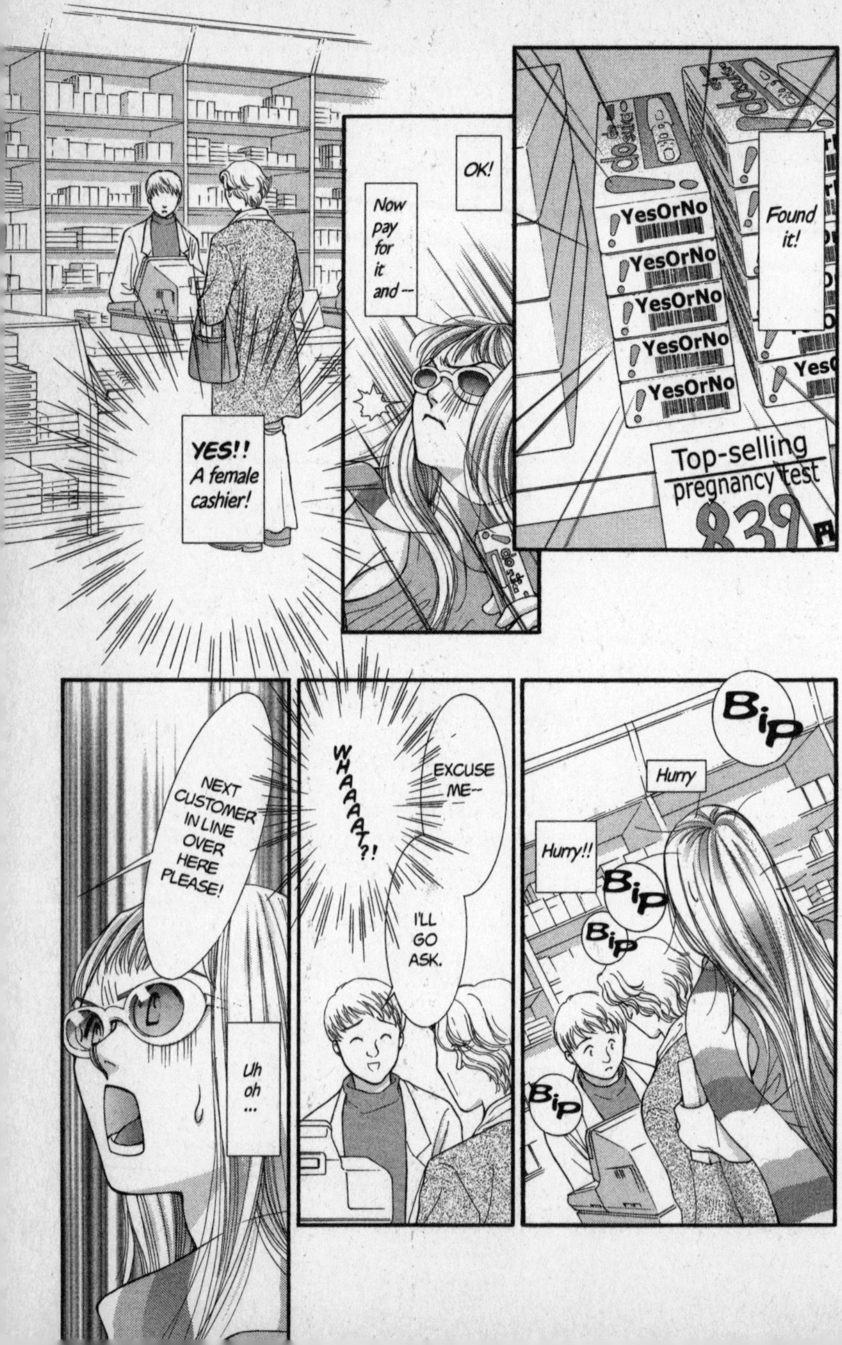
Found it!
YesOrNo
Top-selling pregnancy test 839円
OK!
Now pay for it and --
YES!! A female cashier!
Bip
Hurry
Hurry!!
Bip
Bip
Bip
EXCUSE ME--
WHAAAAT?!
I'LL GO ASK.
NEXT CUSTOMER IN LINE OVER HERE PLEASE!
Uh oh ...

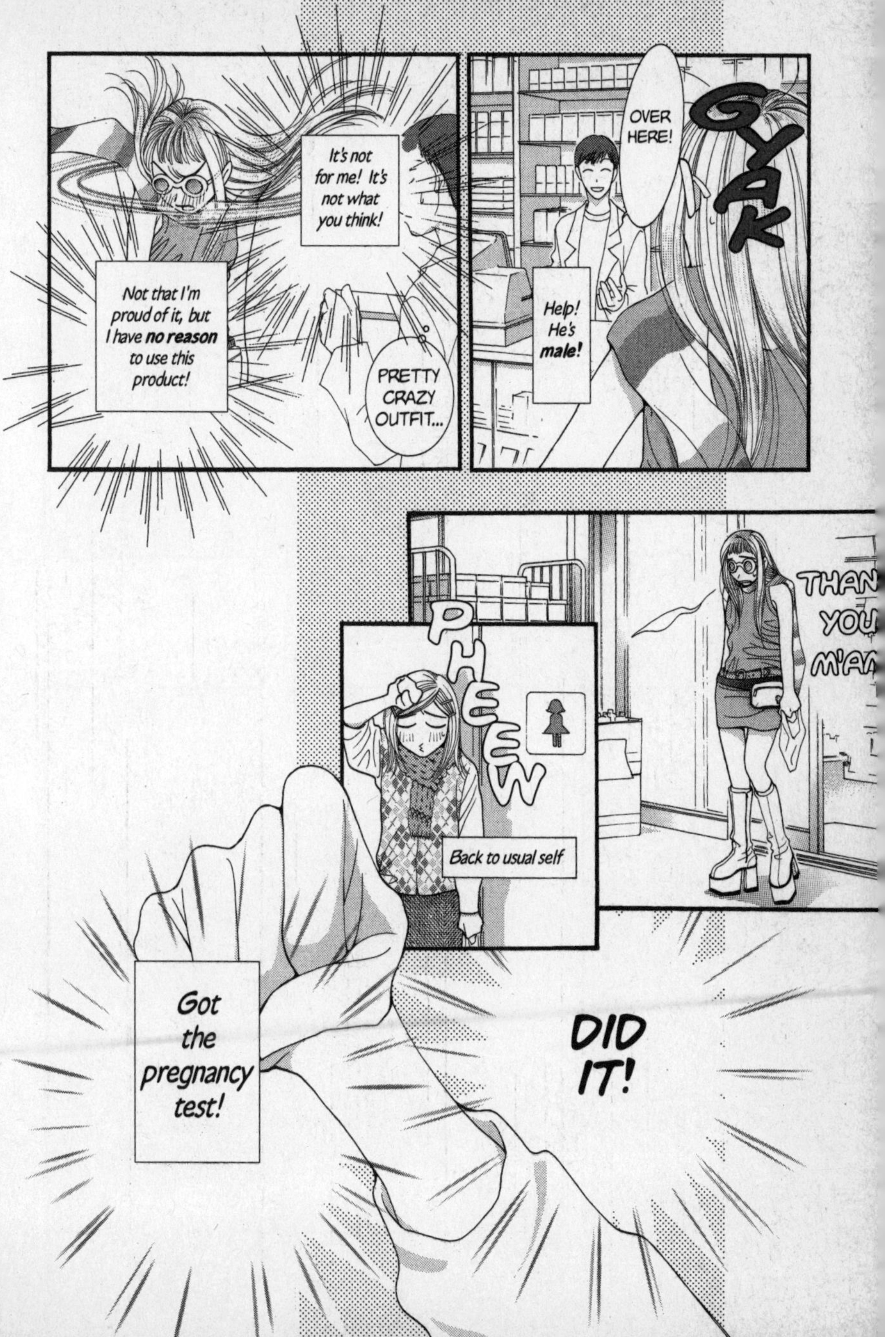
OVER HERE!
GYAK
Help! He's **male!**
It's not for me! It's not what you think!
Not that I'm proud of it, but I have **no reason** to use this product!
PRETTY CRAZY OUTFIT...
THAN
YOU
M'A
PHEW
Back to usual self
Got the pregnancy test!
DID IT!

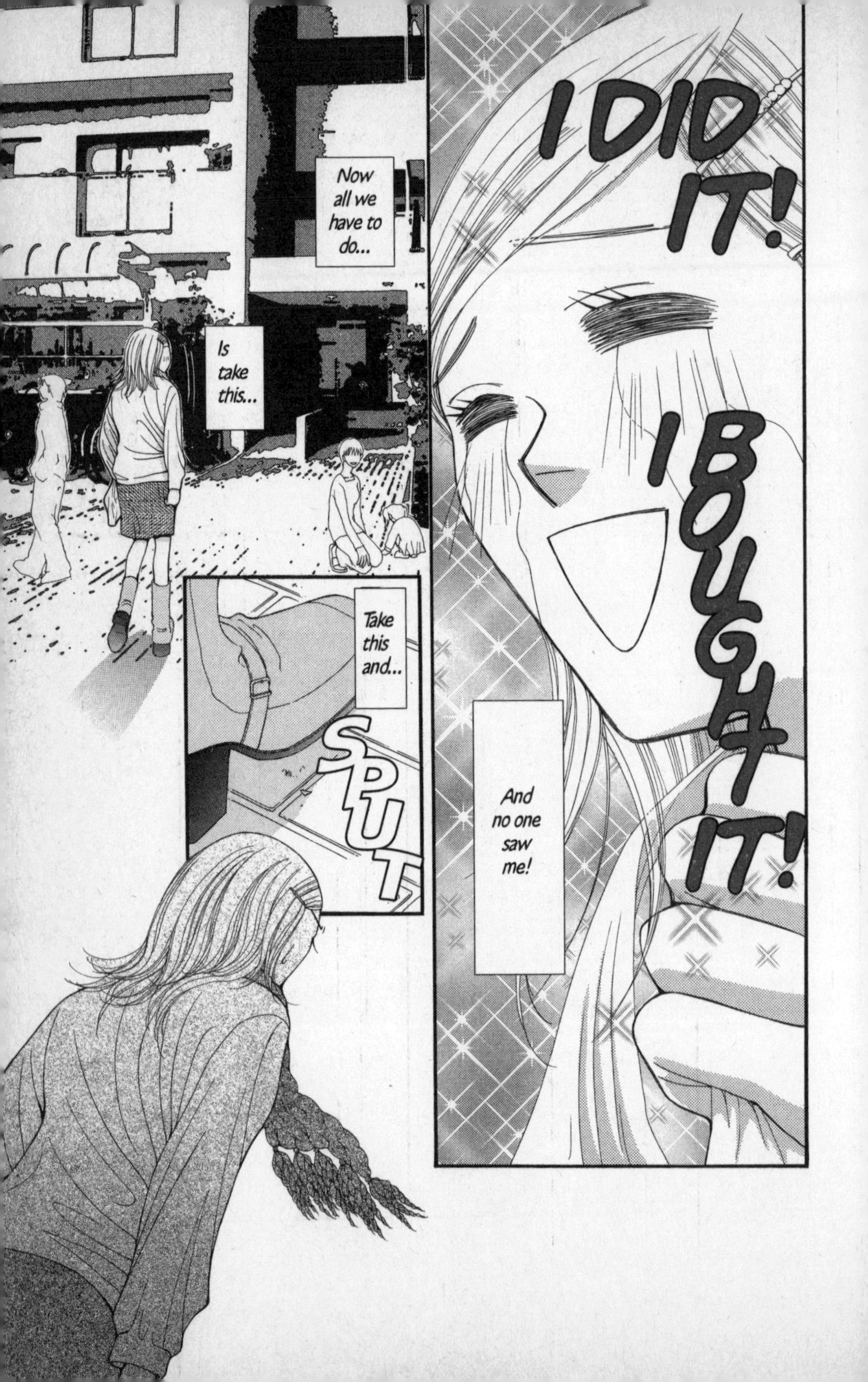
I DID IT!
I BOUGHT IT!
And no one saw me!
Now all we have to do...
Is take this...
Take this and...
SPUT

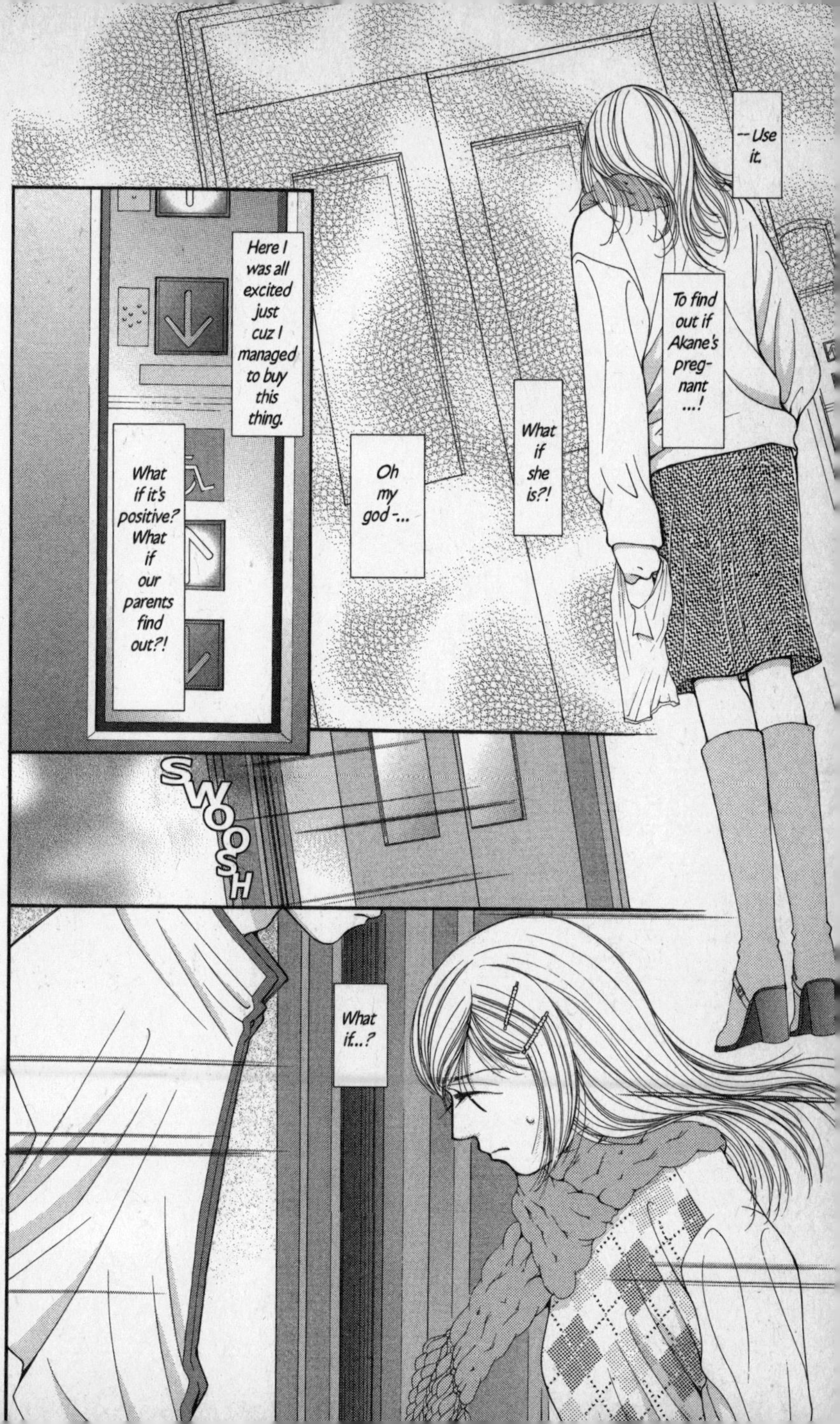
--Use it.
To find out if Akane's pregnant ...!
What if she is?!
Oh my god-...
Here I was all excited just cuz I managed to buy this thing.
What if it's positive? What if our parents find out?!
SWOOSH
What if...?

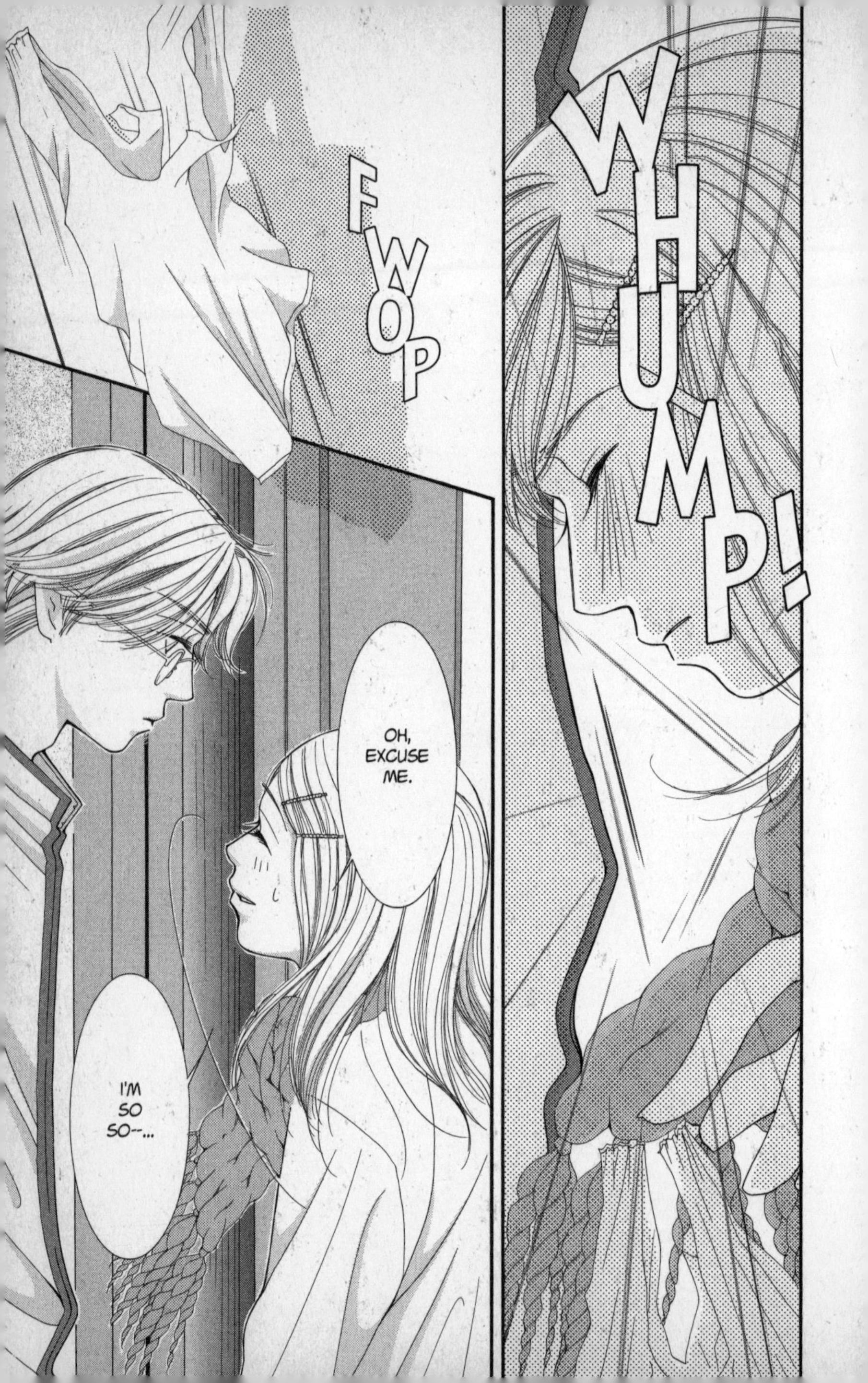
WHUMP!
FWOP
OH, EXCUSE ME.
I'M SO SO--...

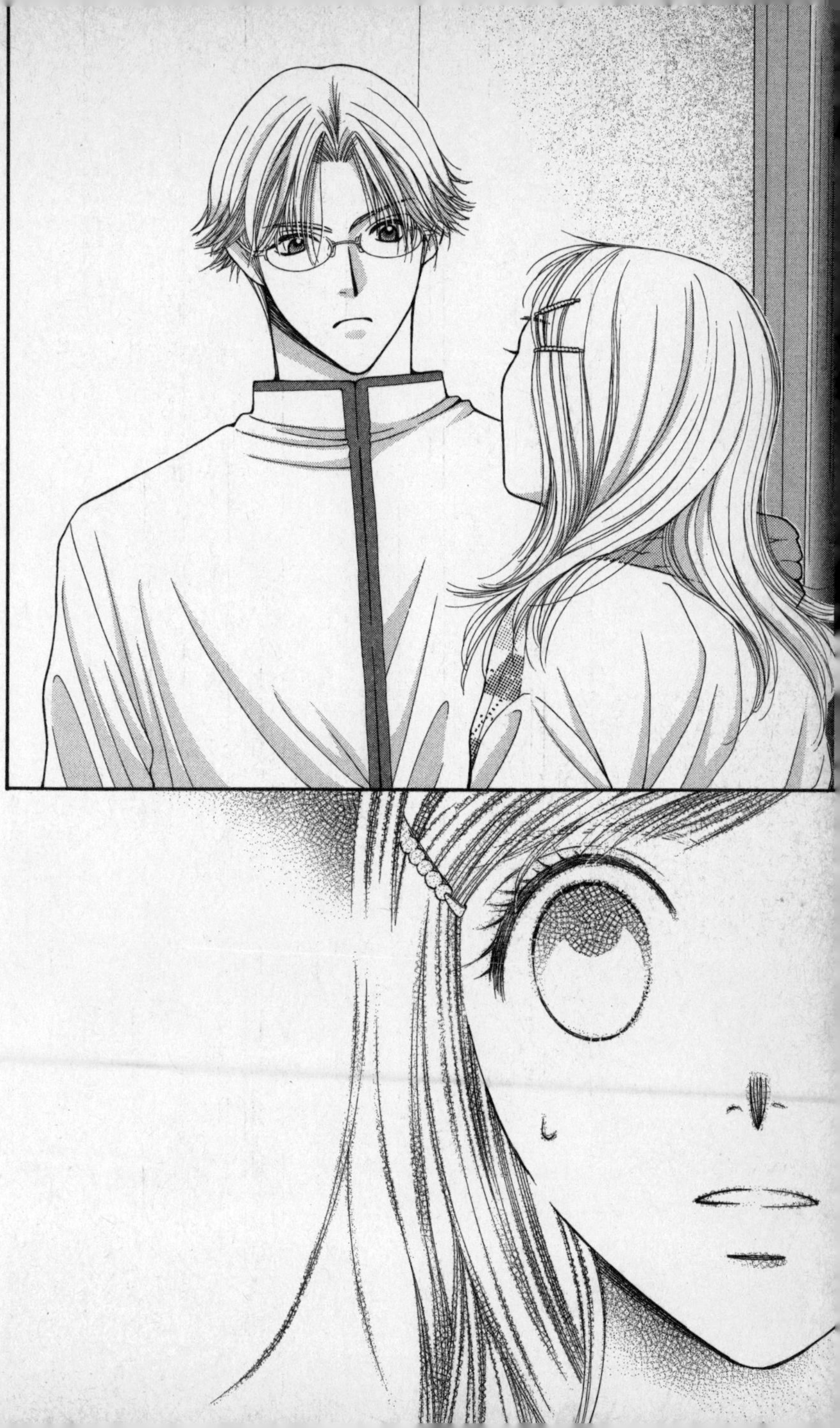

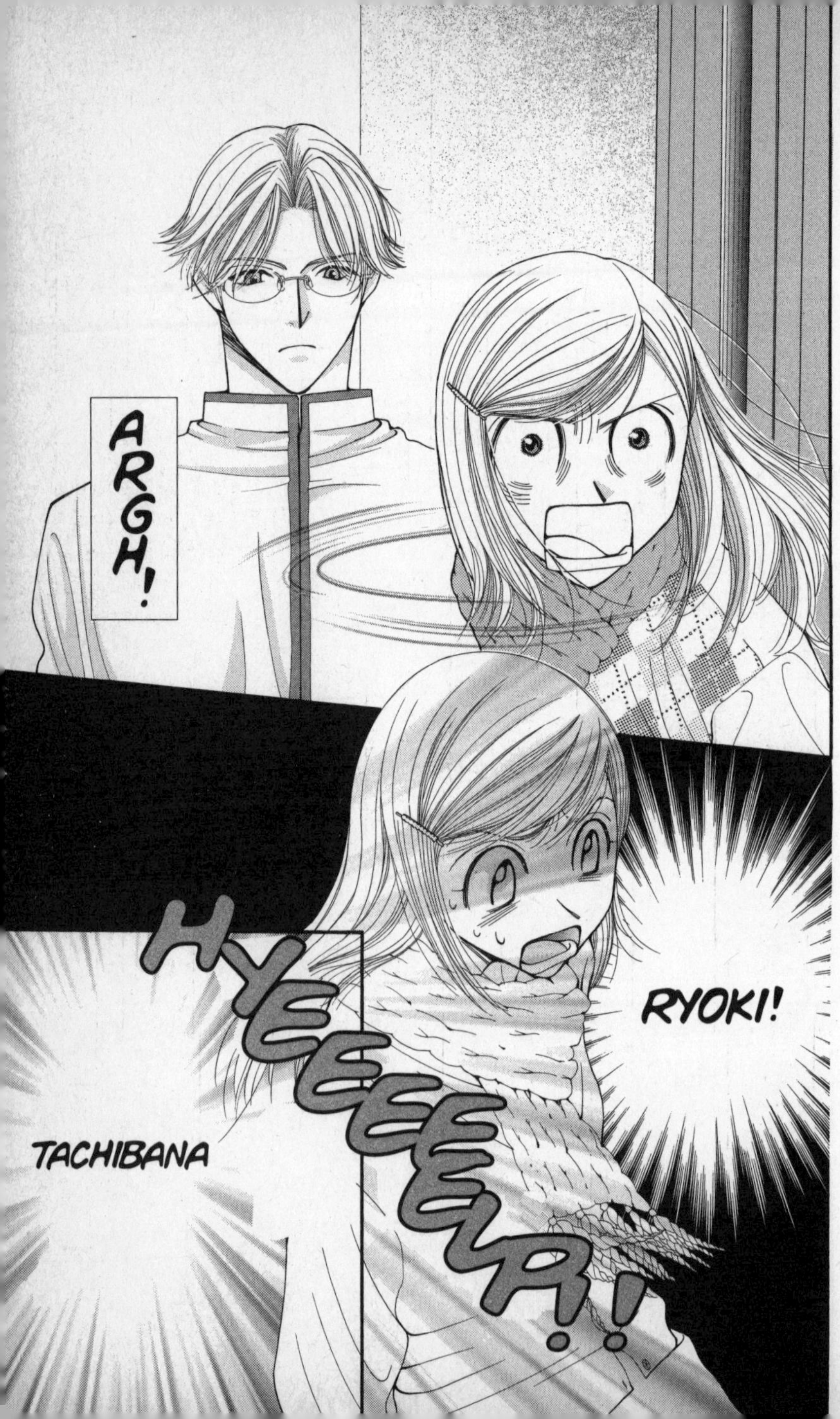
ARGH!
RYOKI!
HYEEEEEAR!!
TACHIBANA

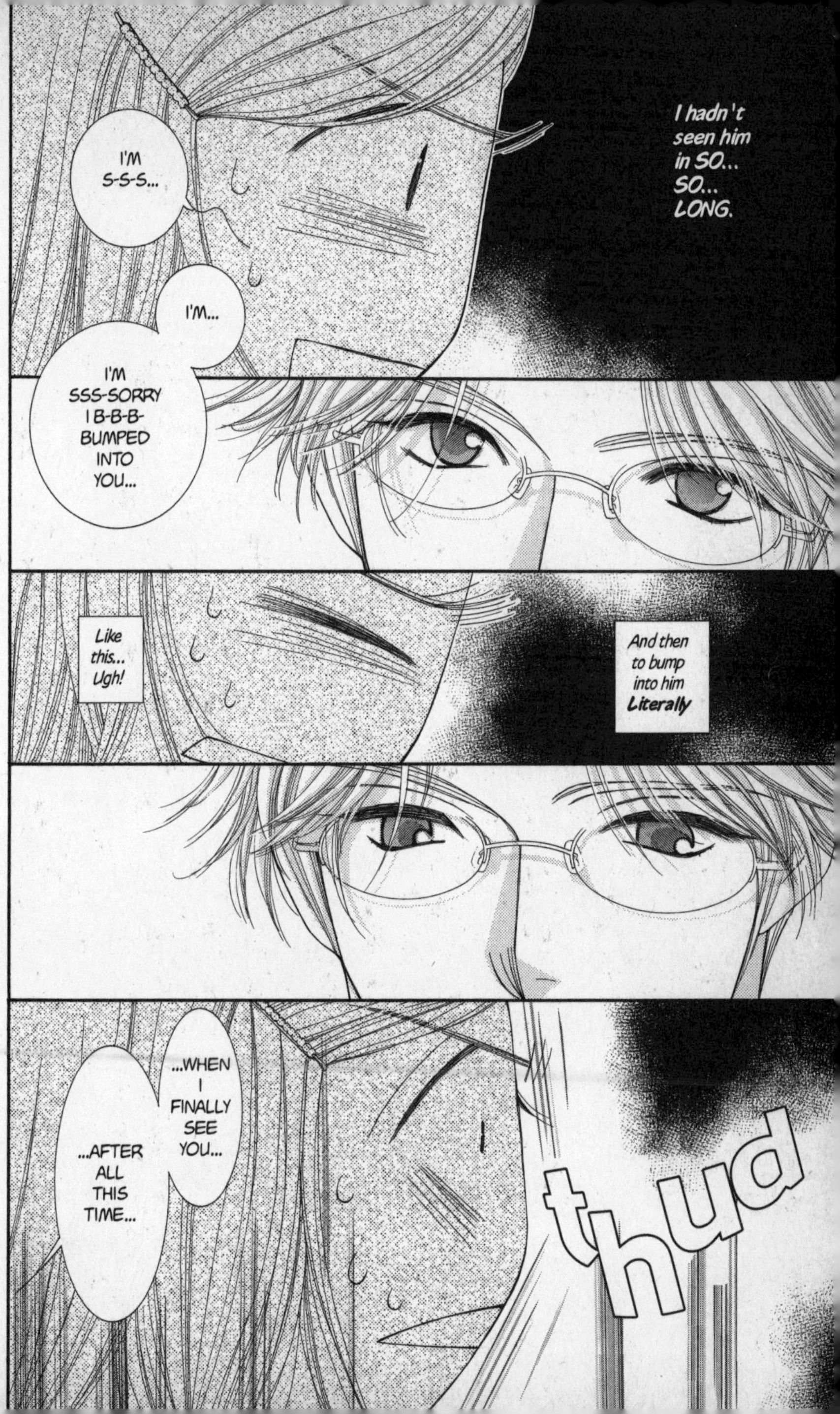
I hadn't seen him in SO... SO... LONG.
I'M S-S-S...
I'M...
I'M SSS-SORRY I B-B-B-BUMPED INTO YOU...
And then to bump into him Literally
Like this... Ugh!
thud
...WHEN I FINALLY SEE YOU...
...AFTER ALL THIS TIME...

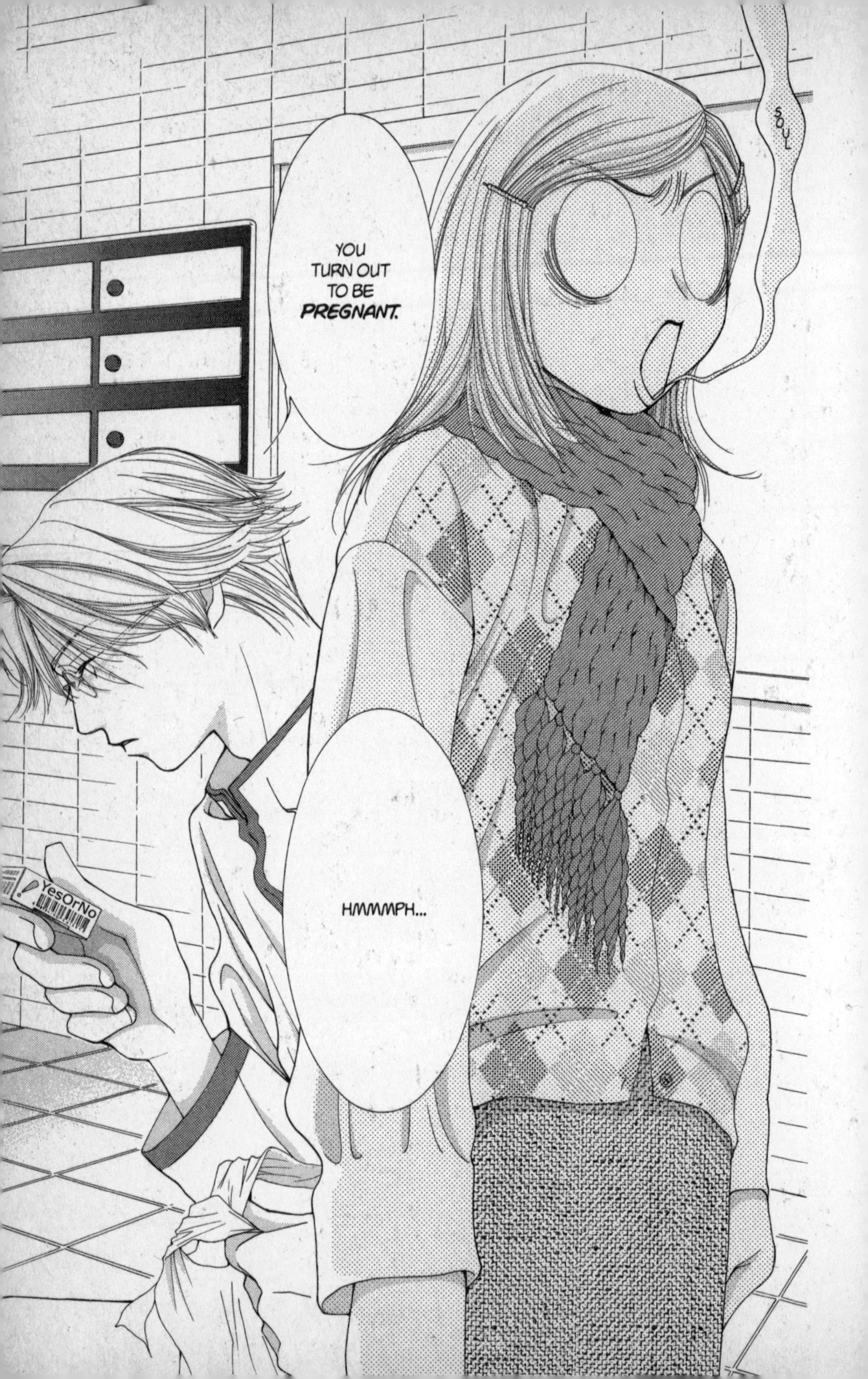
SOUL
YOU TURN OUT TO BE PREGNANT.
HMMMPH...
YesOrNo

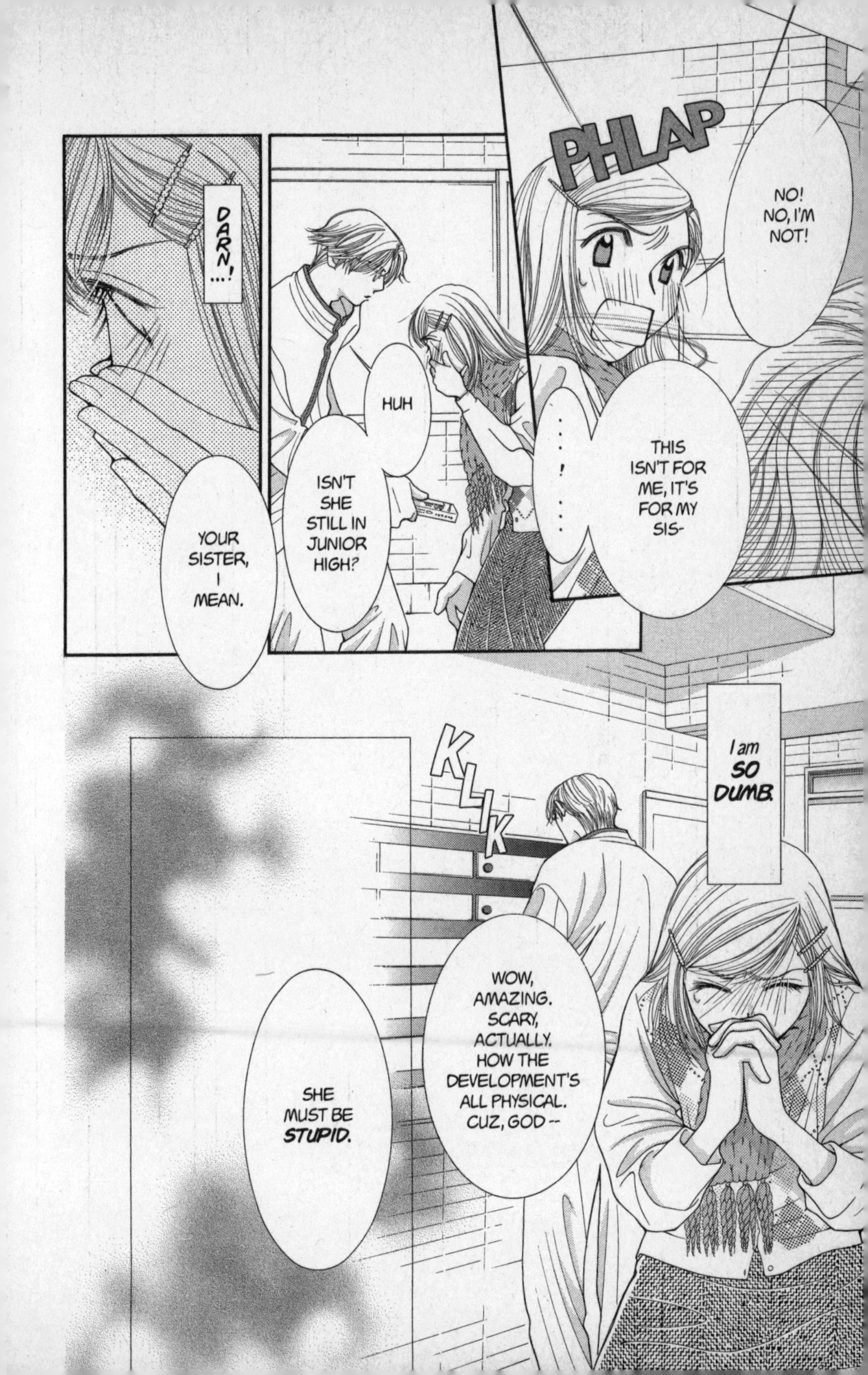
PHLAP
NO! NO, I'M NOT!
THIS ISN'T FOR ME, IT'S FOR MY SIS-
...!...
HUH
ISN'T SHE STILL IN JUNIOR HIGH?
DARN, ...!
YOUR SISTER, I MEAN.
KLIK
I am **SO DUMB.**
WOW, AMAZING. SCARY, ACTUALLY. HOW THE DEVELOPMENT'S ALL PHYSICAL. CUZ, GOD --
SHE MUST BE **STUPID.**

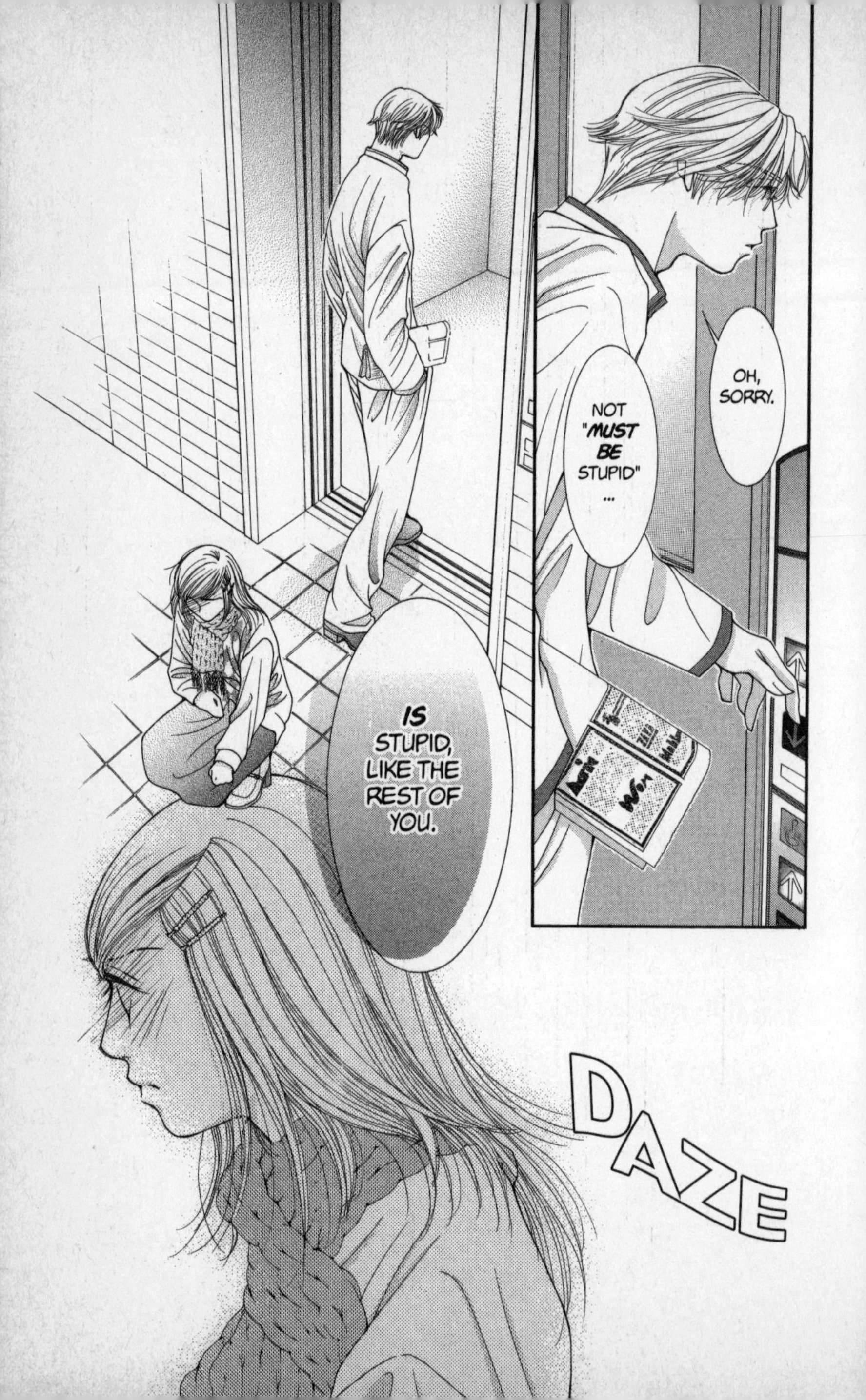
OH, SORRY.
NOT "MUST BE STUPID" ...
IS STUPID, LIKE THE REST OF YOU.
DAZE

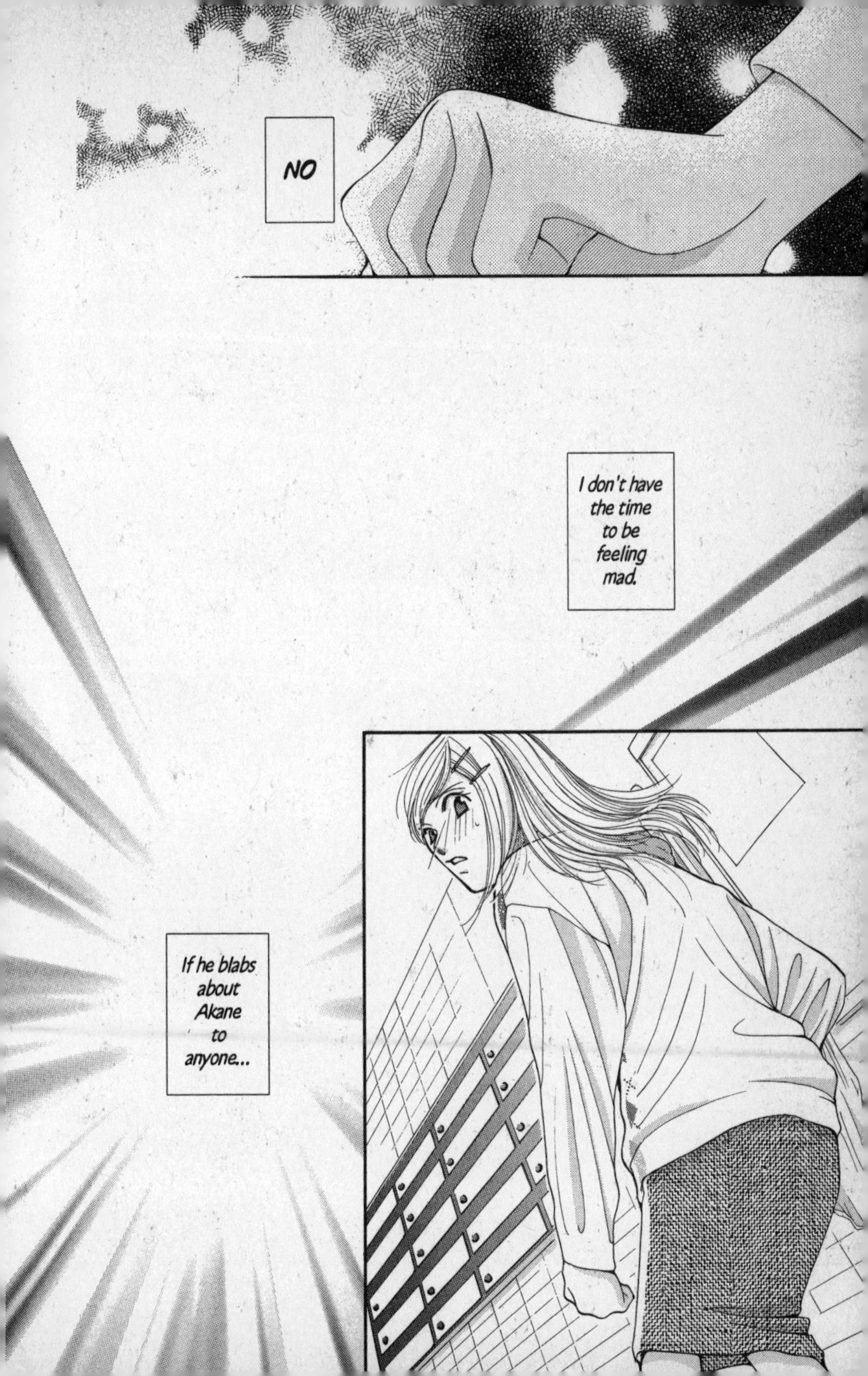
NO
I don't have the time to be feeling mad.
If he blabs about Akane to anyone...

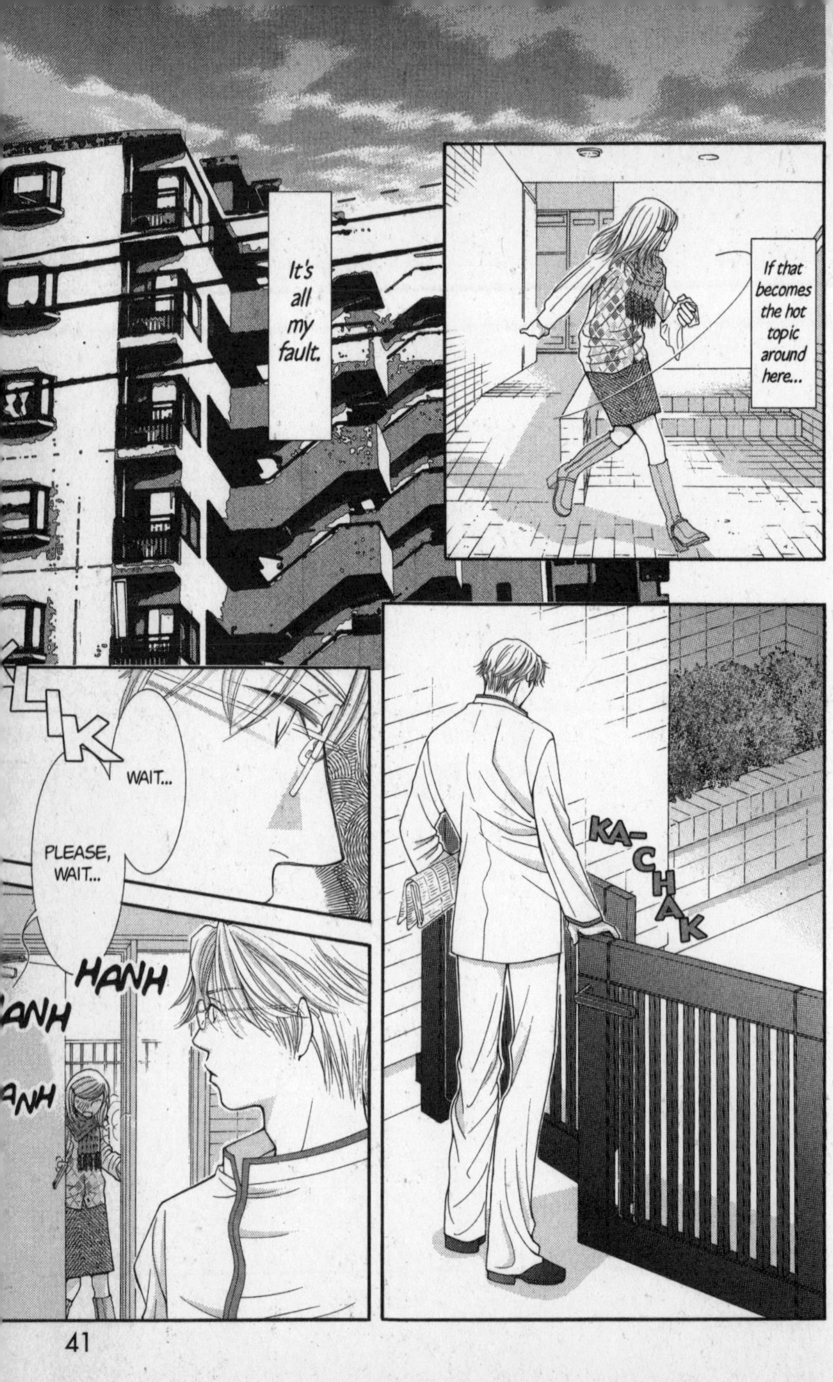

If that becomes the hot topic around here...
It's all my fault.
KA-CHAK
LIK
WAIT...
PLEASE, WAIT...
HANH
ANH
ANH

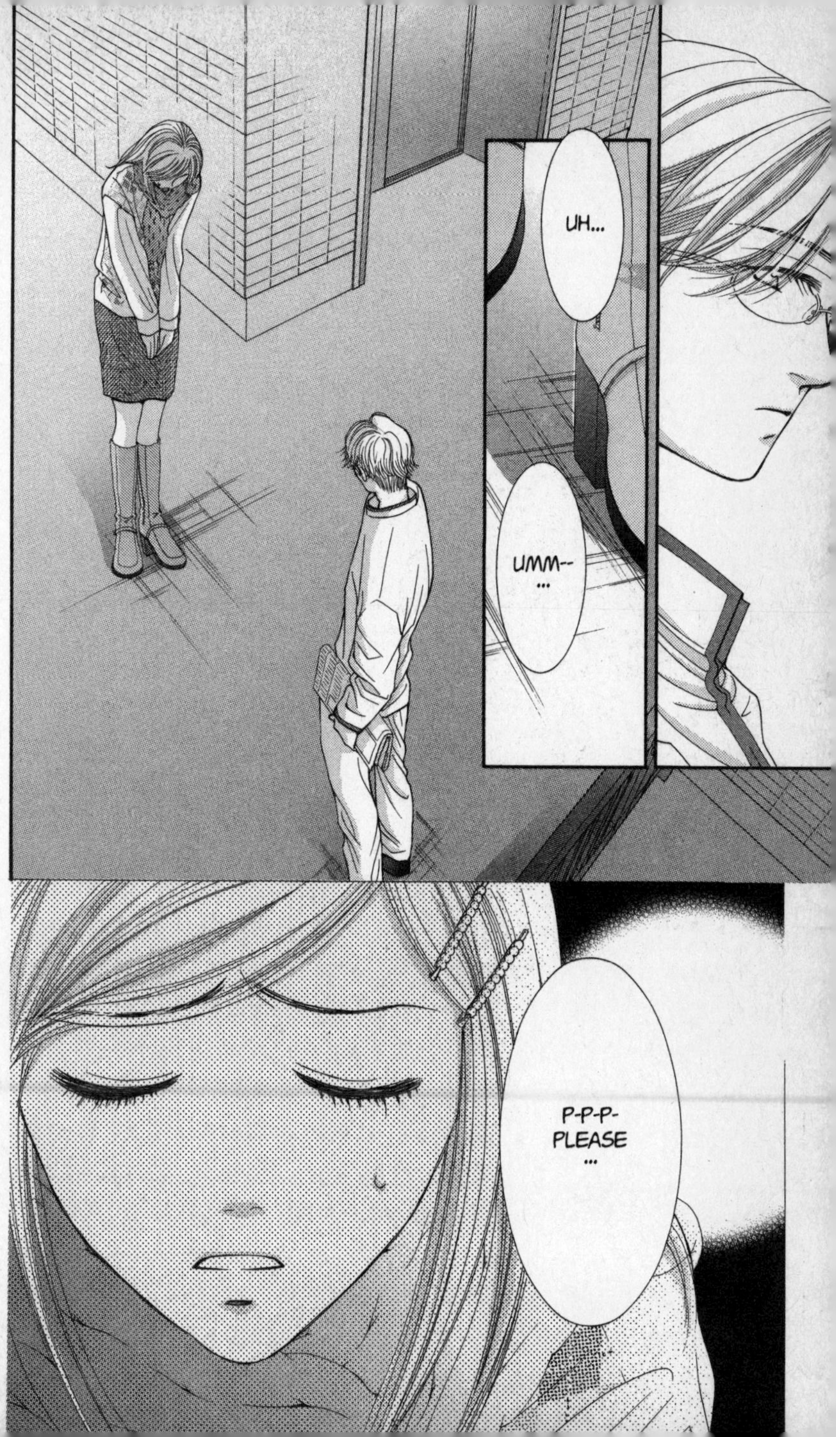
UH...
UMM--
...
P-P-P-
PLEASE
...

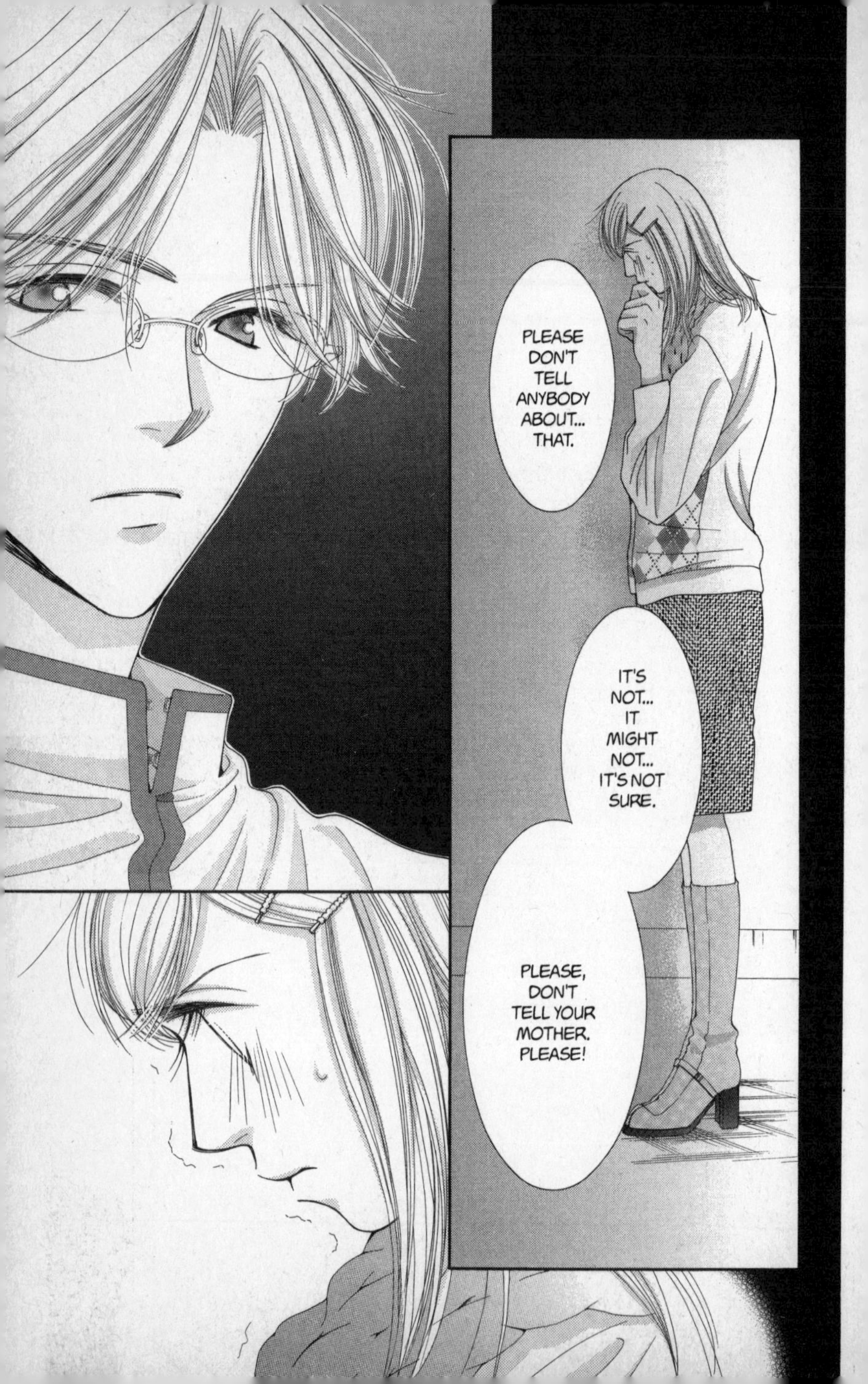
PLEASE DON'T TELL ANYBODY ABOUT... THAT.
IT'S NOT... IT MIGHT NOT... IT'S NOT SURE.
PLEASE, DON'T TELL YOUR MOTHER. PLEASE!

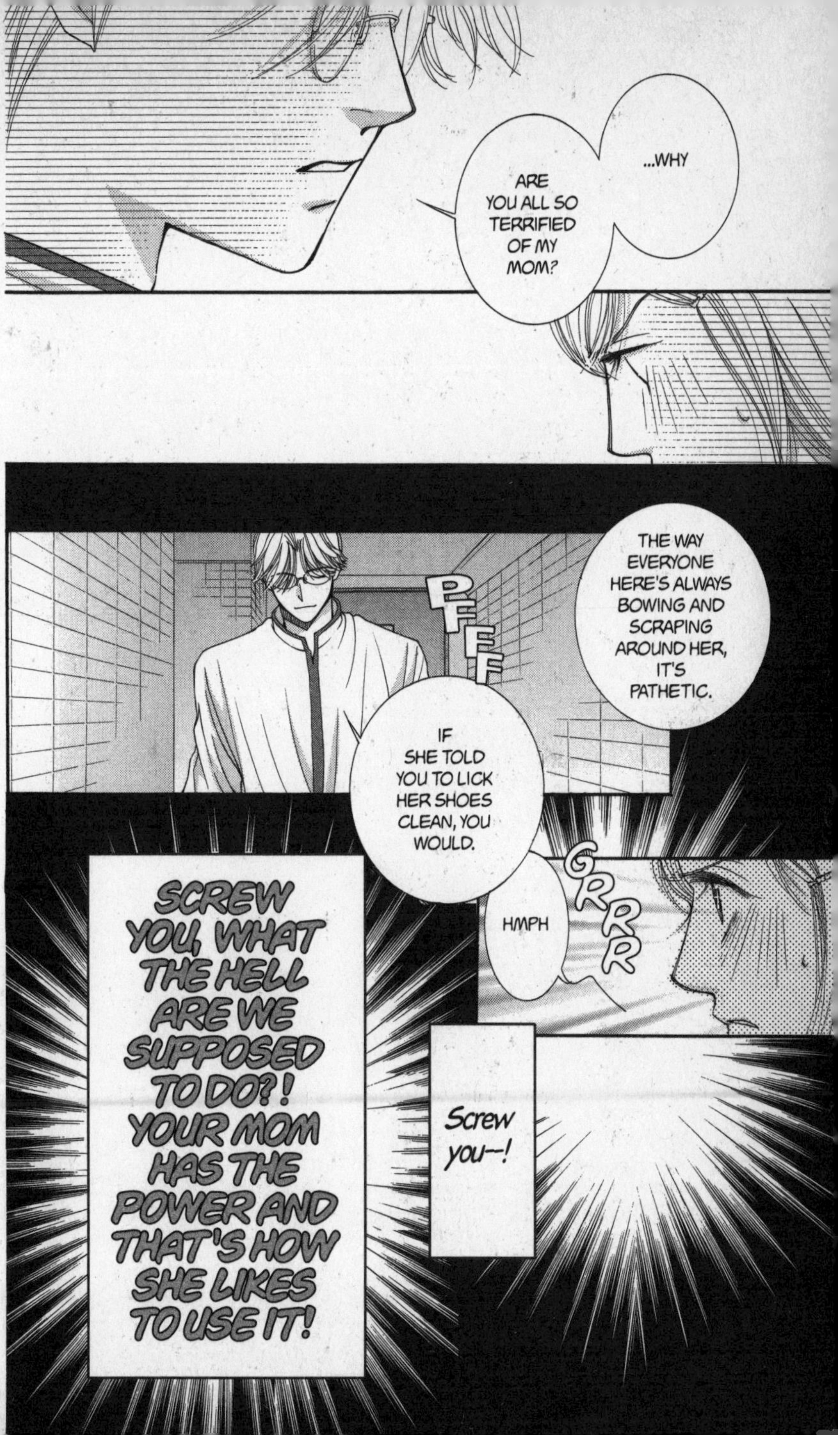
...WHY ARE YOU ALL SO TERRIFIED OF MY MOM?
THE WAY EVERYONE HERE'S ALWAYS BOWING AND SCRAPING AROUND HER, IT'S PATHETIC.
PFFF
IF SHE TOLD YOU TO LICK HER SHOES CLEAN, YOU WOULD.
GRRR
HMPH
Screw you--!
SCREW YOU, WHAT THE HELL ARE WE SUPPOSED TO DO?! YOUR MOM HAS THE POWER AND THAT'S HOW SHE LIKES TO USE IT!

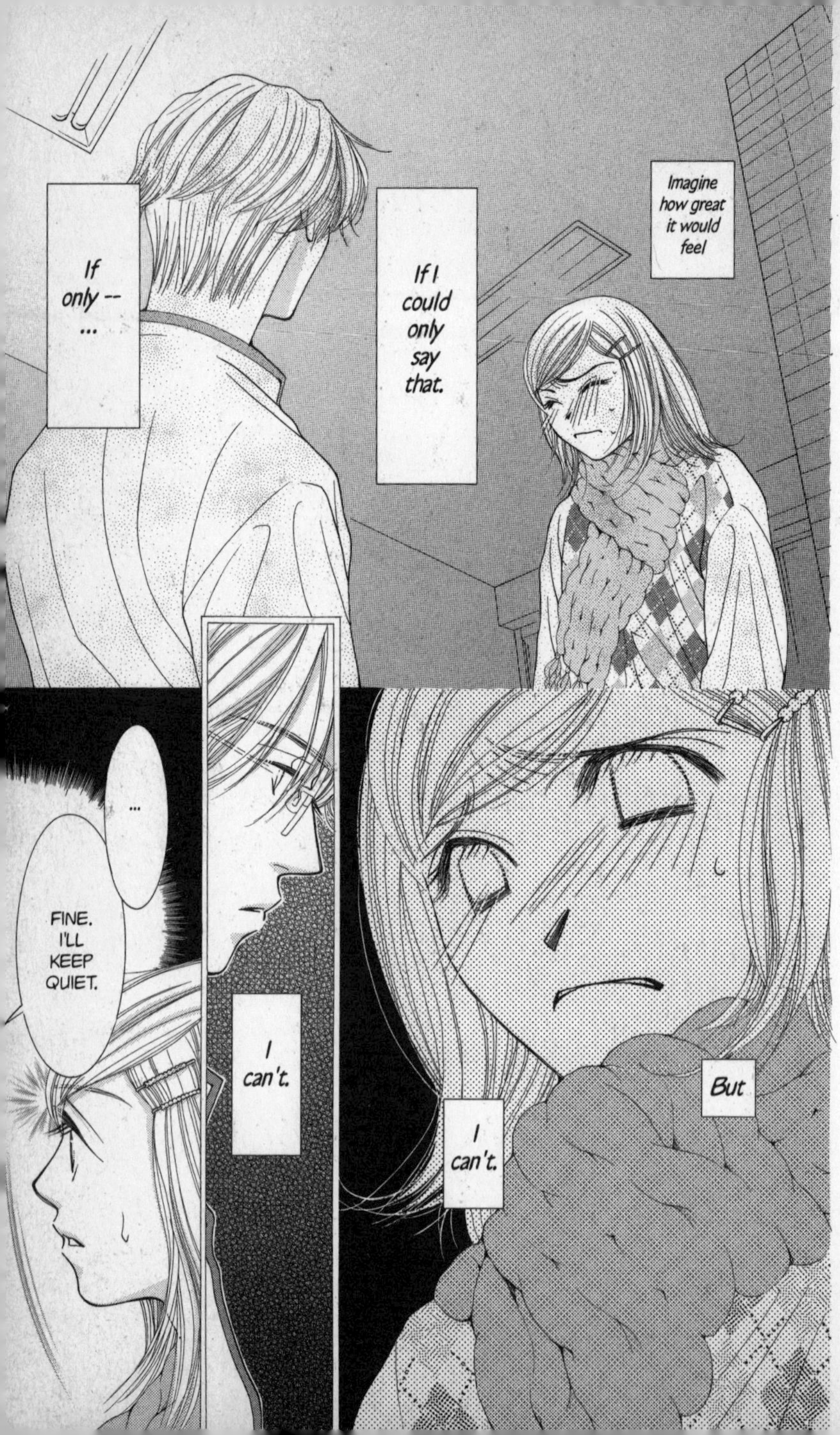
Imagine how great it would feel
If I could only say that.
If only -- ...
But
I can't.
I can't.
...
FINE. I'LL KEEP QUIET.

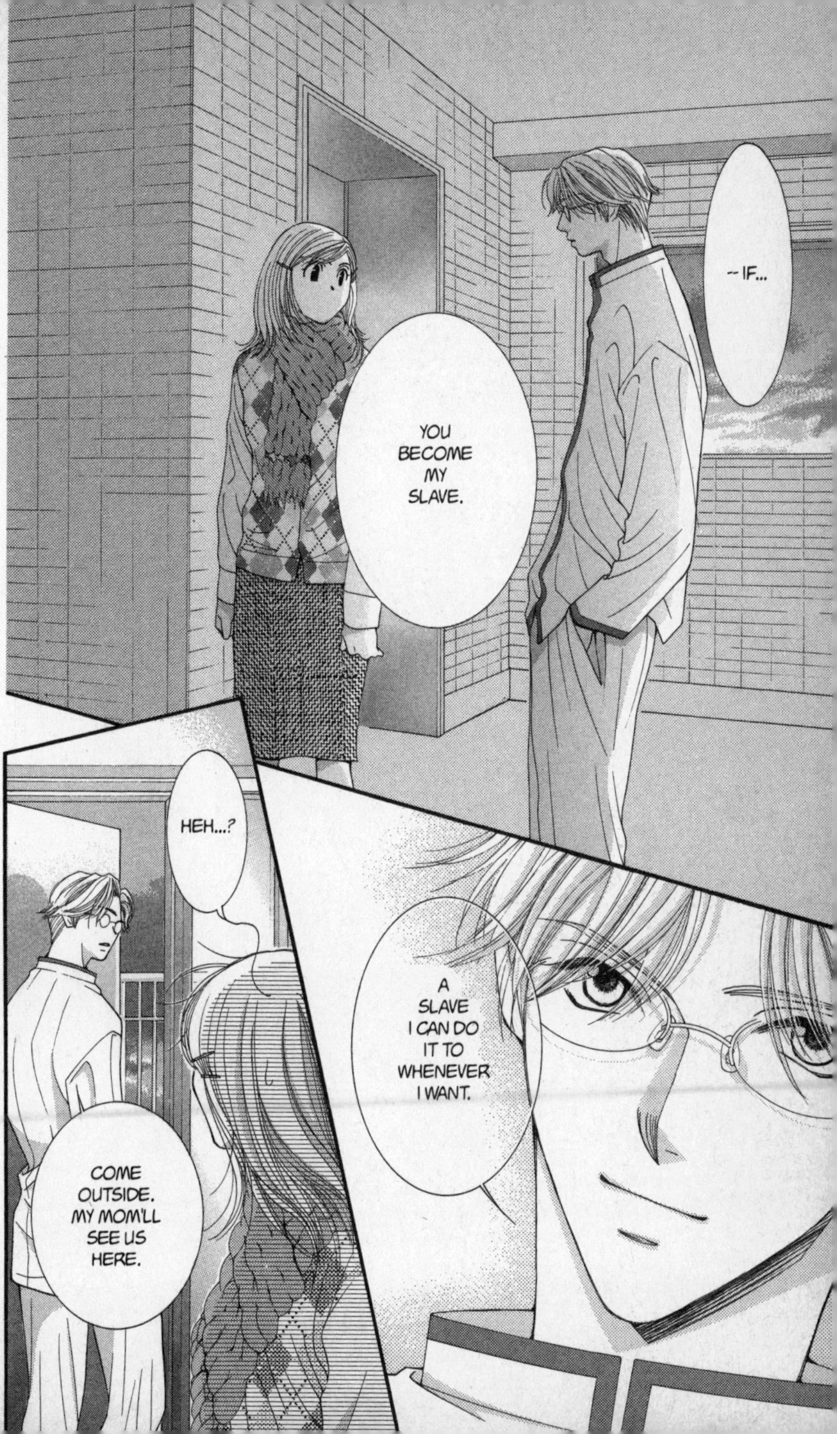
--IF...
YOU BECOME MY SLAVE.
A SLAVE I CAN DO IT TO WHENEVER I WANT.
HEH...?
COME OUTSIDE. MY MOM'LL SEE US HERE.

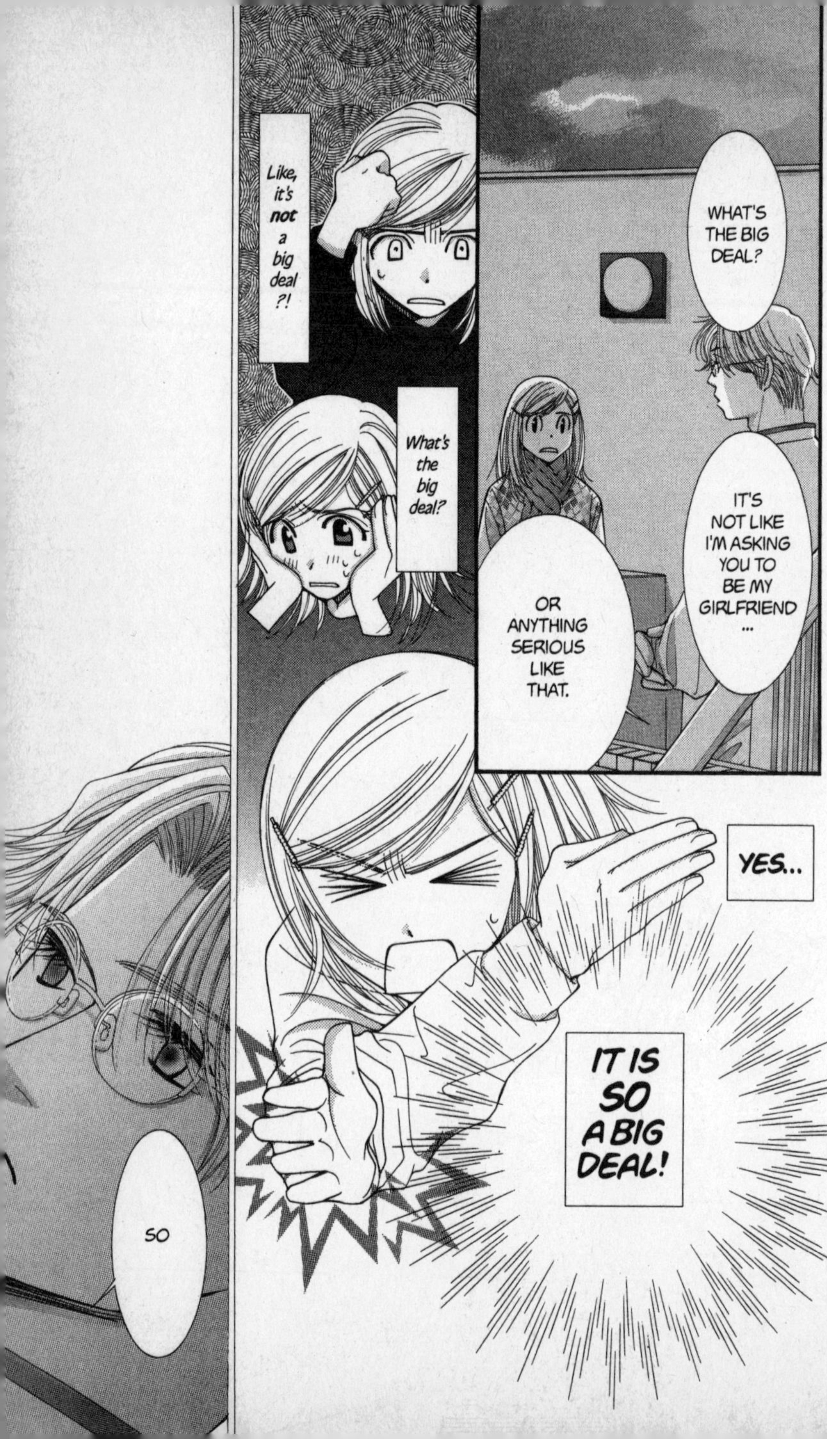
WHAT'S THE BIG DEAL?
IT'S NOT LIKE I'M ASKING YOU TO BE MY GIRLFRIEND ...
OR ANYTHING SERIOUS LIKE THAT.
Like, it's **not** a big deal ?!
What's the big deal?
YES...
IT IS SO A BIG DEAL!
SO

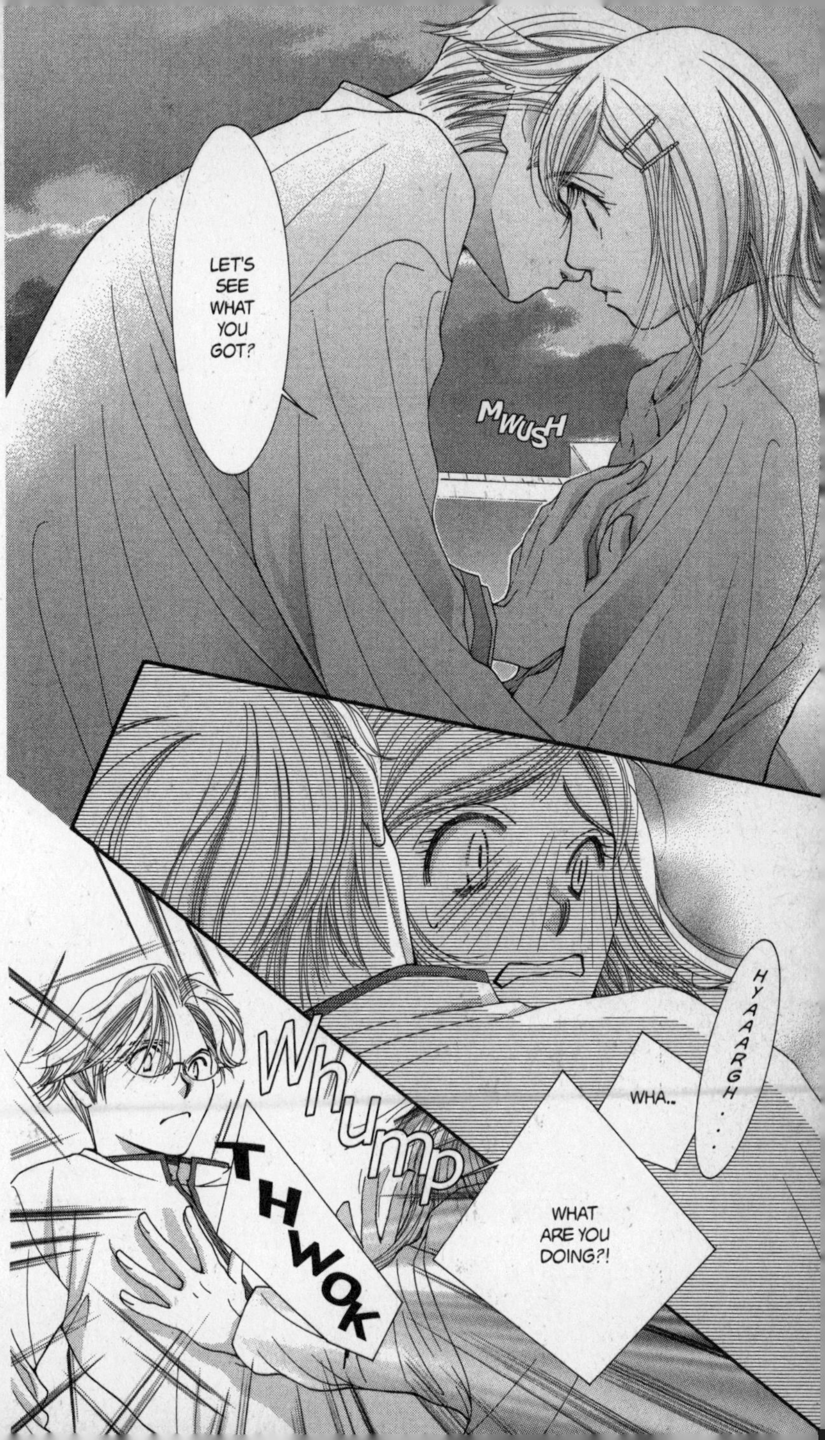

LET'S SEE WHAT YOU GOT?
MWUSH
HYAAARGH . . .
WHA..
WHAT ARE YOU DOING?!
Whump
THWOK

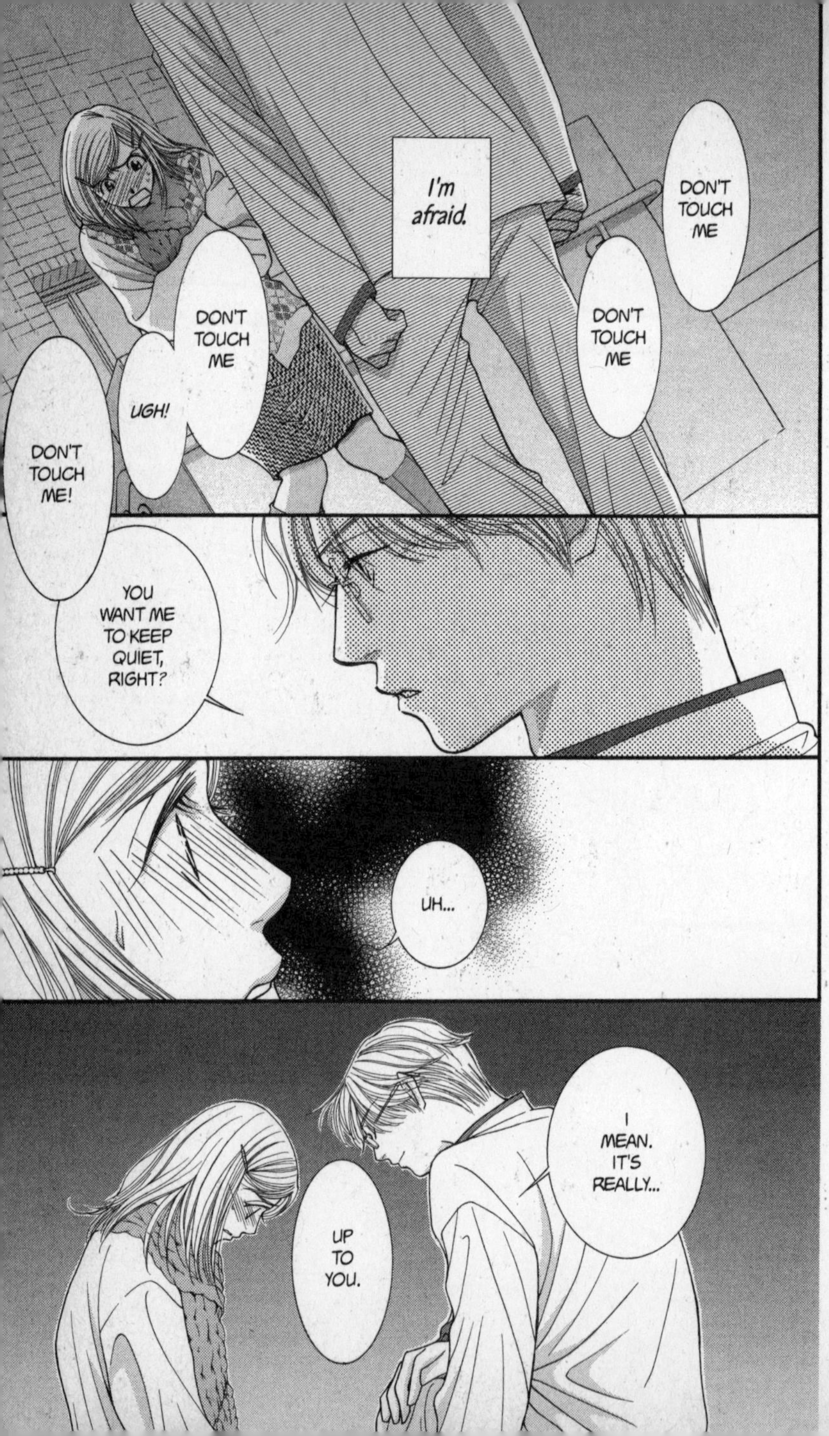
DON'T TOUCH ME
I'm afraid.
DON'T TOUCH ME
DON'T TOUCH ME
UGH!
DON'T TOUCH ME!
YOU WANT ME TO KEEP QUIET, RIGHT?
UH...
I MEAN. IT'S REALLY...
UP TO YOU.

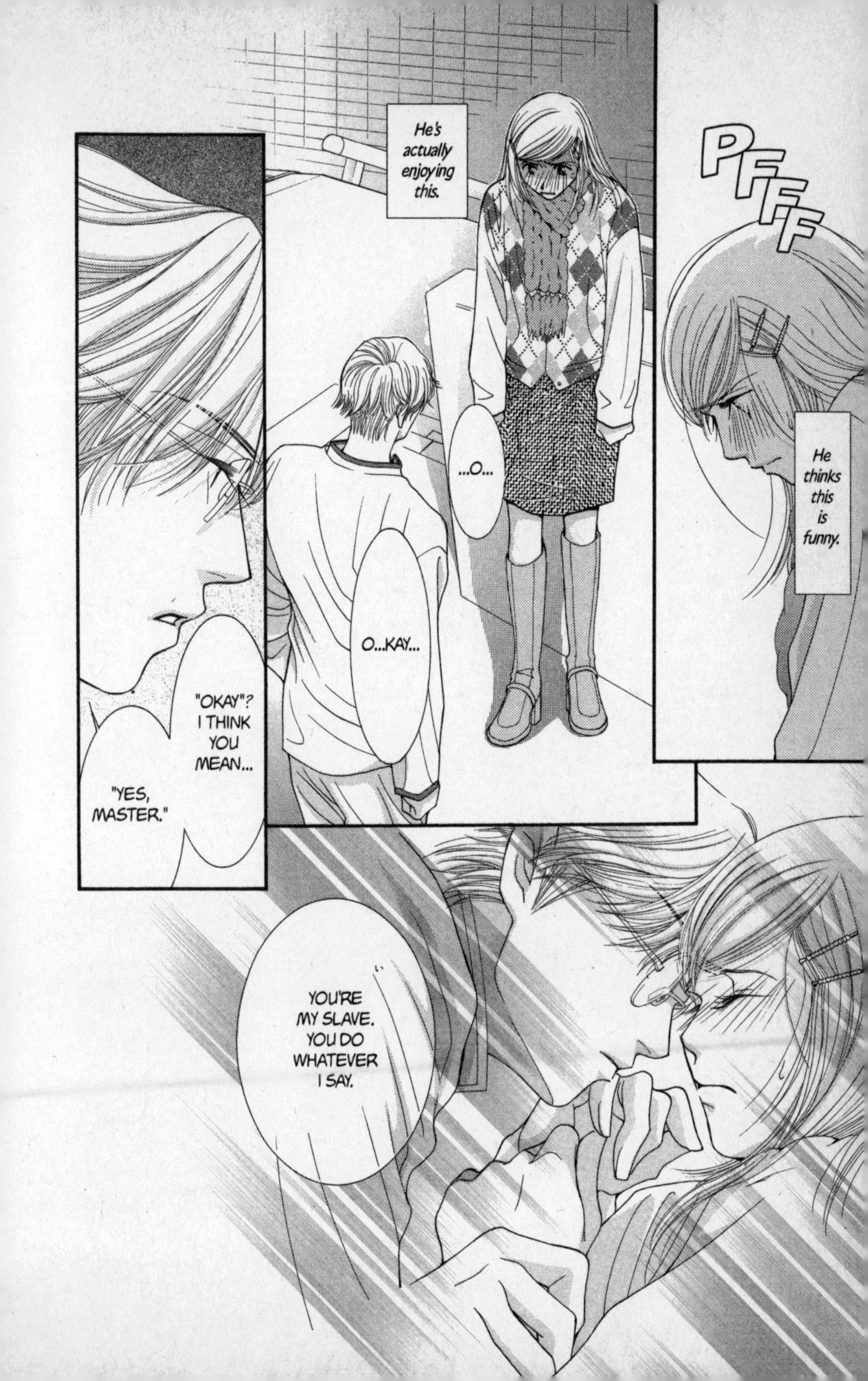
PFFFF
He thinks this is funny.
He's actually enjoying this.
...O...
O...KAY...
"OKAY"? I THINK YOU MEAN...
"YES, MASTER."
YOU'RE MY SLAVE. YOU DO WHATEVER I SAY.

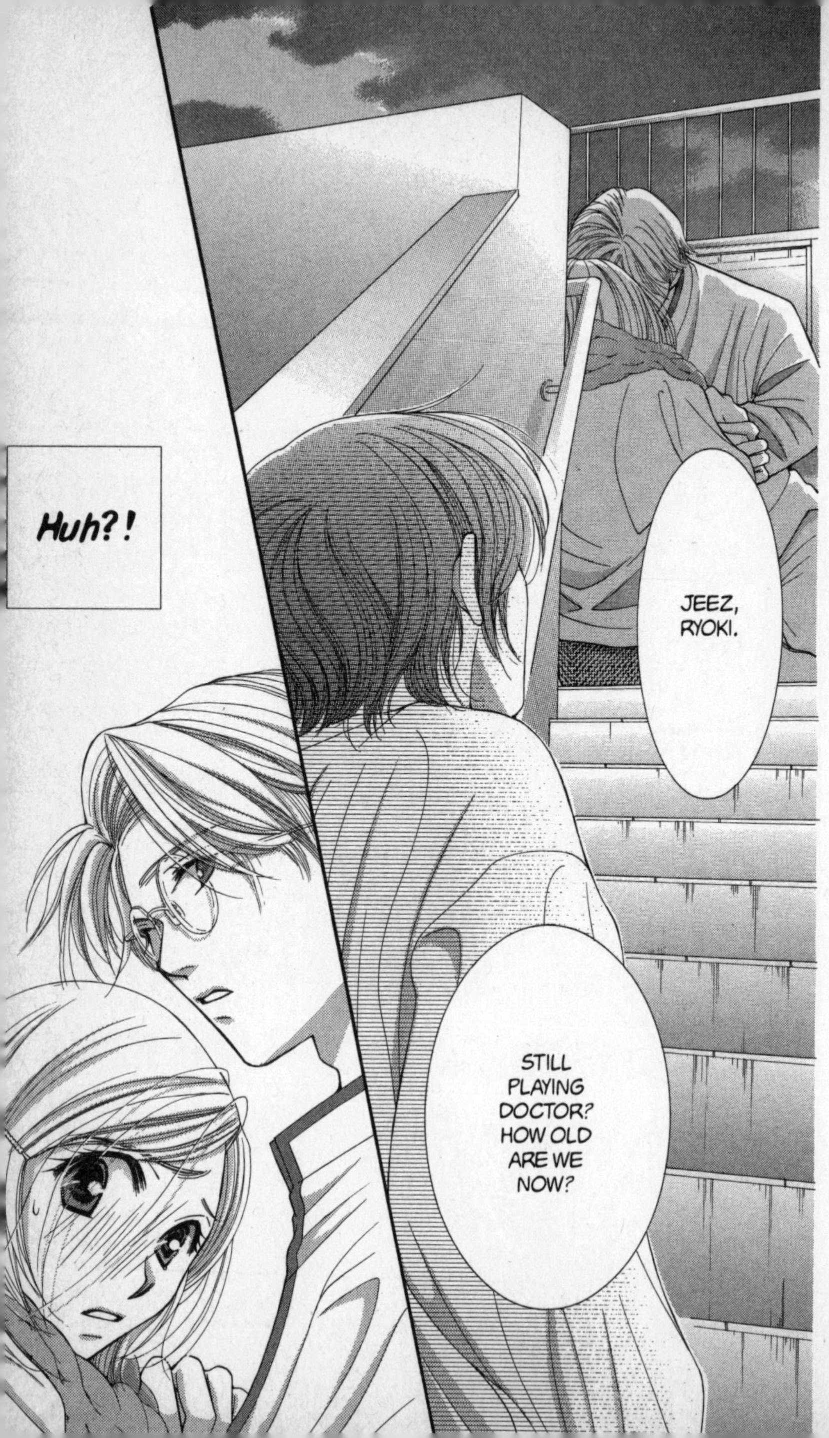
JEEZ, RYOKI.
STILL PLAYING DOCTOR? HOW OLD ARE WE NOW?
Huh?!

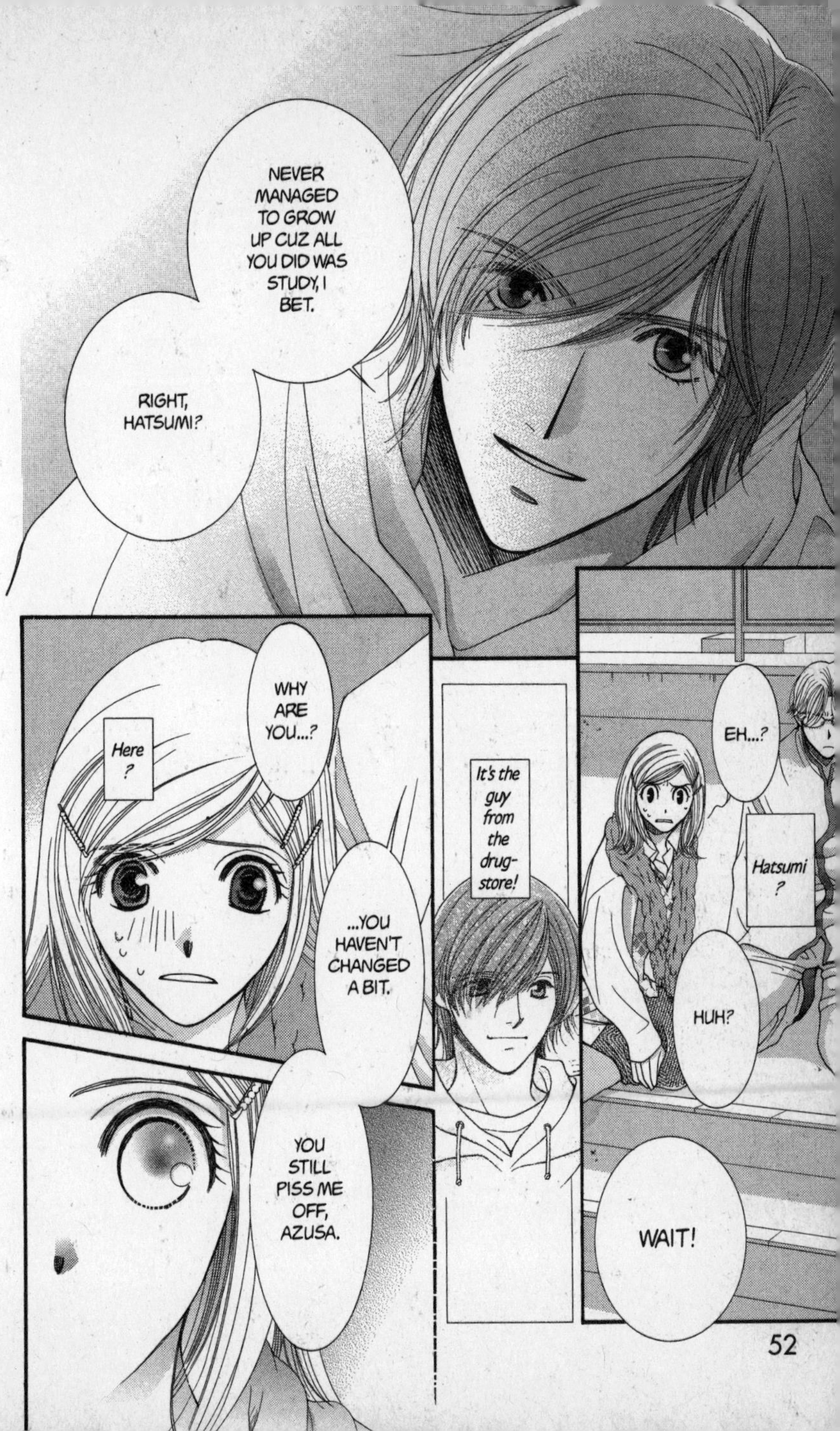
NEVER MANAGED TO GROW UP CUZ ALL YOU DID WAS STUDY, I BET.
RIGHT, HATSUMI?
EH...?
Hatsumi?
HUH?
WAIT!
It's the guy from the drug-store!
WHY ARE YOU...?
Here?
...YOU HAVEN'T CHANGED A BIT.
YOU STILL PISS ME OFF, AZUSA.

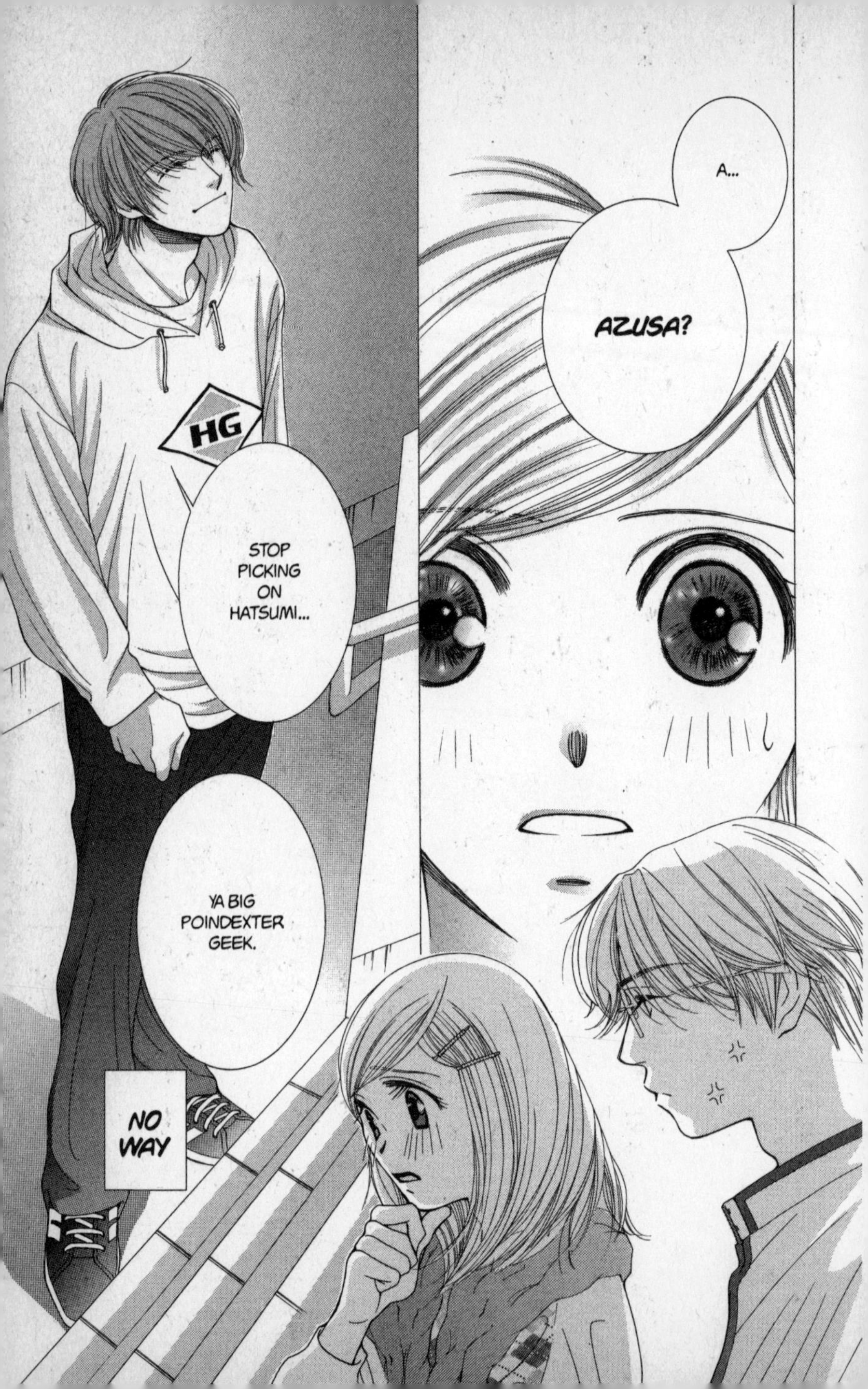
A...
AZUSA?
STOP PICKING ON HATSUMI...
YA BIG POINDEXTER GEEK.
NO WAY

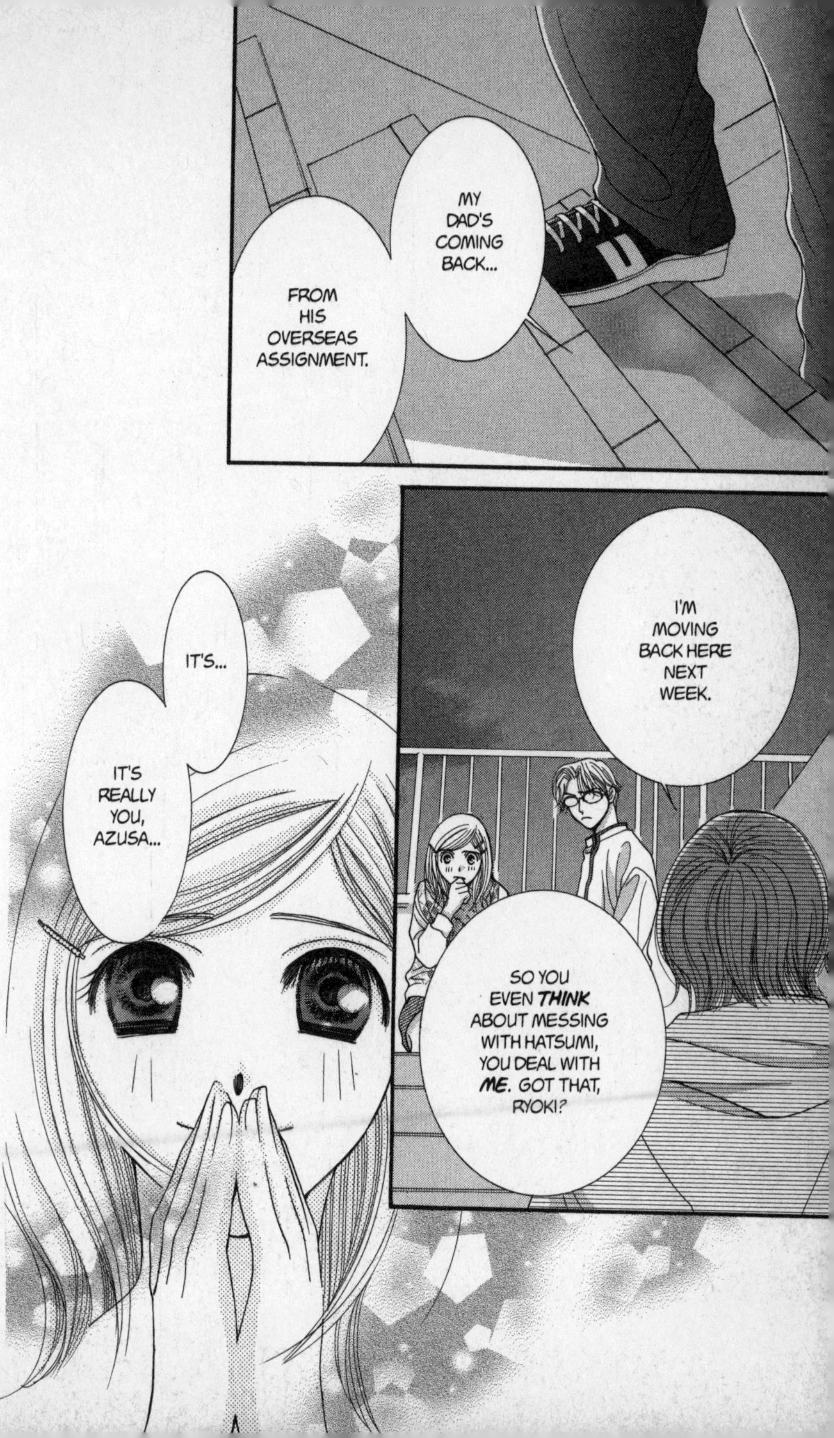
MY DAD'S COMING BACK...
FROM HIS OVERSEAS ASSIGNMENT.
I'M MOVING BACK HERE NEXT WEEK.
SO YOU EVEN **THINK** ABOUT MESSING WITH HATSUMI, YOU DEAL WITH **ME**. GOT THAT, RYOKI?
IT'S...
IT'S REALLY YOU, AZUSA...

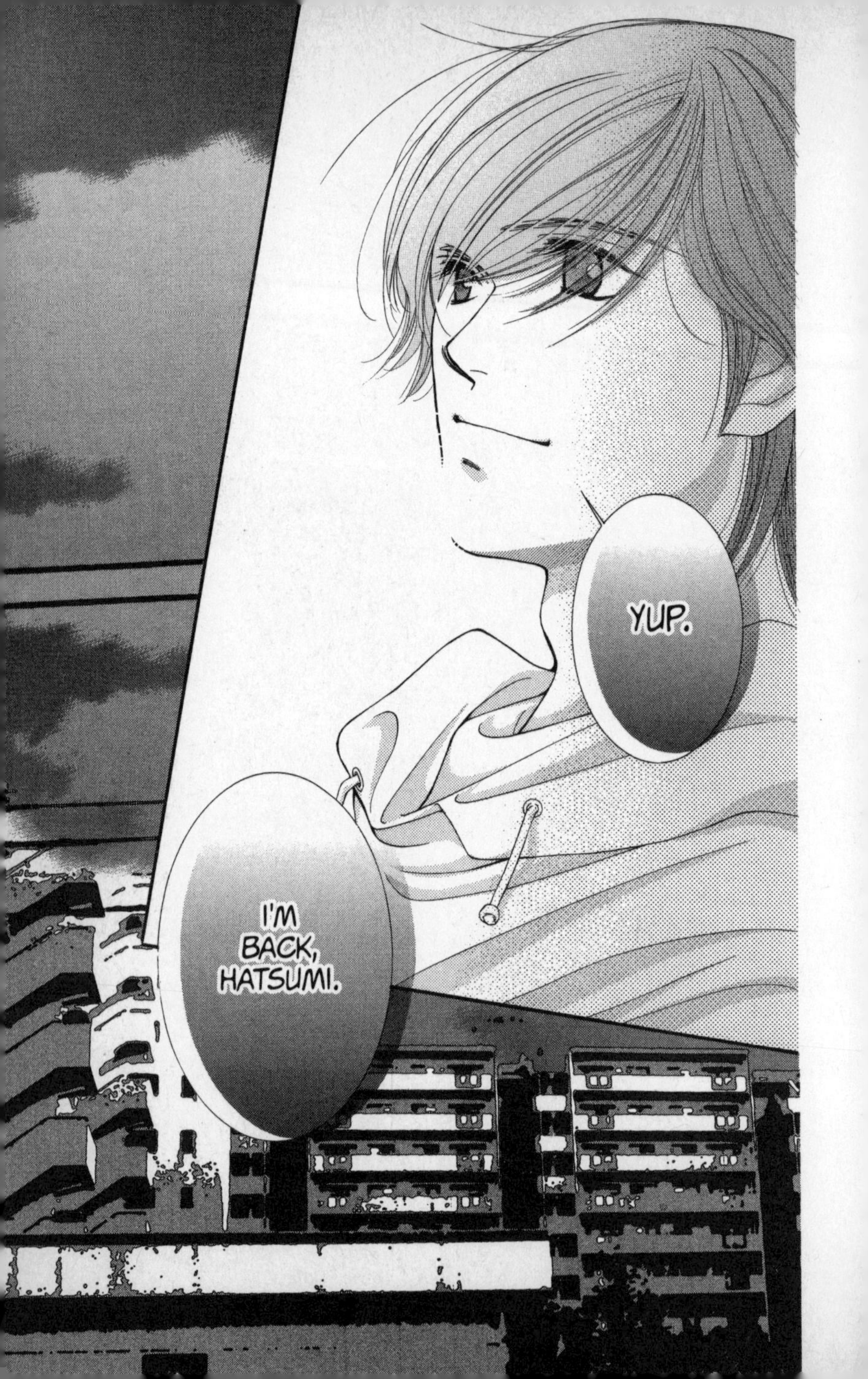
YUP.
I'M BACK, HATSUMI.

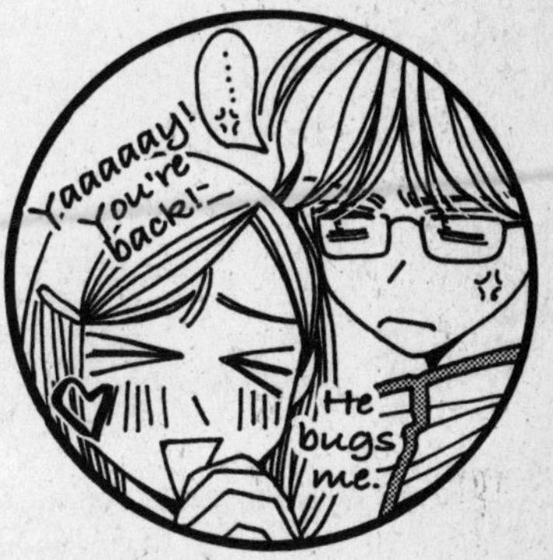
Yaaaaay! You're back!
......
He bugs me.

Chapter 2

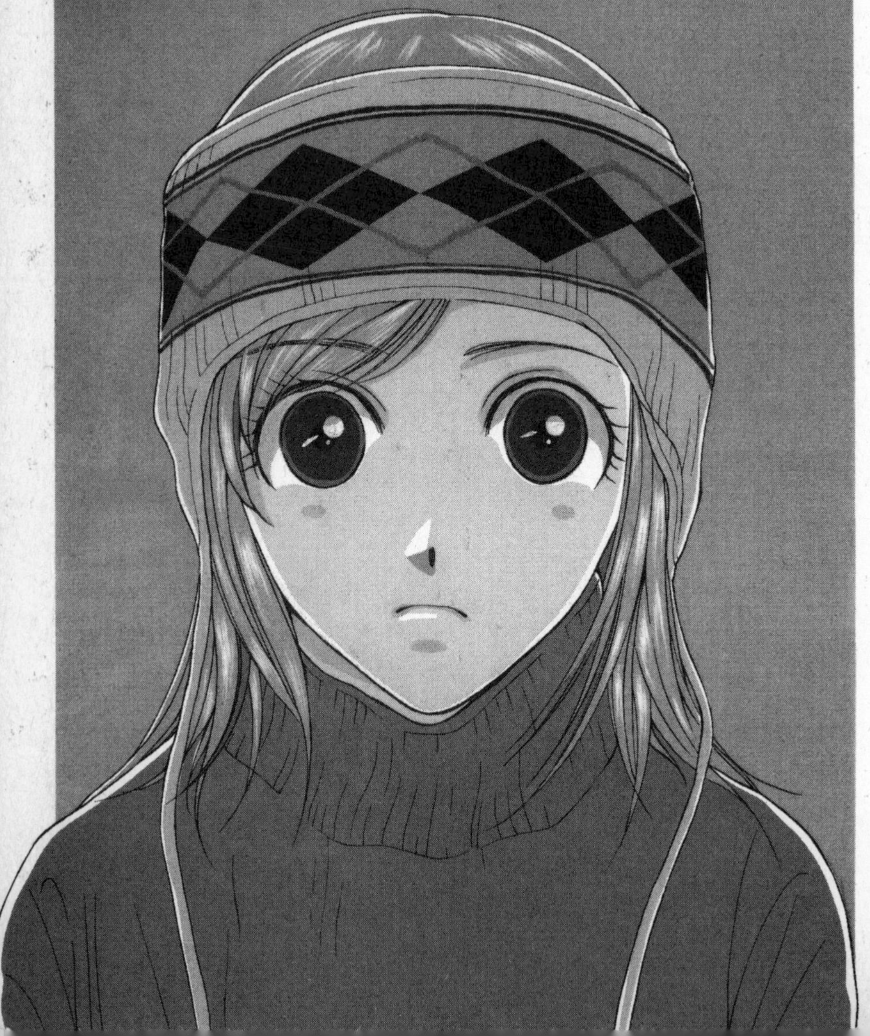

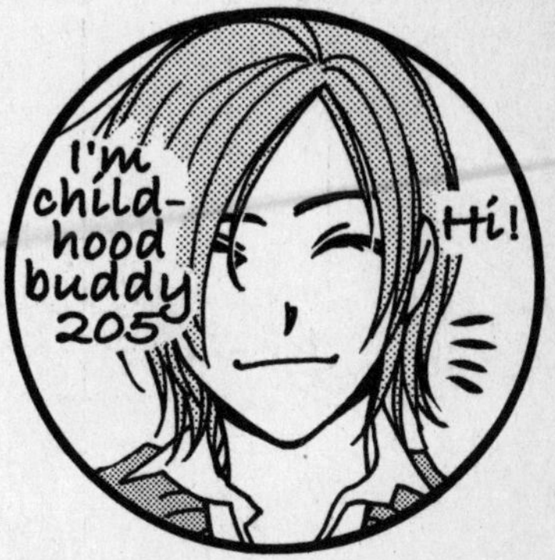
I'm childhood buddy 205
Hi!

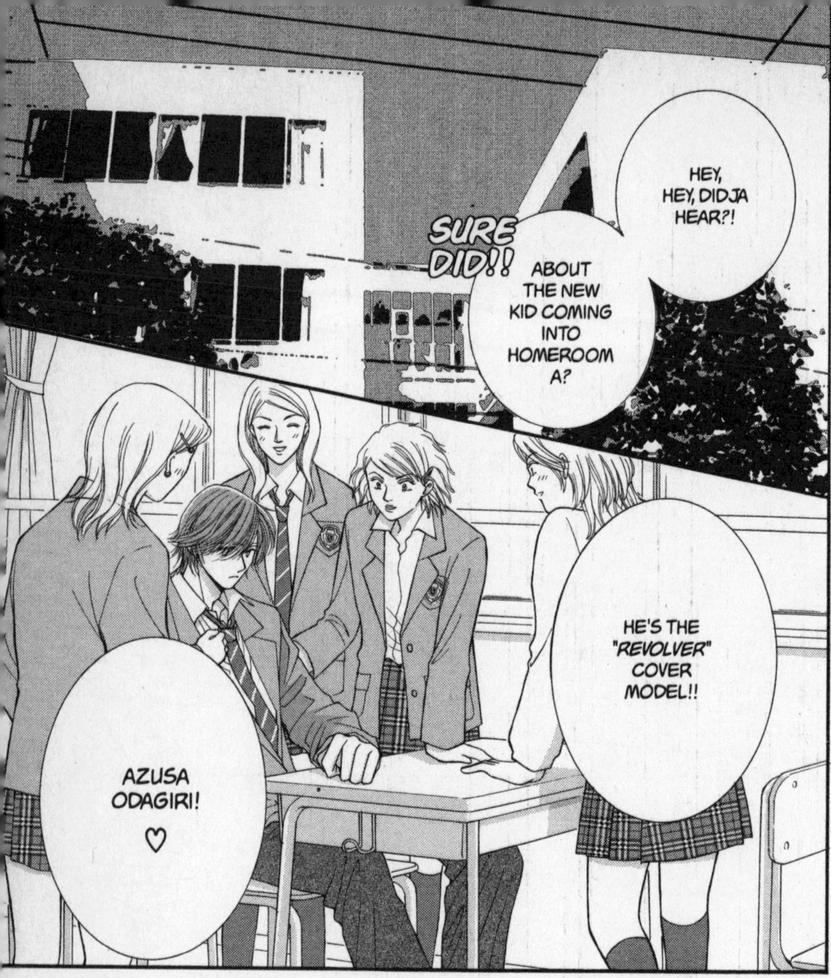
HEY, HEY, DIDJA HEAR?!
SURE DID!!
ABOUT THE NEW KID COMING INTO HOMEROOM A?
HE'S THE "REVOLVER" COVER MODEL!!
AZUSA ODAGIRI! ♡

hot gimmick

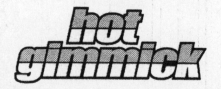

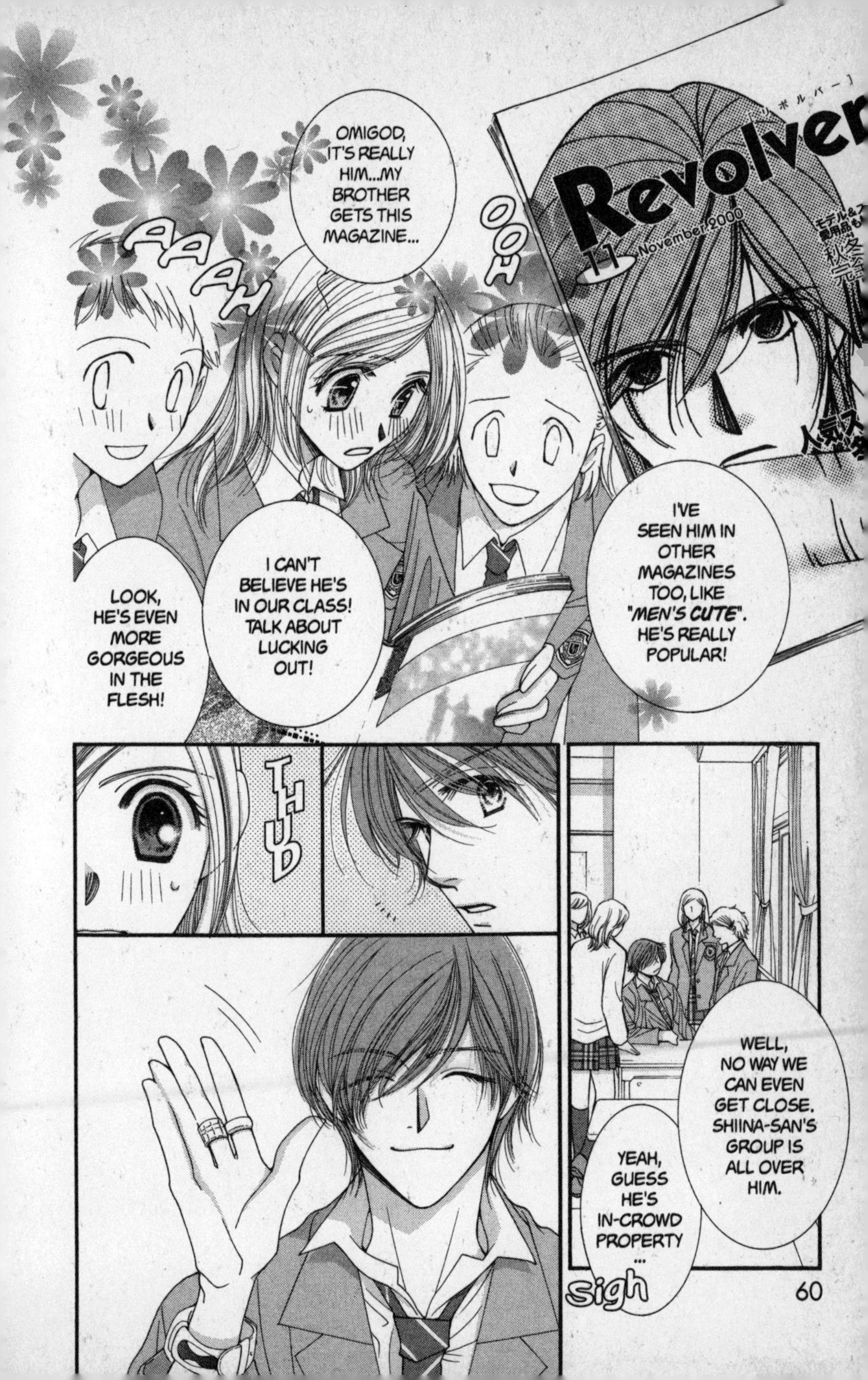
Revolver
11
November 2000
OOOH
OMIGOD, IT'S REALLY HIM...MY BROTHER GETS THIS MAGAZINE...
AAAH
I'VE SEEN HIM IN OTHER MAGAZINES TOO, LIKE "*MEN'S CUTE*". HE'S REALLY POPULAR!
I CAN'T BELIEVE HE'S IN OUR CLASS! TALK ABOUT LUCKING OUT!
LOOK, HE'S EVEN MORE GORGEOUS IN THE FLESH!
WELL, NO WAY WE CAN EVEN GET CLOSE. SHIINA-SAN'S GROUP IS ALL OVER HIM.
YEAH, GUESS HE'S IN-CROWD PROPERTY ...
sigh
THUD

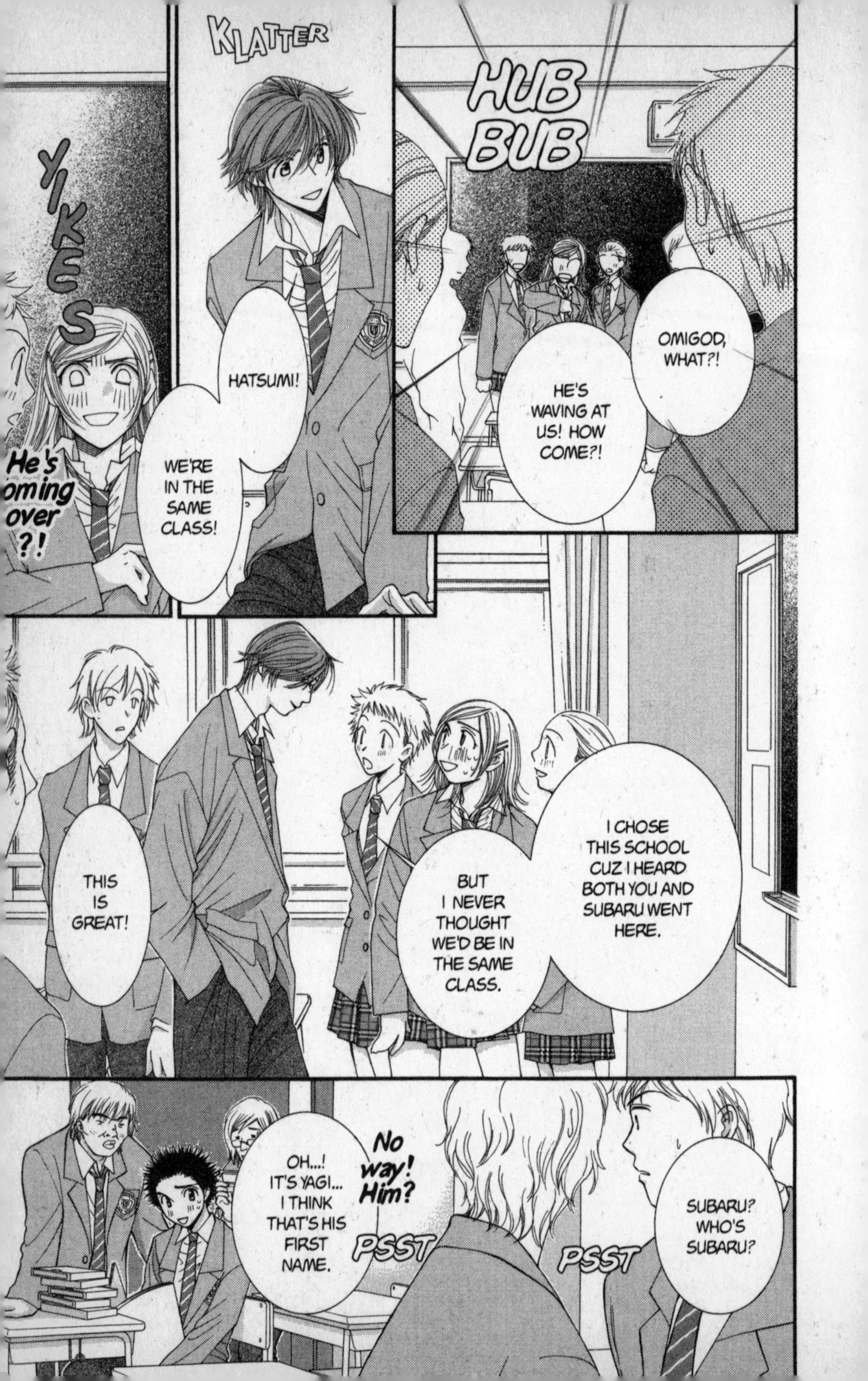
HUB BUB
OMIGOD, WHAT?!
HE'S WAVING AT US! HOW COME?!
KLATTER
HATSUMI!
WE'RE IN THE SAME CLASS!
YIKES
He's oming over ?!
I CHOSE THIS SCHOOL CUZ I HEARD BOTH YOU AND SUBARU WENT HERE.
BUT I NEVER THOUGHT WE'D BE IN THE SAME CLASS.
THIS IS GREAT!
SUBARU? WHO'S SUBARU?
PSST
PSST
No way! Him?
OH...! IT'S YAGI... I THINK THAT'S HIS FIRST NAME.

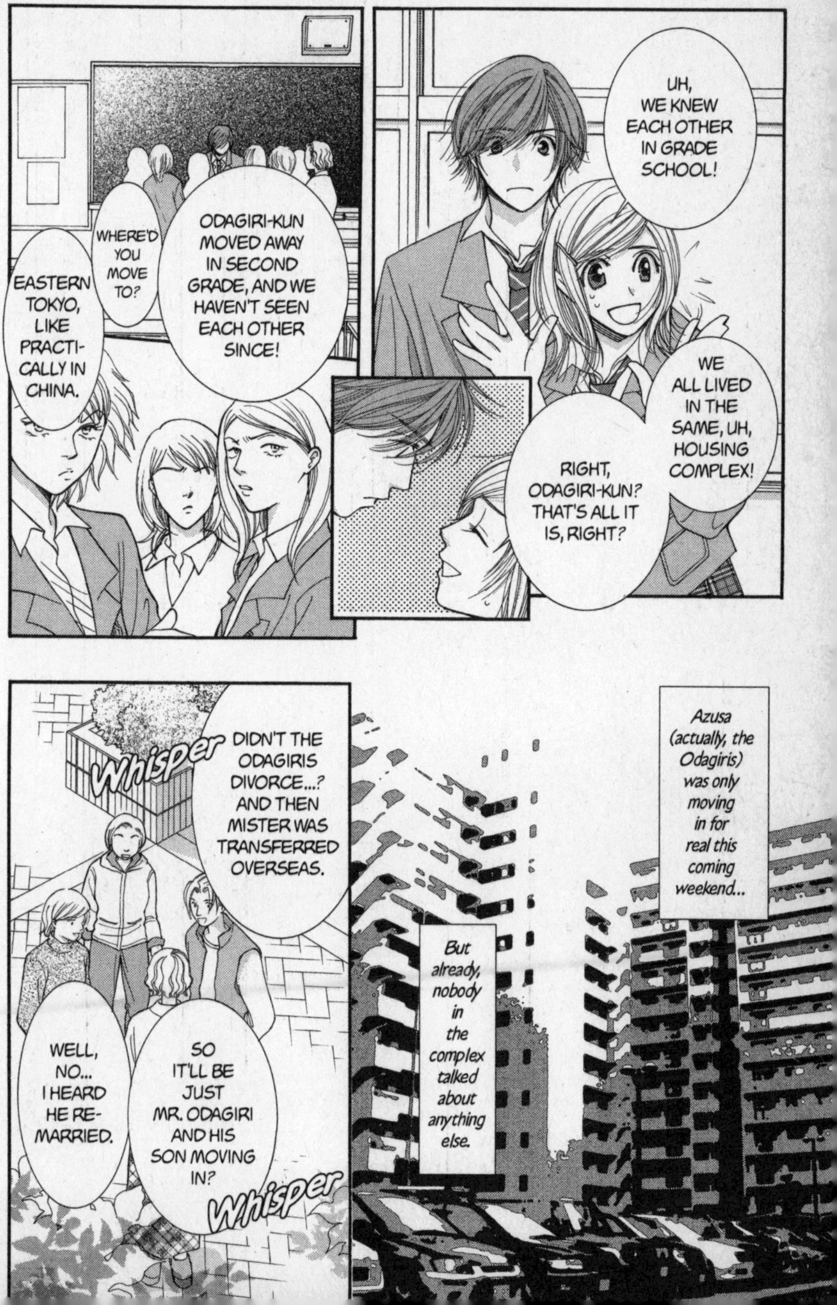
UH, WE KNEW EACH OTHER IN GRADE SCHOOL!
WE ALL LIVED IN THE SAME, UH, HOUSING COMPLEX!
RIGHT, ODAGIRI-KUN? THAT'S ALL IT IS, RIGHT?
ODAGIRI-KUN MOVED AWAY IN SECOND GRADE, AND WE HAVEN'T SEEN EACH OTHER SINCE!
WHERE'D YOU MOVE TO?
EASTERN TOKYO, LIKE PRACTI-CALLY IN CHINA.
Azusa (actually, the Odagiris) was only moving in for real this coming weekend...
But already, nobody in the complex talked about anything else.
Whisper
DIDN'T THE ODAGIRIS DIVORCE...? AND THEN MISTER WAS TRANSFERRED OVERSEAS.
SO IT'LL BE JUST MR. ODAGIRI AND HIS SON MOVING IN?
WELL, NO... I HEARD HE RE-MARRIED.
Whisper

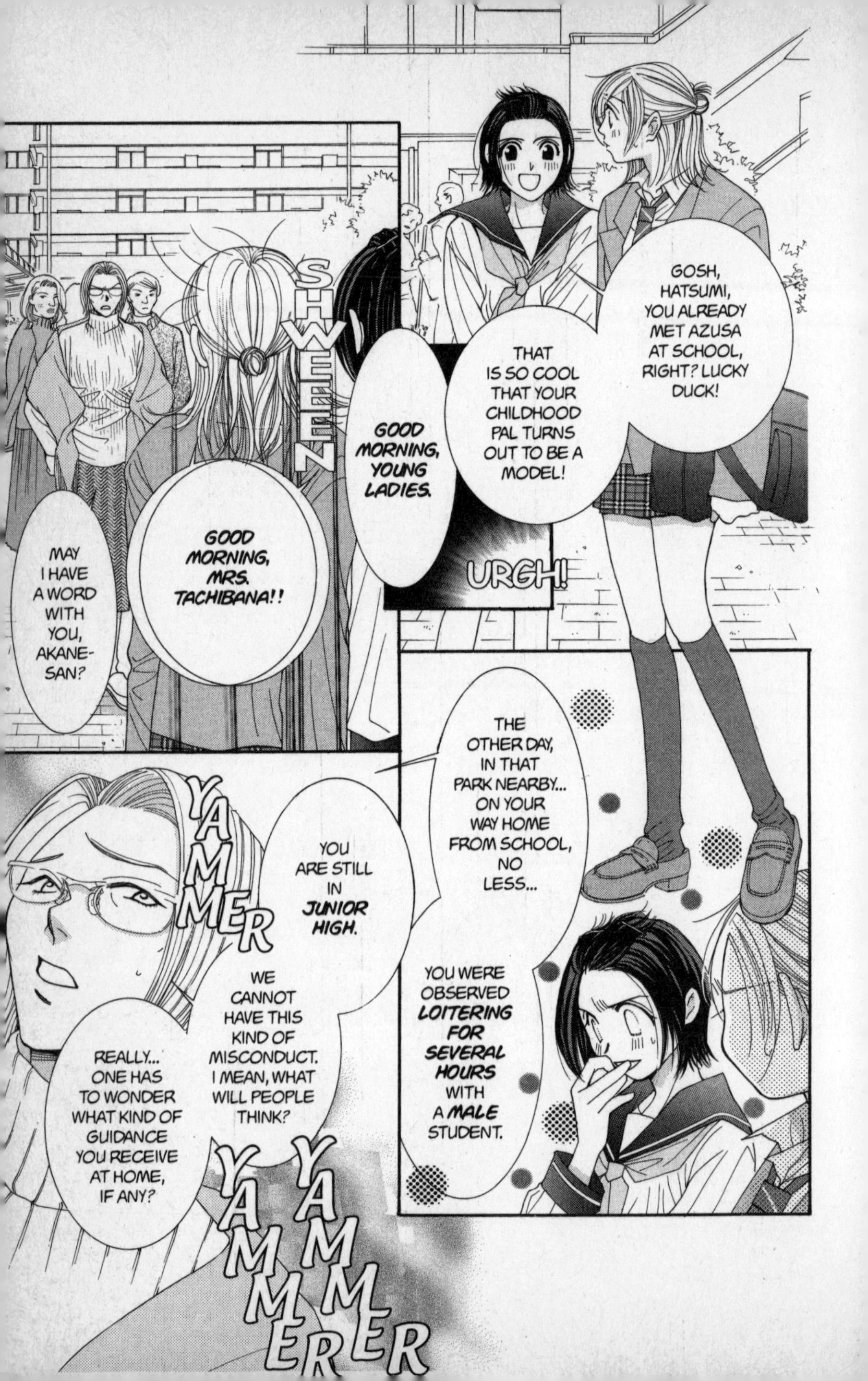
GOSH, HATSUMI, YOU ALREADY MET AZUSA AT SCHOOL, RIGHT? LUCKY DUCK!
THAT IS SO COOL THAT YOUR CHILDHOOD PAL TURNS OUT TO BE A MODEL!
URGH!
GOOD MORNING, YOUNG LADIES.
SHWEEEN
GOOD MORNING, MRS. TACHIBANA!!
MAY I HAVE A WORD WITH YOU, AKANE-SAN?
THE OTHER DAY, IN THAT PARK NEARBY... ON YOUR WAY HOME FROM SCHOOL, NO LESS...
YOU WERE OBSERVED LOITERING FOR SEVERAL HOURS WITH A MALE STUDENT.
YOU ARE STILL IN JUNIOR HIGH.
WE CANNOT HAVE THIS KIND OF MISCONDUCT. I MEAN, WHAT WILL PEOPLE THINK?
YAMMER
REALLY... ONE HAS TO WONDER WHAT KIND OF GUIDANCE YOU RECEIVE AT HOME, IF ANY?
YAMMER
YAMMER

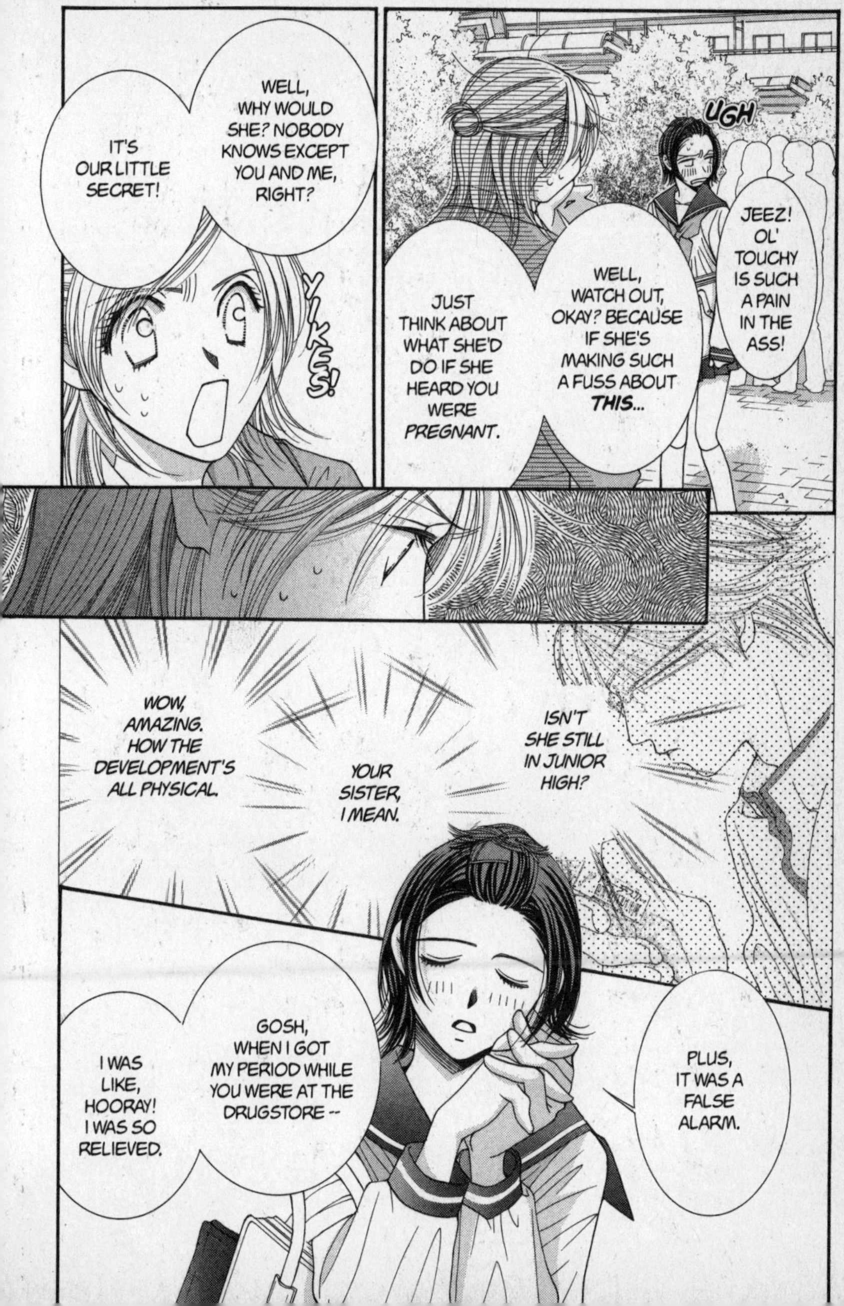
UGH
JEEZ! OL' TOUCHY IS SUCH A PAIN IN THE ASS!
WELL, WATCH OUT, OKAY? BECAUSE IF SHE'S MAKING SUCH A FUSS ABOUT **THIS...**
JUST THINK ABOUT WHAT SHE'D DO IF SHE HEARD YOU WERE *PREGNANT*.
WELL, WHY WOULD SHE? NOBODY KNOWS EXCEPT YOU AND ME, RIGHT?
IT'S OUR LITTLE SECRET!
YIKES!
ISN'T SHE STILL IN JUNIOR HIGH?
YOUR SISTER, I MEAN.
WOW, AMAZING. HOW THE DEVELOPMENT'S ALL PHYSICAL.
PLUS, IT WAS A FALSE ALARM.
GOSH, WHEN I GOT MY PERIOD WHILE YOU WERE AT THE DRUGSTORE --
I WAS LIKE, HOORAY! I WAS SO RELIEVED.

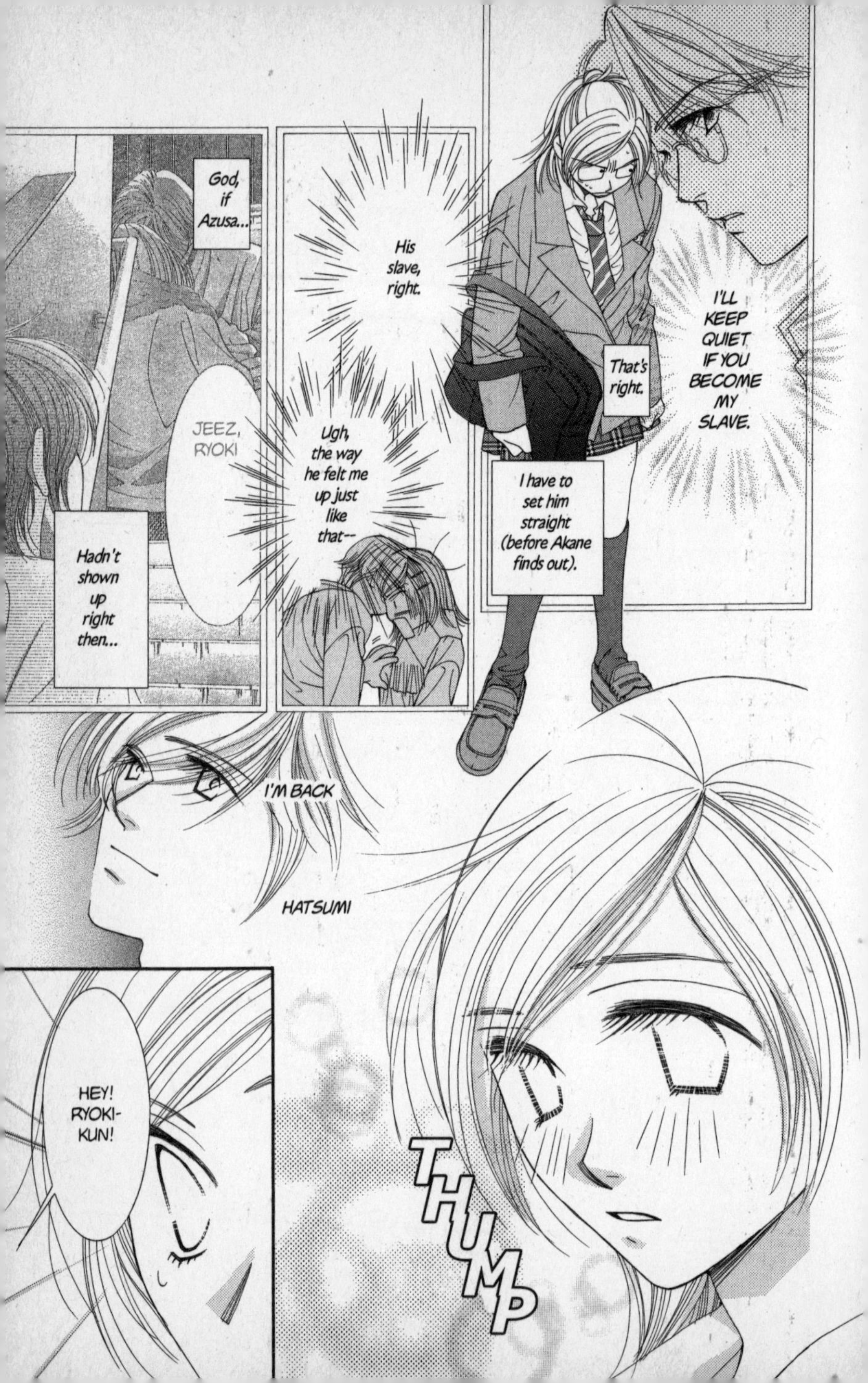
I'LL KEEP QUIET IF YOU BECOME MY SLAVE.
That's right.
I have to set him straight (before Akane finds out).
His slave, right.
Ugh, the way he felt me up just like that--
God, if Azusa...
JEEZ, RYOKI
Hadn't shown up right then...
THUMP
I'M BACK
HATSUMI
HEY! RYOKI-KUN!

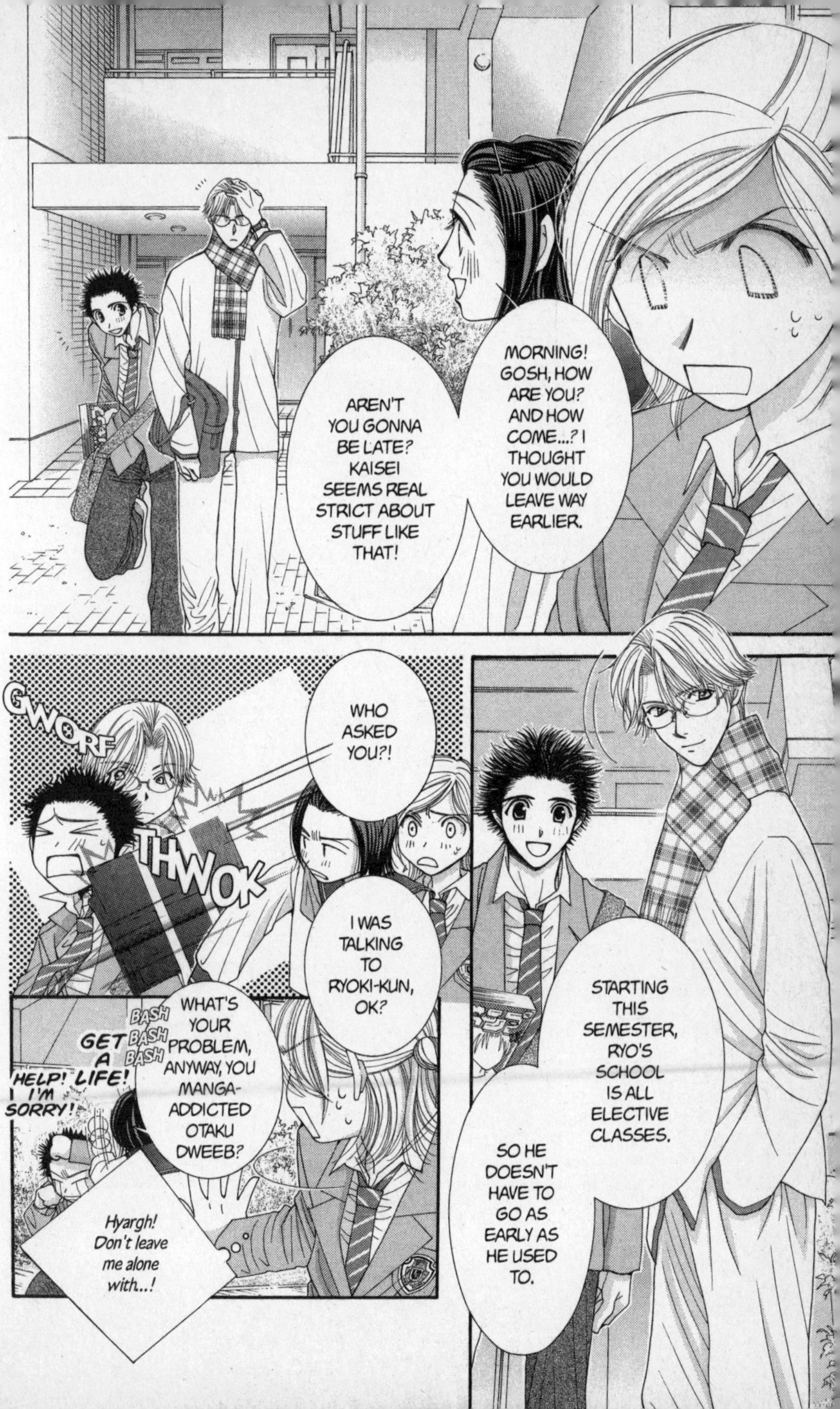
MORNING! GOSH, HOW ARE YOU? AND HOW COME...? I THOUGHT YOU WOULD LEAVE WAY EARLIER.
AREN'T YOU GONNA BE LATE? KAISEI SEEMS REAL STRICT ABOUT STUFF LIKE THAT!
STARTING THIS SEMESTER, RYO'S SCHOOL IS ALL ELECTIVE CLASSES.
SO HE DOESN'T HAVE TO GO AS EARLY AS HE USED TO.
WHO ASKED YOU?!
GWORF
THWOK
I WAS TALKING TO RYOKI-KUN, OK?
WHAT'S YOUR PROBLEM, ANYWAY, YOU MANGA-ADDICTED OTAKU DWEEB?
BASH BASH BASH
GET A LIFE!
HELP! I'M SORRY!
Hyargh! Don't leave me alone with...!

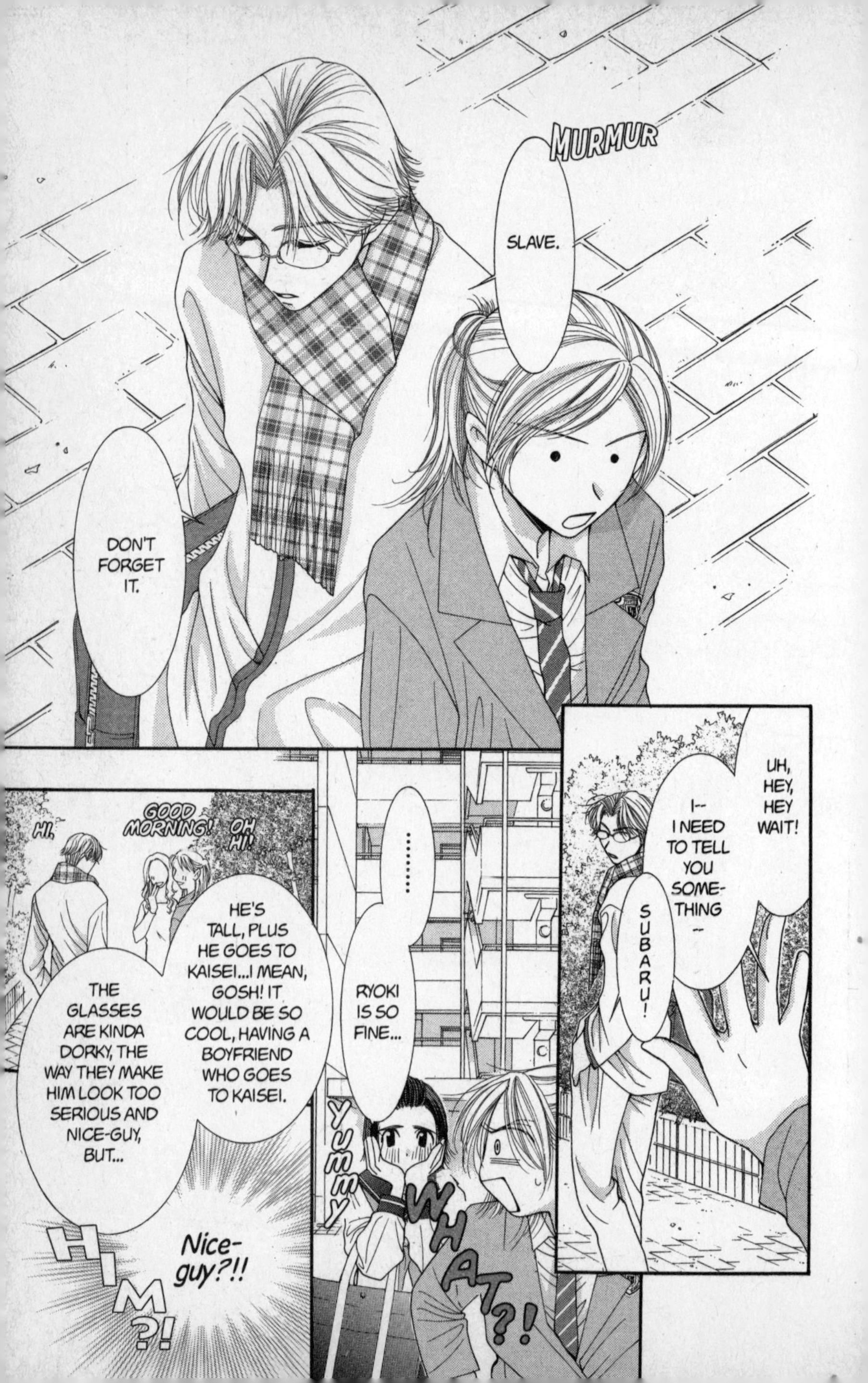
MURMUR
SLAVE.
DON'T FORGET IT.
UH, HEY, HEY WAIT!
I-- I NEED TO TELL YOU SOME-THING --
SUBARU!
......
RYOKI IS SO FINE...
YUMMY
WHAT?!
GOOD MORNING!
OH HI!
HI.
HE'S TALL, PLUS HE GOES TO KAISEI...I MEAN, GOSH! IT WOULD BE SO COOL, HAVING A BOYFRIEND WHO GOES TO KAISEI.
THE GLASSES ARE KINDA DORKY, THE WAY THEY MAKE HIM LOOK TOO SERIOUS AND NICE-GUY, BUT...
Nice-guy?!!
HIM?!

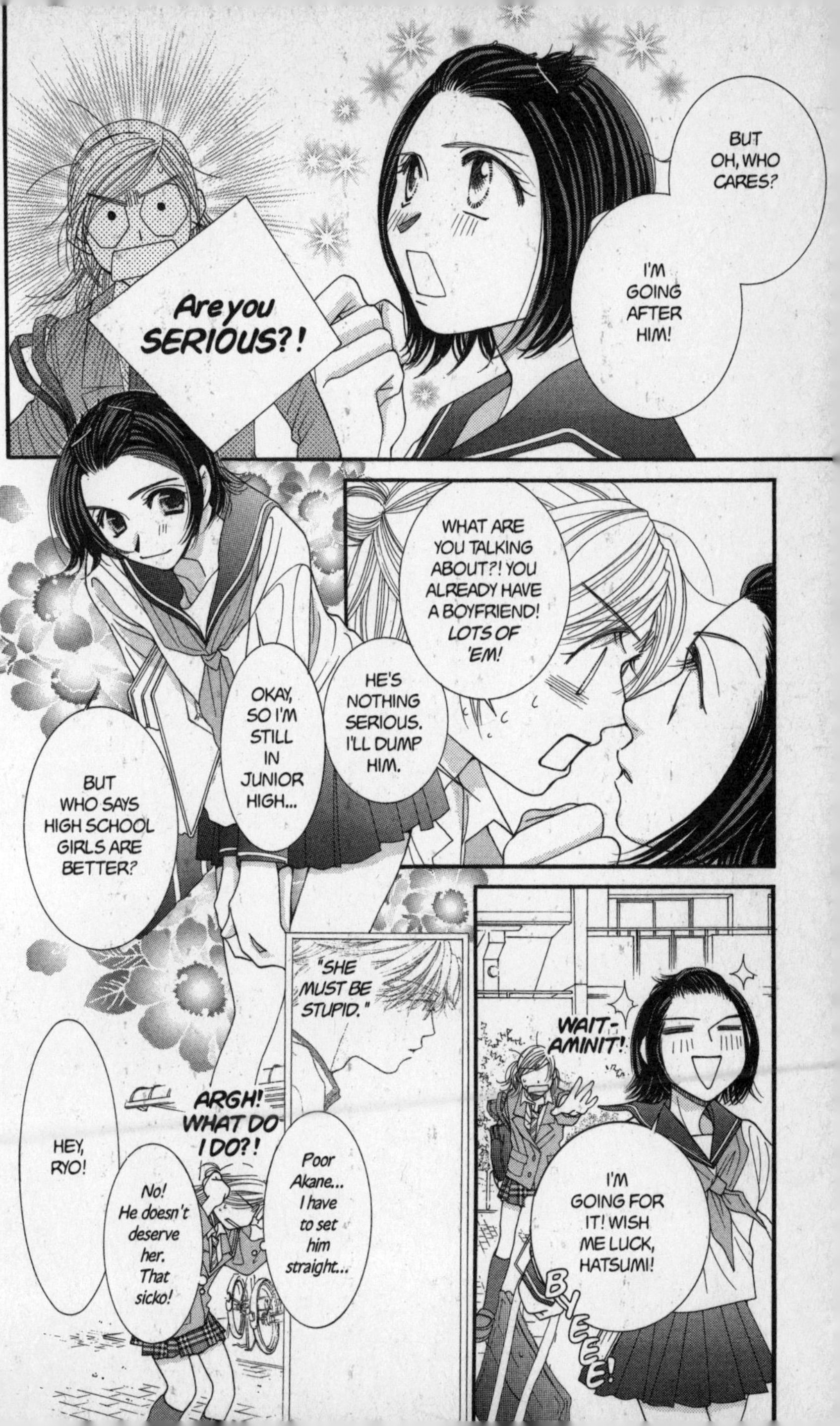
BUT OH, WHO CARES?
I'M GOING AFTER HIM!
Are you SERIOUS?!
WHAT ARE YOU TALKING ABOUT?! YOU ALREADY HAVE A BOYFRIEND! LOTS OF 'EM!
HE'S NOTHING SERIOUS. I'LL DUMP HIM.
OKAY, SO I'M STILL IN JUNIOR HIGH...
BUT WHO SAYS HIGH SCHOOL GIRLS ARE BETTER?
I'M GOING FOR IT! WISH ME LUCK, HATSUMI!
BYEEE!
WAIT-AMINIT!
"SHE MUST BE STUPID."
Poor Akane... I have to set him straight...
ARGH! WHAT DO I DO?!
No! He doesn't deserve her. That sicko!
HEY, RYO!

hot gimmick

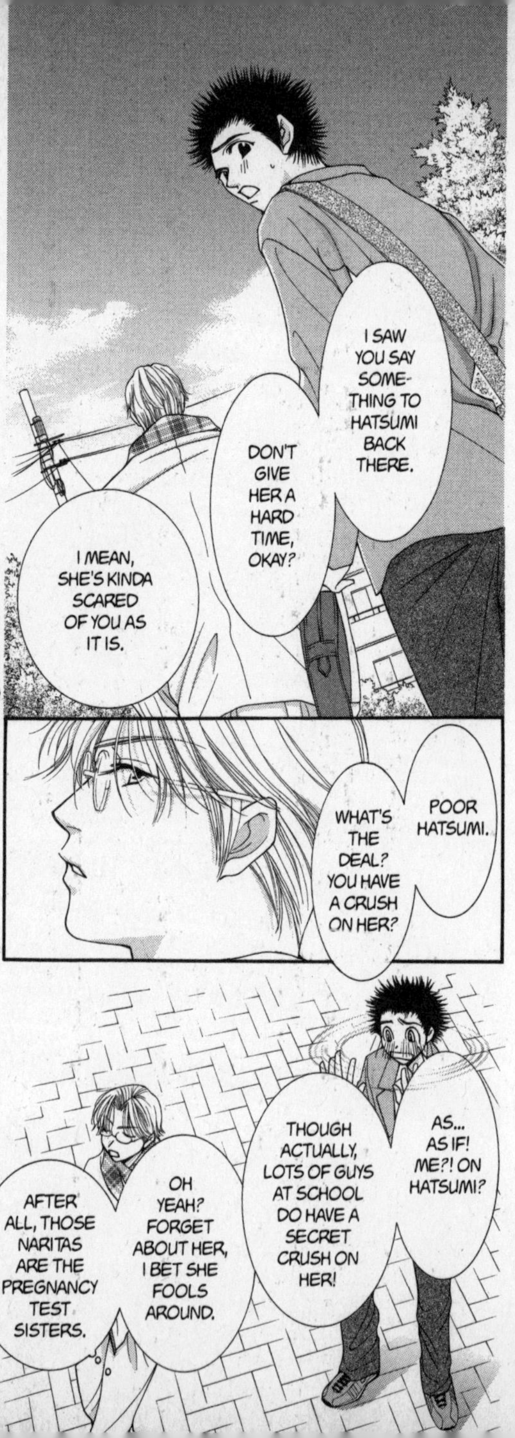
I SAW YOU SAY SOME-THING TO HATSUMI BACK THERE.
DON'T GIVE HER A HARD TIME, OKAY?
I MEAN, SHE'S KINDA SCARED OF YOU AS IT IS.
POOR HATSUMI.
WHAT'S THE DEAL? YOU HAVE A CRUSH ON HER?
AS... AS IF! ME?! ON HATSUMI?
THOUGH ACTUALLY, LOTS OF GUYS AT SCHOOL DO HAVE A SECRET CRUSH ON HER!
OH YEAH? FORGET ABOUT HER, I BET SHE FOOLS AROUND.
AFTER ALL, THOSE NARITAS ARE THE PREGNANCY TEST SISTERS.

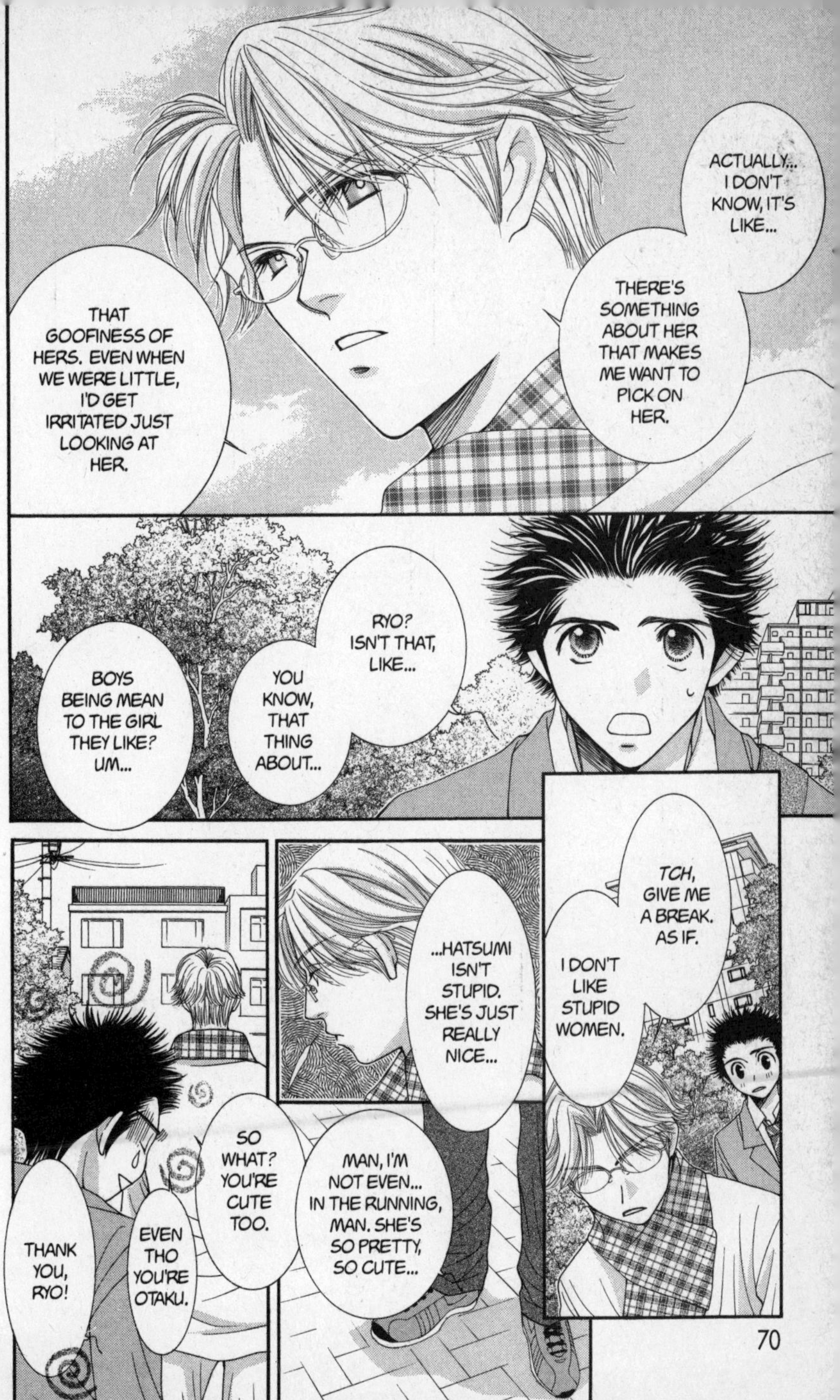
ACTUALLY... I DON'T KNOW, IT'S LIKE...
THERE'S SOMETHING ABOUT HER THAT MAKES ME WANT TO PICK ON HER.
THAT GOOFINESS OF HERS. EVEN WHEN WE WERE LITTLE, I'D GET IRRITATED JUST LOOKING AT HER.
RYO? ISN'T THAT, LIKE...
YOU KNOW, THAT THING ABOUT...
BOYS BEING MEAN TO THE GIRL THEY LIKE? UM...
TCH, GIVE ME A BREAK. AS IF.
I DON'T LIKE STUPID WOMEN.
...HATSUMI ISN'T STUPID. SHE'S JUST REALLY NICE...
MAN, I'M NOT EVEN... IN THE RUNNING, MAN. SHE'S SO PRETTY, SO CUTE...
SO WHAT? YOU'RE CUTE TOO.
EVEN THO YOU'RE OTAKU.
THANK YOU, RYO!

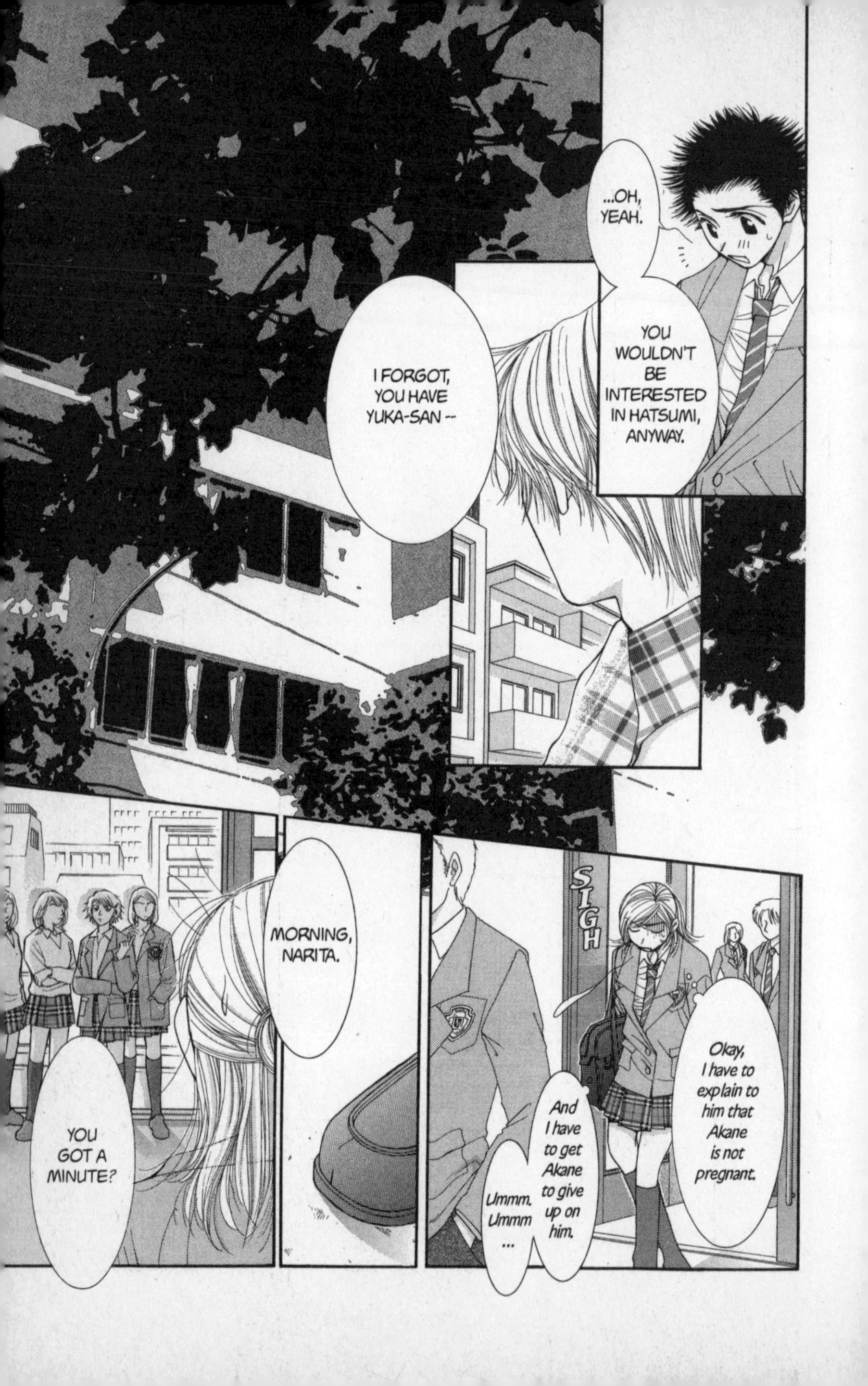
...OH, YEAH.
I FORGOT, YOU HAVE YUKA-SAN --
YOU WOULDN'T BE INTERESTED IN HATSUMI, ANYWAY.
SIGH
Okay, I have to explain to him that Akane is not pregnant.
And I have to get Akane to give up on him.
Ummm. Ummm ...
MORNING, NARITA.
YOU GOT A MINUTE?

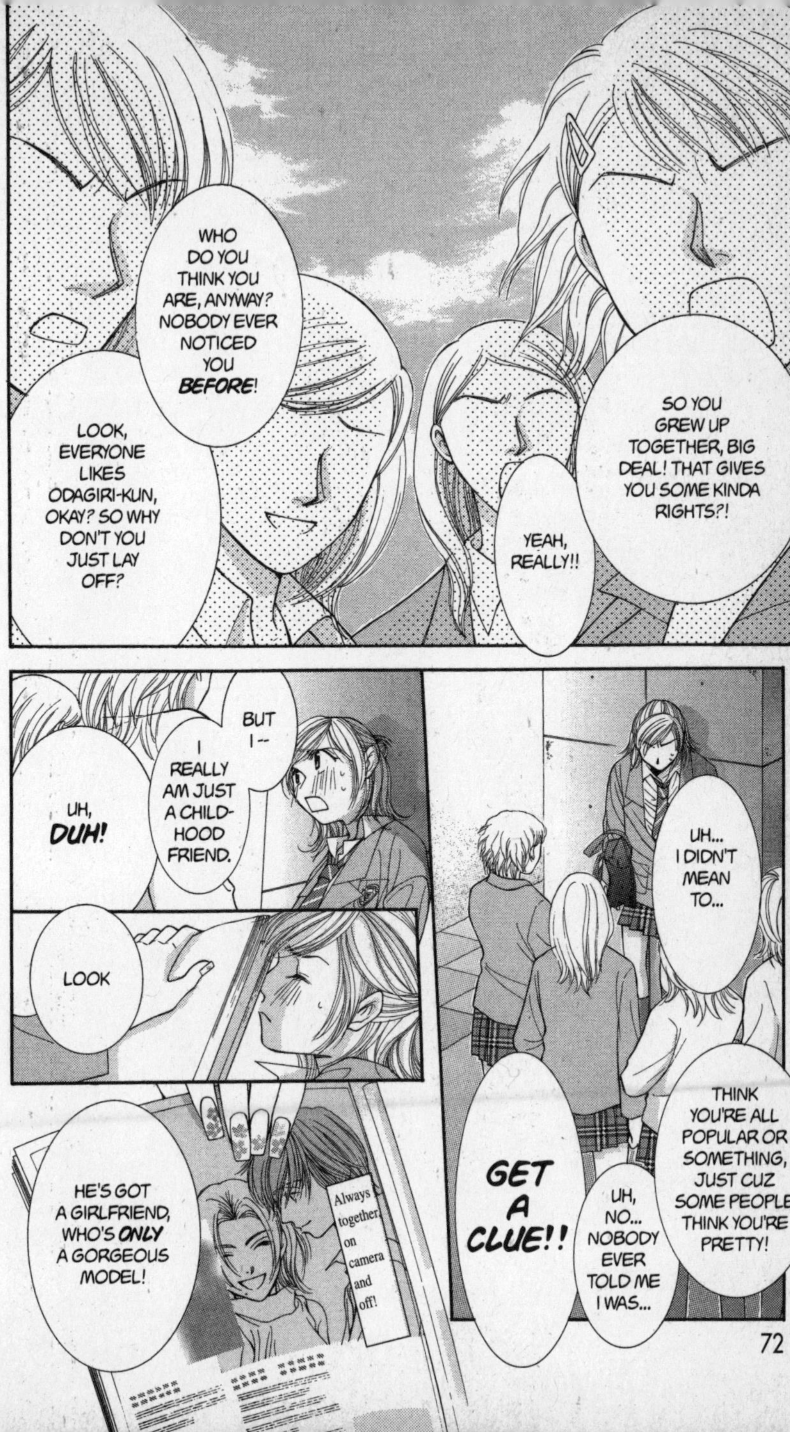
SO YOU GREW UP TOGETHER, BIG DEAL! THAT GIVES YOU SOME KINDA RIGHTS?!
YEAH, REALLY!!
WHO DO YOU THINK YOU ARE, ANYWAY? NOBODY EVER NOTICED YOU ***BEFORE***!
LOOK, EVERYONE LIKES ODAGIRI-KUN, OKAY? SO WHY DON'T YOU JUST LAY OFF?
UH... I DIDN'T MEAN TO...
THINK YOU'RE ALL POPULAR OR SOMETHING, JUST CUZ SOME PEOPLE THINK YOU'RE PRETTY!
UH, NO... NOBODY EVER TOLD ME I WAS...
GET A CLUE!!
BUT I--
I REALLY AM JUST A CHILD-HOOD FRIEND.
UH, ***DUH!***
LOOK
Always together on camera and off!
HE'S GOT A GIRLFRIEND, WHO'S ***ONLY*** A GORGEOUS MODEL!

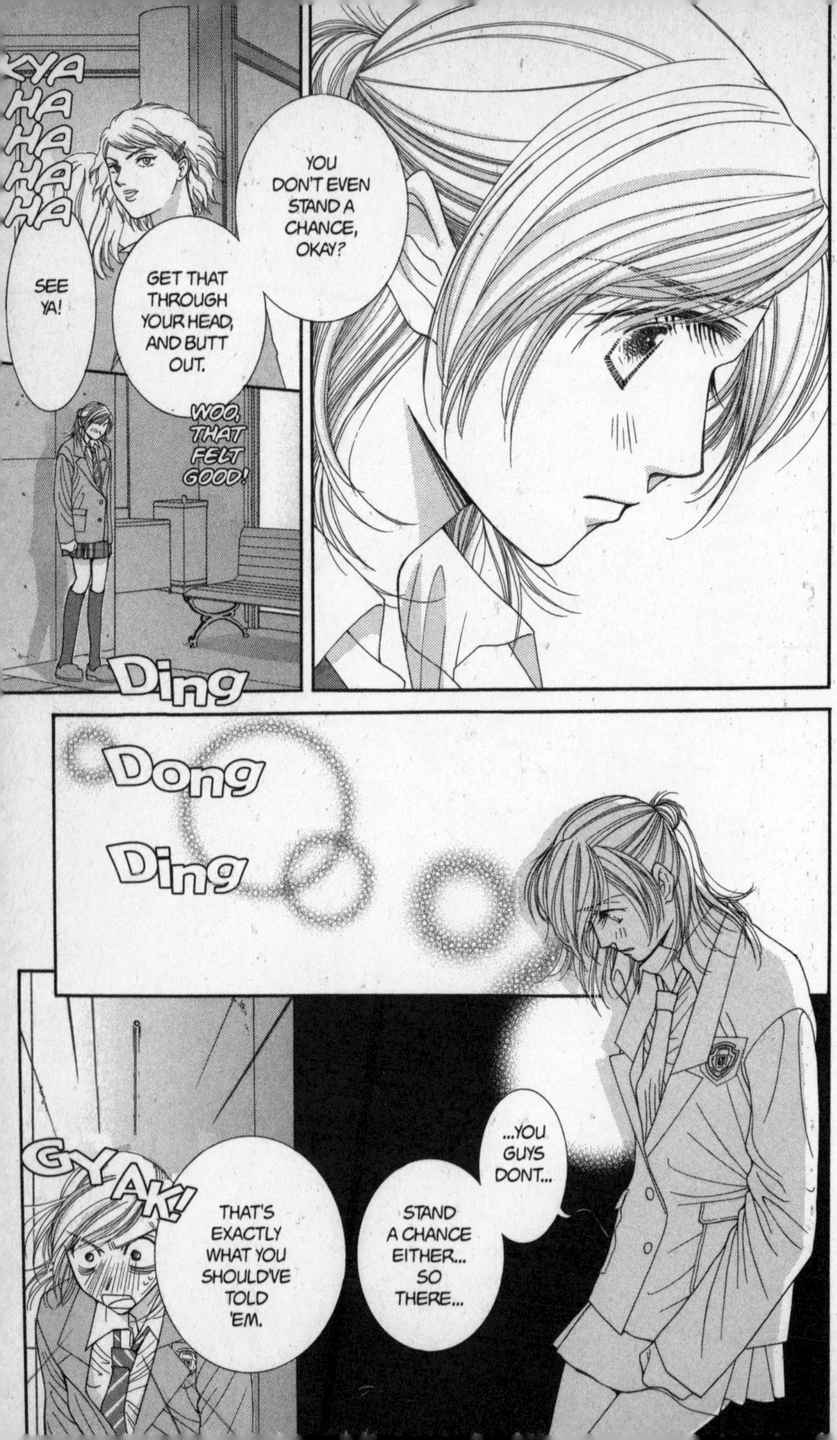
YOU DON'T EVEN STAND A CHANCE, OKAY?
GET THAT THROUGH YOUR HEAD, AND BUTT OUT.
SEE YA!
KYA HA HA HA HA HA
WOO, THAT FELT GOOD!
Ding
Dong
Ding
...YOU GUYS DONT...
STAND A CHANCE EITHER... SO THERE...
GYAK!
THAT'S EXACTLY WHAT YOU SHOULD'VE TOLD 'EM.

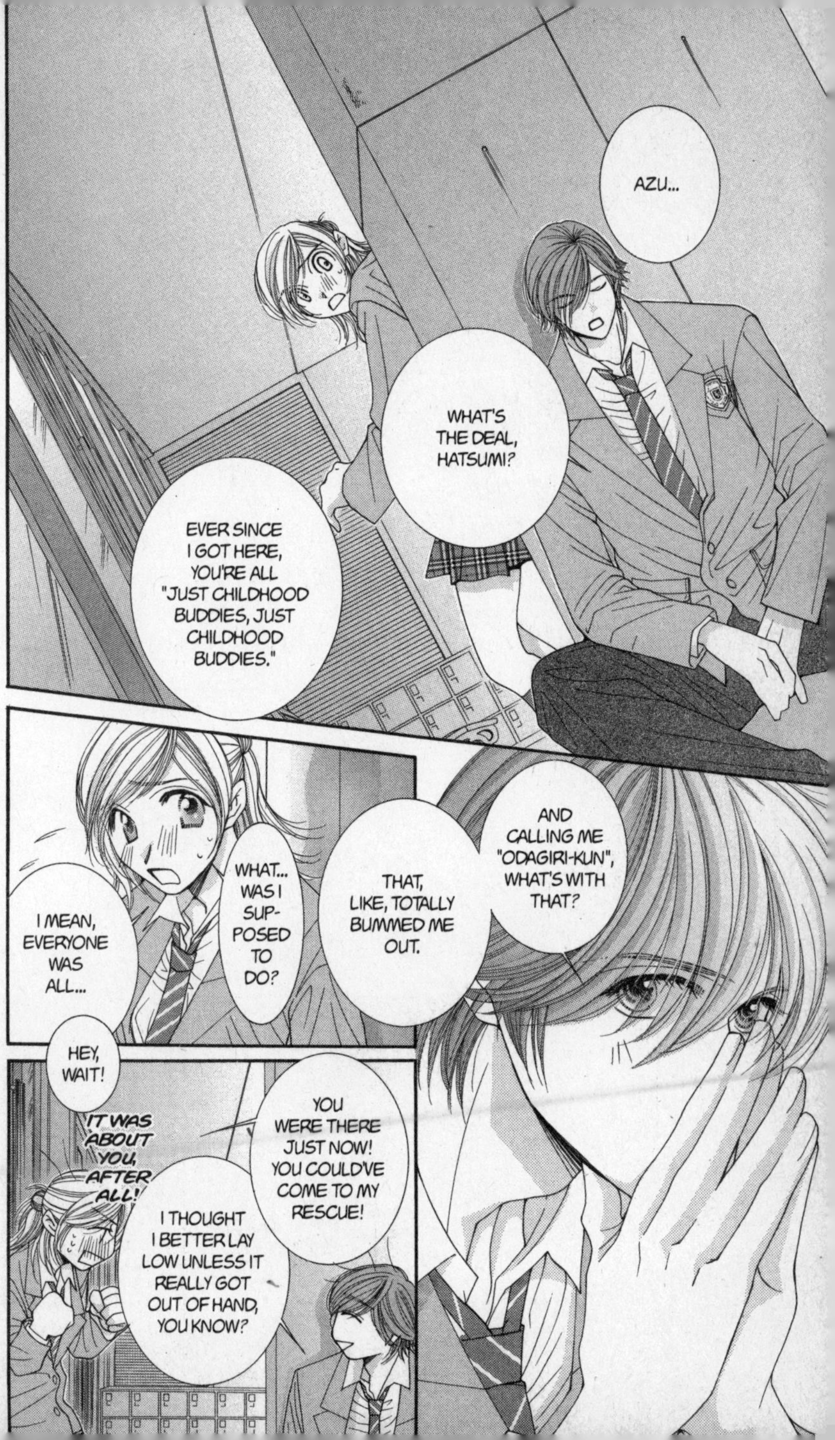

AZU...
WHAT'S THE DEAL, HATSUMI?
EVER SINCE I GOT HERE, YOU'RE ALL "JUST CHILDHOOD BUDDIES, JUST CHILDHOOD BUDDIES."
AND CALLING ME "ODAGIRI-KUN", WHAT'S WITH THAT?
THAT, LIKE, TOTALLY BUMMED ME OUT.
WHAT... WAS I SUP-POSED TO DO?
I MEAN, EVERYONE WAS ALL...
HEY, WAIT!
YOU WERE THERE JUST NOW! YOU COULD'VE COME TO MY RESCUE!
IT WAS ABOUT YOU, AFTER ALL!
I THOUGHT I BETTER LAY LOW UNLESS IT REALLY GOT OUT OF HAND, YOU KNOW?

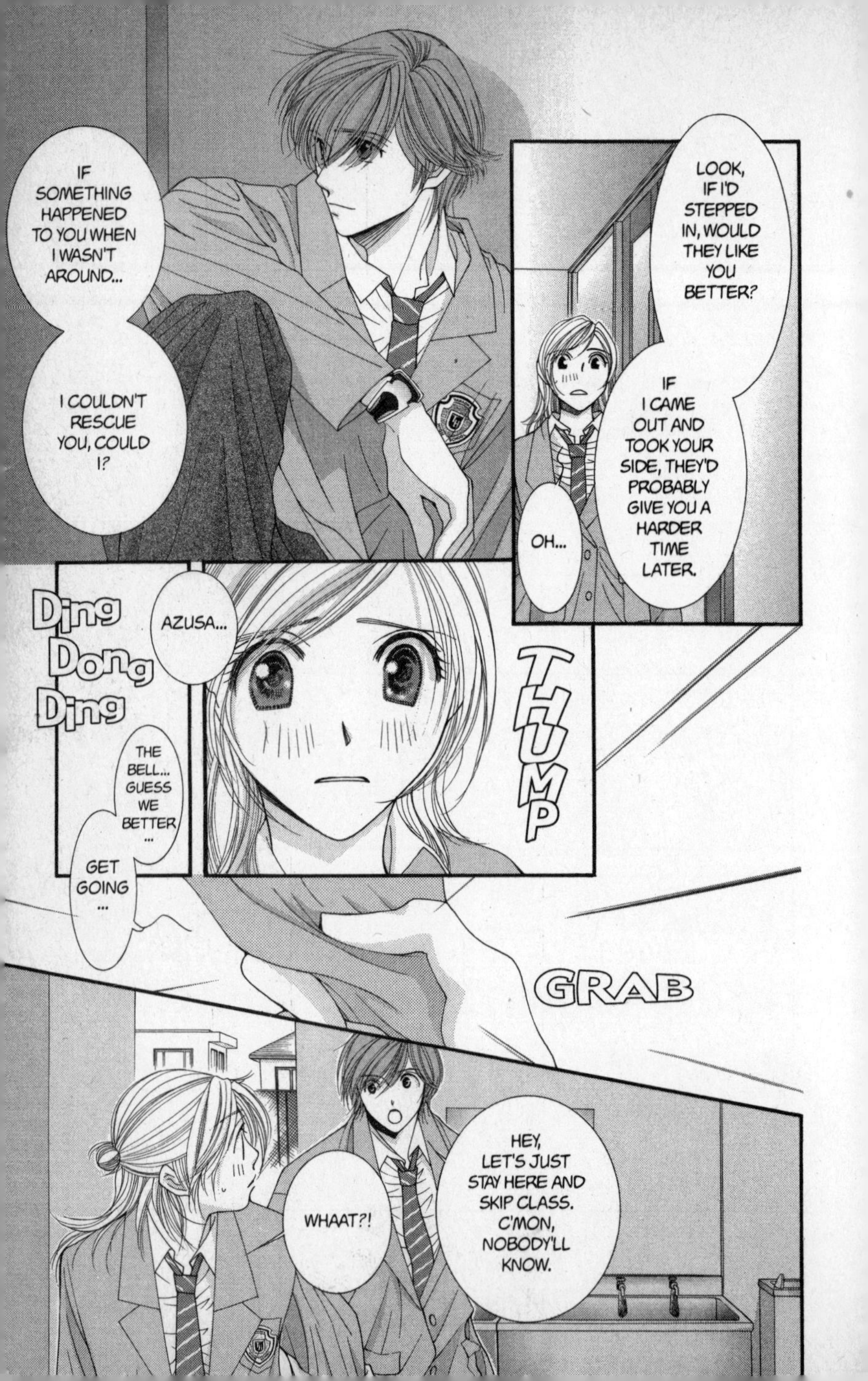
LOOK, IF I'D STEPPED IN, WOULD THEY LIKE YOU BETTER?
IF I CAME OUT AND TOOK YOUR SIDE, THEY'D PROBABLY GIVE YOU A HARDER TIME LATER.
OH...
IF SOMETHING HAPPENED TO YOU WHEN I WASN'T AROUND...
I COULDN'T RESCUE YOU, COULD I?
THUMP
AZUSA...
Ding Dong Ding
THE BELL... GUESS WE BETTER...
GET GOING...
GRAB
HEY, LET'S JUST STAY HERE AND SKIP CLASS. C'MON, NOBODY'LL KNOW.
WHAAT?!

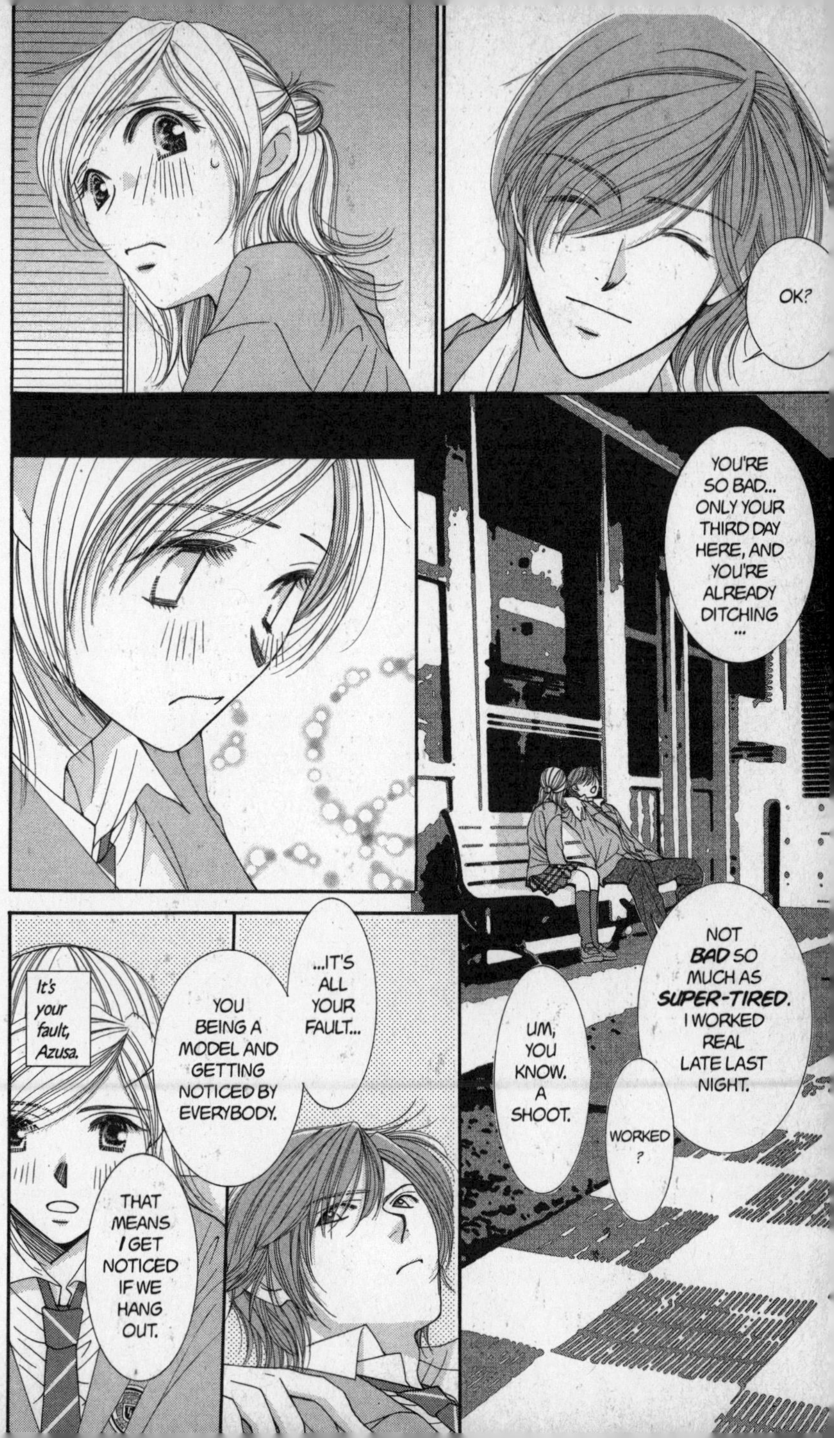
OK?
YOU'RE SO BAD... ONLY YOUR THIRD DAY HERE, AND YOU'RE ALREADY DITCHING...
NOT BAD SO MUCH AS SUPER-TIRED. I WORKED REAL LATE LAST NIGHT.
WORKED?
UM, YOU KNOW. A SHOOT.
...IT'S ALL YOUR FAULT...
YOU BEING A MODEL AND GETTING NOTICED BY EVERYBODY.
It's your fault, Azusa.
THAT MEANS I GET NOTICED IF WE HANG OUT.

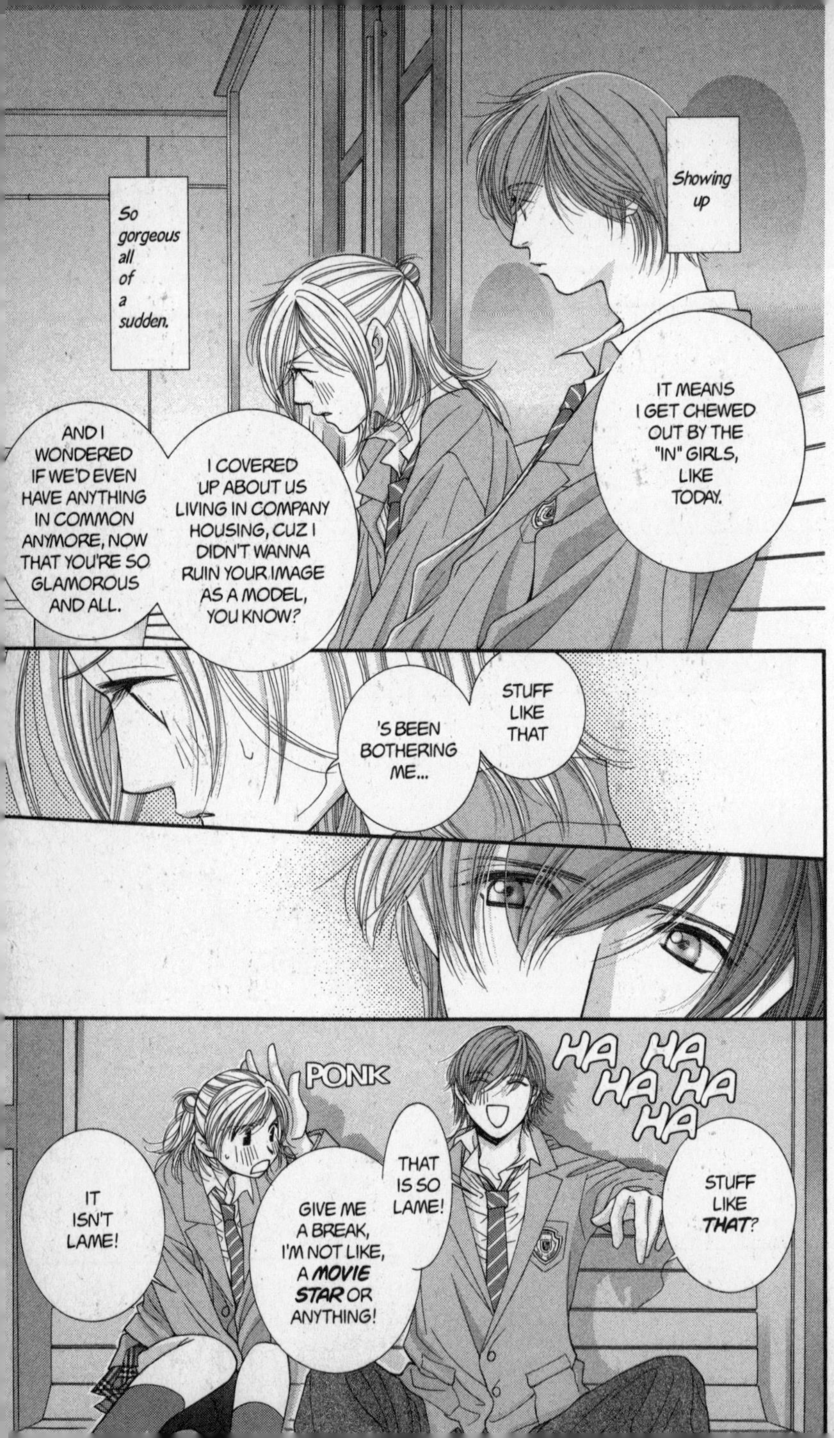
Showing up
So gorgeous all of a sudden.
IT MEANS I GET CHEWED OUT BY THE "IN" GIRLS, LIKE TODAY.
I COVERED UP ABOUT US LIVING IN COMPANY HOUSING, CUZ I DIDN'T WANNA RUIN YOUR IMAGE AS A MODEL, YOU KNOW?
AND I WONDERED IF WE'D EVEN HAVE ANYTHING IN COMMON ANYMORE, NOW THAT YOU'RE SO GLAMOROUS AND ALL.
STUFF LIKE THAT
'S BEEN BOTHERING ME...
HA HA HA HA HA
STUFF LIKE *THAT*?
THAT IS SO LAME!
PONK
GIVE ME A BREAK, I'M NOT LIKE, A ***MOVIE STAR*** OR ANYTHING!
IT ISN'T LAME!

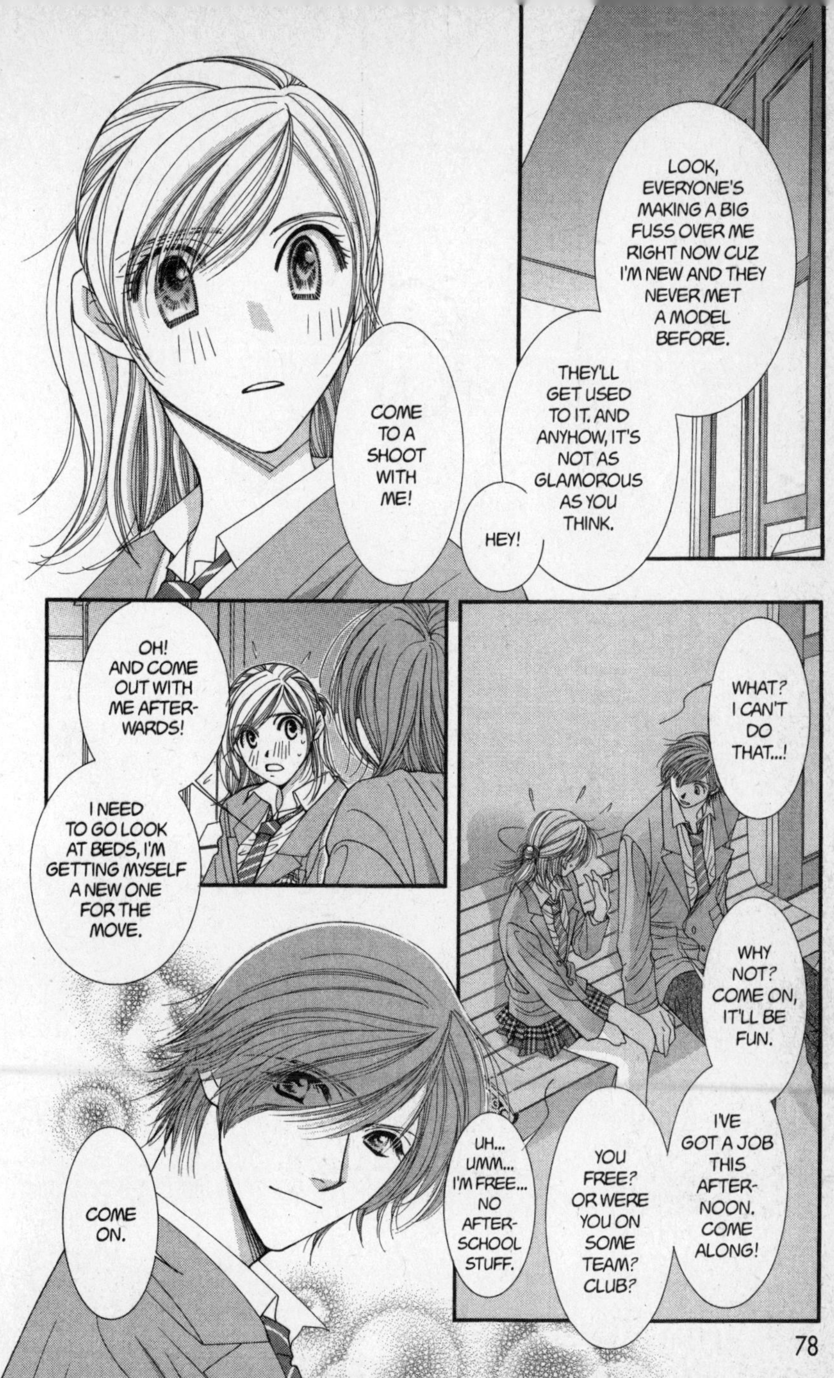
LOOK, EVERYONE'S MAKING A BIG FUSS OVER ME RIGHT NOW CUZ I'M NEW AND THEY NEVER MET A MODEL BEFORE.
THEY'LL GET USED TO IT. AND ANYHOW, IT'S NOT AS GLAMOROUS AS YOU THINK.
HEY!
COME TO A SHOOT WITH ME!
WHAT? I CAN'T DO THAT...!
WHY NOT? COME ON, IT'LL BE FUN.
I'VE GOT A JOB THIS AFTER-NOON. COME ALONG!
YOU FREE? OR WERE YOU ON SOME TEAM? CLUB?
UH... UMM... I'M FREE... NO AFTER-SCHOOL STUFF.
OH! AND COME OUT WITH ME AFTER-WARDS!
I NEED TO GO LOOK AT BEDS, I'M GETTING MYSELF A NEW ONE FOR THE MOVE.
COME ON.

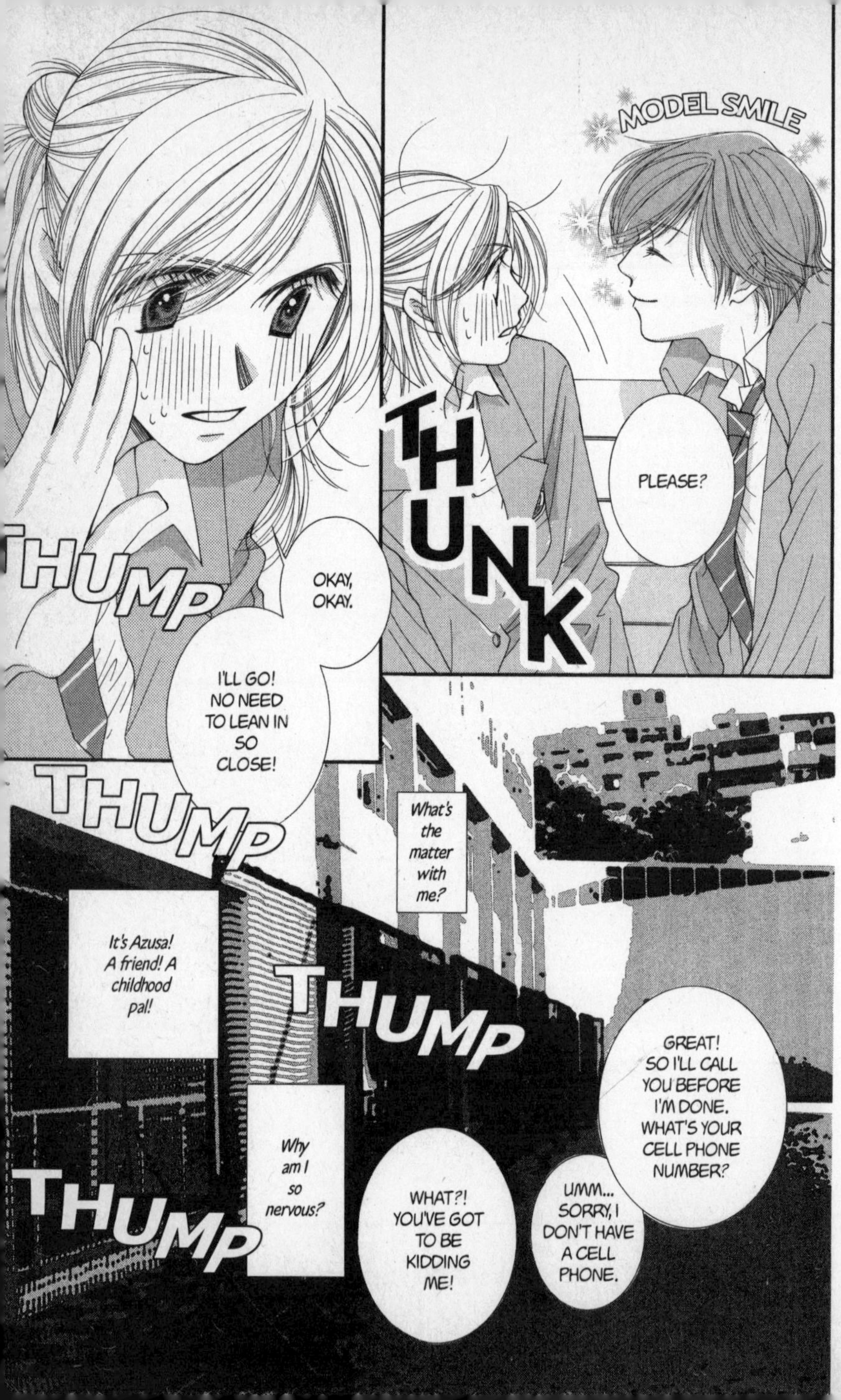
MODEL SMILE
PLEASE?
THUNK
THUMP
OKAY, OKAY.
I'LL GO! NO NEED TO LEAN IN SO CLOSE!
What's the matter with me?
THUMP
It's Azusa! A friend! A childhood pal!
THUMP
GREAT! SO I'LL CALL YOU BEFORE I'M DONE. WHAT'S YOUR CELL PHONE NUMBER?
UMM... SORRY, I DON'T HAVE A CELL PHONE.
WHAT?! YOU'VE GOT TO BE KIDDING ME!
Why am I so nervous?
THUMP

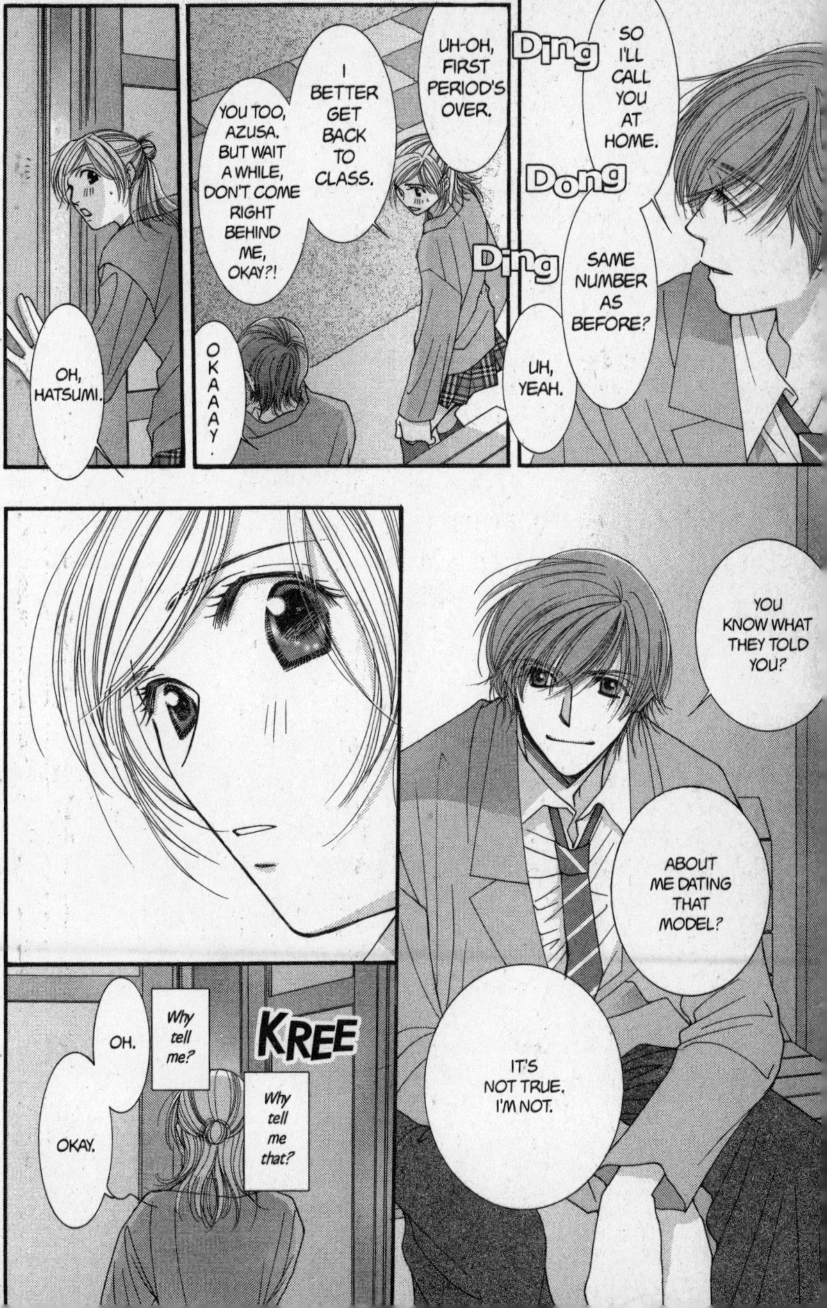
SO I'LL CALL YOU AT HOME.
Ding
Dong
Ding
SAME NUMBER AS BEFORE?
UH, YEAH.
UH-OH, FIRST PERIOD'S OVER.
I BETTER GET BACK TO CLASS.
YOU TOO, AZUSA. BUT WAIT A WHILE, DON'T COME RIGHT BEHIND ME, OKAY?!
OKAAAAY.
OH, HATSUMI.
YOU KNOW WHAT THEY TOLD YOU?
ABOUT ME DATING THAT MODEL?
IT'S NOT TRUE. I'M NOT.
KREE
Why tell me?
OH.
Why tell me that?
OKAY.

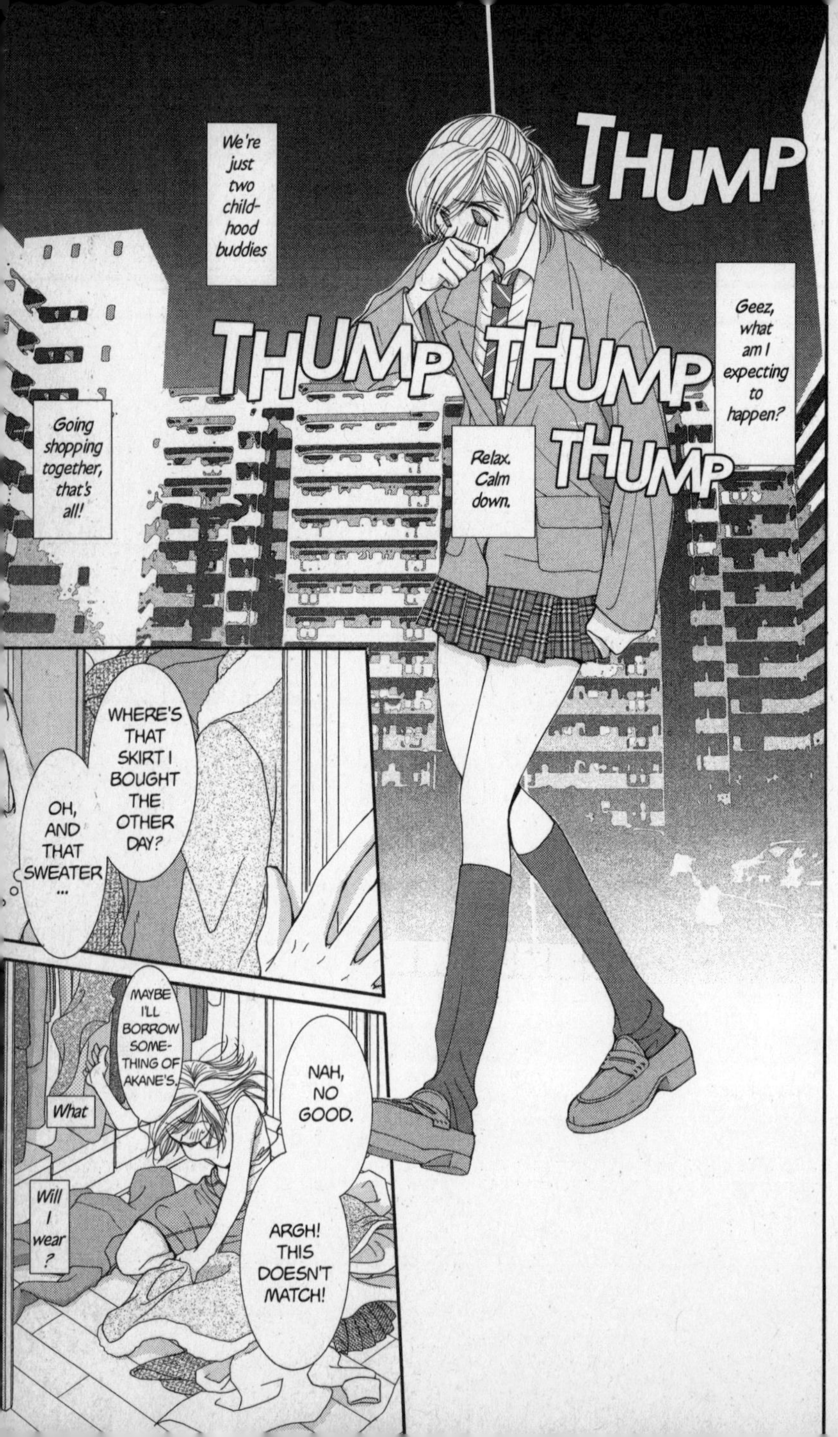
THUMP
Geez, what am I expecting to happen?
THUMP THUMP THUMP
Relax. Calm down.
We're just two child-hood buddies
Going shopping together, that's all!
WHERE'S THAT SKIRT I BOUGHT THE OTHER DAY?
OH, AND THAT SWEATER...
NAH, NO GOOD.
MAYBE I'LL BORROW SOME-THING OF AKANE'S.
ARGH! THIS DOESN'T MATCH!
What
Will I wear?

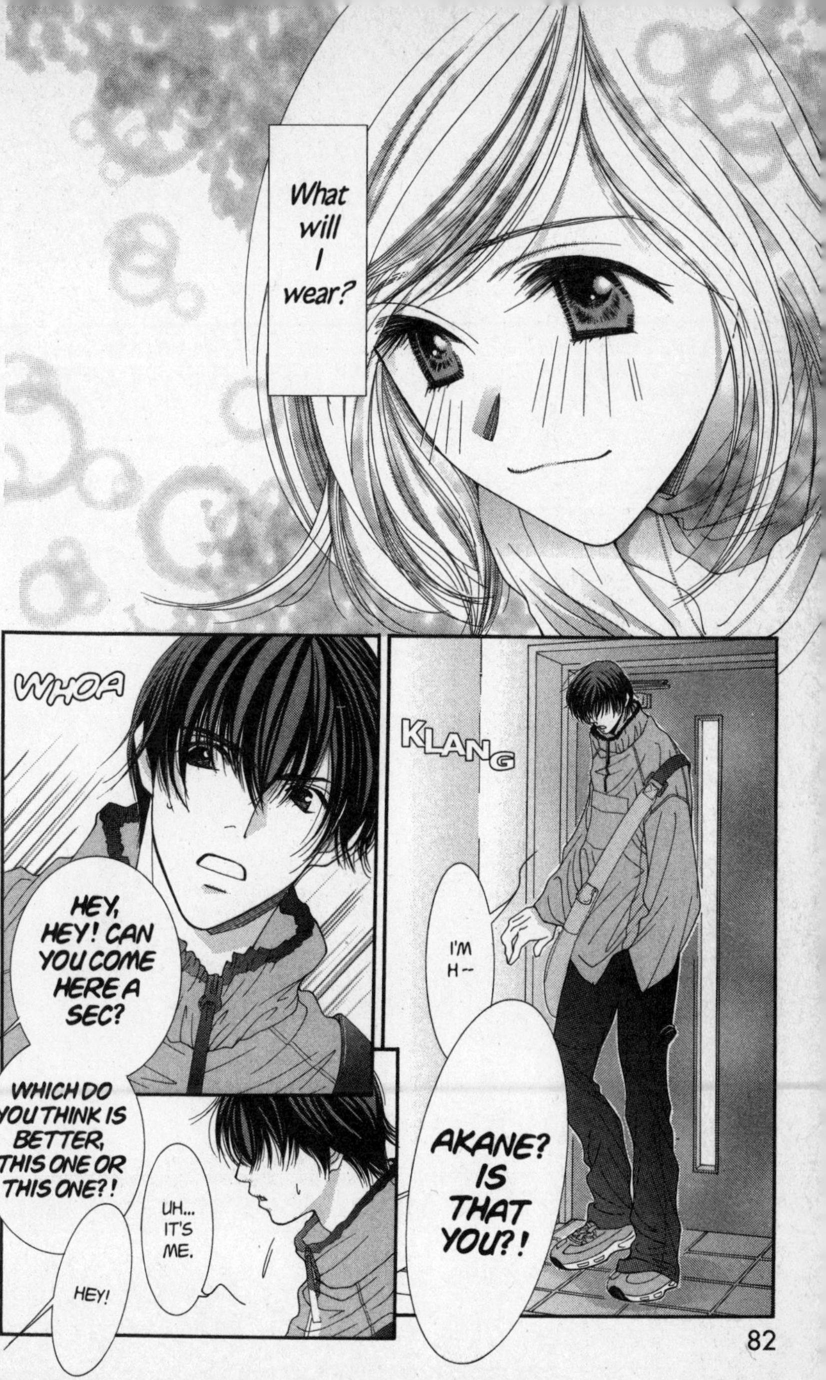
What will I wear?
KLANG
I'M H--
AKANE? IS THAT YOU?!
WHOA
HEY, HEY! CAN YOU COME HERE A SEC?
WHICH DO YOU THINK IS BETTER, THIS ONE OR THIS ONE?!
UH... IT'S ME.
HEY!

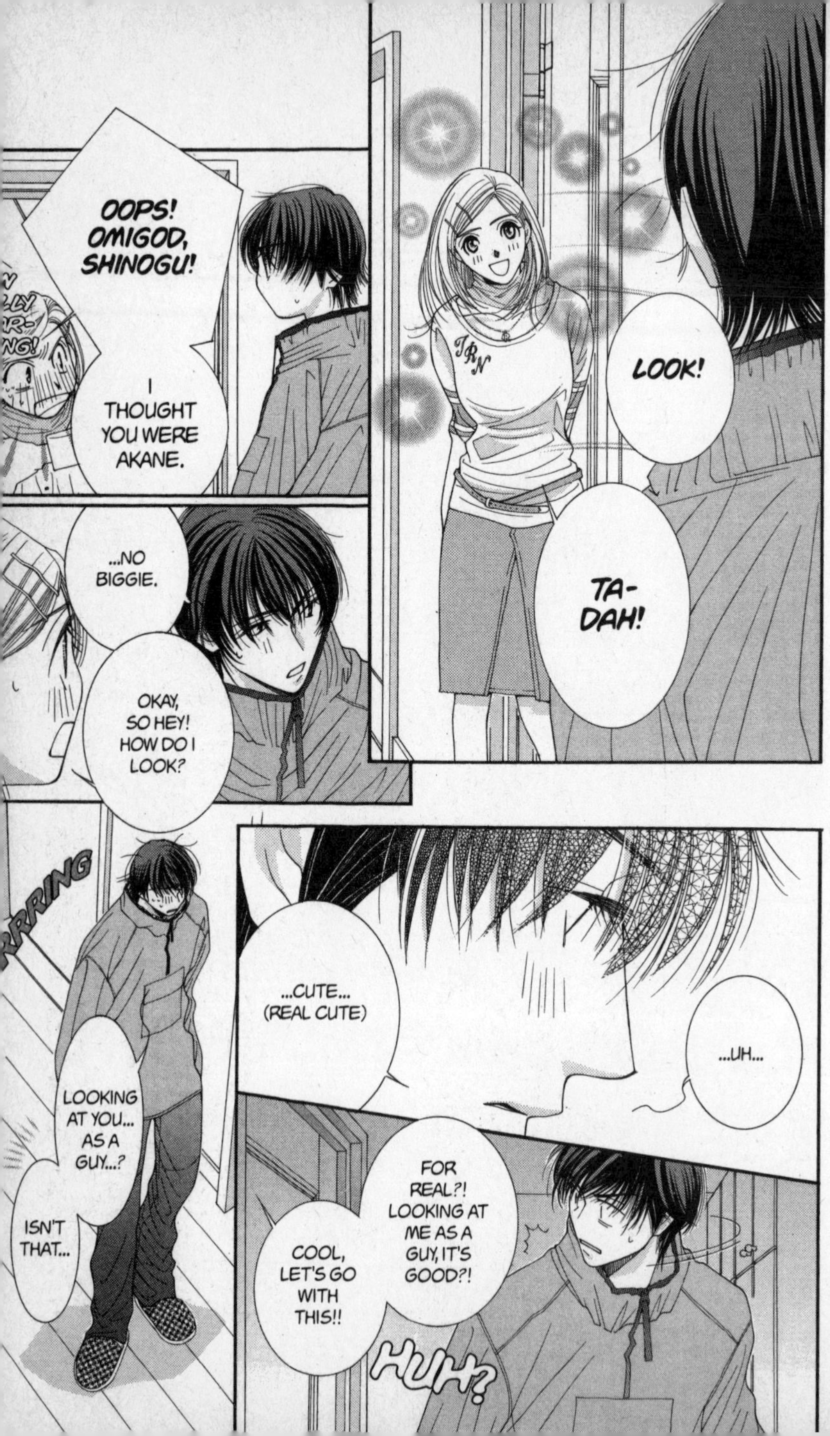
LOOK!
TA-DAH!
OOPS! OMIGOD, SHINOGU!
I THOUGHT YOU WERE AKANE.
...NO BIGGIE.
OKAY, SO HEY! HOW DO I LOOK?
...UH...
...CUTE... (REAL CUTE)
FOR REAL?! LOOKING AT ME AS A GUY, IT'S GOOD?!
COOL, LET'S GO WITH THIS!!
HUH?
RRRRING
LOOKING AT YOU... AS A GUY...?
ISN'T THAT...

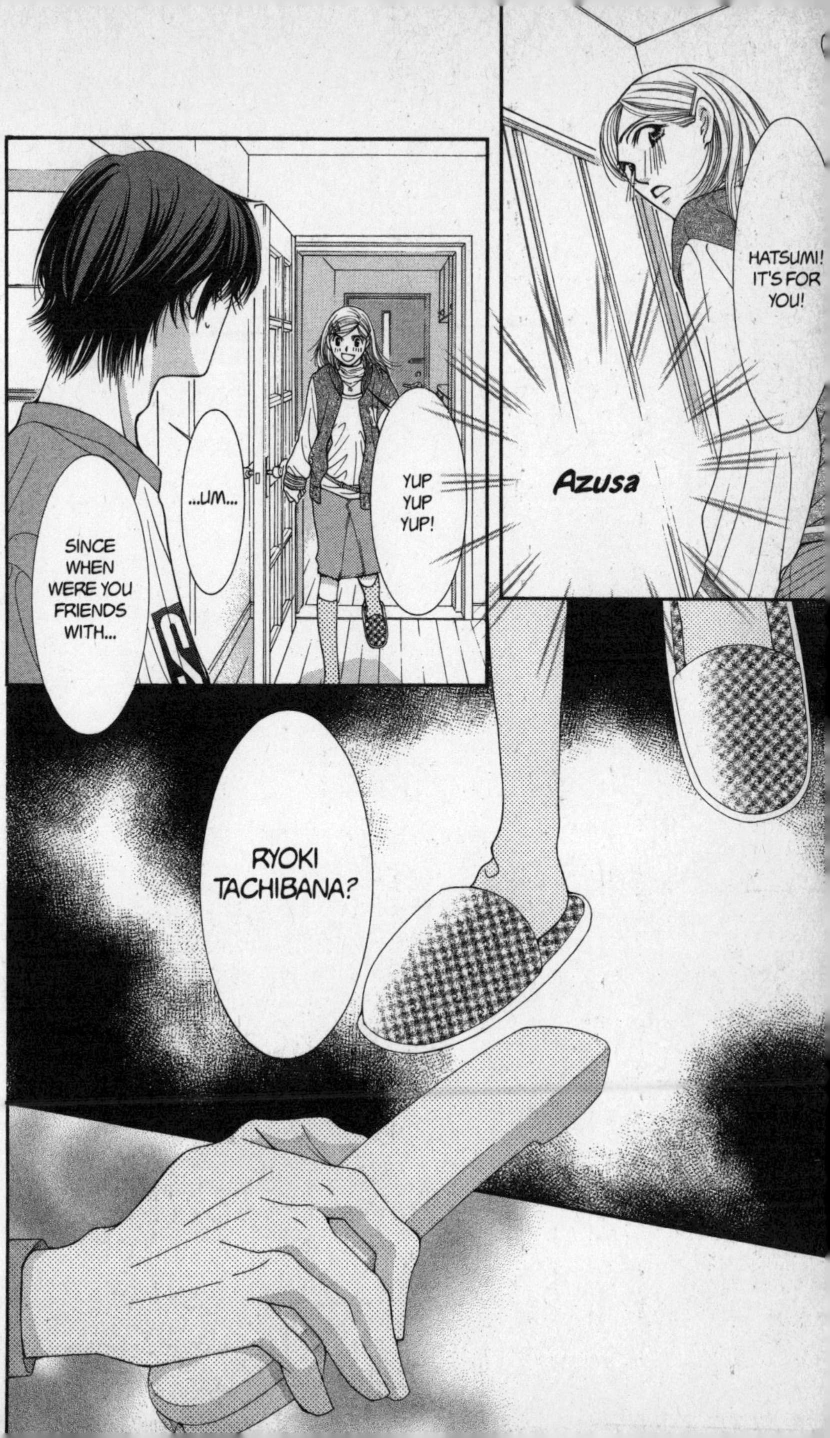
HATSUMI! IT'S FOR YOU!
Azusa
YUP YUP YUP!
...UM...
SINCE WHEN WERE YOU FRIENDS WITH...
RYOKI TACHIBANA?

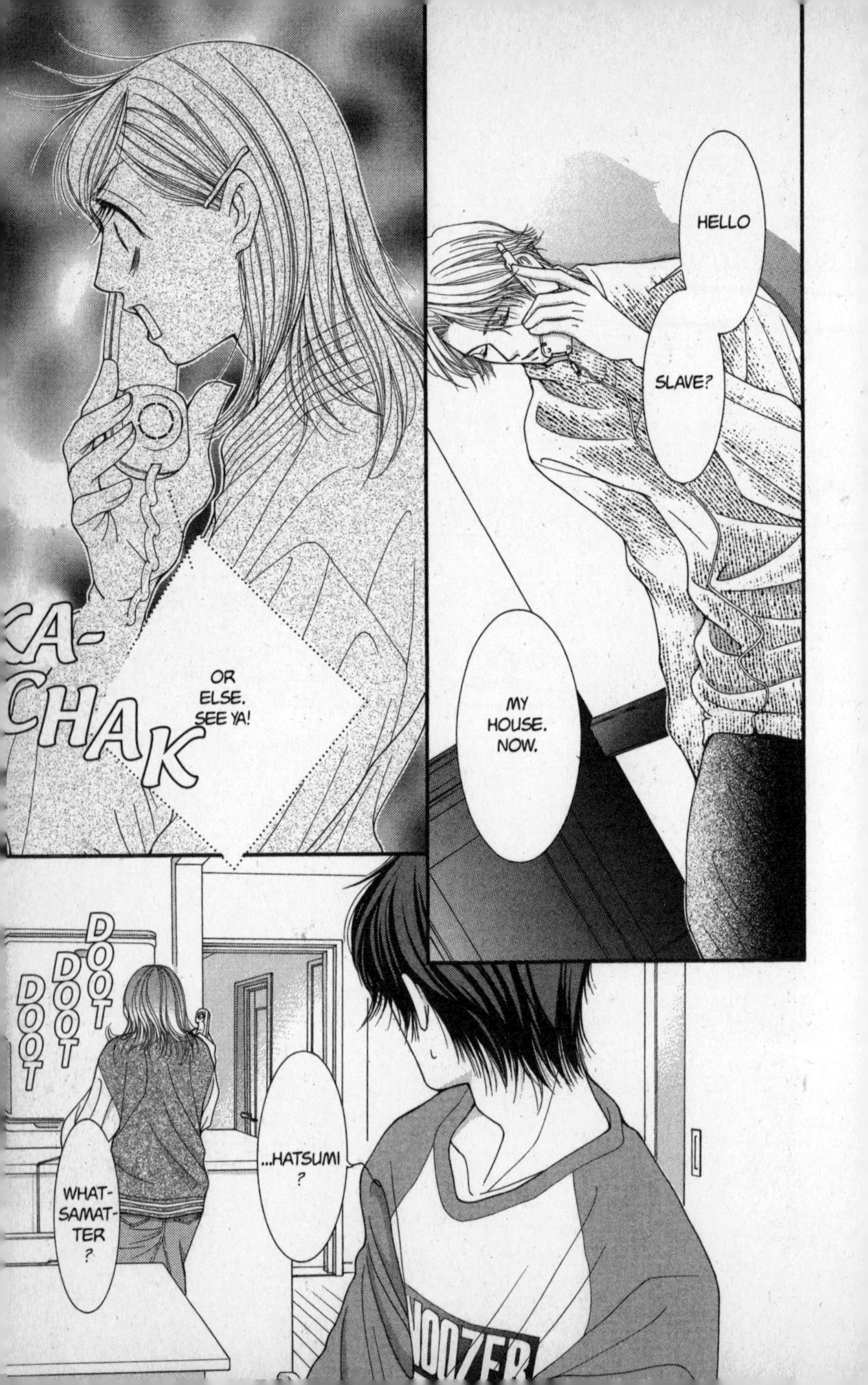
HELLO
SLAVE?
MY HOUSE. NOW.
OR ELSE. SEE YA!
KA-CHAK
...HATSUMI?
DOOT DOOT DOOT
WHAT-SAMATTER?

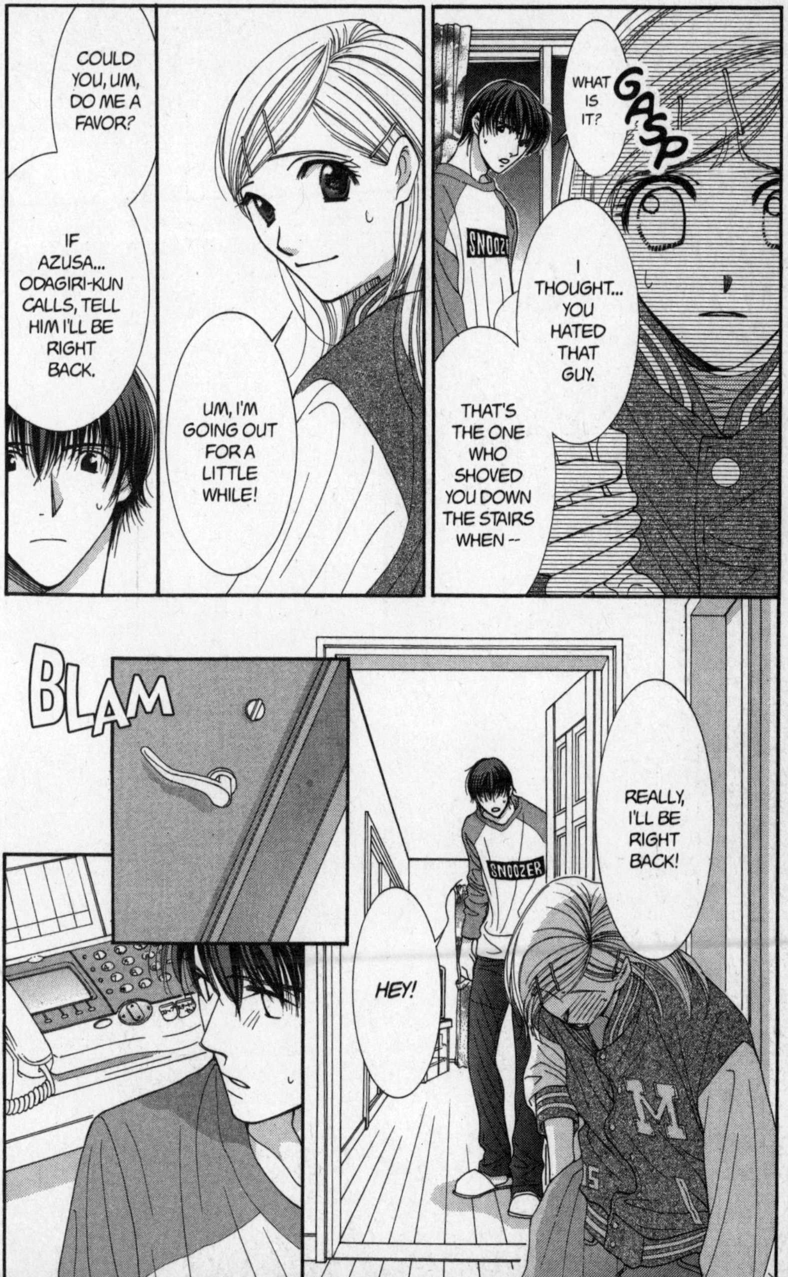
WHAT IS IT?
GASP
I THOUGHT... YOU HATED THAT GUY.
THAT'S THE ONE WHO SHOVED YOU DOWN THE STAIRS WHEN --
UM, I'M GOING OUT FOR A LITTLE WHILE!
COULD YOU, UM, DO ME A FAVOR?
IF AZUSA... ODAGIRI-KUN CALLS, TELL HIM I'LL BE RIGHT BACK.
REALLY, I'LL BE RIGHT BACK!
HEY!
BLAM

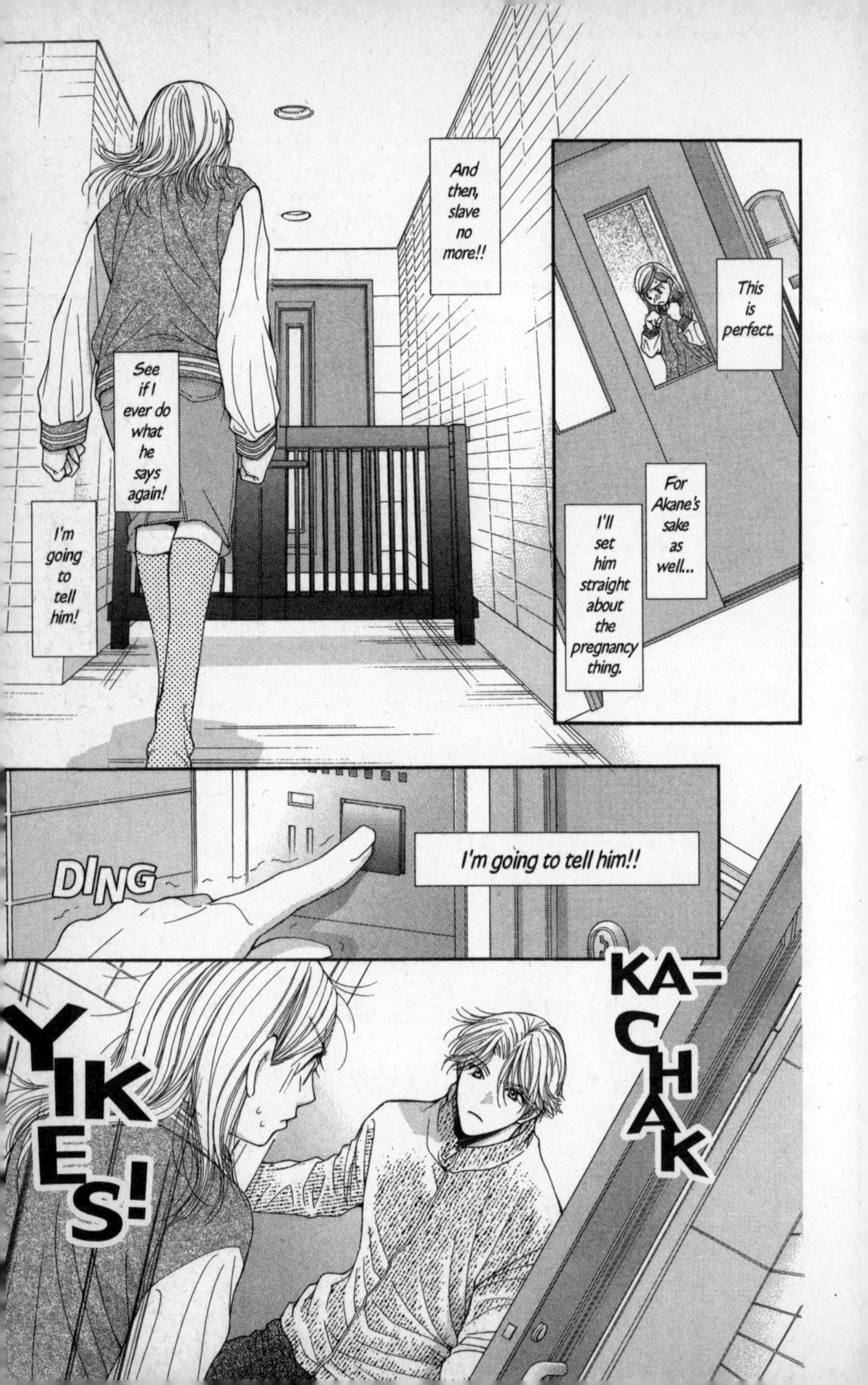
This is perfect.
For Akane's sake as well...
I'll set him straight about the pregnancy thing.
And then, slave no more!!
See if I ever do what he says again!
I'm going to tell him!
I'm going to tell him!!
DING
KA-CHAK
YIKES!

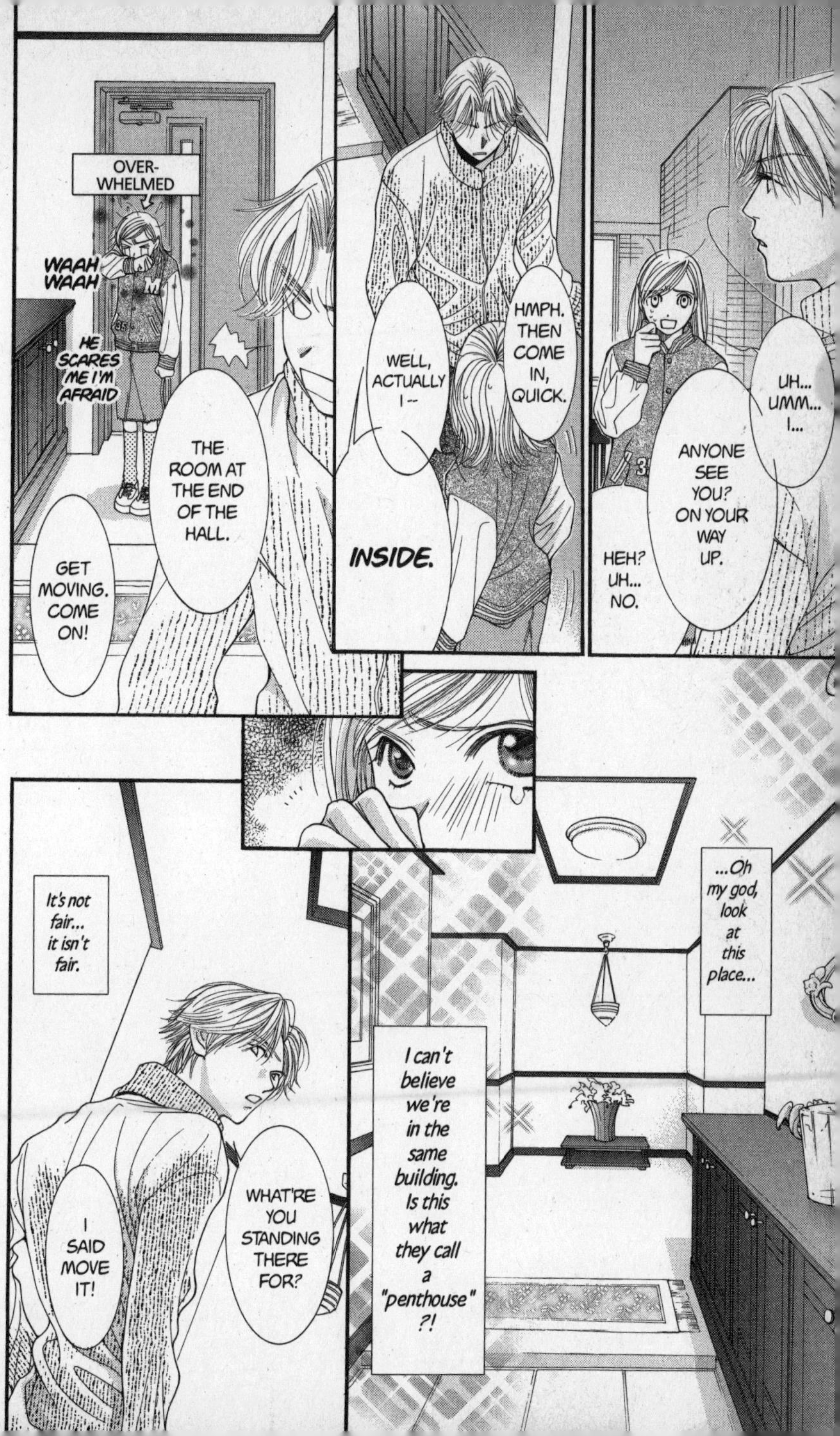
UH... UMM... I...
ANYONE SEE YOU? ON YOUR WAY UP.
HEH? UH... NO.
HMPH. THEN COME IN, QUICK.
WELL, ACTUALLY I--
INSIDE.
OVER-WHELMED
WAAH WAAH
HE SCARES ME I'M AFRAID
THE ROOM AT THE END OF THE HALL.
GET MOVING. COME ON!
...Oh my god, look at this place...
I can't believe we're in the same building. Is this what they call a "penthouse"?!
It's not fair... it isn't fair.
WHAT'RE YOU STANDING THERE FOR?
I SAID MOVE IT!

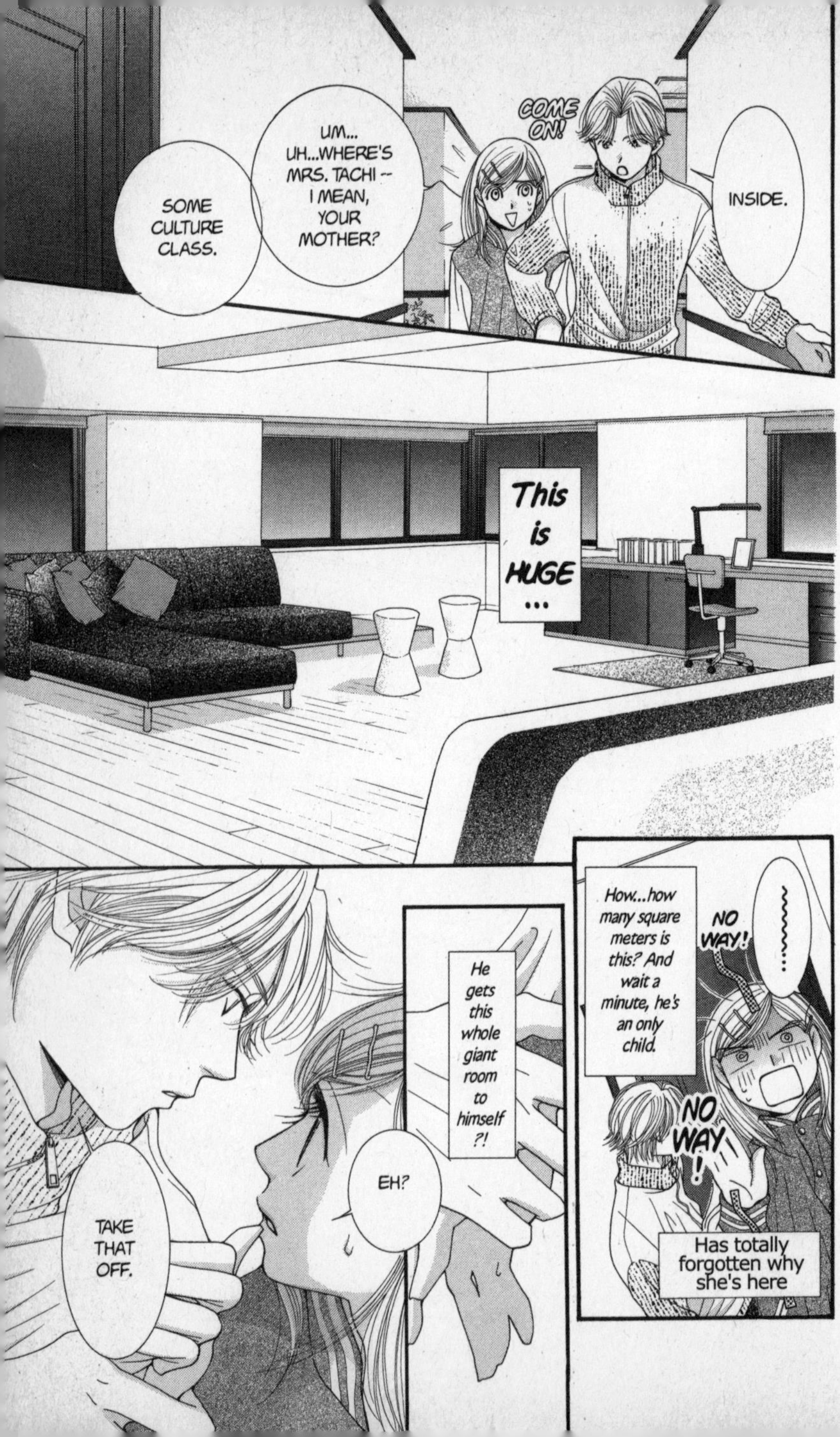
INSIDE.
COME ON!
UM... UH...WHERE'S MRS. TACHI -- I MEAN, YOUR MOTHER?
SOME CULTURE CLASS.
This is HUGE ...
NO WAY!
How...how many square meters is this? And wait a minute, he's an only child.
NO WAY!
Has totally forgotten why she's here
He gets this whole giant room to himself?!
EH?
TAKE THAT OFF.

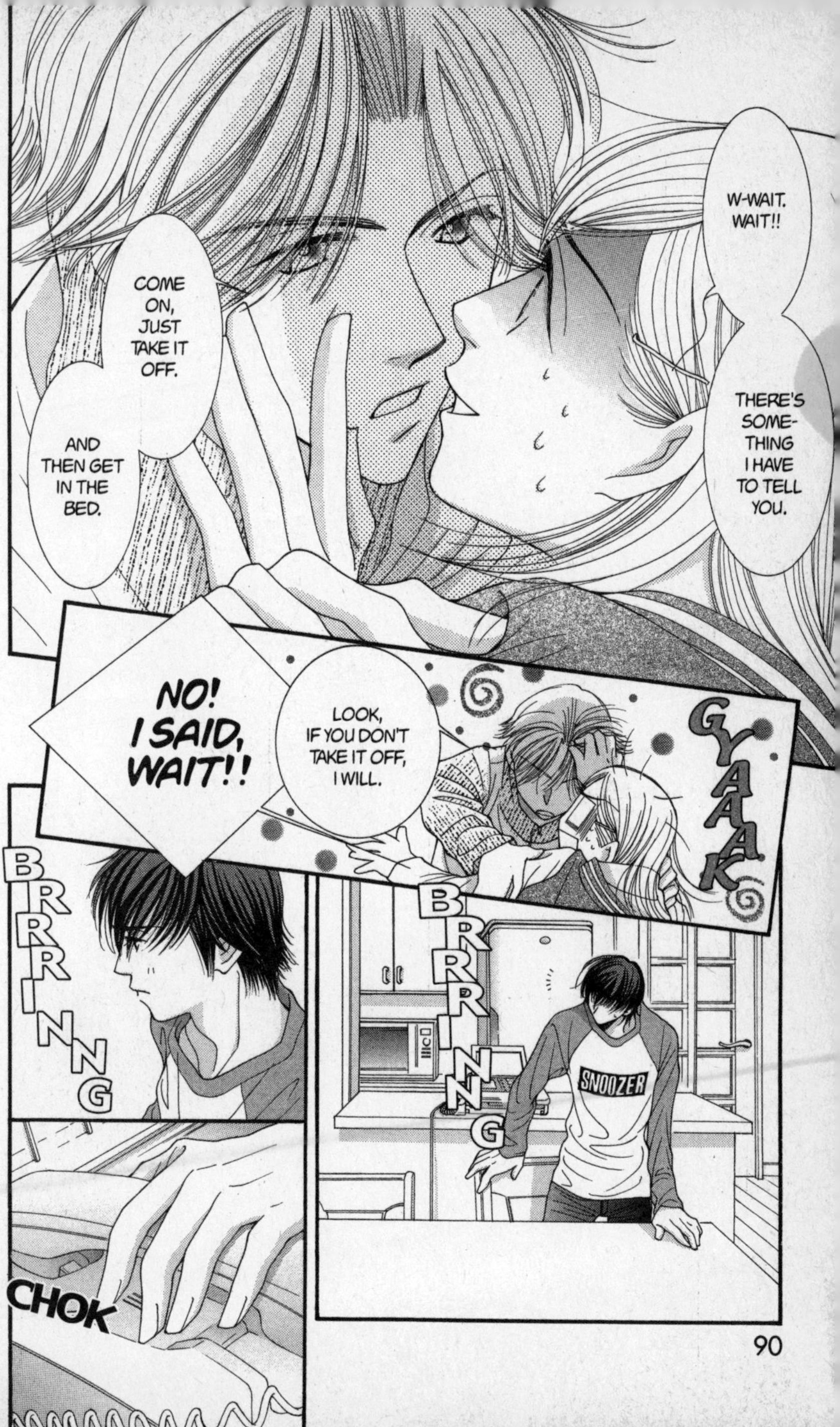
W-WAIT. WAIT!!
THERE'S SOME-THING I HAVE TO TELL YOU.
COME ON, JUST TAKE IT OFF.
AND THEN GET IN THE BED.
GYAAAK
LOOK, IF YOU DON'T TAKE IT OFF, I WILL.
NO! I SAID, WAIT!!
BRRRINNNG
BRRRINNNG
SNOOZER
CHOK

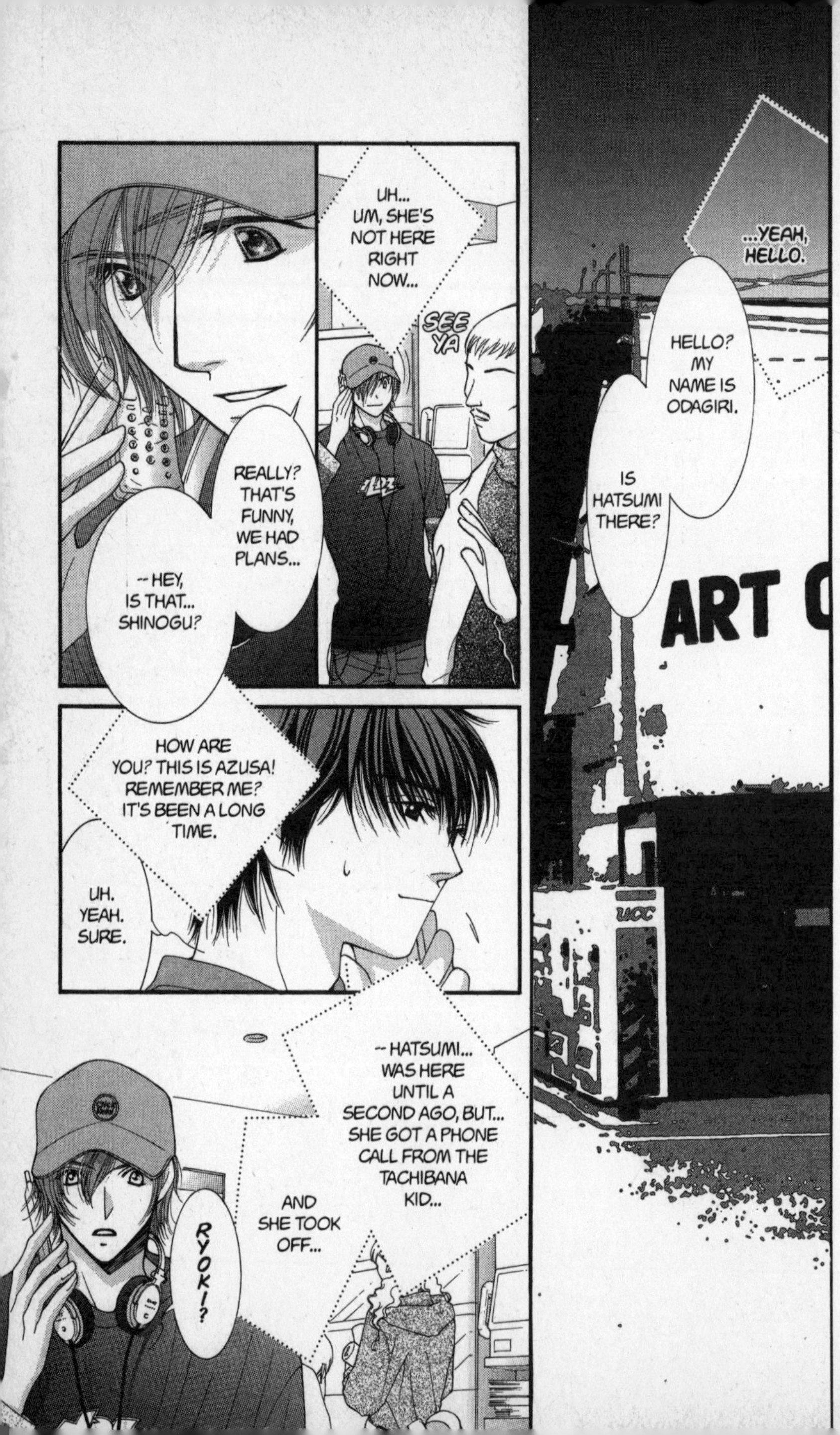
...YEAH, HELLO.
HELLO? MY NAME IS ODAGIRI.
IS HATSUMI THERE?
ART
UH... UM, SHE'S NOT HERE RIGHT NOW...
SEE YA
REALLY? THAT'S FUNNY, WE HAD PLANS...
--HEY, IS THAT... SHINOGU?
HOW ARE YOU? THIS IS AZUSA! REMEMBER ME? IT'S BEEN A LONG TIME.
UH. YEAH. SURE.
--HATSUMI... WAS HERE UNTIL A SECOND AGO, BUT... SHE GOT A PHONE CALL FROM THE TACHIBANA KID...
AND SHE TOOK OFF...
RYOKI?

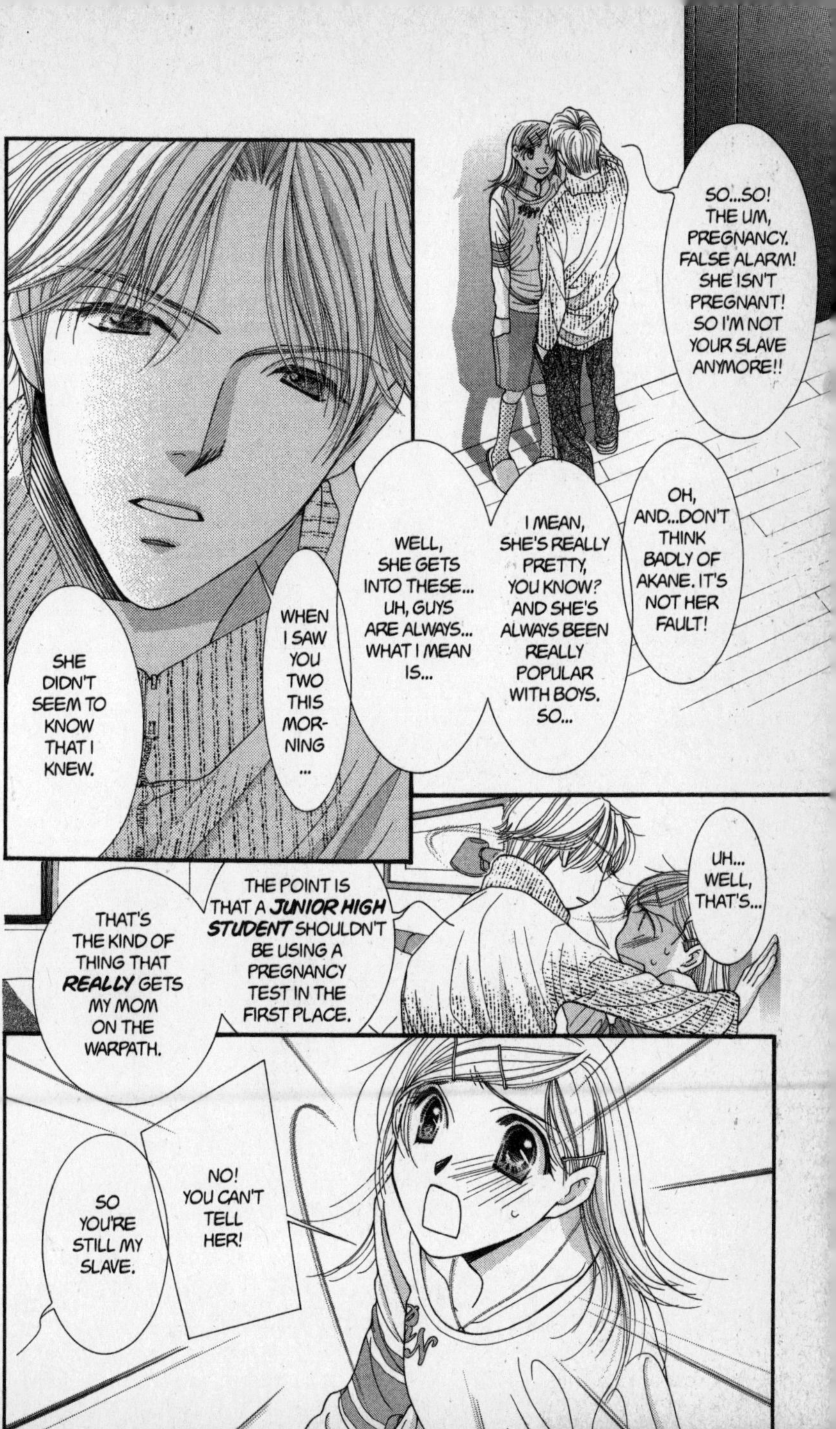
SO...SO! THE UM, PREGNANCY. FALSE ALARM! SHE ISN'T PREGNANT! SO I'M NOT YOUR SLAVE ANYMORE!!
OH, AND...DON'T THINK BADLY OF AKANE. IT'S NOT HER FAULT!
I MEAN, SHE'S REALLY PRETTY, YOU KNOW? AND SHE'S ALWAYS BEEN REALLY POPULAR WITH BOYS. SO...
WELL, SHE GETS INTO THESE... UH, GUYS ARE ALWAYS... WHAT I MEAN IS...
WHEN I SAW YOU TWO THIS MORNING...
SHE DIDN'T SEEM TO KNOW THAT I KNEW.
UH... WELL, THAT'S...
THE POINT IS THAT A ***JUNIOR HIGH STUDENT*** SHOULDN'T BE USING A PREGNANCY TEST IN THE FIRST PLACE.
THAT'S THE KIND OF THING THAT ***REALLY*** GETS MY MOM ON THE WARPATH.
NO! YOU CAN'T TELL HER!
SO YOU'RE STILL MY SLAVE.

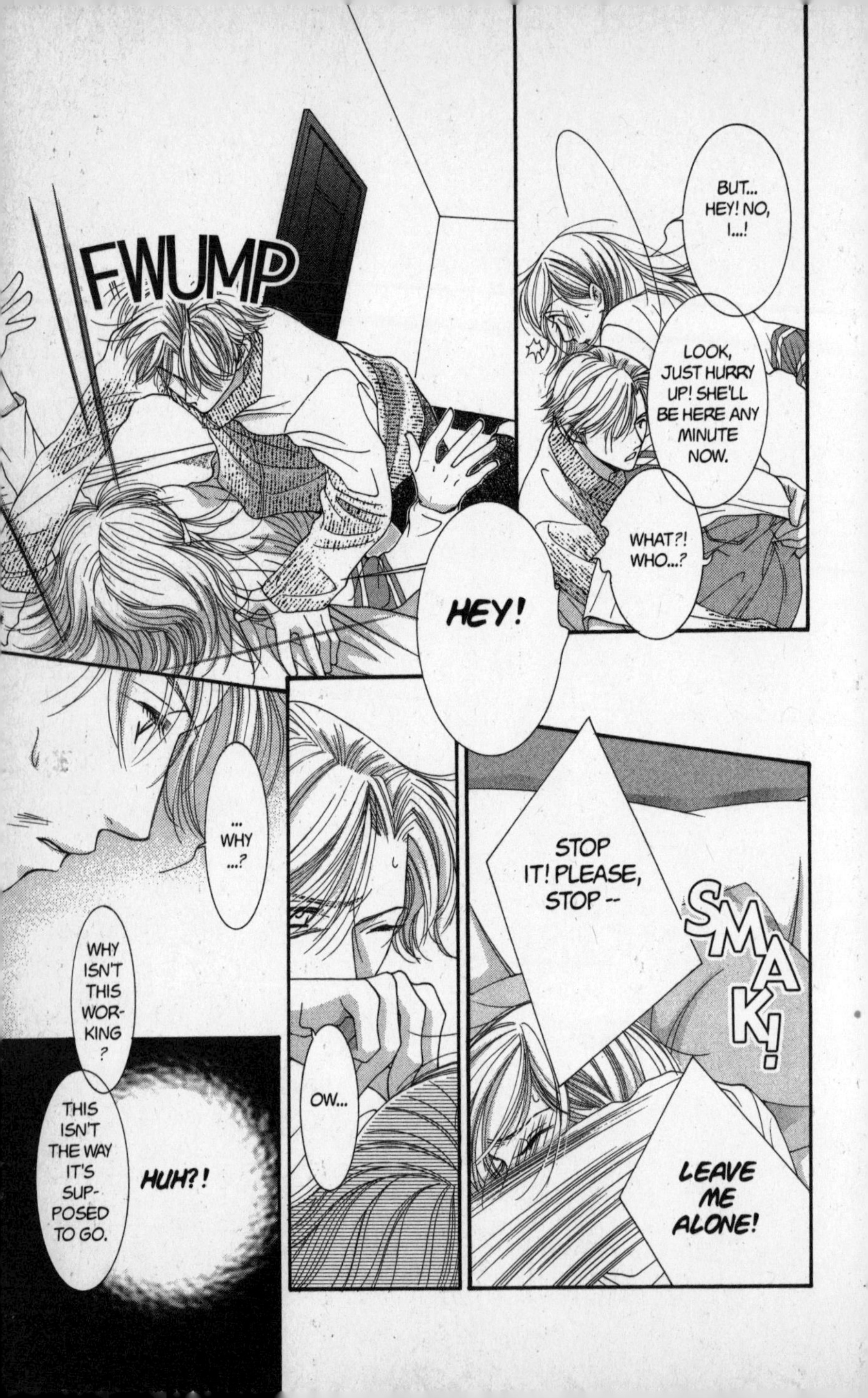
BUT... HEY! NO, I...!
LOOK, JUST HURRY UP! SHE'LL BE HERE ANY MINUTE NOW.
WHAT?! WHO...?
FWUMP
HEY!
STOP IT! PLEASE, STOP --
SMAK!
LEAVE ME ALONE!
OW...
... WHY ...?
WHY ISN'T THIS WOR-KING?
THIS ISN'T THE WAY IT'S SUP-POSED TO GO.
HUH?!

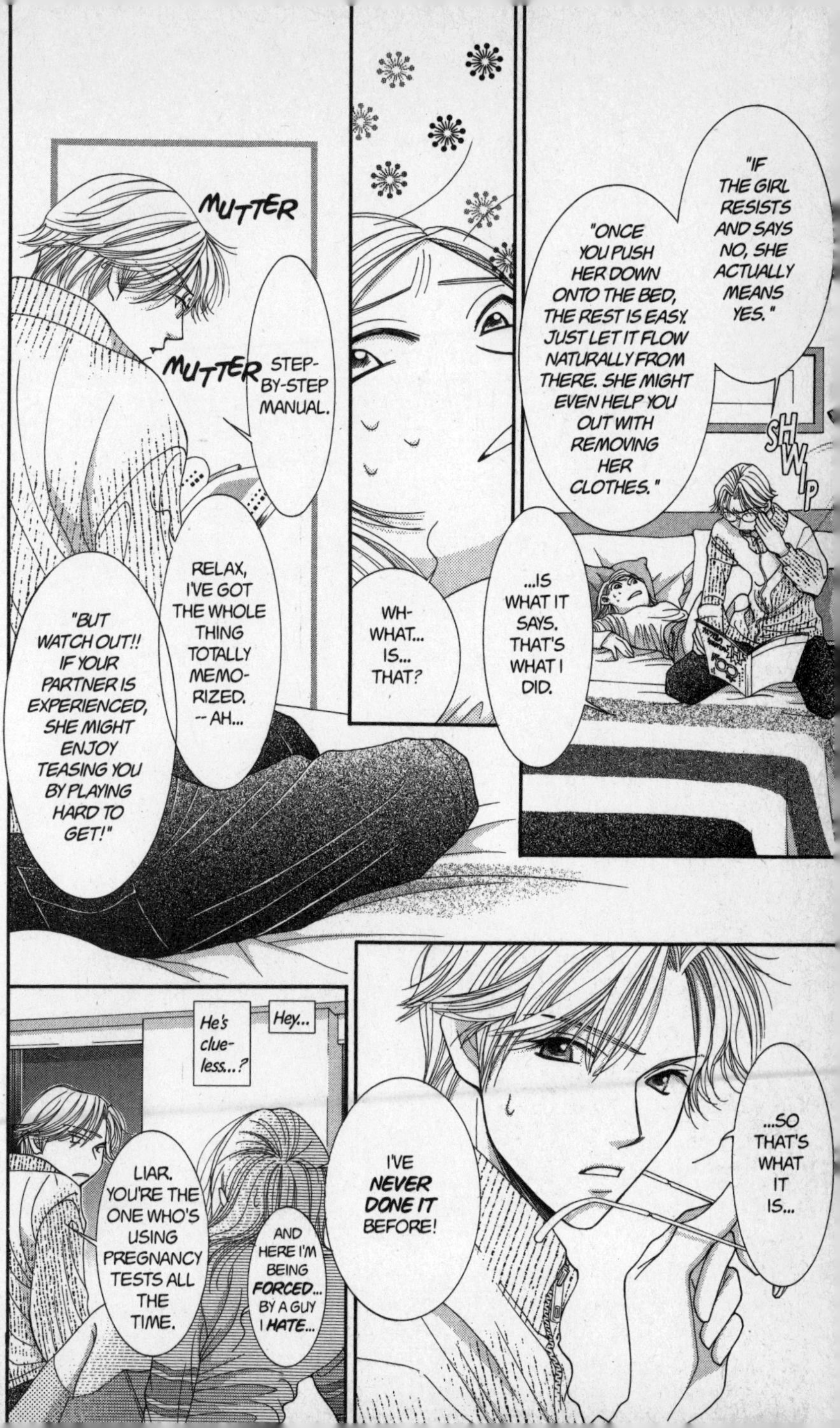
"IF THE GIRL RESISTS AND SAYS NO, SHE ACTUALLY MEANS YES."
"ONCE YOU PUSH HER DOWN ONTO THE BED, THE REST IS EASY. JUST LET IT FLOW NATURALLY FROM THERE. SHE MIGHT EVEN HELP YOU OUT WITH REMOVING HER CLOTHES."
SHWIP
...IS WHAT IT SAYS. THAT'S WHAT I DID.
WH- WHAT... IS... THAT?
MUTTER
STEP-BY-STEP MANUAL.
MUTTER
RELAX, I'VE GOT THE WHOLE THING TOTALLY MEMORIZED. -- AH...
"BUT WATCH OUT!! IF YOUR PARTNER IS EXPERIENCED, SHE MIGHT ENJOY TEASING YOU BY PLAYING HARD TO GET!"
...SO THAT'S WHAT IT IS...
I'VE **NEVER DONE IT** BEFORE!
Hey...
He's clueless...?
AND HERE I'M BEING **FORCED**... BY A GUY I **HATE**...
LIAR. YOU'RE THE ONE WHO'S USING PREGNANCY TESTS ALL THE TIME.

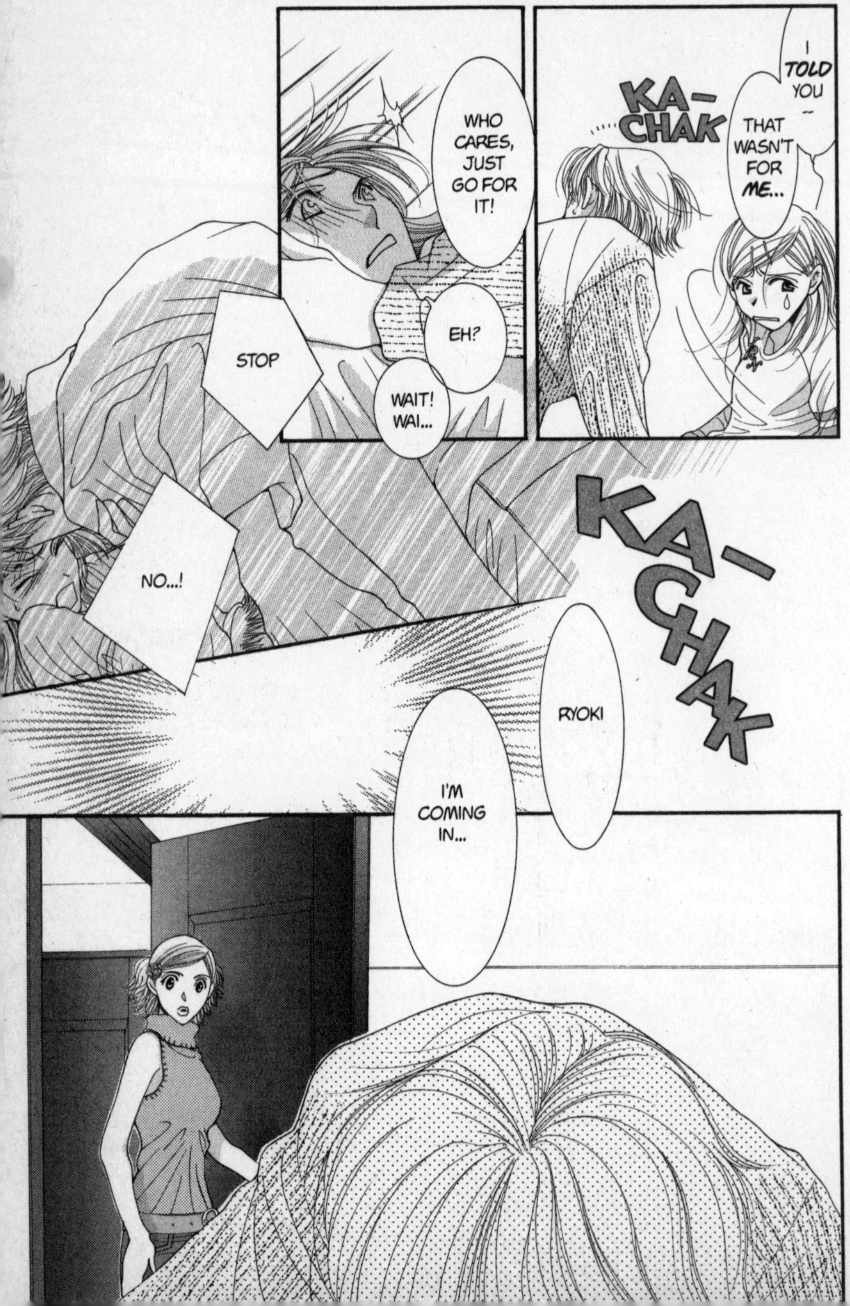
I TOLD YOU --
THAT WASN'T FOR ME...
KA-CHAK
WHO CARES, JUST GO FOR IT!
EH?
WAIT! WAI...
KA-CHAK
STOP
NO...!
RYOKI
I'M COMING IN...

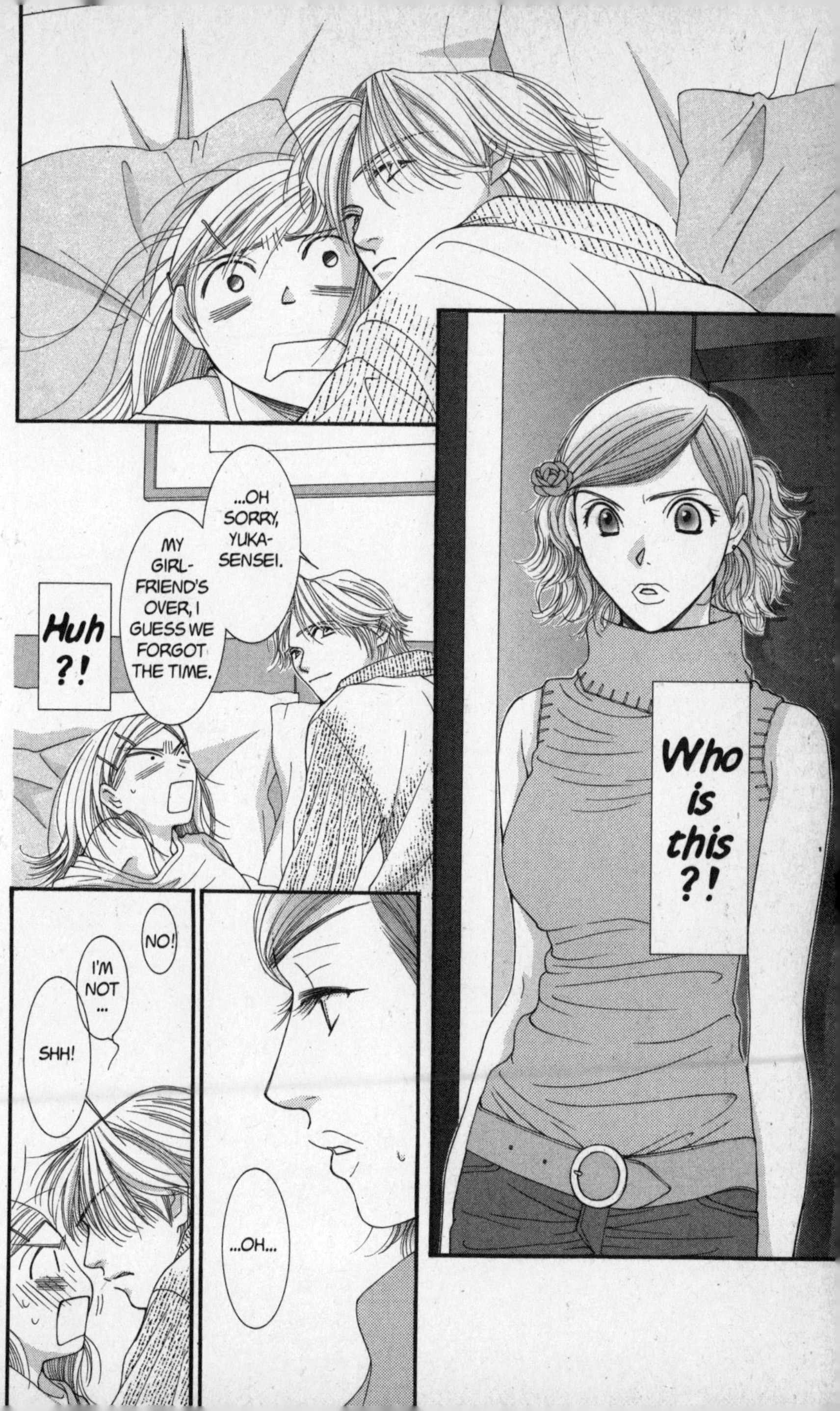
Who is this?!
...OH SORRY, YUKA-SENSEI.
MY GIRLFRIEND'S OVER, I GUESS WE FORGOT THE TIME.
Huh?!
...OH...
NO!
I'M NOT ...
SHH!

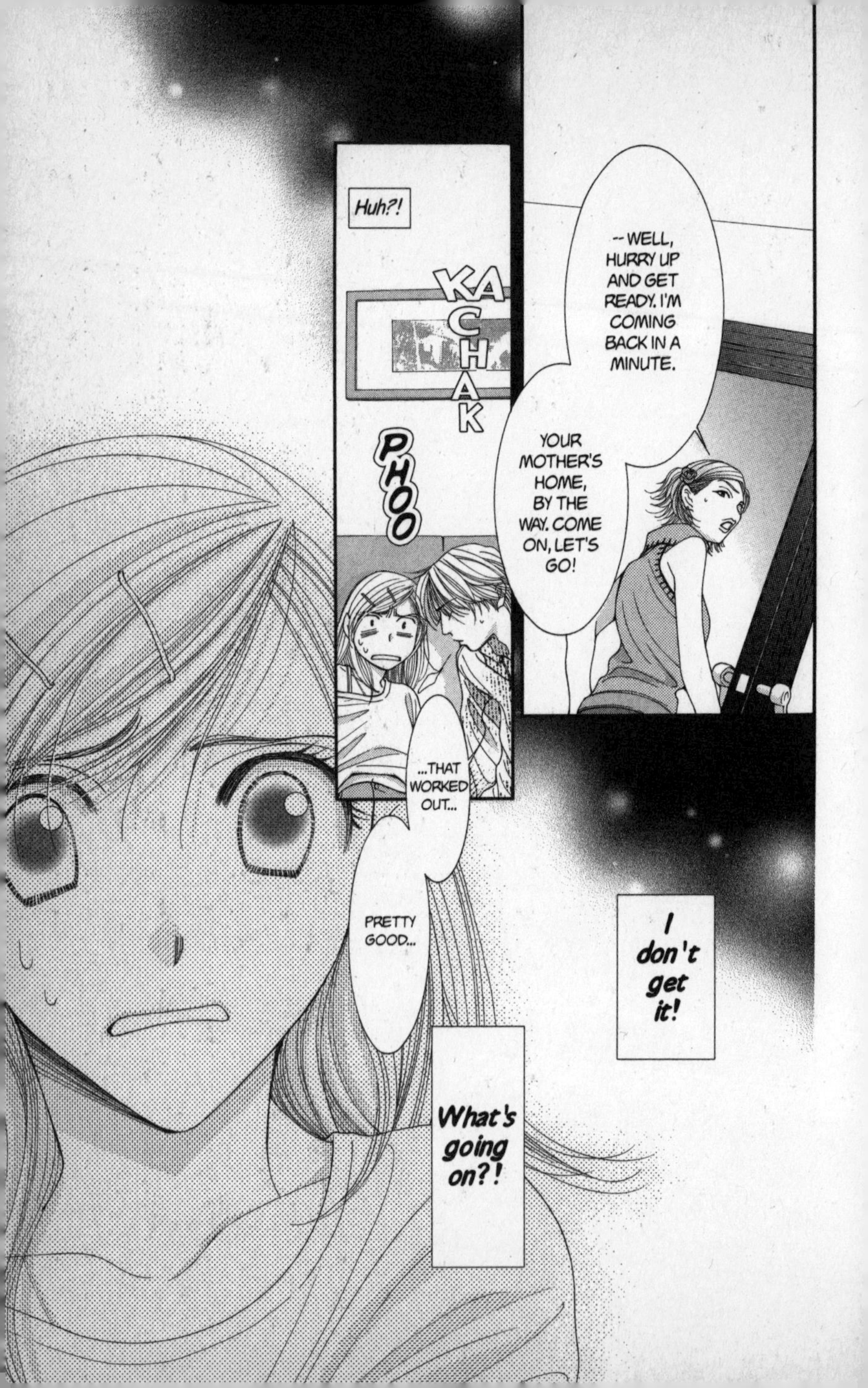
--WELL, HURRY UP AND GET READY. I'M COMING BACK IN A MINUTE.
YOUR MOTHER'S HOME, BY THE WAY. COME ON, LET'S GO!
Huh?!
KACHAK
PHOO
...THAT WORKED OUT...
PRETTY GOOD...
I don't get it!
What's going on?!

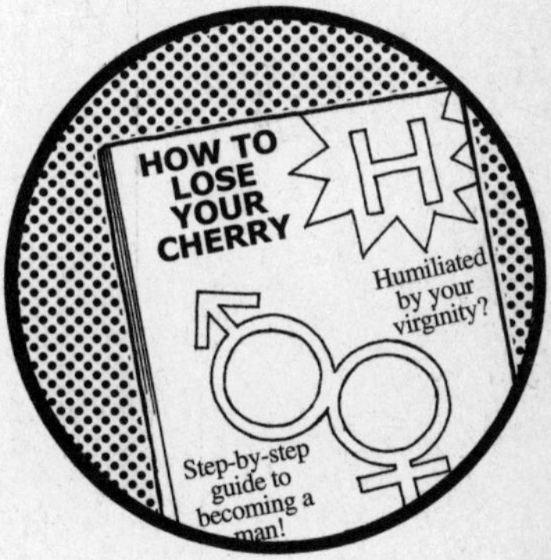
HOW TO LOSE YOUR CHERRY
H
Humiliated by your virginity?
Step-by-step guide to becoming a man!

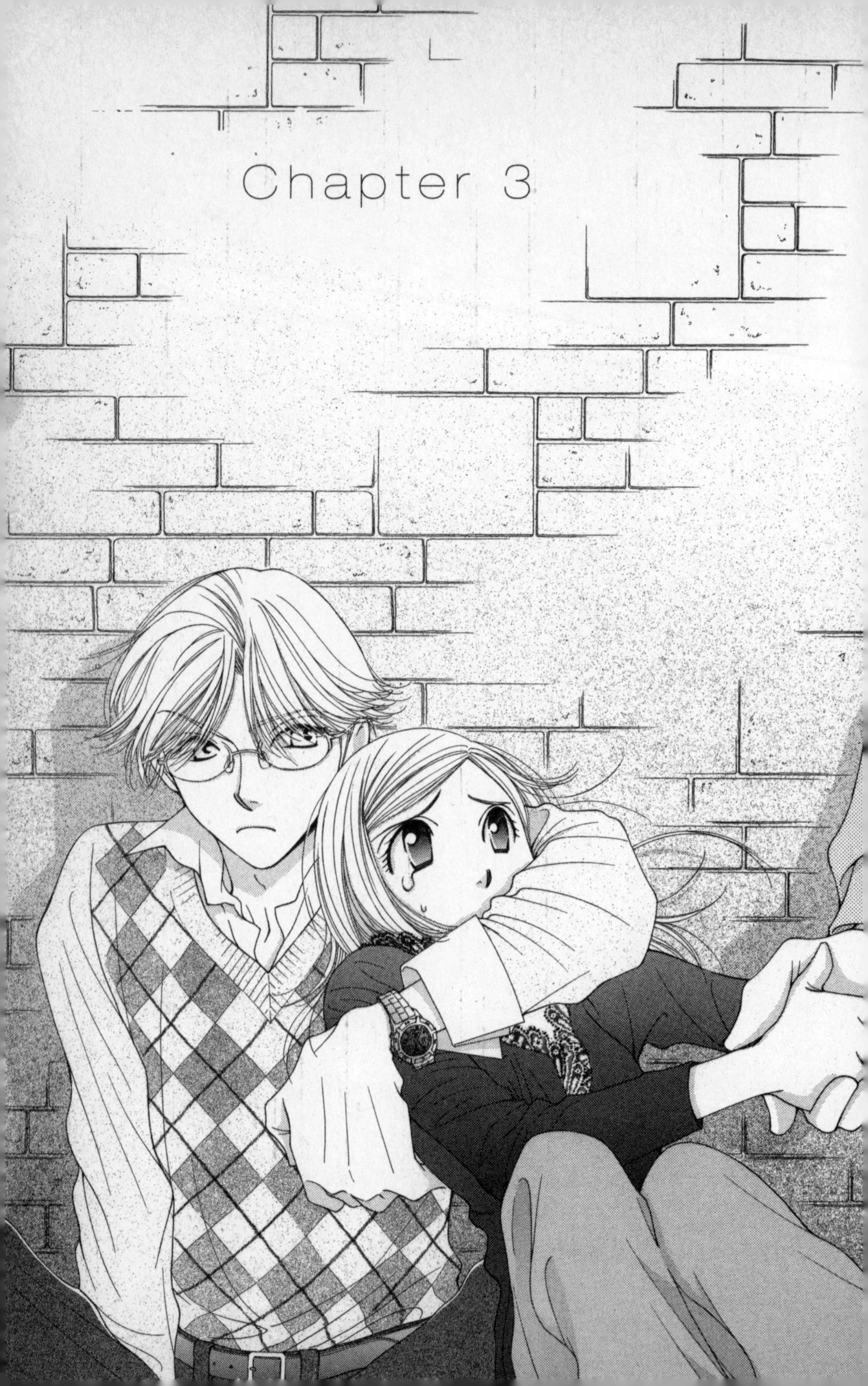
Chapter 3

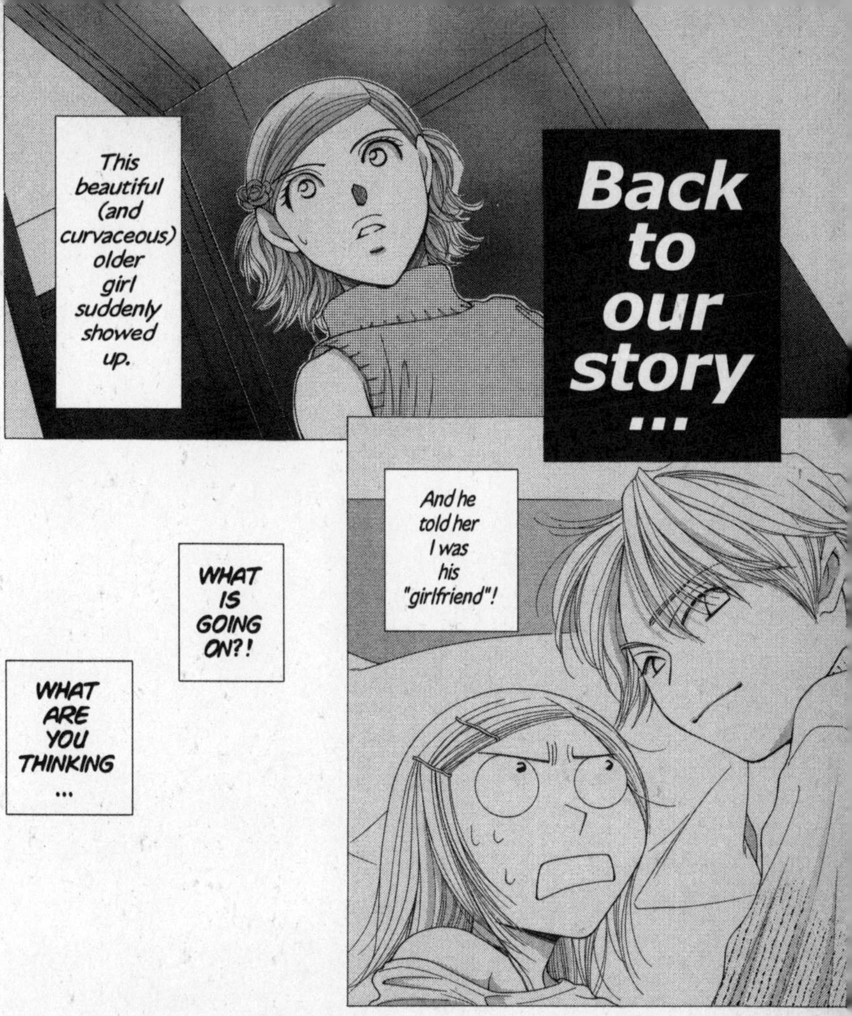
Back to our story ...
This beautiful (and curvaceous) older girl suddenly showed up.
And he told her I was his "girlfriend"!
WHAT IS GOING ON?!
WHAT ARE YOU THINKING ...

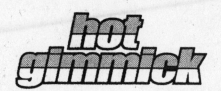

hot gimmick

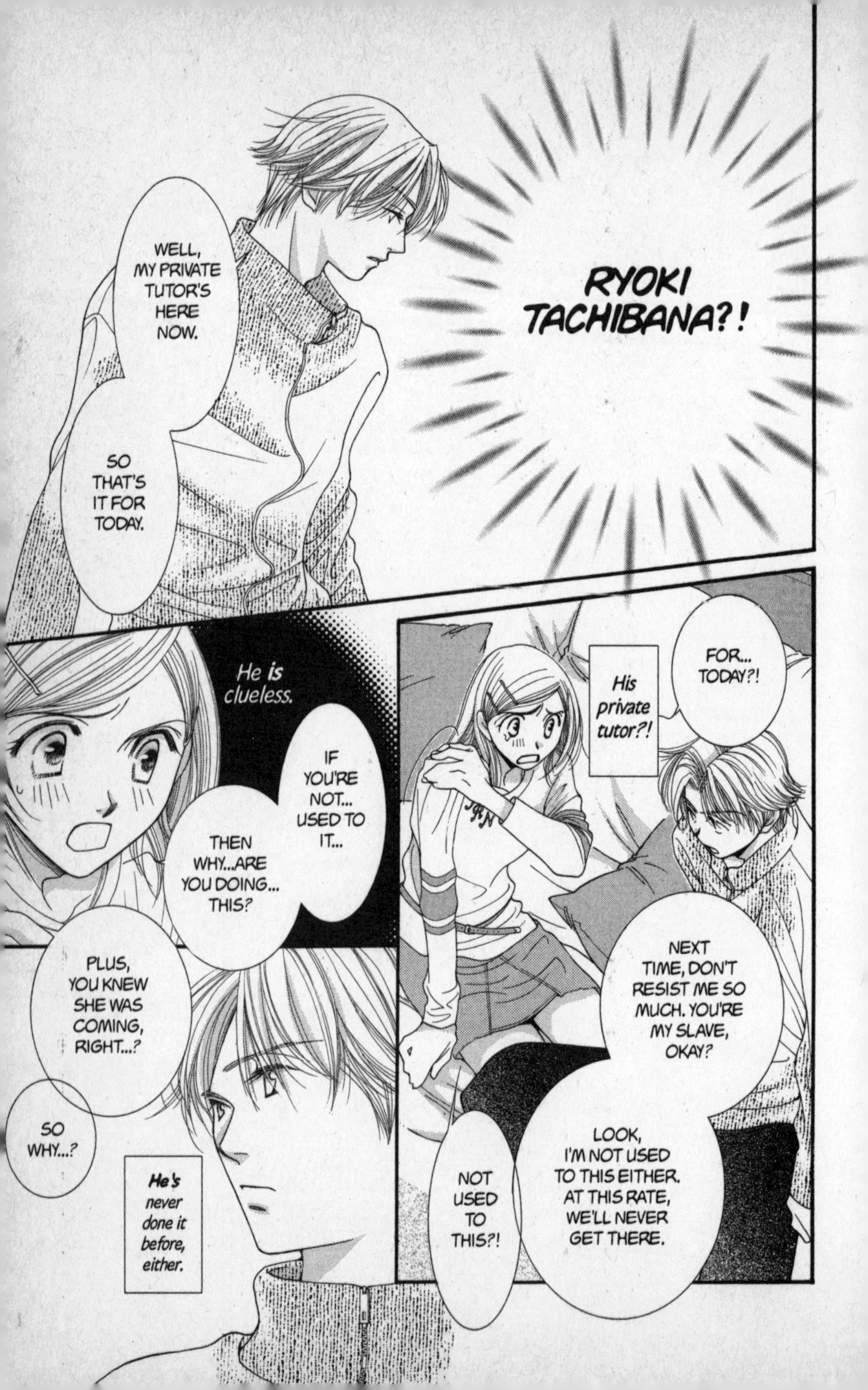
RYOKI TACHIBANA?!
WELL, MY PRIVATE TUTOR'S HERE NOW.
SO THAT'S IT FOR TODAY.
FOR... TODAY?!
His private tutor?!
NEXT TIME, DON'T RESIST ME SO MUCH. YOU'RE MY SLAVE, OKAY?
LOOK, I'M NOT USED TO THIS EITHER. AT THIS RATE, WE'LL NEVER GET THERE.
NOT USED TO THIS?!
He *is* clueless.
IF YOU'RE NOT... USED TO IT...
THEN WHY...ARE YOU DOING... THIS?
PLUS, YOU KNEW SHE WAS COMING, RIGHT...?
SO WHY...?
He's never done it before, either.

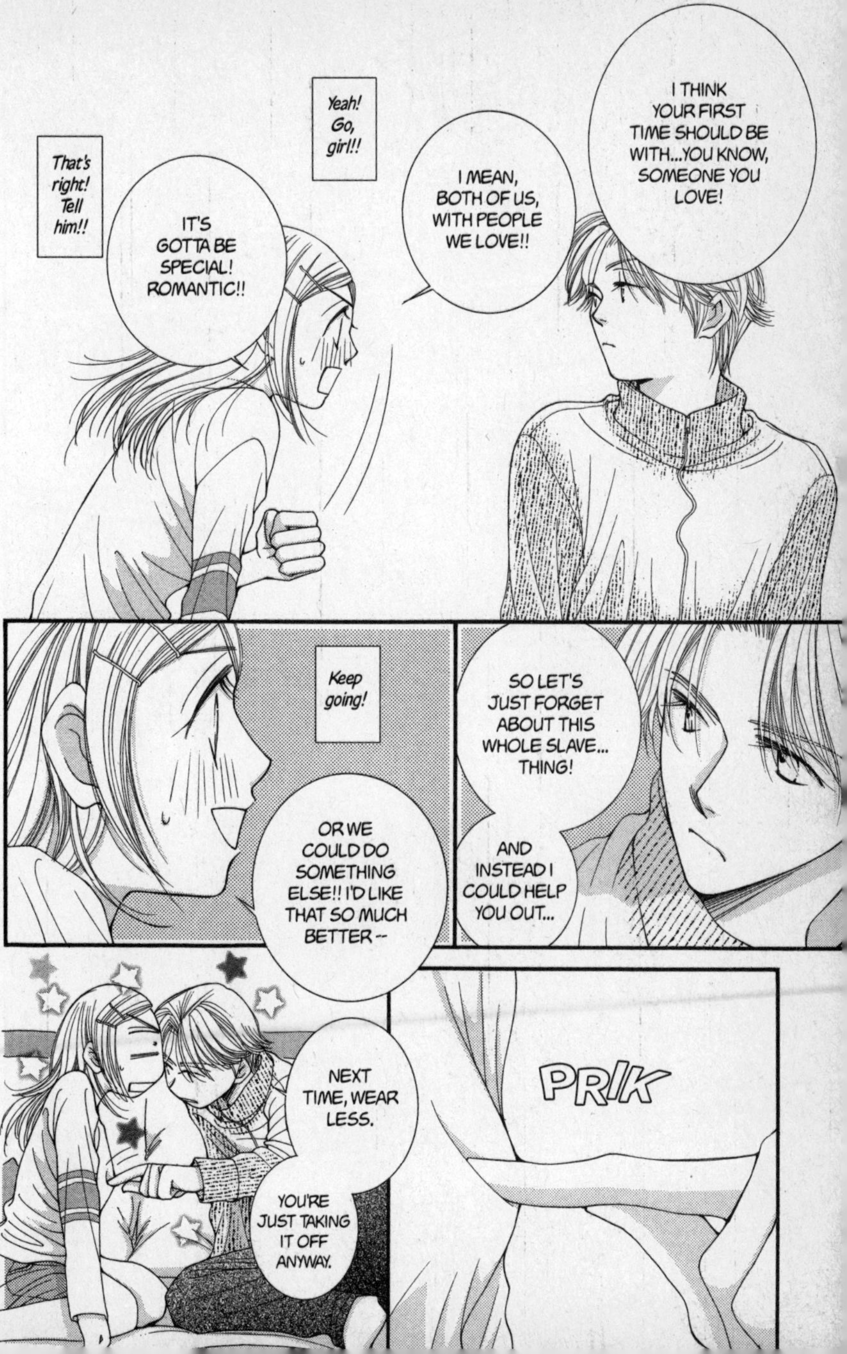
I THINK YOUR FIRST TIME SHOULD BE WITH...YOU KNOW, SOMEONE YOU LOVE!
I MEAN, BOTH OF US, WITH PEOPLE WE LOVE!!
Yeah! Go, girl!!
IT'S GOTTA BE SPECIAL! ROMANTIC!!
That's right! Tell him!!
SO LET'S JUST FORGET ABOUT THIS WHOLE SLAVE... THING!
AND INSTEAD I COULD HELP YOU OUT...
Keep going!
OR WE COULD DO SOMETHING ELSE!! I'D LIKE THAT SO MUCH BETTER --
PRIK
NEXT TIME, WEAR LESS.
YOU'RE JUST TAKING IT OFF ANYWAY.

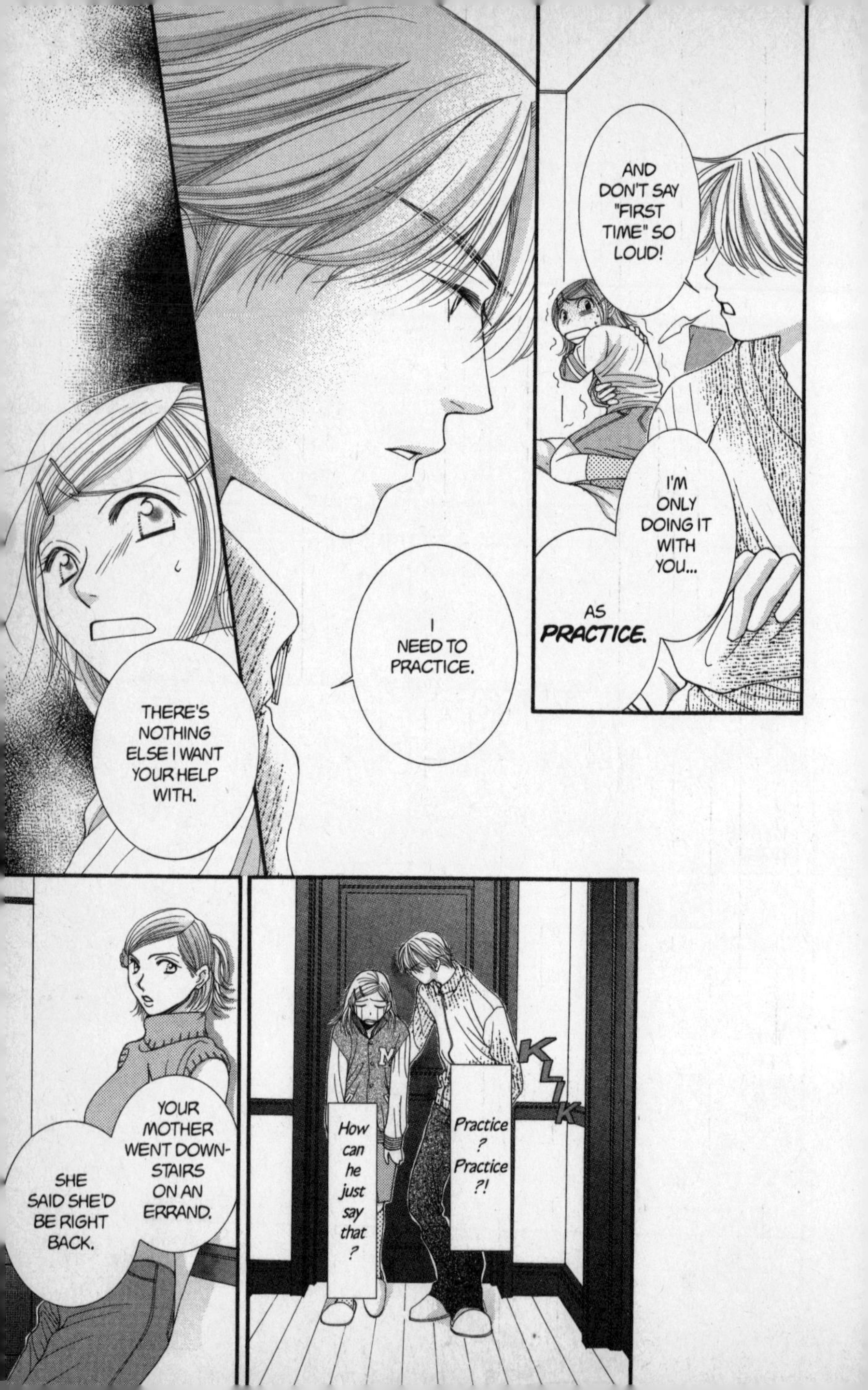
AND DON'T SAY "FIRST TIME" SO LOUD!
I'M ONLY DOING IT WITH YOU...
AS PRACTICE.
I NEED TO PRACTICE.
THERE'S NOTHING ELSE I WANT YOUR HELP WITH.
KLIK
Practice? Practice?!
How can he just say that?
YOUR MOTHER WENT DOWN-STAIRS ON AN ERRAND.
SHE SAID SHE'D BE RIGHT BACK.

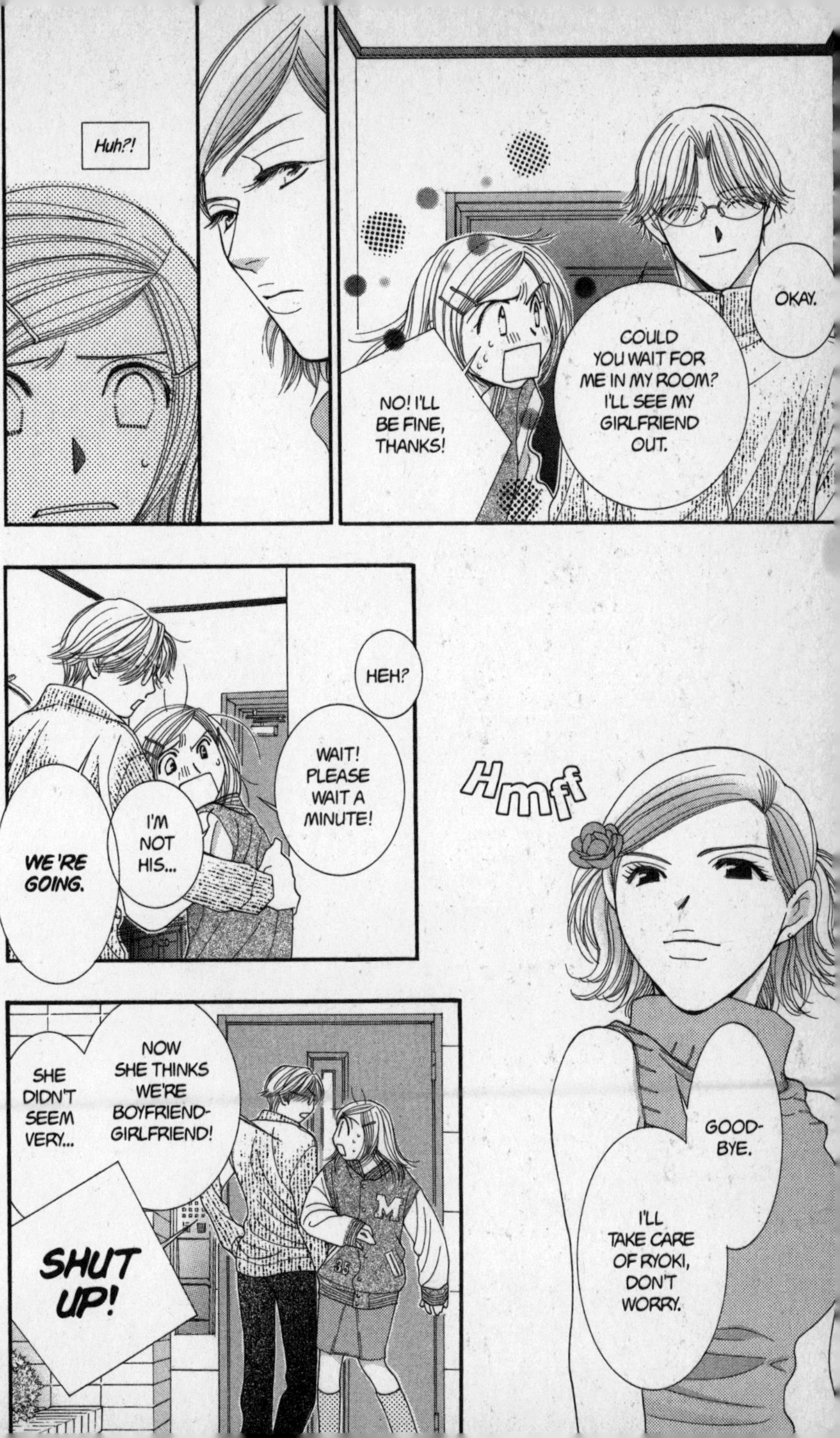
OKAY.
COULD YOU WAIT FOR ME IN MY ROOM? I'LL SEE MY GIRLFRIEND OUT.
NO! I'LL BE FINE, THANKS!
Huh?!
Hmf
GOOD-BYE.
I'LL TAKE CARE OF RYOKI, DON'T WORRY.
HEH?
WAIT! PLEASE WAIT A MINUTE!
I'M NOT HIS...
WE'RE GOING.
NOW SHE THINKS WE'RE BOYFRIEND-GIRLFRIEND!
SHE DIDN'T SEEM VERY...
SHUT UP!

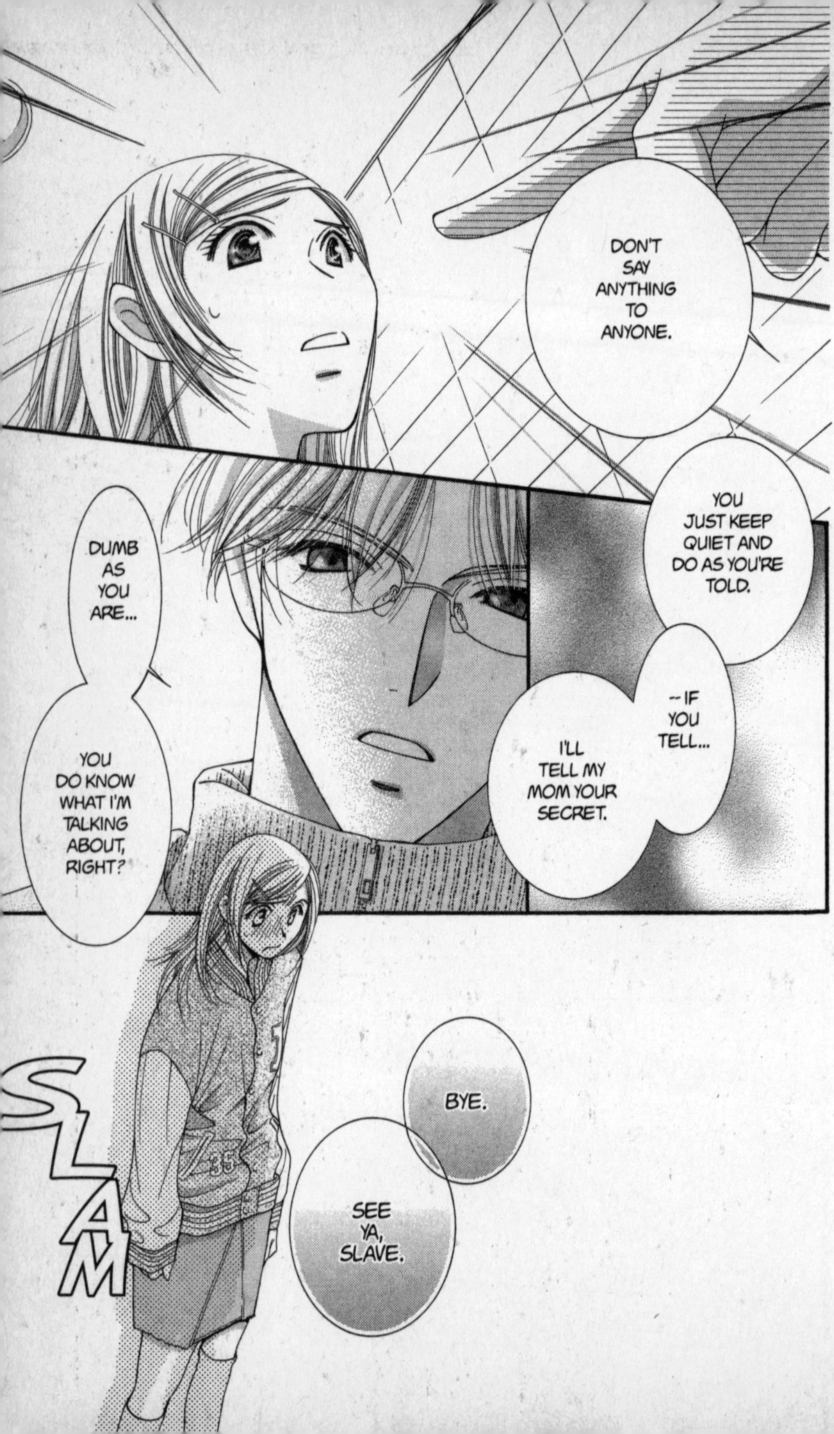
DON'T SAY ANYTHING TO ANYONE.
YOU JUST KEEP QUIET AND DO AS YOU'RE TOLD.
--IF YOU TELL...
I'LL TELL MY MOM YOUR SECRET.
DUMB AS YOU ARE...
YOU DO KNOW WHAT I'M TALKING ABOUT, RIGHT?
BYE.
SEE YA, SLAVE.
SLAM

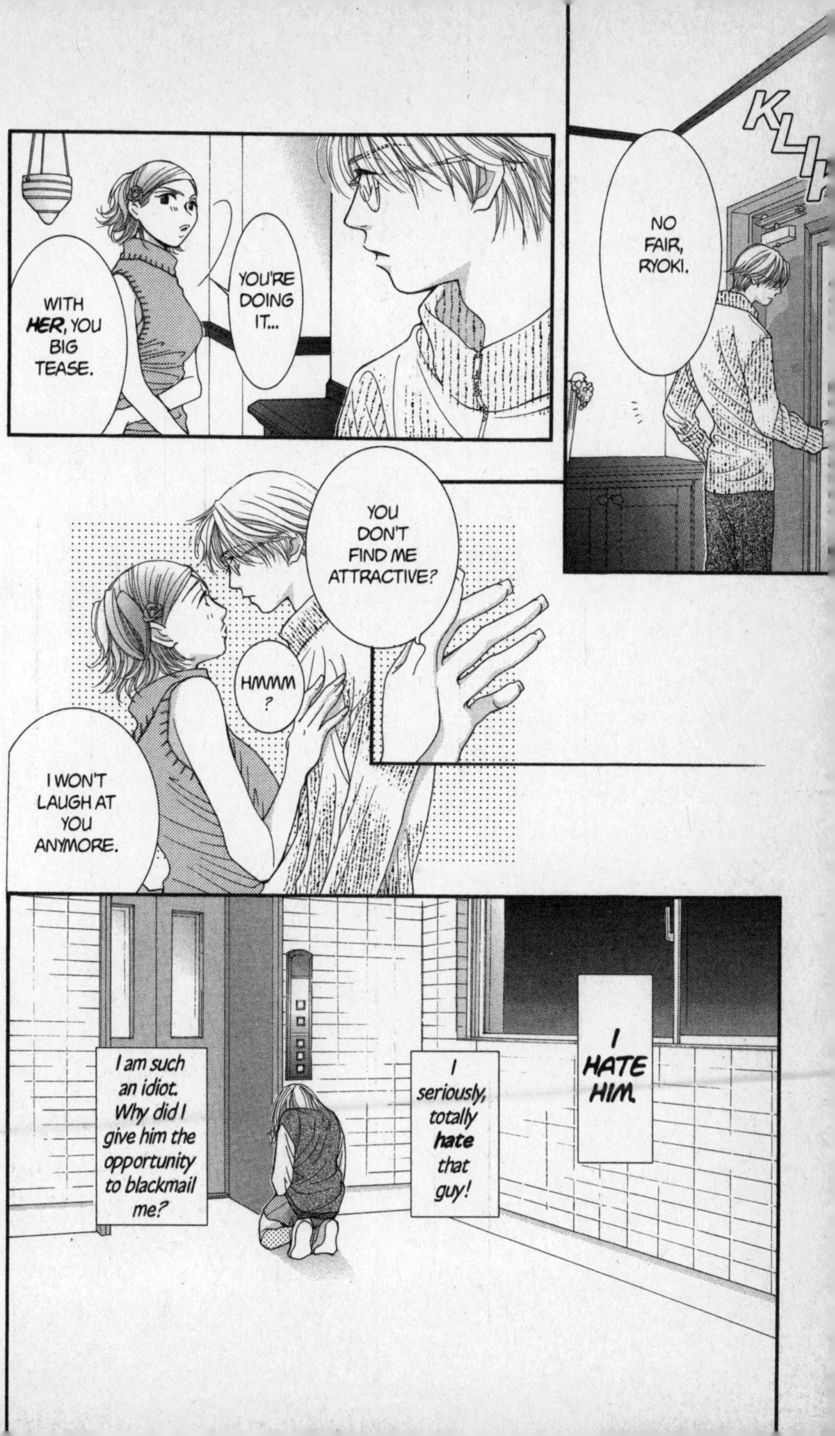
KLIK
NO FAIR, RYOKI.
YOU'RE DOING IT...
WITH HER, YOU BIG TEASE.
YOU DON'T FIND ME ATTRACTIVE?
HMMM?
I WON'T LAUGH AT YOU ANYMORE.
I HATE HIM.
I seriously, totally hate that guy!
I am such an idiot. Why did I give him the opportunity to blackmail me?

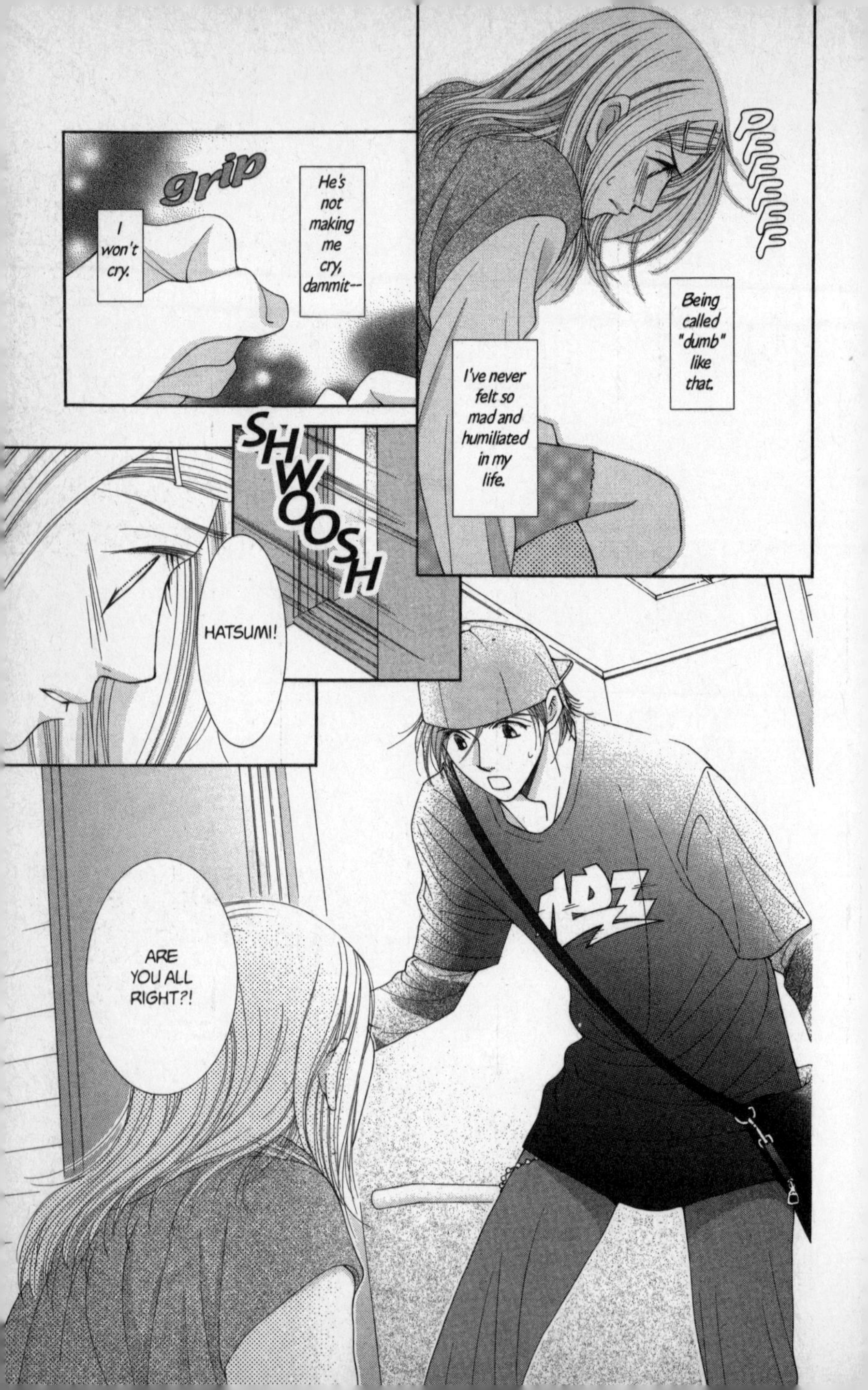
PFFFF
Being called "dumb" like that.
I've never felt so mad and humiliated in my life.
grip
He's not making me cry, dammit--
I won't cry.
SHWOOSH
HATSUMI!
ARE YOU ALL RIGHT?!

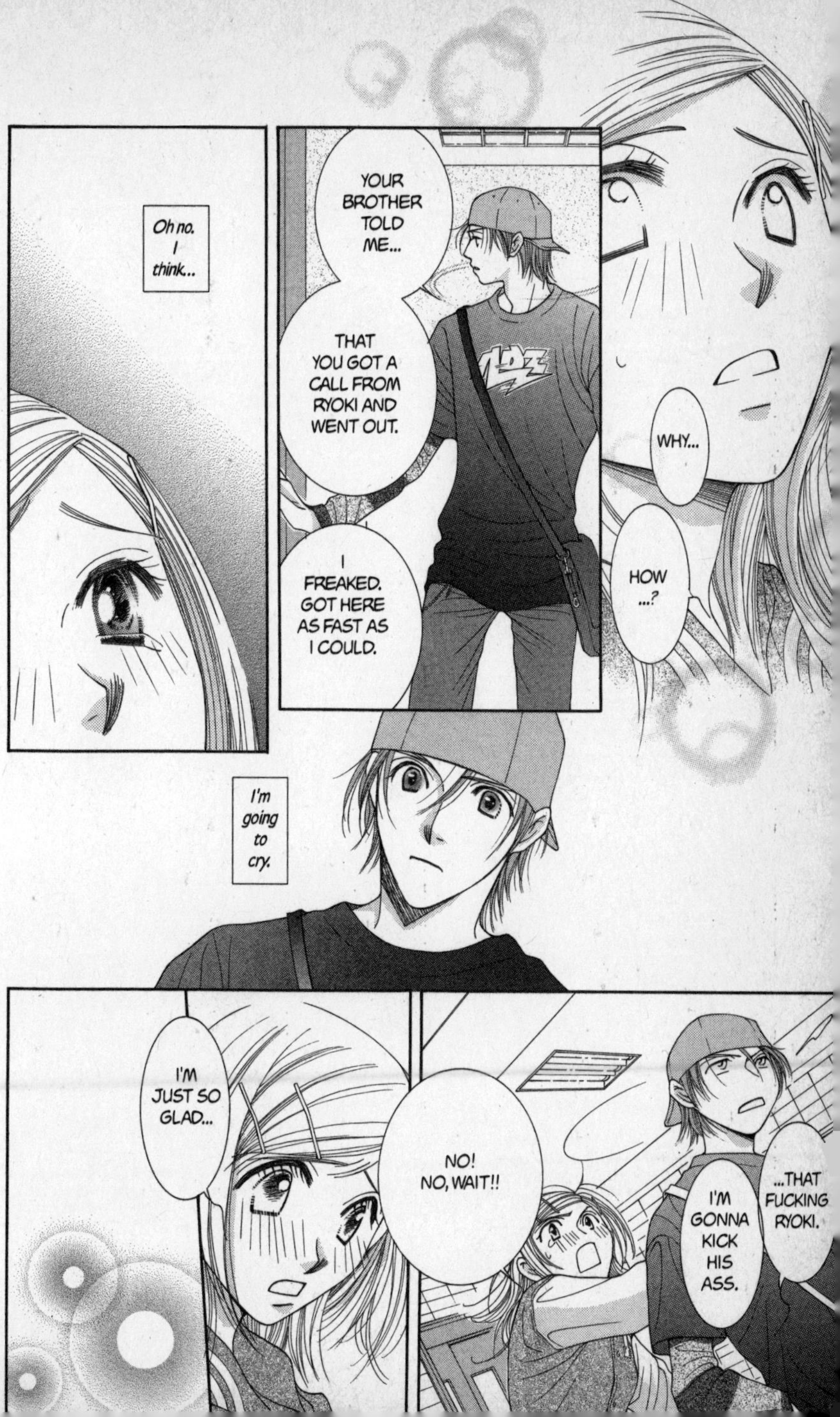
WHY...
HOW ...?
YOUR BROTHER TOLD ME...
THAT YOU GOT A CALL FROM RYOKI AND WENT OUT.
I FREAKED. GOT HERE AS FAST AS I COULD.
Oh no. I think...
I'm going to cry.
...THAT FUCKING RYOKI.
I'M GONNA KICK HIS ASS.
NO! NO, WAIT!!
I'M JUST SO GLAD...

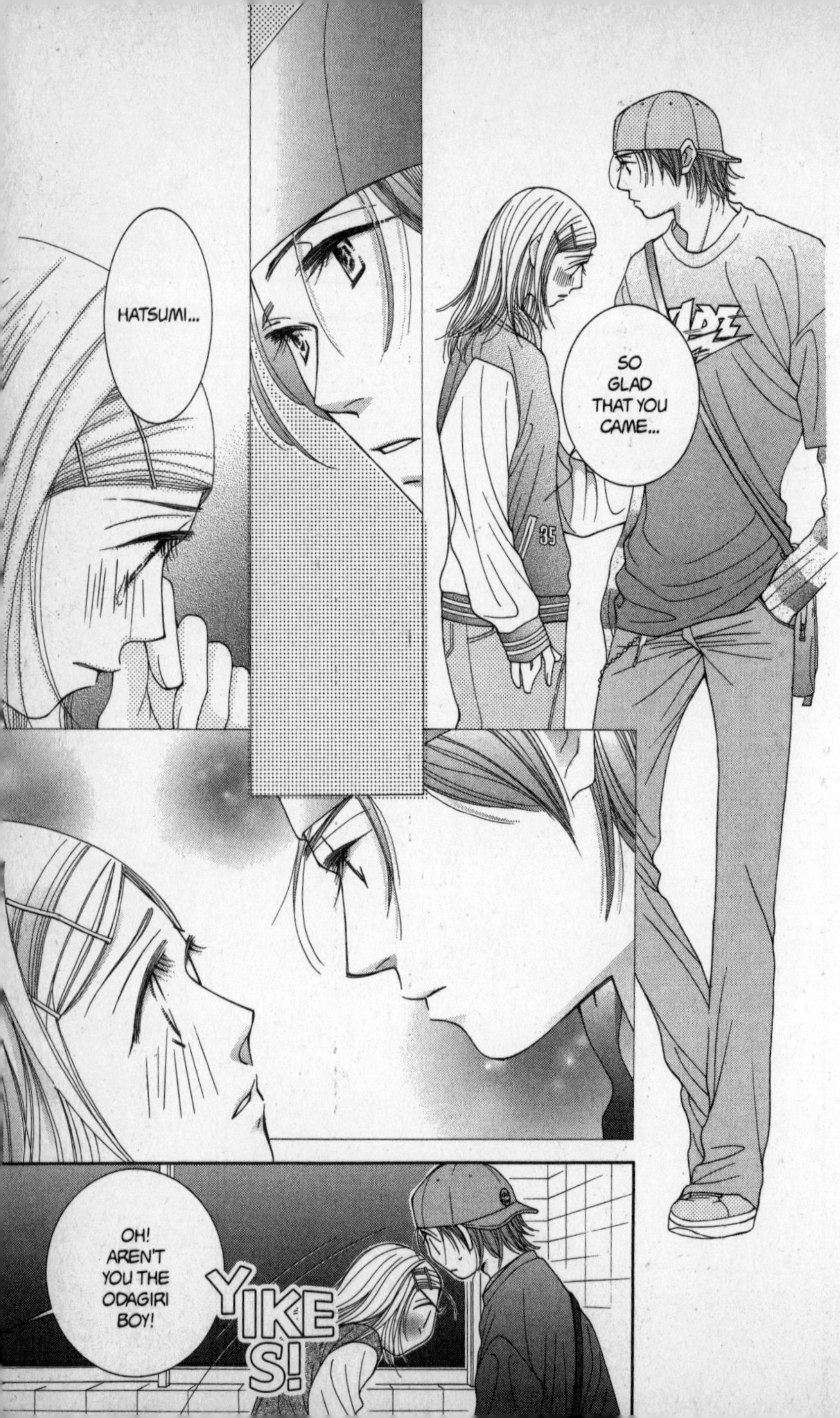
SO GLAD THAT YOU CAME...
HATSUMI...
OH! AREN'T YOU THE ODAGIRI BOY!
YIKES!

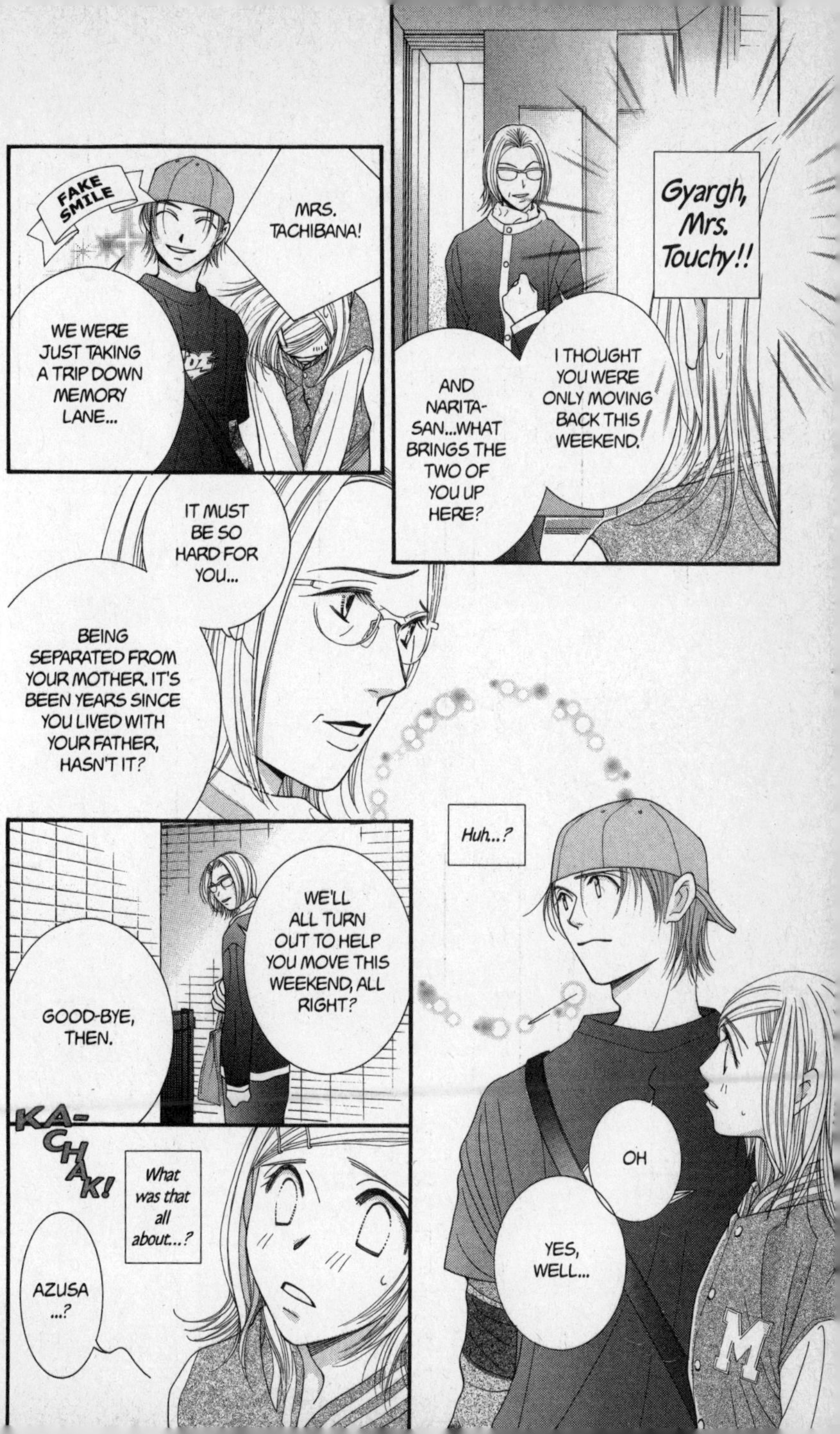
Gyargh, Mrs. Touchy!!
I THOUGHT YOU WERE ONLY MOVING BACK THIS WEEKEND.
AND NARITA-SAN...WHAT BRINGS THE TWO OF YOU UP HERE?
MRS. TACHIBANA!
FAKE SMILE
WE WERE JUST TAKING A TRIP DOWN MEMORY LANE...
IT MUST BE SO HARD FOR YOU...
BEING SEPARATED FROM YOUR MOTHER. IT'S BEEN YEARS SINCE YOU LIVED WITH YOUR FATHER, HASN'T IT?
Huh...?
OH
YES, WELL...
WE'LL ALL TURN OUT TO HELP YOU MOVE THIS WEEKEND, ALL RIGHT?
GOOD-BYE, THEN.
KA-CHAK!
What was that all about...?
AZUSA ...?

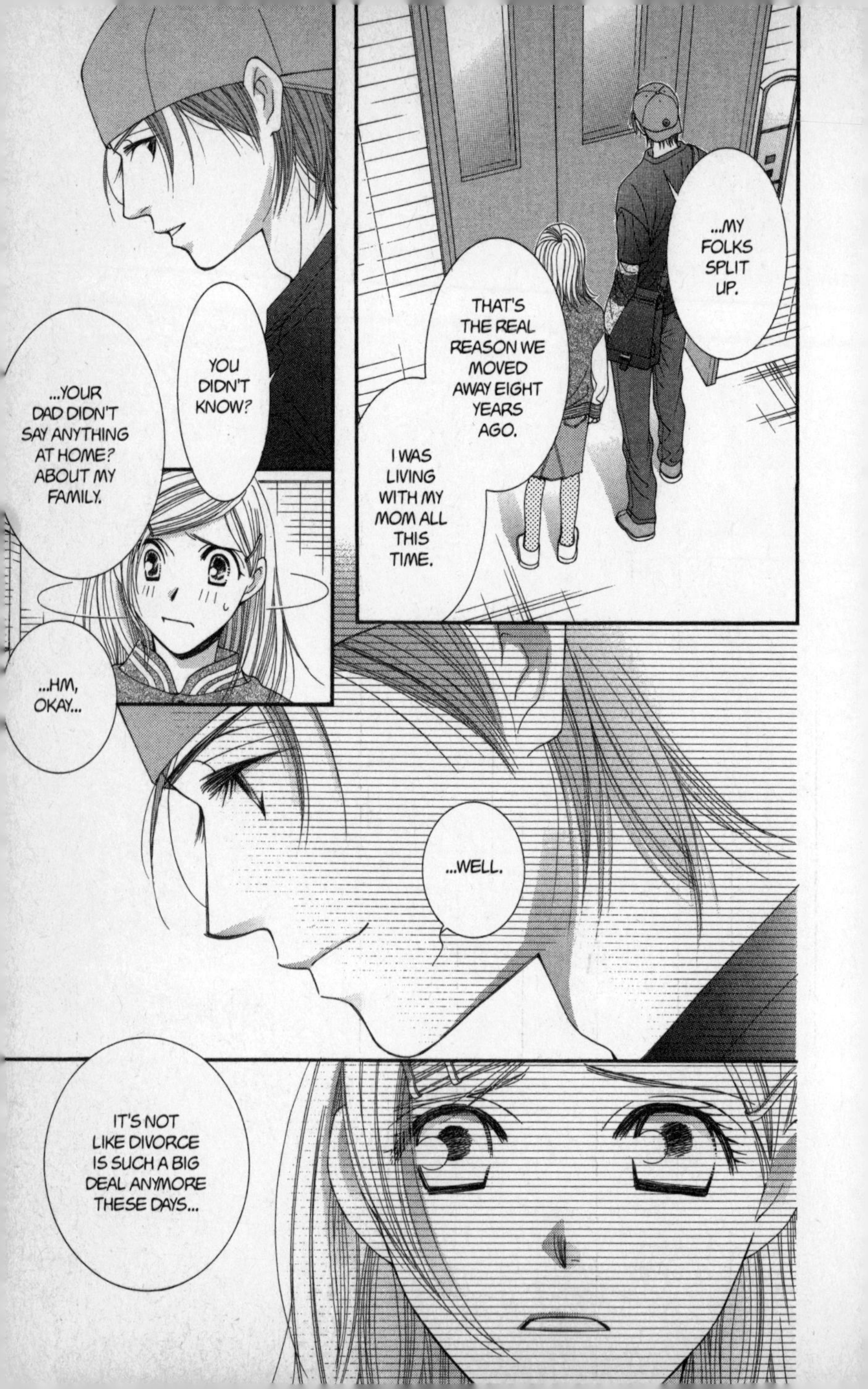
...MY FOLKS SPLIT UP.
THAT'S THE REAL REASON WE MOVED AWAY EIGHT YEARS AGO.
I WAS LIVING WITH MY MOM ALL THIS TIME.
YOU DIDN'T KNOW?
...YOUR DAD DIDN'T SAY ANYTHING AT HOME? ABOUT MY FAMILY.
...HM, OKAY...
...WELL.
IT'S NOT LIKE DIVORCE IS SUCH A BIG DEAL ANYMORE THESE DAYS...

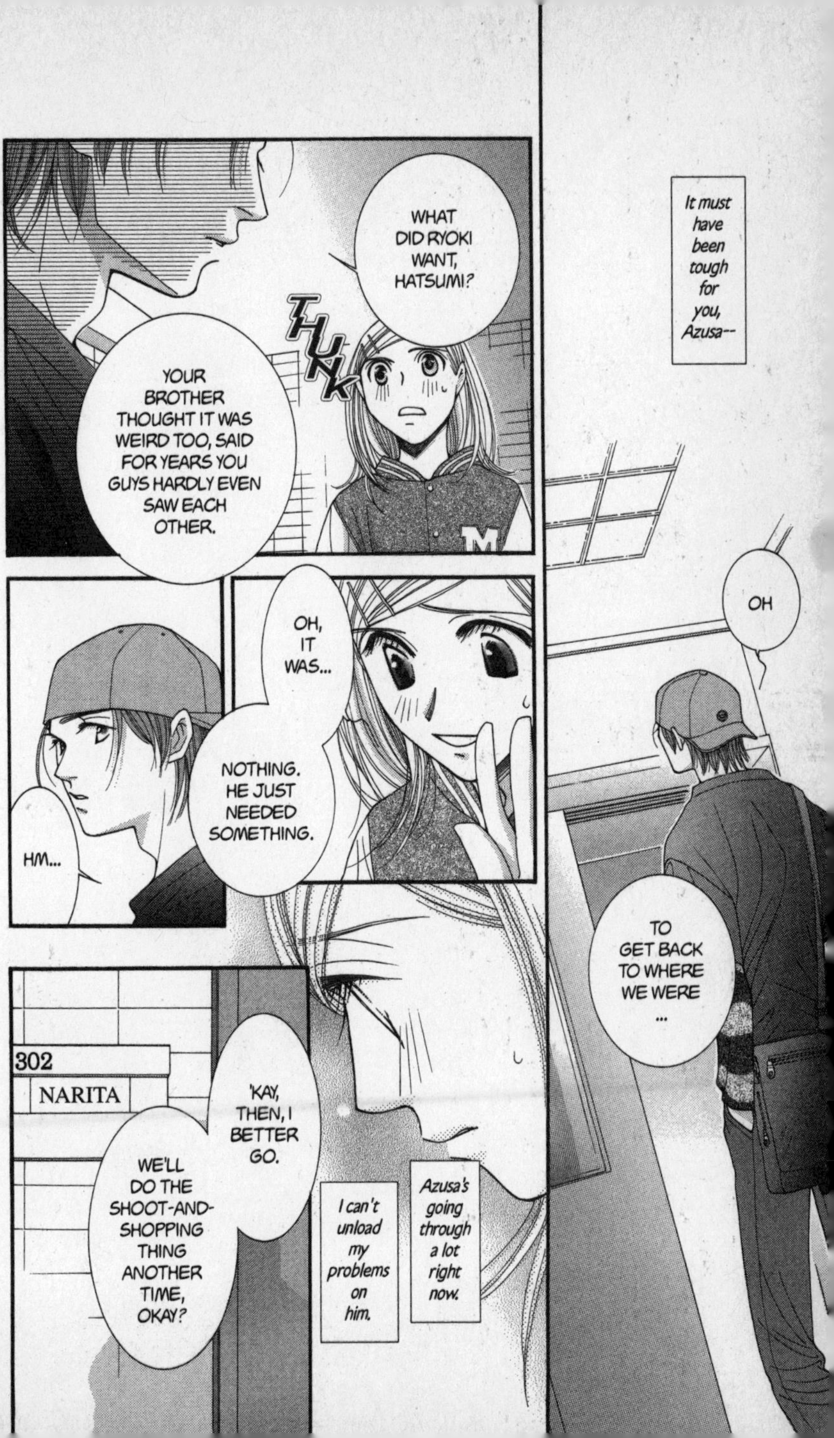
It must have been tough for you, Azusa--
OH
TO GET BACK TO WHERE WE WERE ...
WHAT DID RYOKI WANT, HATSUMI?
THUNK
YOUR BROTHER THOUGHT IT WAS WEIRD TOO, SAID FOR YEARS YOU GUYS HARDLY EVEN SAW EACH OTHER.
OH, IT WAS...
NOTHING. HE JUST NEEDED SOMETHING.
HM...
Azusa's going through a lot right now.
I can't unload my problems on him.
'KAY, THEN, I BETTER GO.
302
NARITA
WE'LL DO THE SHOOT-AND-SHOPPING THING ANOTHER TIME, OKAY?

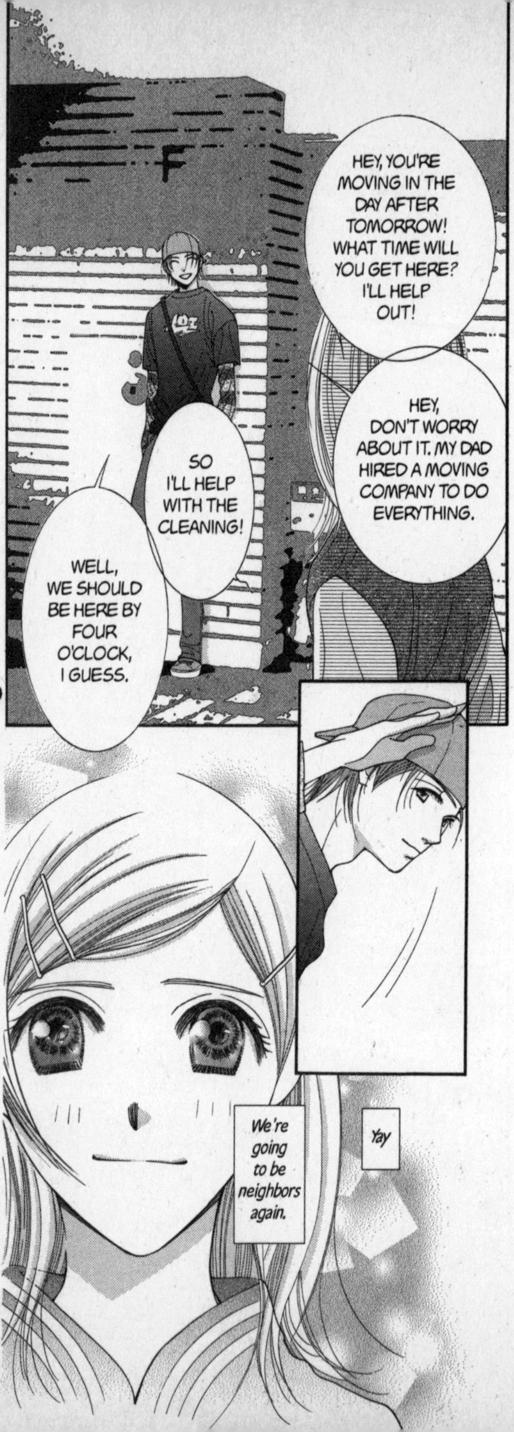
HEY, YOU'RE MOVING IN THE DAY AFTER TOMORROW! WHAT TIME WILL YOU GET HERE? I'LL HELP OUT!
HEY, DON'T WORRY ABOUT IT. MY DAD HIRED A MOVING COMPANY TO DO EVERYTHING.
WELL, WE SHOULD BE HERE BY FOUR O'CLOCK, I GUESS.
SO I'LL HELP WITH THE CLEANING!
Yay
We're going to be neighbors again.

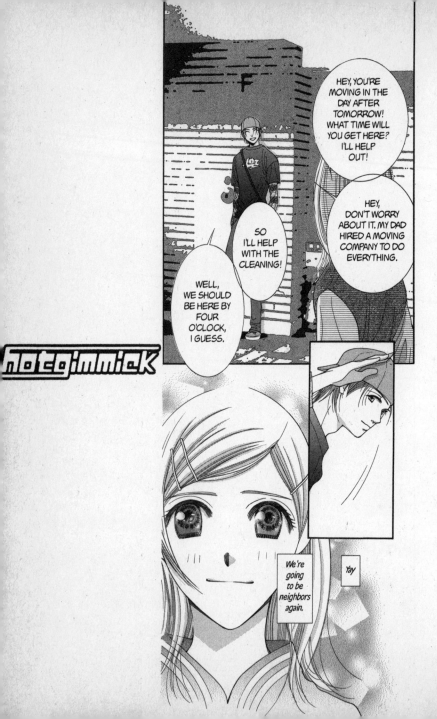

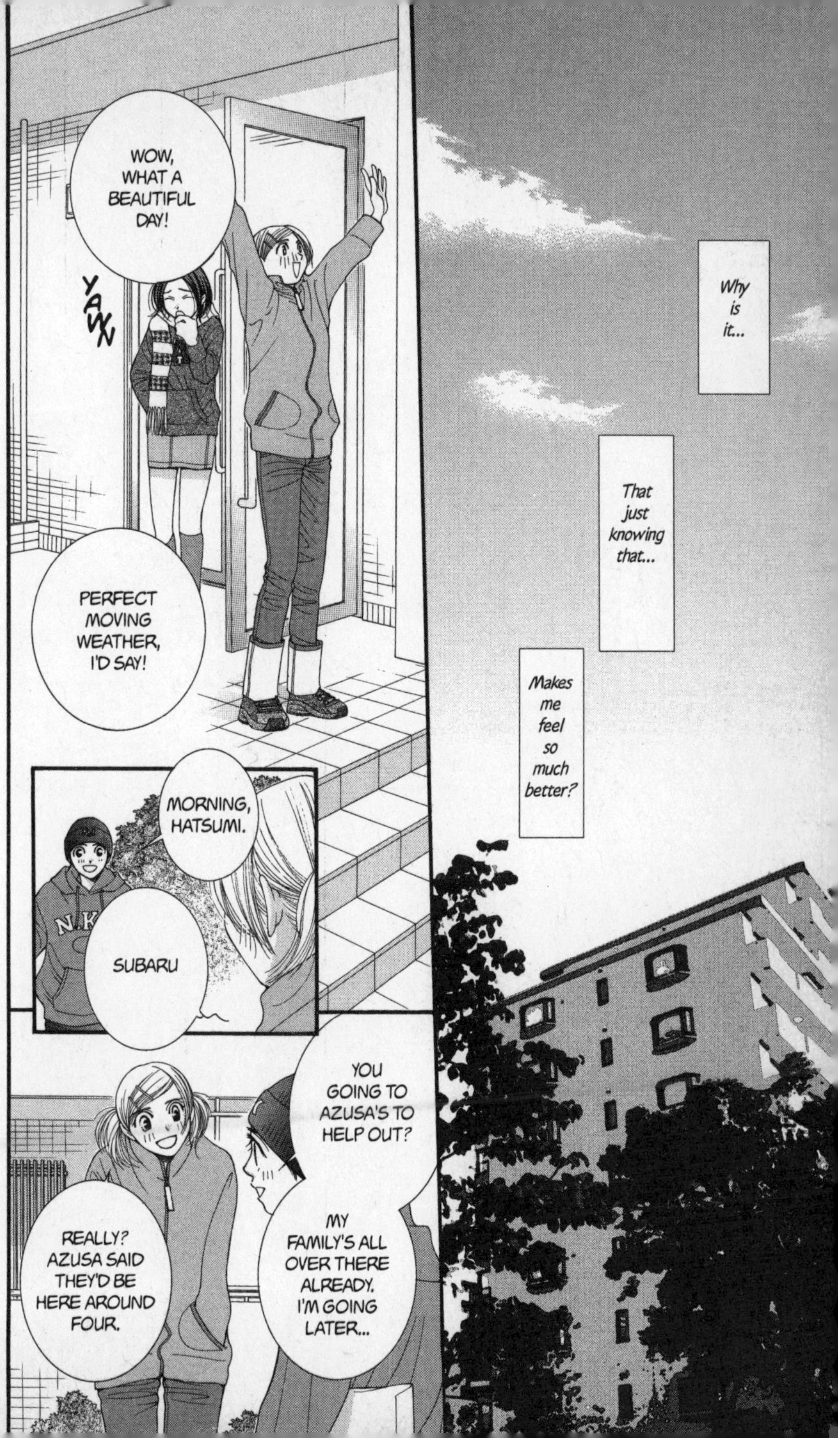
Why is it...
That just knowing that...
Makes me feel so much better?
WOW, WHAT A BEAUTIFUL DAY!
YAWN
PERFECT MOVING WEATHER, I'D SAY!
MORNING, HATSUMI.
SUBARU
YOU GOING TO AZUSA'S TO HELP OUT?
MY FAMILY'S ALL OVER THERE ALREADY. I'M GOING LATER...
REALLY? AZUSA SAID THEY'D BE HERE AROUND FOUR.

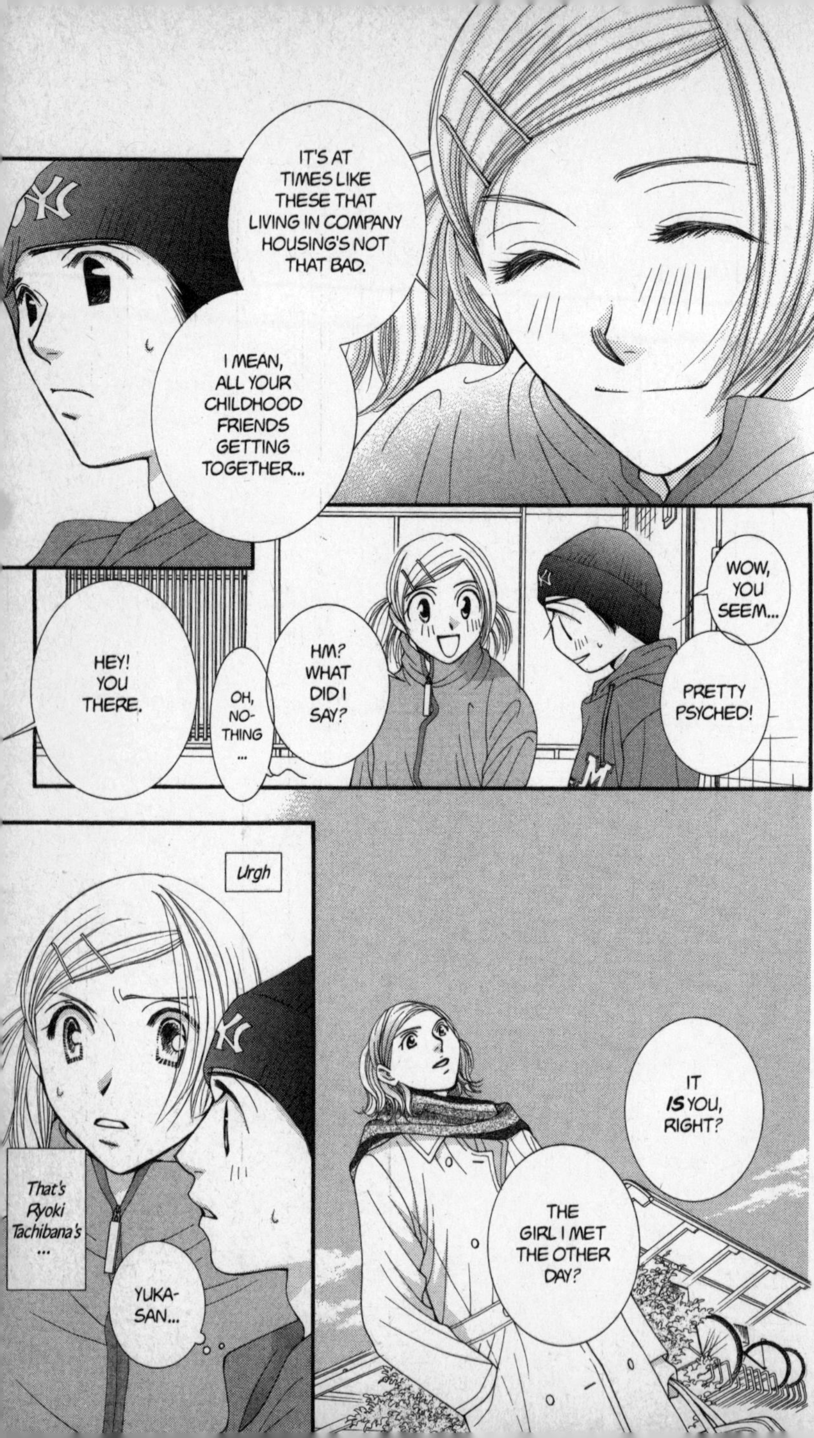
IT'S AT TIMES LIKE THESE THAT LIVING IN COMPANY HOUSING'S NOT THAT BAD.
I MEAN, ALL YOUR CHILDHOOD FRIENDS GETTING TOGETHER...
WOW, YOU SEEM...
PRETTY PSYCHED!
HM? WHAT DID I SAY?
OH, NO-THING...
HEY! YOU THERE.
IT *IS* YOU, RIGHT?
THE GIRL I MET THE OTHER DAY?
Urgh
That's Ryoki Tachibana's...
YUKA-SAN...

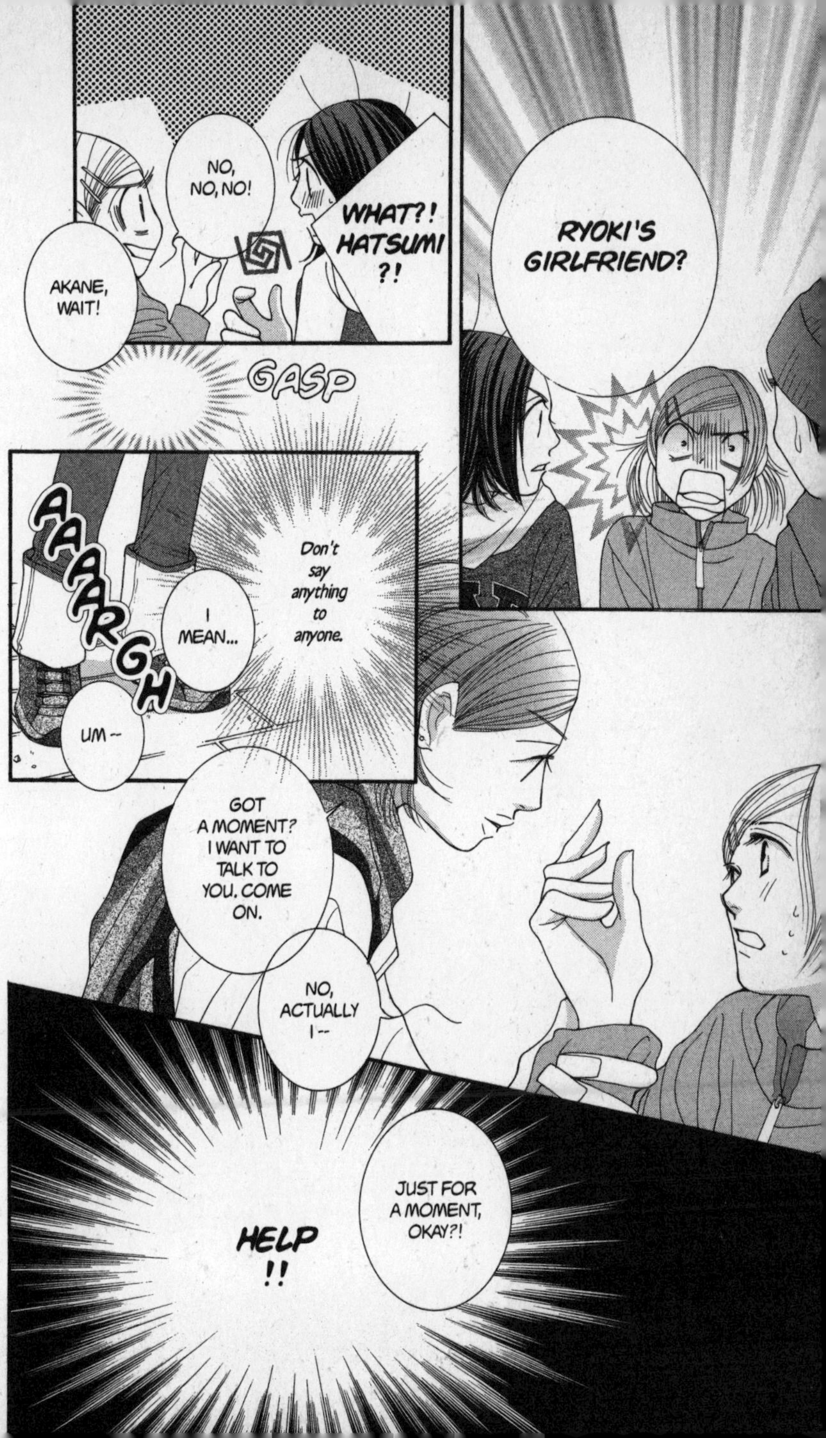
RYOKI'S GIRLFRIEND?
WHAT?! HATSUMI ?!
NO, NO, NO!
AKANE, WAIT!
GASP
Don't say anything to anyone.
I MEAN...
AAAARGH
UM --
GOT A MOMENT? I WANT TO TALK TO YOU. COME ON.
NO, ACTUALLY I --
JUST FOR A MOMENT, OKAY?!
HELP !!

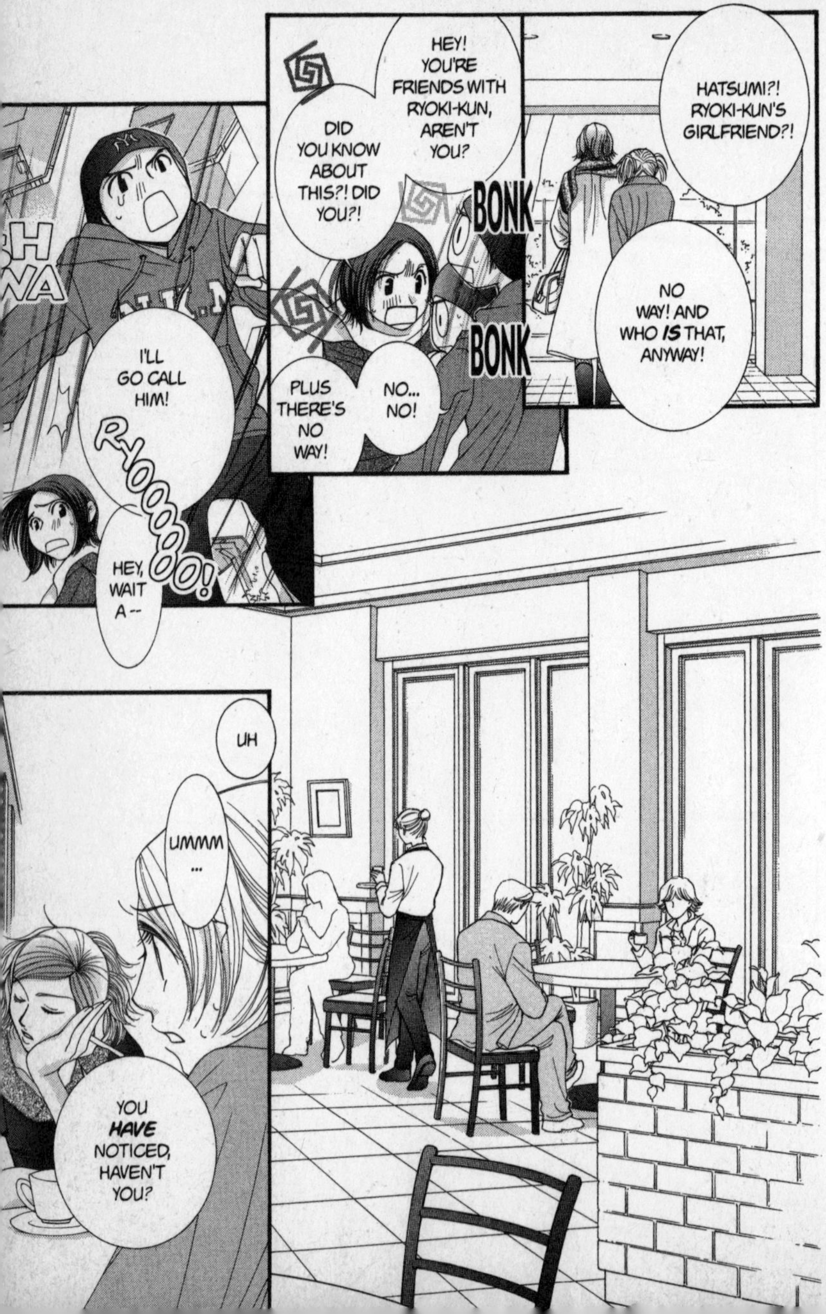
HATSUMI?! RYOKI-KUN'S GIRLFRIEND?!
NO WAY! AND WHO ***IS*** THAT, ANYWAY!
HEY! YOU'RE FRIENDS WITH RYOKI-KUN, AREN'T YOU?
DID YOU KNOW ABOUT THIS?! DID YOU?!
BONK
BONK
NO... NO!
PLUS THERE'S NO WAY!
I'LL GO CALL HIM!
RYOOOOO!
HEY, WAIT A--
UH
UMMM...
YOU ***HAVE*** NOTICED, HAVEN'T YOU?

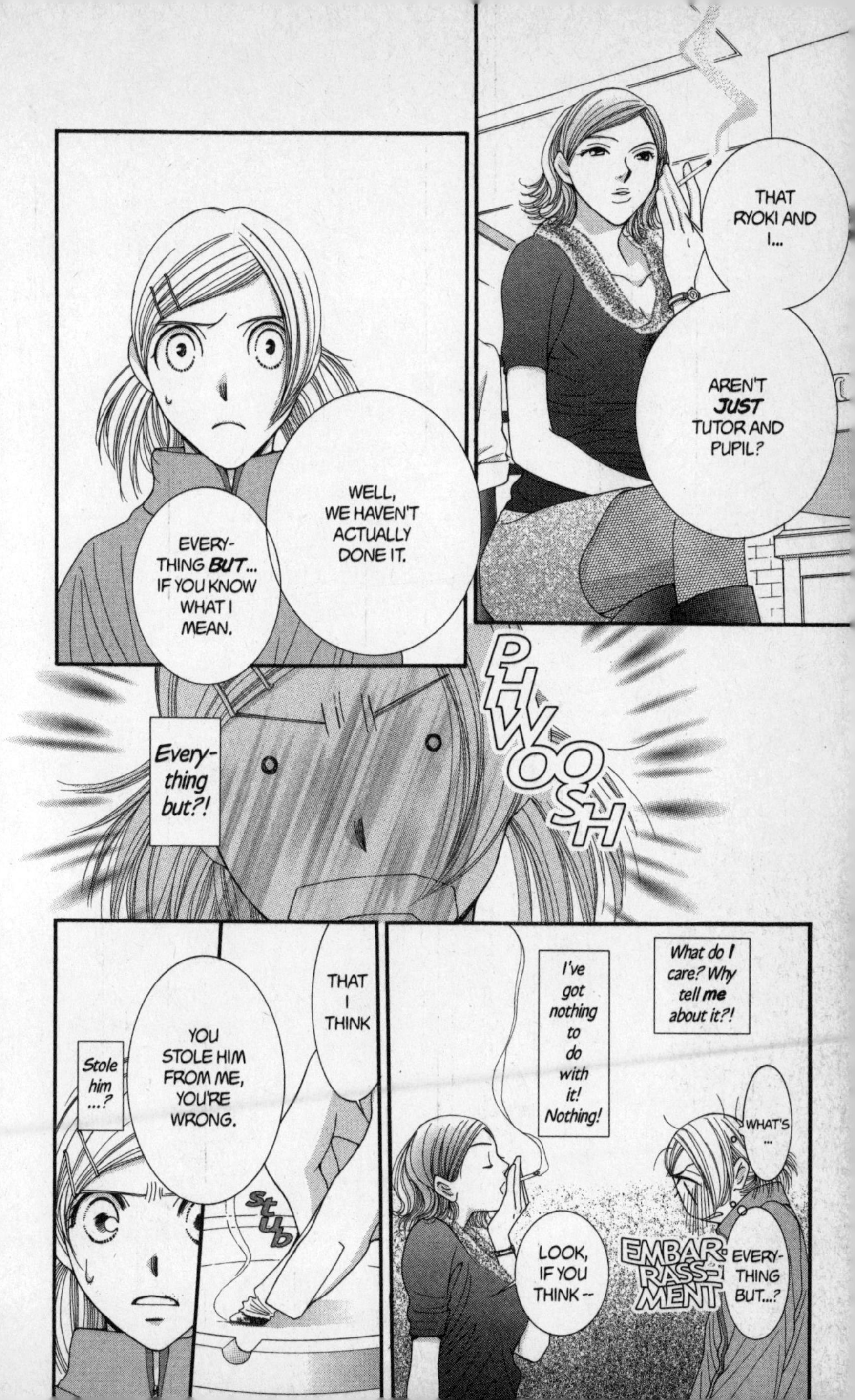
THAT RYOKI AND I...
AREN'T **JUST** TUTOR AND PUPIL?
WELL, WE HAVEN'T ACTUALLY DONE IT.
EVERY-THING **BUT**... IF YOU KNOW WHAT I MEAN.
PHWOOSH
Every-thing but?!
*What do **I** care? Why tell **me** about it?!*
I've got nothing to do with it! Nothing!
WHAT'S ...
EVERY-THING BUT...?
EMBAR-RASS-MENT
LOOK, IF YOU THINK --
THAT I THINK
YOU STOLE HIM FROM ME, YOU'RE WRONG.
stub
Stole him ...?

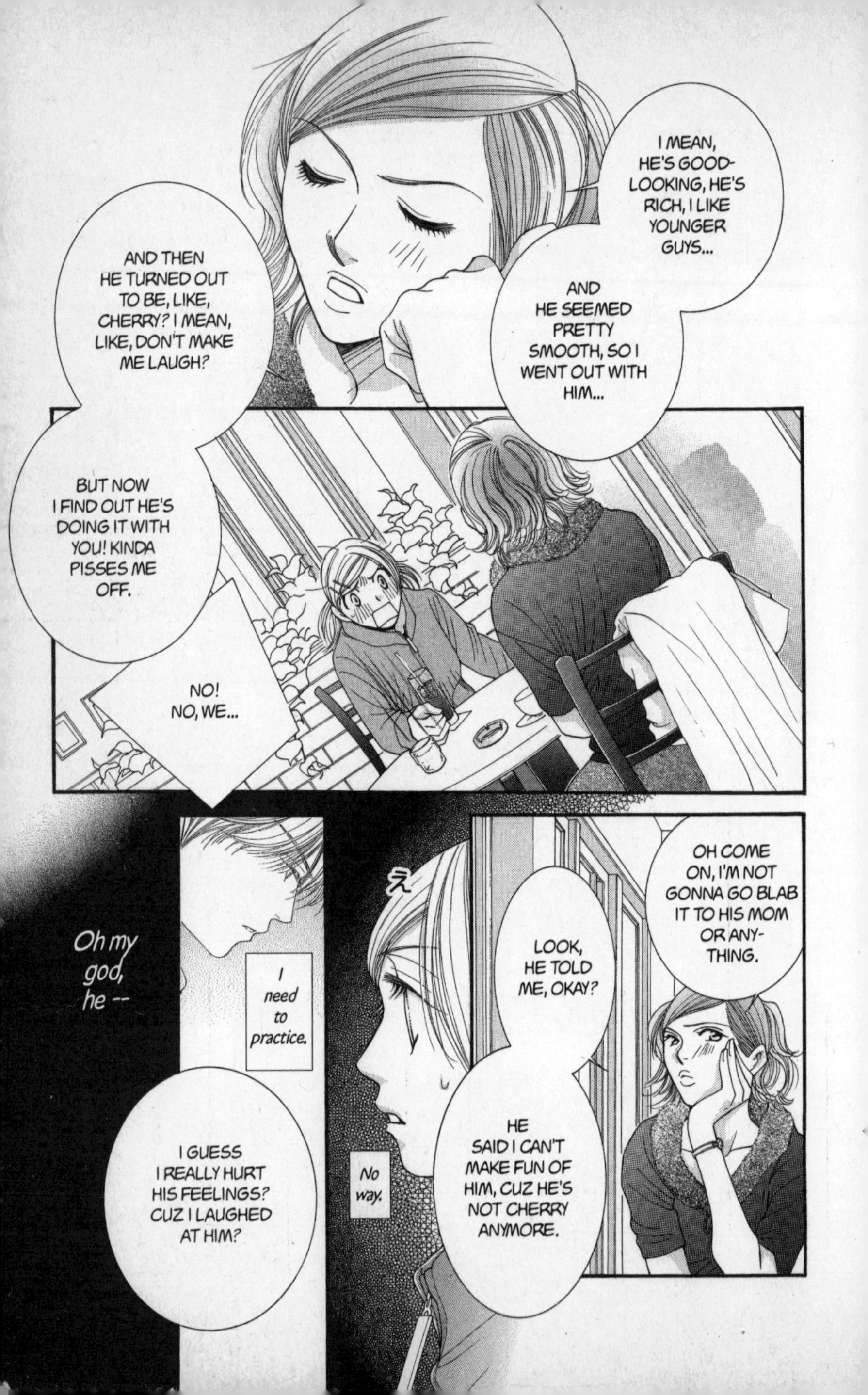
I MEAN, HE'S GOOD-LOOKING, HE'S RICH, I LIKE YOUNGER GUYS...
AND HE SEEMED PRETTY SMOOTH, SO I WENT OUT WITH HIM...
AND THEN HE TURNED OUT TO BE, LIKE, CHERRY? I MEAN, LIKE, DON'T MAKE ME LAUGH?
BUT NOW I FIND OUT HE'S DOING IT WITH YOU! KINDA PISSES ME OFF.
NO! NO, WE...
え
OH COME ON, I'M NOT GONNA GO BLAB IT TO HIS MOM OR ANY-THING.
LOOK, HE TOLD ME, OKAY?
HE SAID I CAN'T MAKE FUN OF HIM, CUZ HE'S NOT CHERRY ANYMORE.
No way.
I need to practice.
I GUESS I REALLY HURT HIS FEELINGS? CUZ I LAUGHED AT HIM?
Oh my god, he --

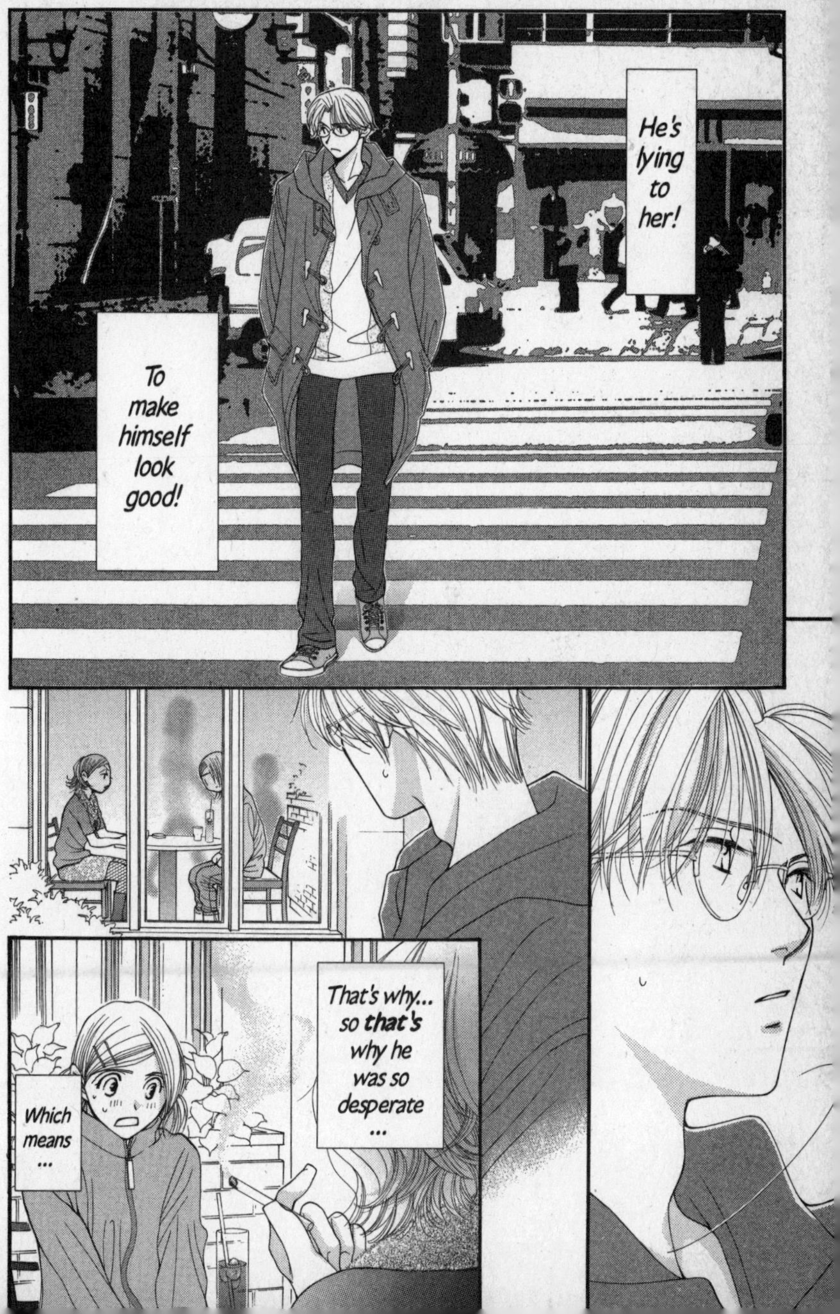
He's lying to her!
To make himself look good!
That's why... so **that's** why he was so desperate...
Which means...

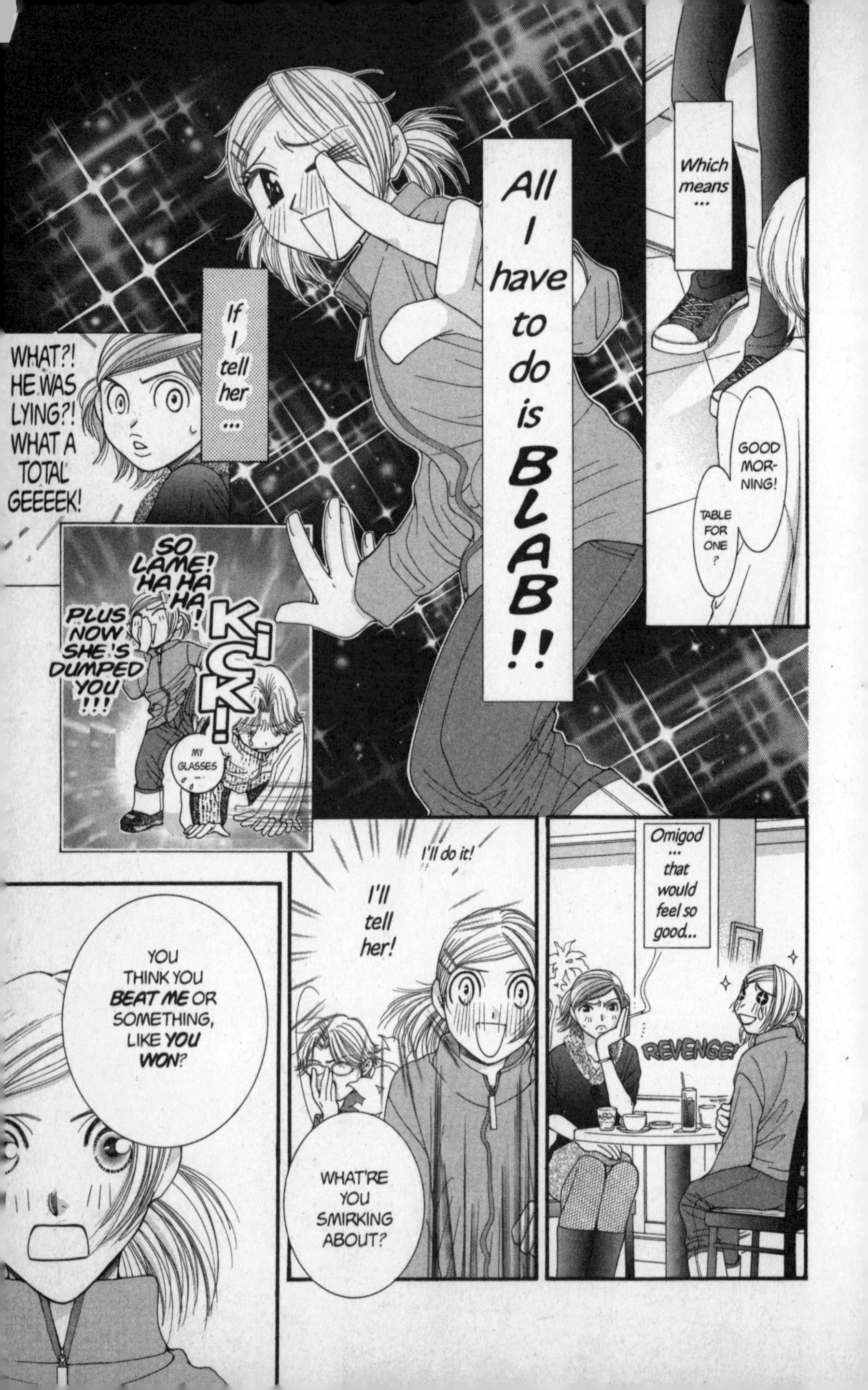

Which means ...
GOOD MORNING!
TABLE FOR ONE?
All I have to do is BLAB!!
If I tell her ...
WHAT?! HE WAS LYING?! WHAT A TOTAL GEEEEK!
SO LAME! HA HA HA!
PLUS NOW SHE'S DUMPED YOU!!!
KICK!
MY GLASSES ...
Omigod ... that would feel so good...
REVENGE!
I'll do it!
I'll tell her!
WHAT'RE YOU SMIRKING ABOUT?
YOU THINK YOU BEAT ME OR SOMETHING, LIKE YOU WON?

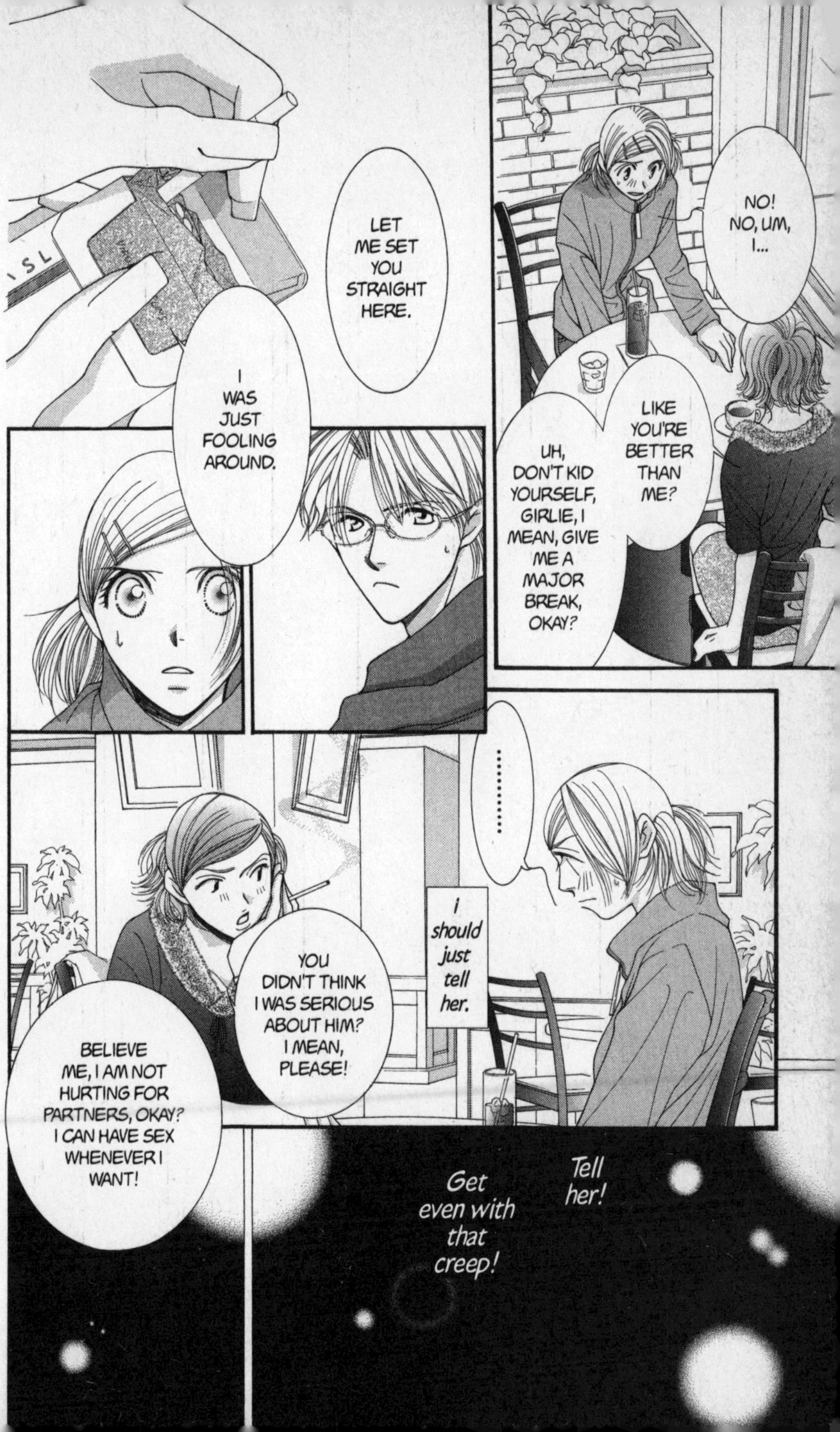
NO! NO, UM, I...
LIKE YOU'RE BETTER THAN ME?
UH, DON'T KID YOURSELF, GIRLIE, I MEAN, GIVE ME A MAJOR BREAK, OKAY?
LET ME SET YOU STRAIGHT HERE.
I WAS JUST FOOLING AROUND.
....
I should just tell her.
YOU DIDN'T THINK I WAS SERIOUS ABOUT HIM? I MEAN, PLEASE!
BELIEVE ME, I AM NOT HURTING FOR PARTNERS, OKAY? I CAN HAVE SEX WHENEVER I WANT!
Tell her!
Get even with that creep!

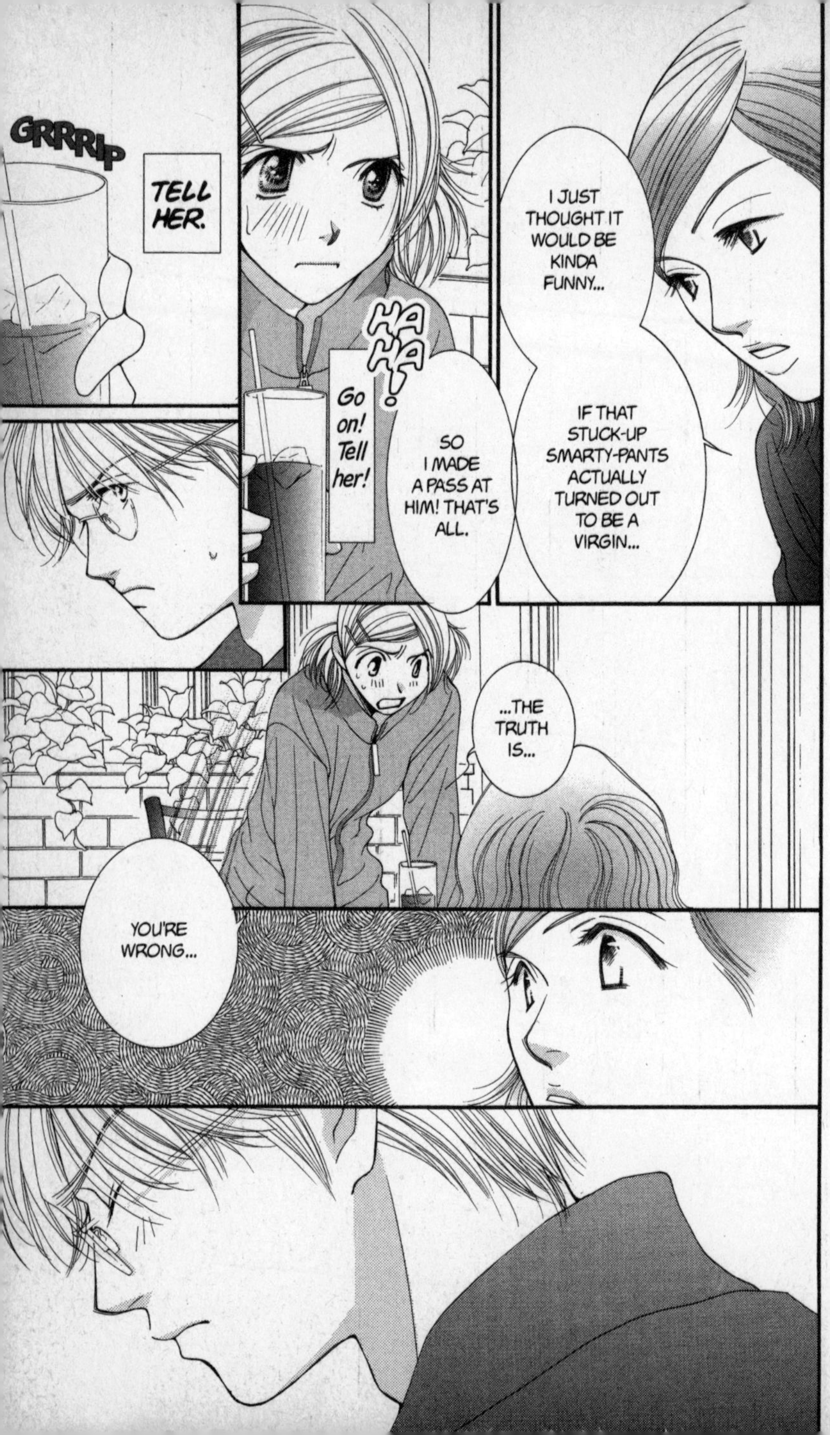
I JUST THOUGHT IT WOULD BE KINDA FUNNY...
IF THAT STUCK-UP SMARTY-PANTS ACTUALLY TURNED OUT TO BE A VIRGIN...
SO I MADE A PASS AT HIM! THAT'S ALL.
HA HA HA!
Go on! Tell her!
GRRRIP
TELL HER.
...THE TRUTH IS...
YOU'RE WRONG...

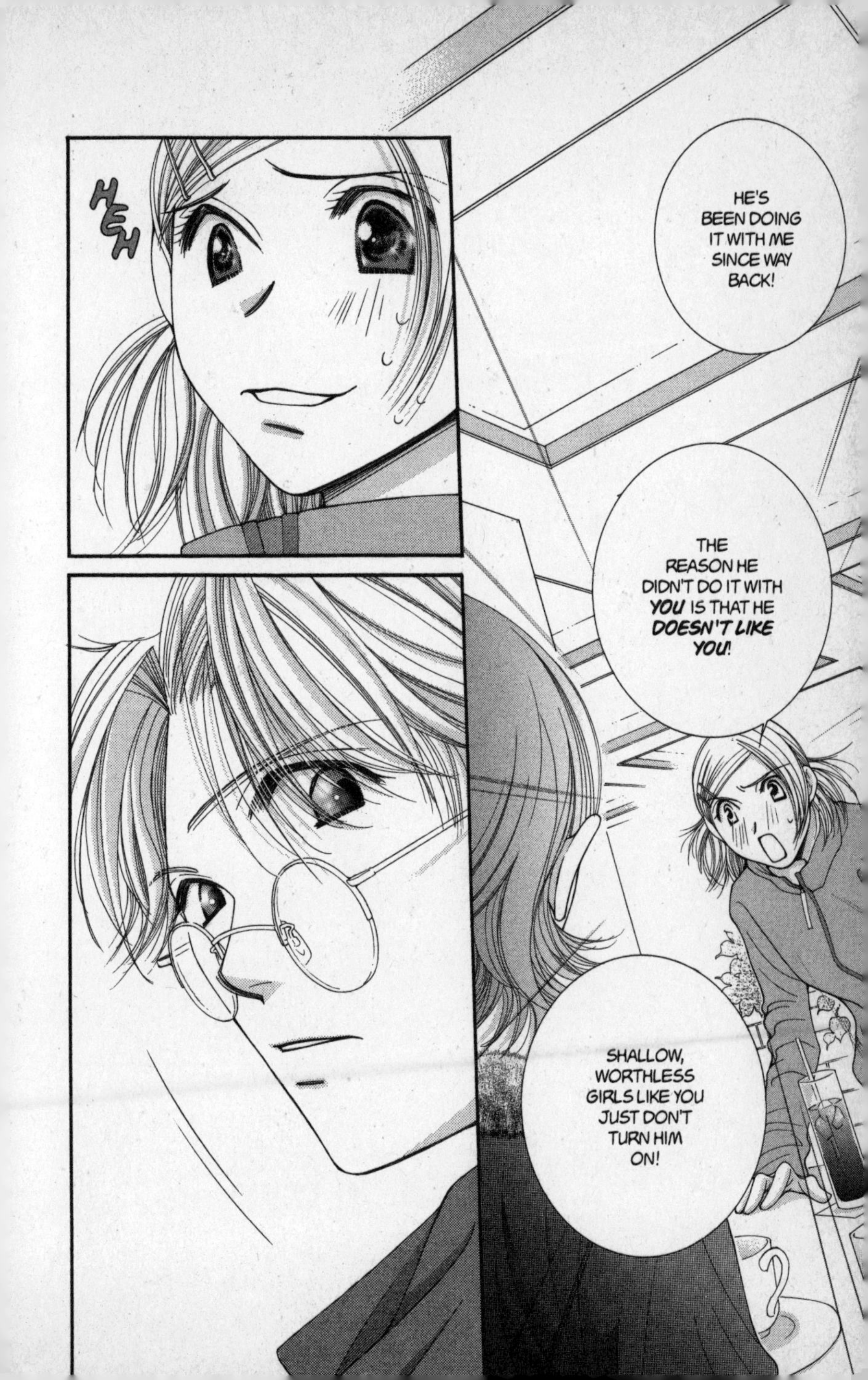
HE'S BEEN DOING IT WITH ME SINCE WAY BACK!
THE REASON HE DIDN'T DO IT WITH *YOU* IS THAT HE ***DOESN'T LIKE YOU***!
SHALLOW, WORTHLESS GIRLS LIKE YOU JUST DON'T TURN HIM ON!
HEH

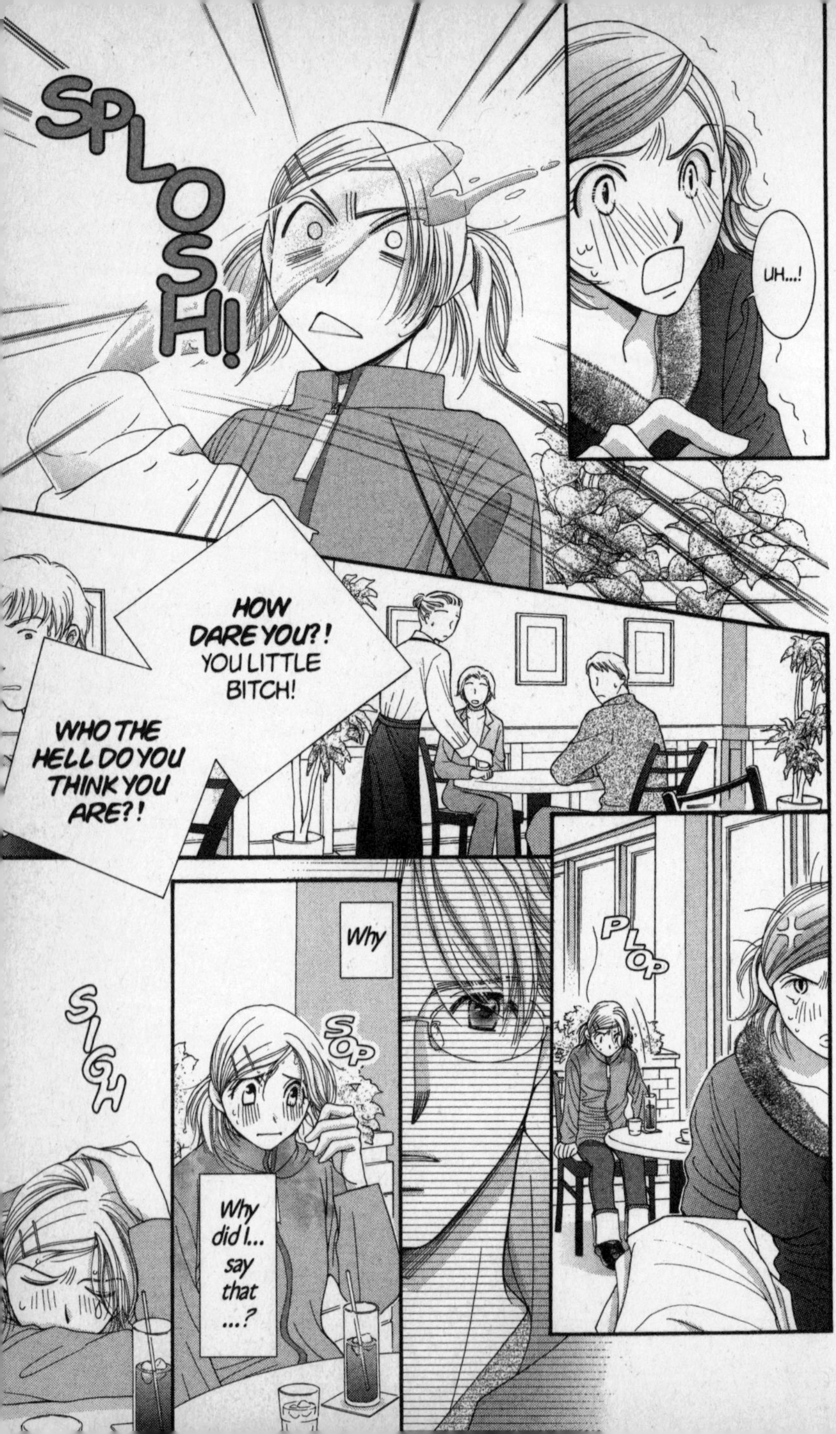
UH...!
SPLOSH!
HOW DARE YOU?! YOU LITTLE BITCH!
WHO THE HELL DO YOU THINK YOU ARE?!
PLOP
Why
SOP
Why did I... say that ...?
SIGH

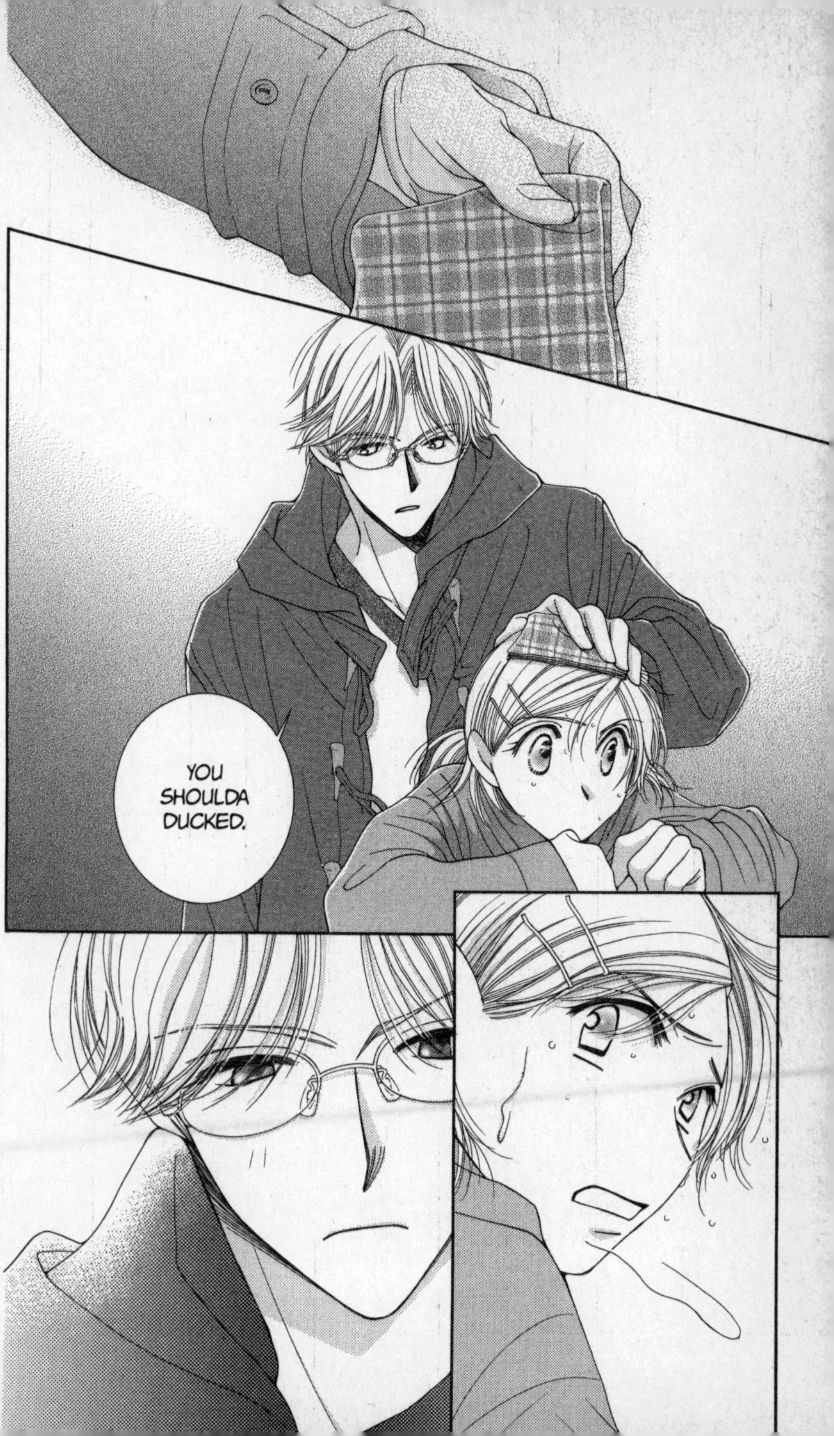
YOU SHOULDA DUCKED.

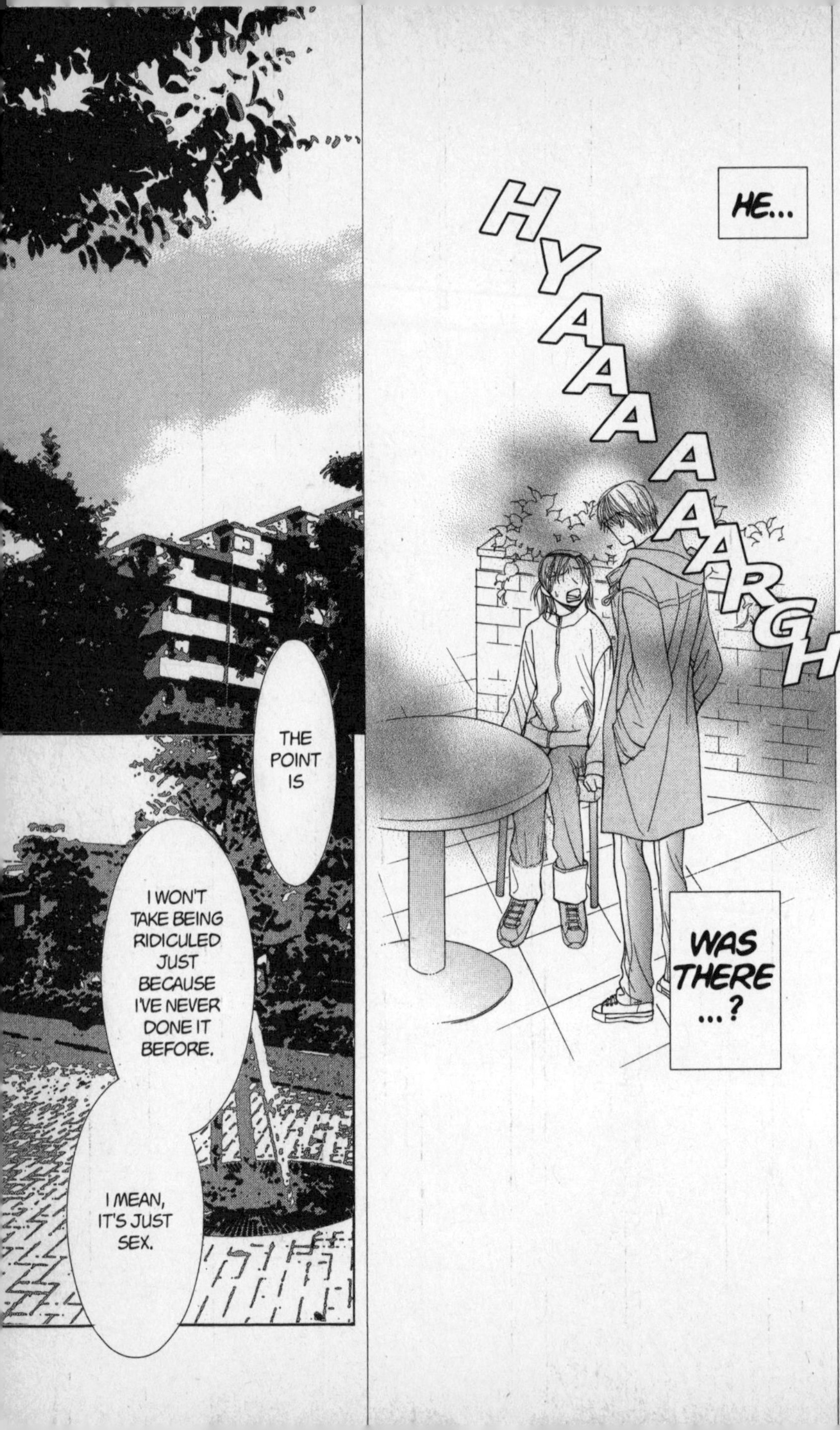
HE...
HYAAAAARGH
WAS THERE ...?
THE POINT IS
I WON'T TAKE BEING RIDICULED JUST BECAUSE I'VE NEVER DONE IT BEFORE.
I MEAN, IT'S JUST SEX.

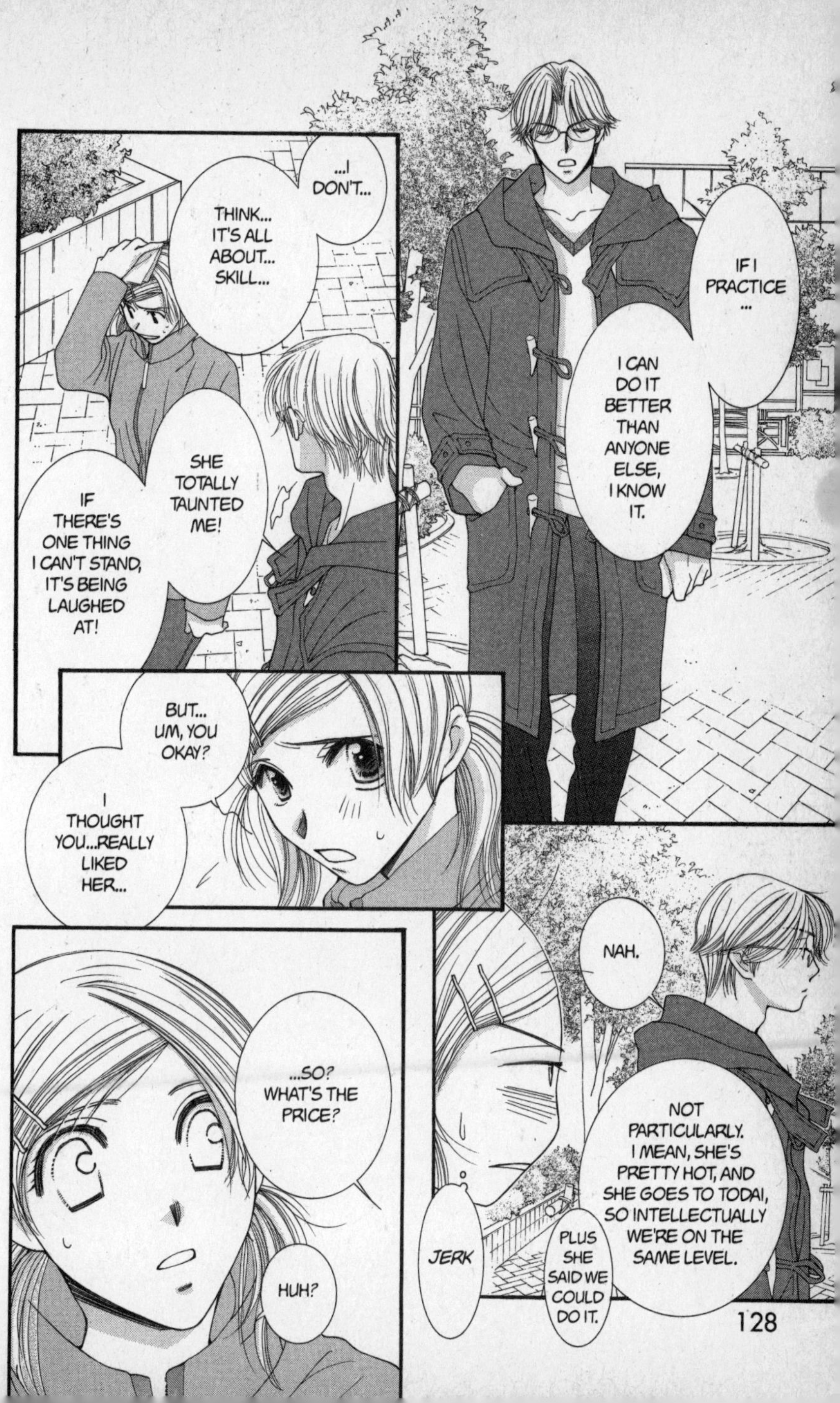
IF I PRACTICE ...
I CAN DO IT BETTER THAN ANYONE ELSE, I KNOW IT.
...I DON'T...
THINK... IT'S ALL ABOUT... SKILL...
SHE TOTALLY TAUNTED ME!
IF THERE'S ONE THING I CAN'T STAND, IT'S BEING LAUGHED AT!
BUT... UM, YOU OKAY?
I THOUGHT YOU...REALLY LIKED HER...
NAH.
NOT PARTICULARLY. I MEAN, SHE'S PRETTY HOT, AND SHE GOES TO TODAI, SO INTELLECTUALLY WE'RE ON THE SAME LEVEL.
PLUS SHE SAID WE COULD DO IT.
JERK
...SO? WHAT'S THE PRICE?
HUH?

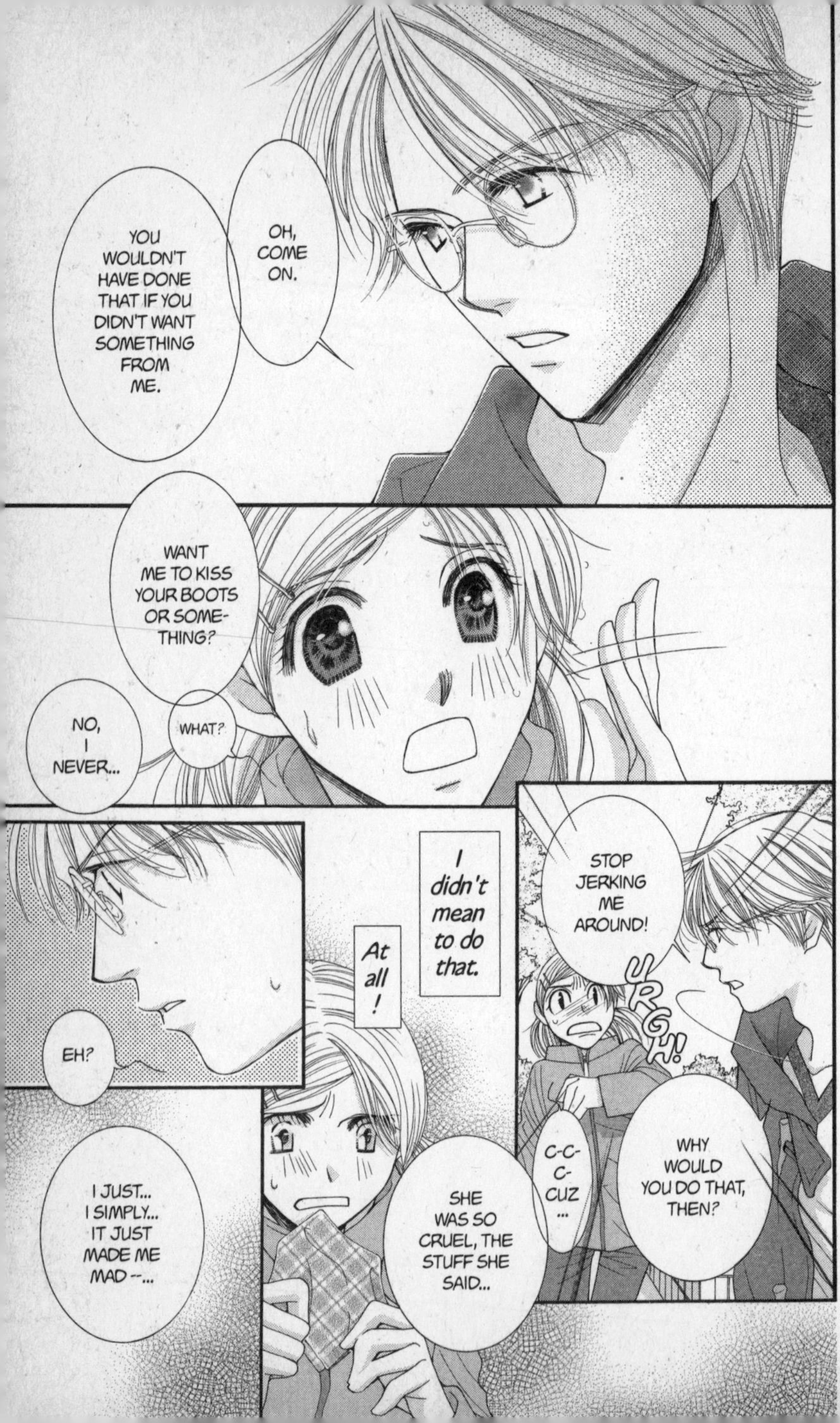
OH, COME ON.
YOU WOULDN'T HAVE DONE THAT IF YOU DIDN'T WANT SOMETHING FROM ME.
WANT ME TO KISS YOUR BOOTS OR SOME-THING?
WHAT?
NO, I NEVER...
STOP JERKING ME AROUND!
URGH!
WHY WOULD YOU DO THAT, THEN?
C-C-C-CUZ...
I didn't mean to do that.
At all!
EH?
SHE WAS SO CRUEL, THE STUFF SHE SAID...
I JUST... I SIMPLY... IT JUST MADE ME MAD --...

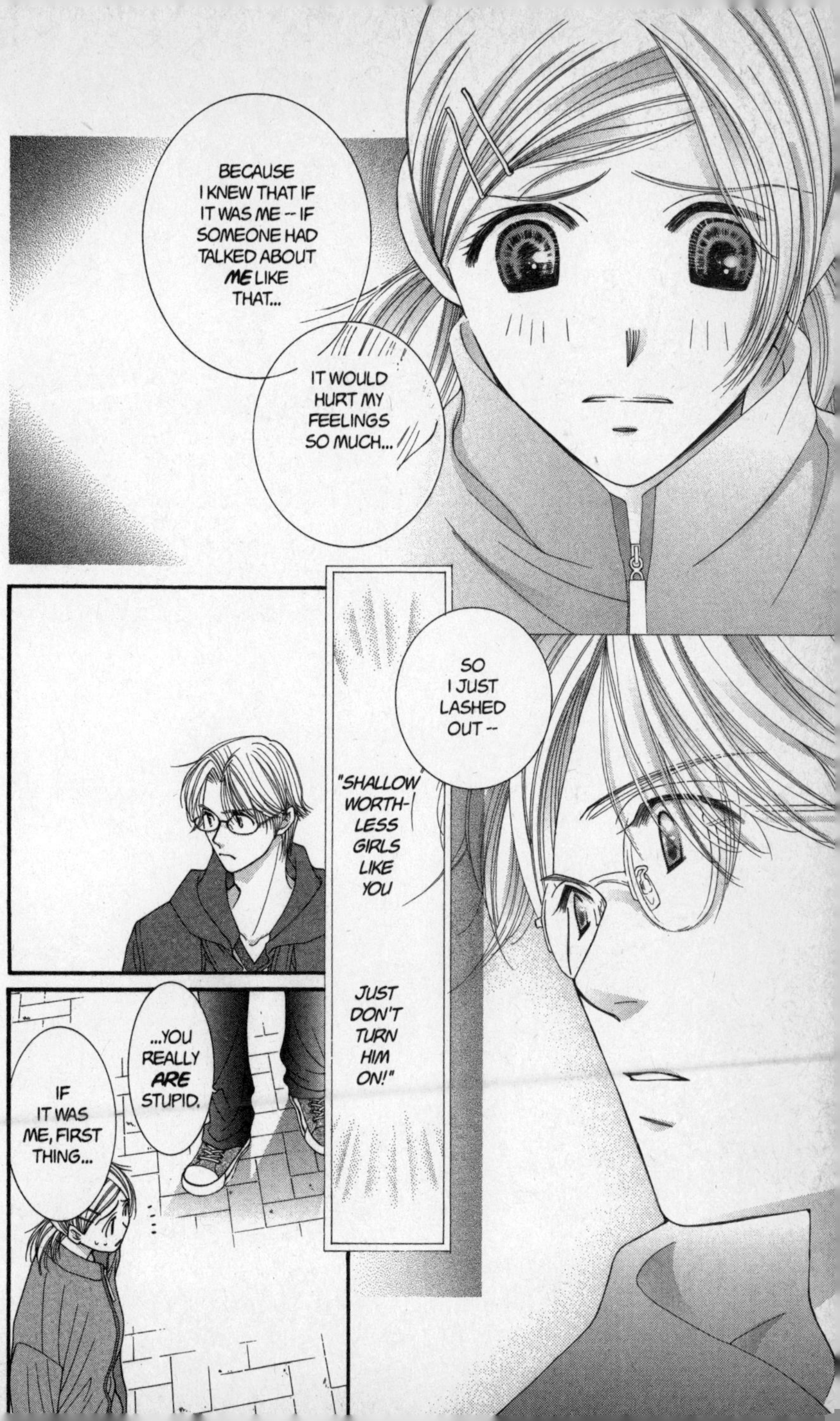
BECAUSE I KNEW THAT IF IT WAS ME -- IF SOMEONE HAD TALKED ABOUT **ME** LIKE THAT...
IT WOULD HURT MY FEELINGS SO MUCH...
SO I JUST LASHED OUT --
"SHALLOW WORTHLESS GIRLS LIKE YOU JUST DON'T TURN HIM ON!"
...YOU REALLY **ARE** STUPID.
IF IT WAS ME, FIRST THING...

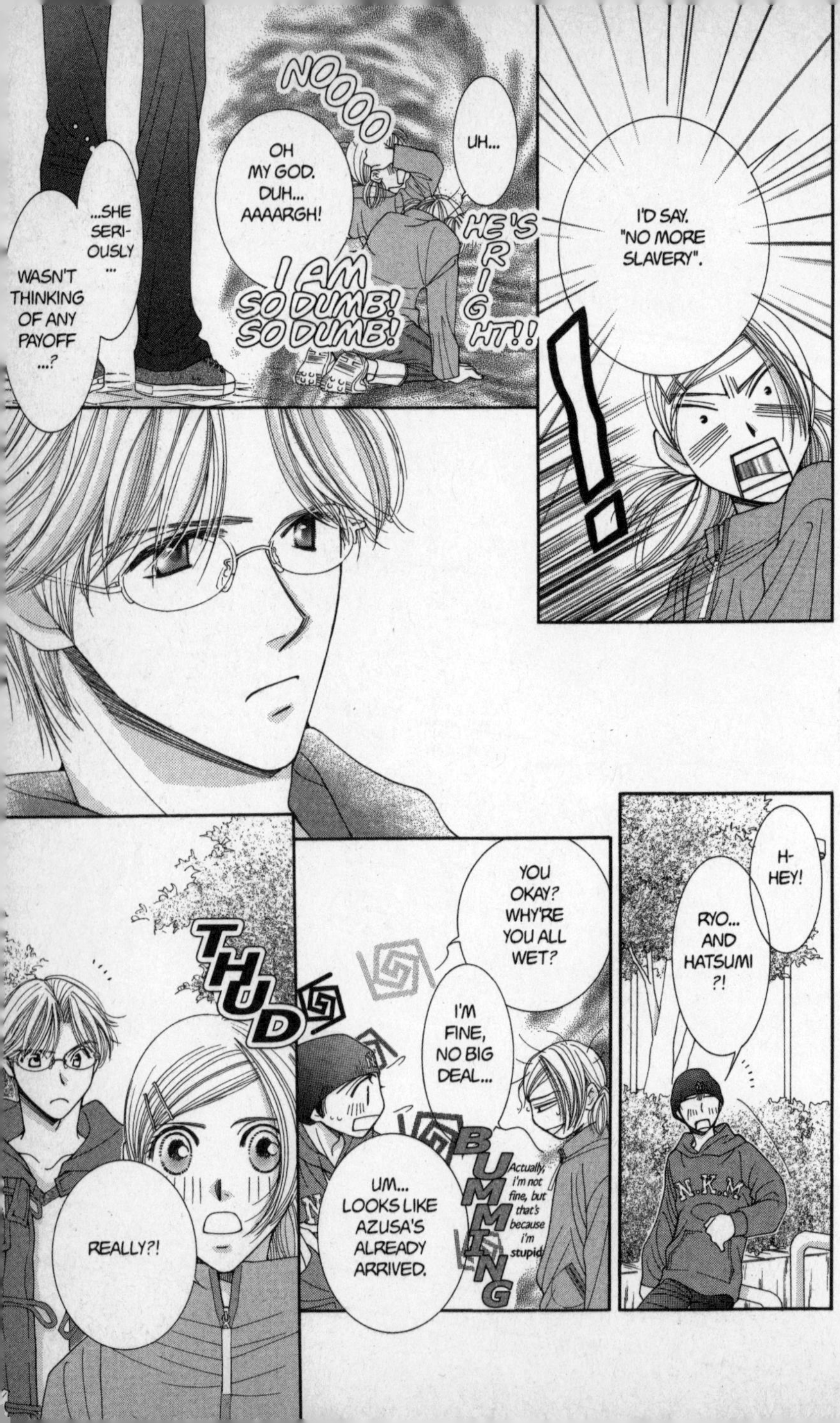
I'D SAY. "NO MORE SLAVERY".
!
UH...
NOOOO
OH MY GOD. DUH... AAAARGH!
HE'S RIGHT!!
I AM SO DUMB! SO DUMB!
...SHE SERIOUSLY ...
WASN'T THINKING OF ANY PAYOFF ...?
H- HEY!
RYO... AND HATSUMI ?!
YOU OKAY? WHY'RE YOU ALL WET?
I'M FINE, NO BIG DEAL...
BUMMING
Actually, I'm not fine, but that's because I'm stupid
UM... LOOKS LIKE AZUSA'S ALREADY ARRIVED.
THUD
REALLY?!

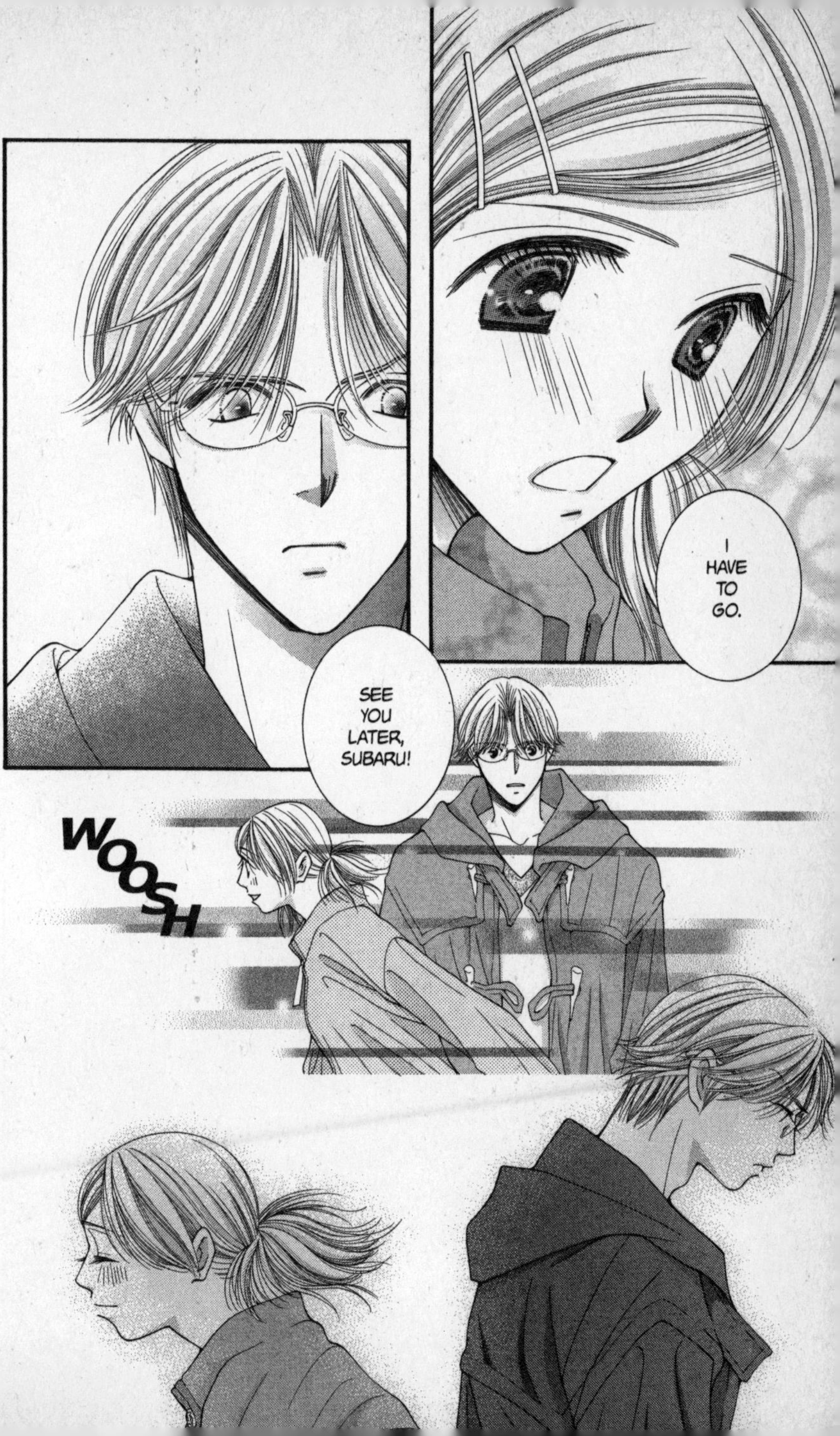
I HAVE TO GO.
SEE YOU LATER, SUBARU!
WOOSH

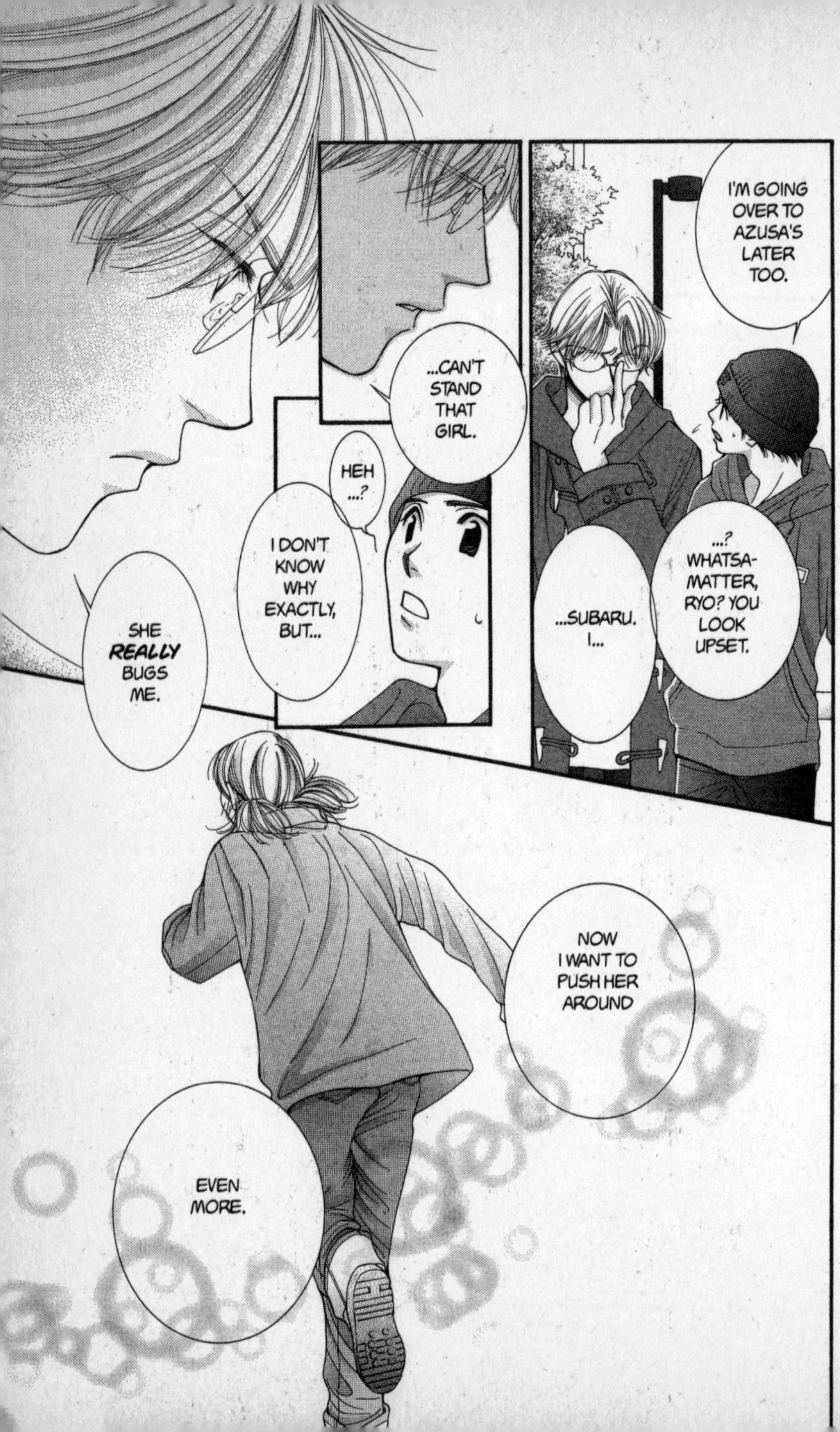
I'M GOING OVER TO AZUSA'S LATER TOO.
...? WHATSA-MATTER, RYO? YOU LOOK UPSET.
...SUBARU. I...
...CAN'T STAND THAT GIRL.
HEH ...?
I DON'T KNOW WHY EXACTLY, BUT...
SHE **REALLY** BUGS ME.
NOW I WANT TO PUSH HER AROUND
EVEN MORE.

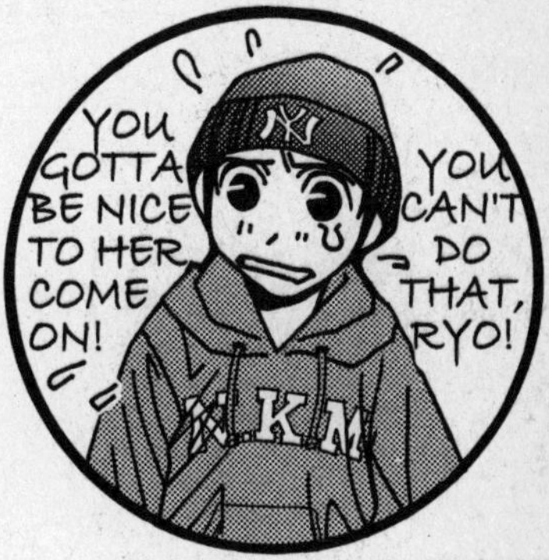
YOU CAN'T DO THAT, RYO!
YOU GOTTA BE NICE TO HER. COME ON!

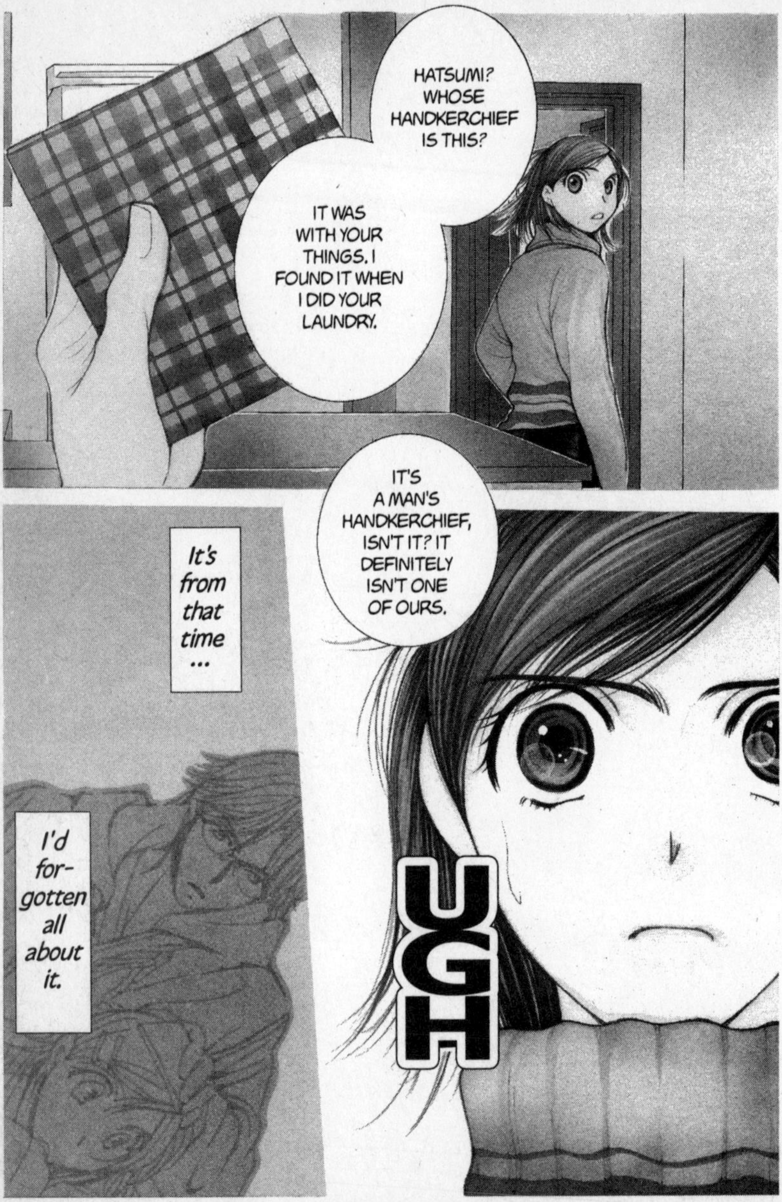
HATSUMI? WHOSE HANDKERCHIEF IS THIS?
IT WAS WITH YOUR THINGS. I FOUND IT WHEN I DID YOUR LAUNDRY.
IT'S A MAN'S HANDKERCHIEF, ISN'T IT? IT DEFINITELY ISN'T ONE OF OURS.
UGH
It's from that time...
I'd for-gotten all about it.

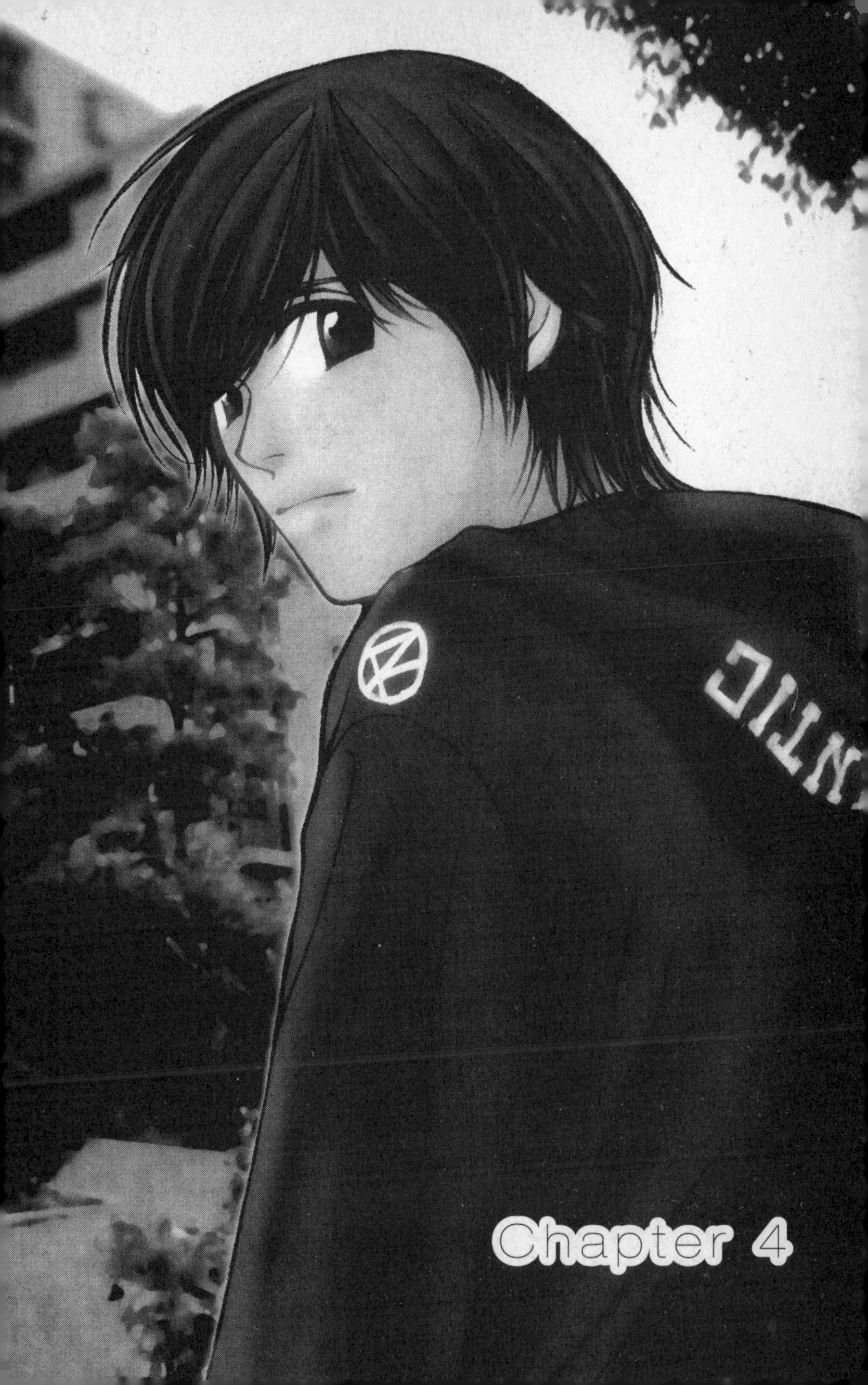
Chapter 4

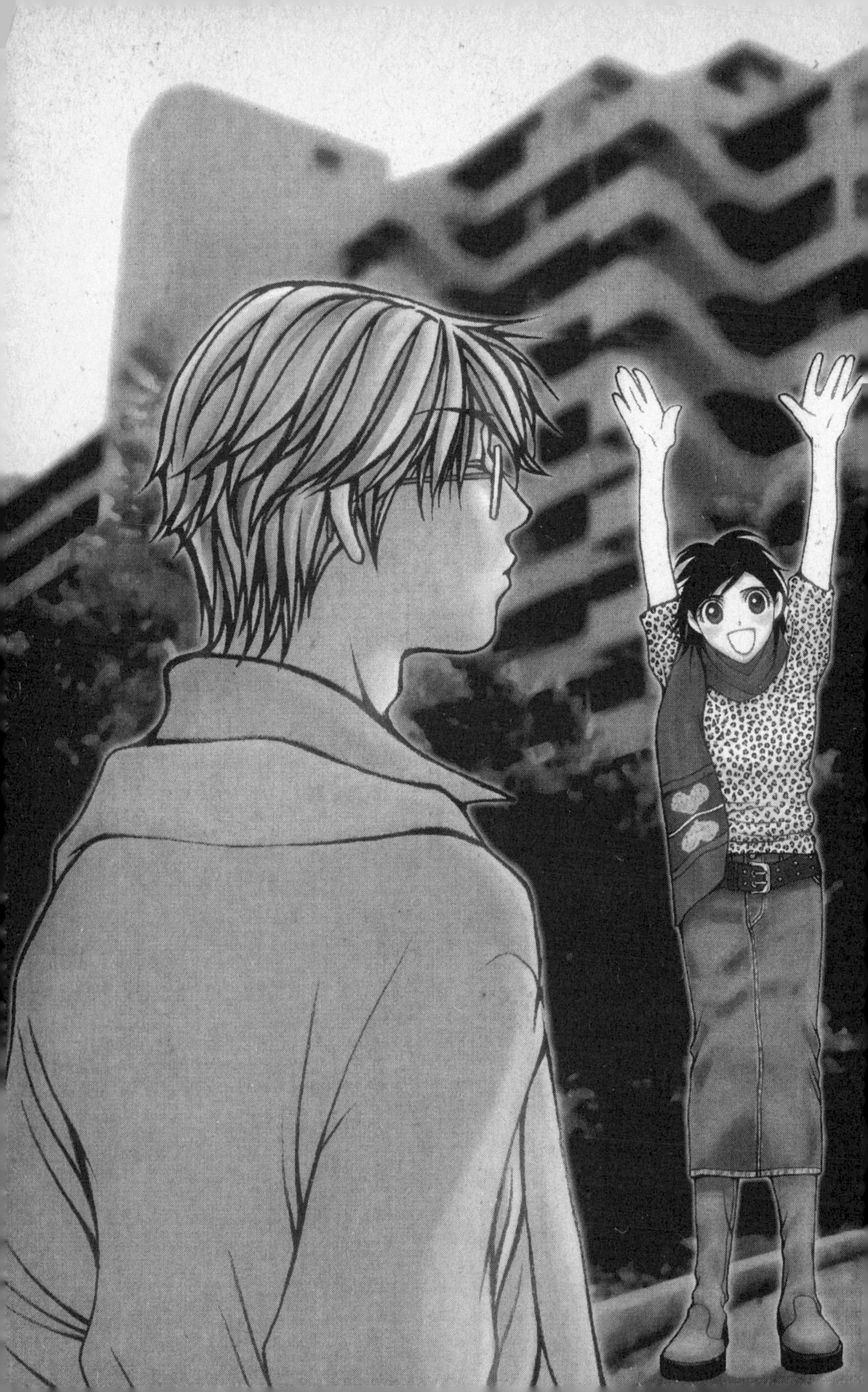

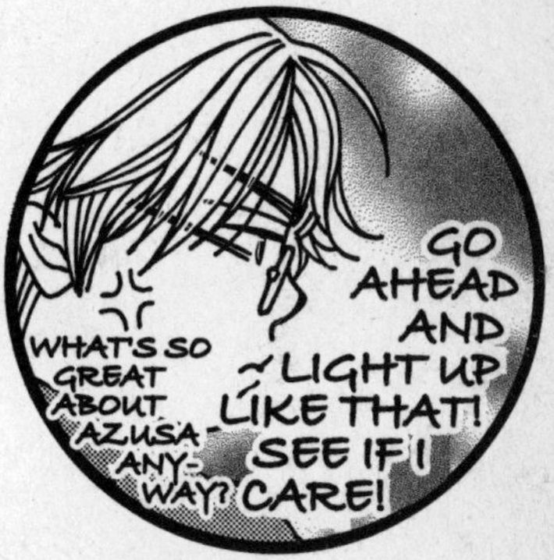
GO AHEAD AND LIGHT UP LIKE THAT! SEE IF I CARE!
WHAT'S SO GREAT ABOUT AZUSA ANY-WAY?

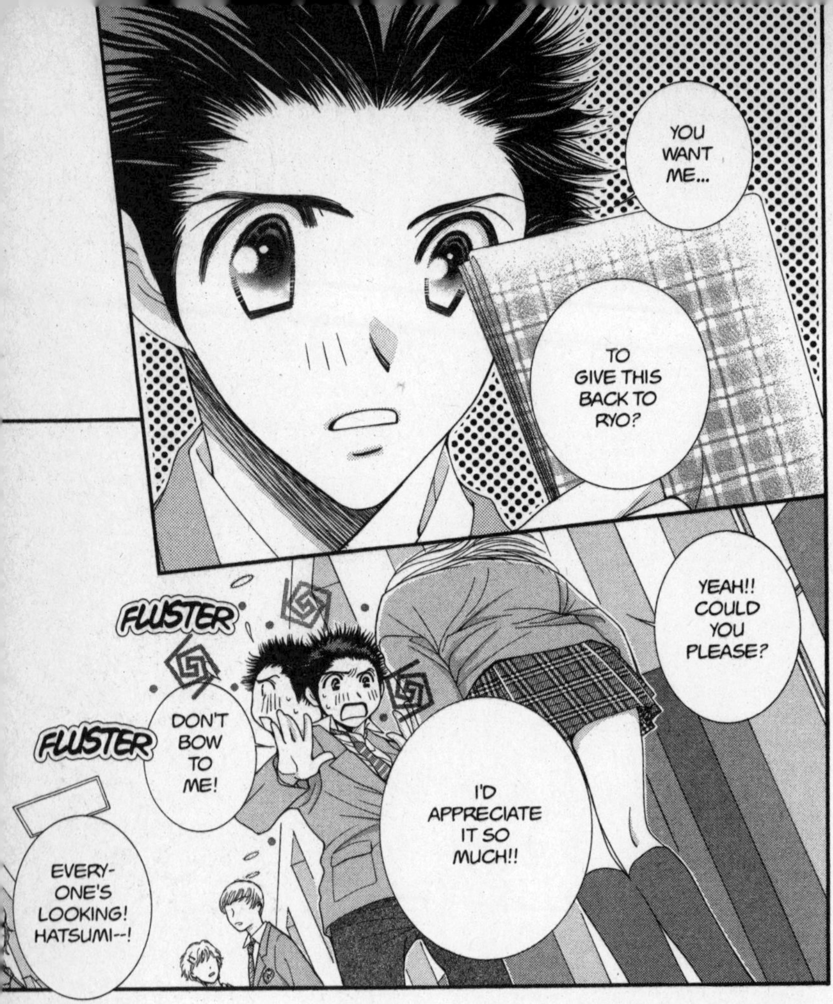
YOU WANT ME...
TO GIVE THIS BACK TO RYO?
YEAH!! COULD YOU PLEASE?
I'D APPRECIATE IT SO MUCH!!
FLUSTER
DON'T BOW TO ME!
FLUSTER
EVERY-ONE'S LOOKING! HATSUMI--!

hot gimmick

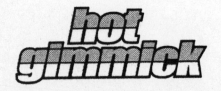

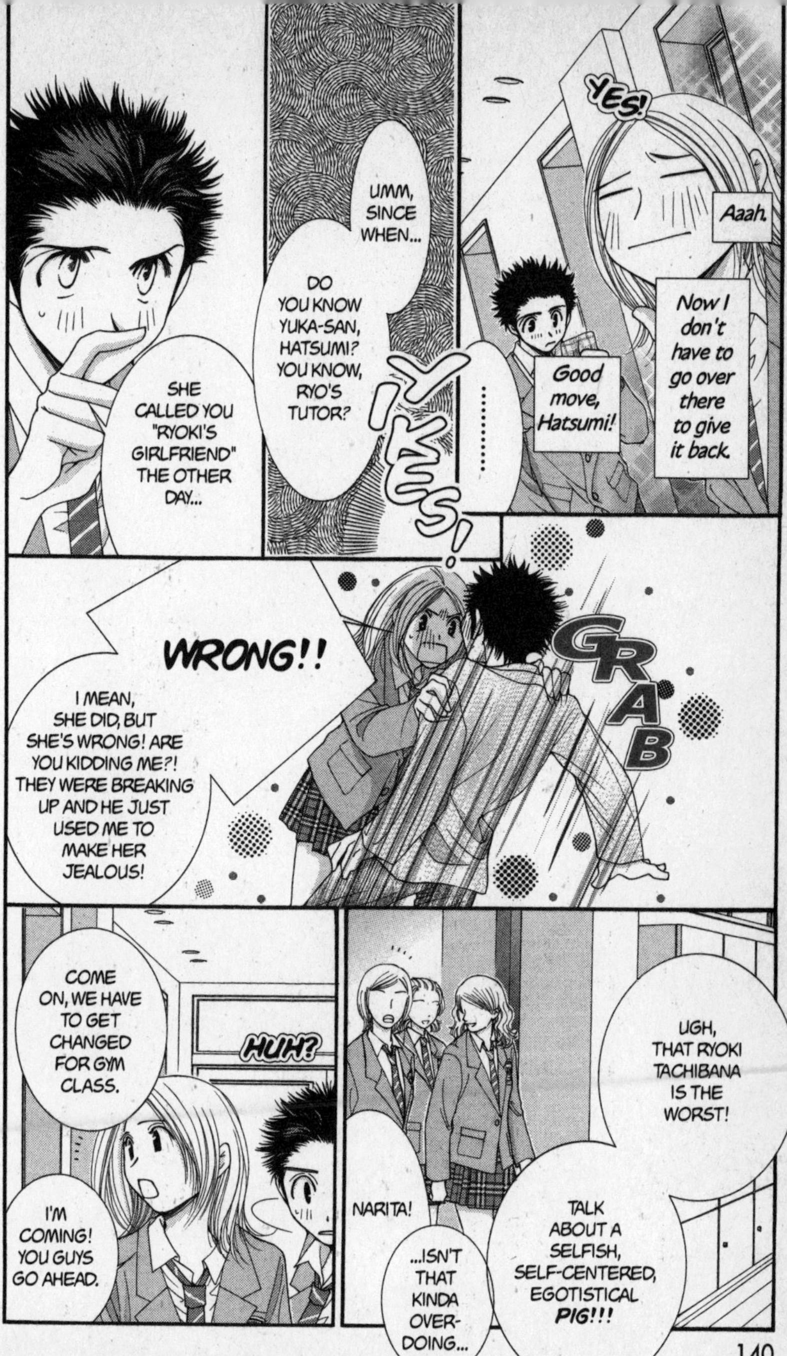
YES!
Aaah.
Now I don't have to go over there to give it back.
Good move, Hatsumi!
UMM, SINCE WHEN...
DO YOU KNOW YUKA-SAN, HATSUMI? YOU KNOW, RYO'S TUTOR?
SHE CALLED YOU "RYOKI'S GIRLFRIEND" THE OTHER DAY...
......
YIKES!
WRONG!!
I MEAN, SHE DID, BUT SHE'S WRONG! ARE YOU KIDDING ME?! THEY WERE BREAKING UP AND HE JUST USED ME TO MAKE HER JEALOUS!
GRAB
UGH, THAT RYOKI TACHIBANA IS THE WORST!
TALK ABOUT A SELFISH, SELF-CENTERED, EGOTISTICAL PIG!!!
NARITA!
...ISN'T THAT KINDA OVER-DOING...
COME ON, WE HAVE TO GET CHANGED FOR GYM CLASS.
HUH?
I'M COMING! YOU GUYS GO AHEAD.

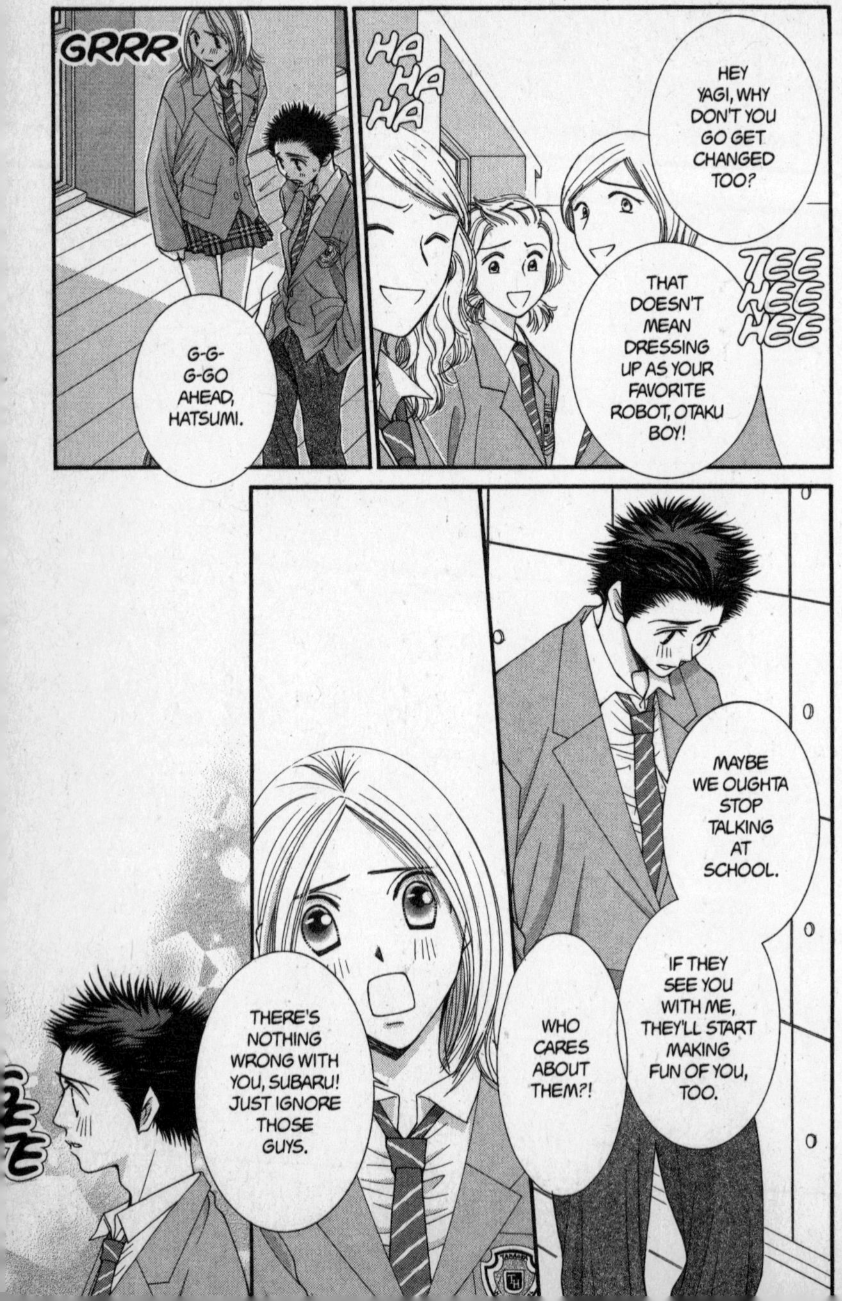
HA HA HA
HEY YAGI, WHY DON'T YOU GO GET CHANGED TOO?
TEE HEE HEE
THAT DOESN'T MEAN DRESSING UP AS YOUR FAVORITE ROBOT, OTAKU BOY!
GRRR
G-G-G-GO AHEAD, HATSUMI.
MAYBE WE OUGHTA STOP TALKING AT SCHOOL.
IF THEY SEE YOU WITH ME, THEY'LL START MAKING FUN OF YOU, TOO.
WHO CARES ABOUT THEM?!
THERE'S NOTHING WRONG WITH YOU, SUBARU! JUST IGNORE THOSE GUYS.

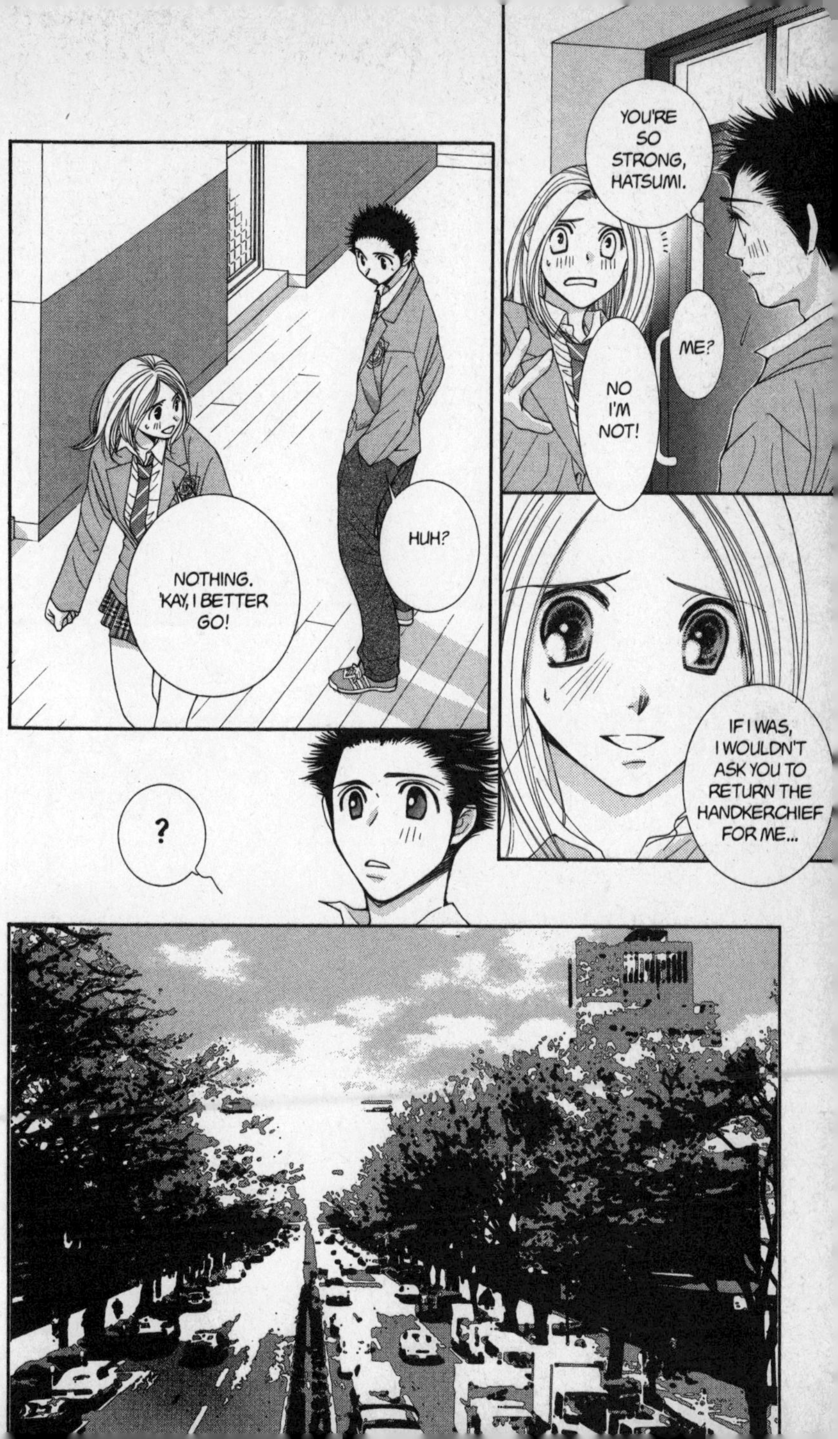
YOU'RE SO STRONG, HATSUMI.
ME?
NO I'M NOT!
IF I WAS, I WOULDN'T ASK YOU TO RETURN THE HANDKERCHIEF FOR ME...
HUH?
NOTHING. 'KAY, I BETTER GO!
?

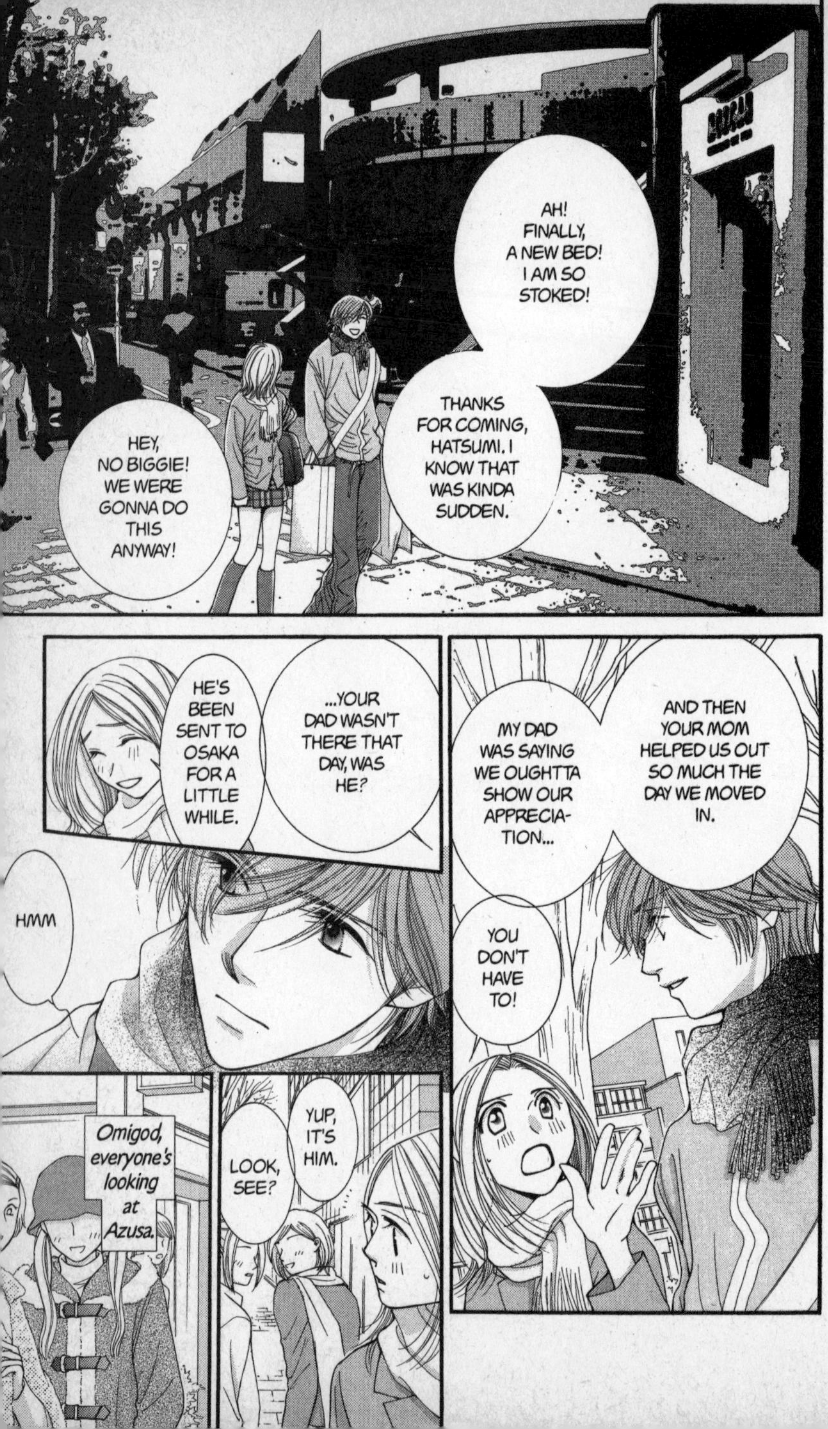
AH! FINALLY, A NEW BED! I AM SO STOKED!
THANKS FOR COMING, HATSUMI. I KNOW THAT WAS KINDA SUDDEN.
HEY, NO BIGGIE! WE WERE GONNA DO THIS ANYWAY!
AND THEN YOUR MOM HELPED US OUT SO MUCH THE DAY WE MOVED IN.
MY DAD WAS SAYING WE OUGHTTA SHOW OUR APPRECIA-TION...
YOU DON'T HAVE TO!
...YOUR DAD WASN'T THERE THAT DAY, WAS HE?
HE'S BEEN SENT TO OSAKA FOR A LITTLE WHILE.
HMM
YUP, IT'S HIM.
LOOK, SEE?
Omigod, everyone's looking at Azusa.

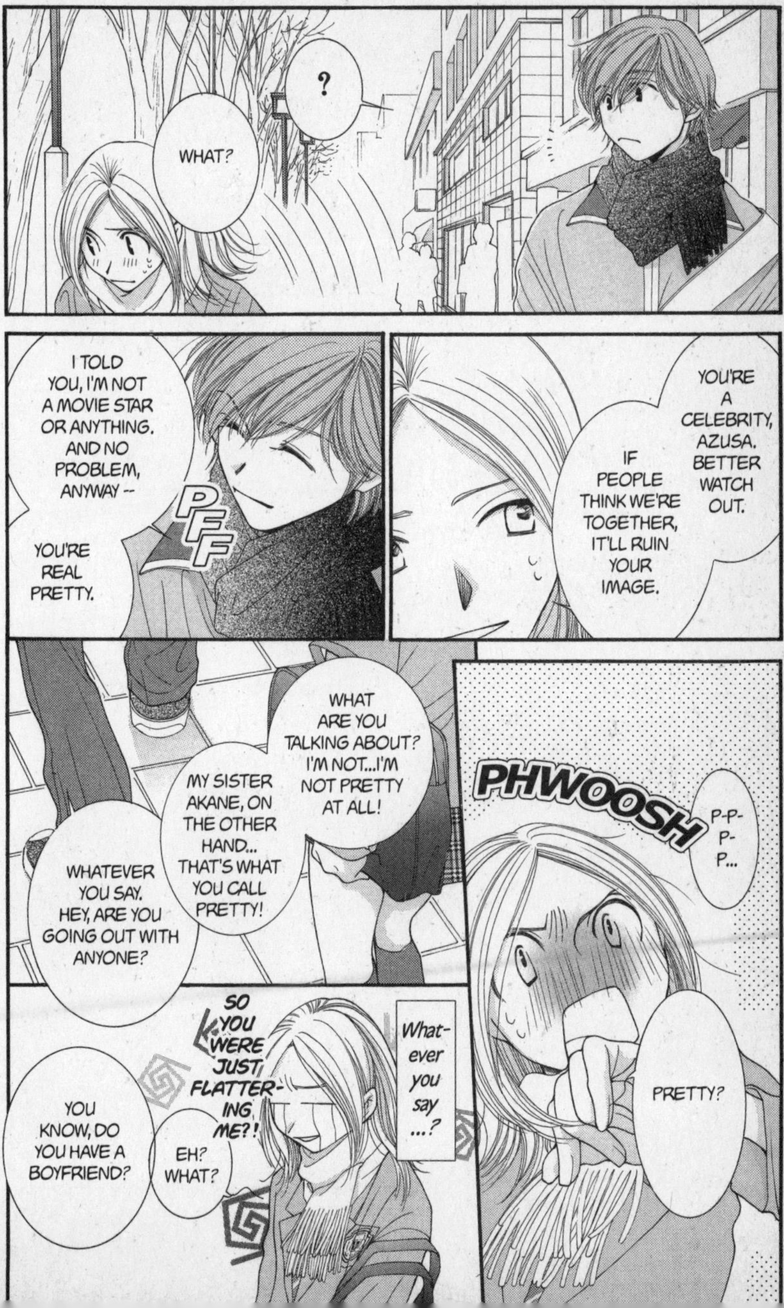
?
WHAT?
YOU'RE A CELEBRITY, AZUSA. BETTER WATCH OUT.
IF PEOPLE THINK WE'RE TOGETHER, IT'LL RUIN YOUR IMAGE.
I TOLD YOU, I'M NOT A MOVIE STAR OR ANYTHING. AND NO PROBLEM, ANYWAY --
PFF
YOU'RE REAL PRETTY.
PHWOOSH
P-P-P-P...
PRETTY?
WHAT ARE YOU TALKING ABOUT? I'M NOT...I'M NOT PRETTY AT ALL!
MY SISTER AKANE, ON THE OTHER HAND... THAT'S WHAT YOU CALL PRETTY!
WHATEVER YOU SAY. HEY, ARE YOU GOING OUT WITH ANYONE?
What-ever you say ...?
SO YOU WERE JUST FLATTERING ME?!
EH? WHAT?
YOU KNOW, DO YOU HAVE A BOYFRIEND?

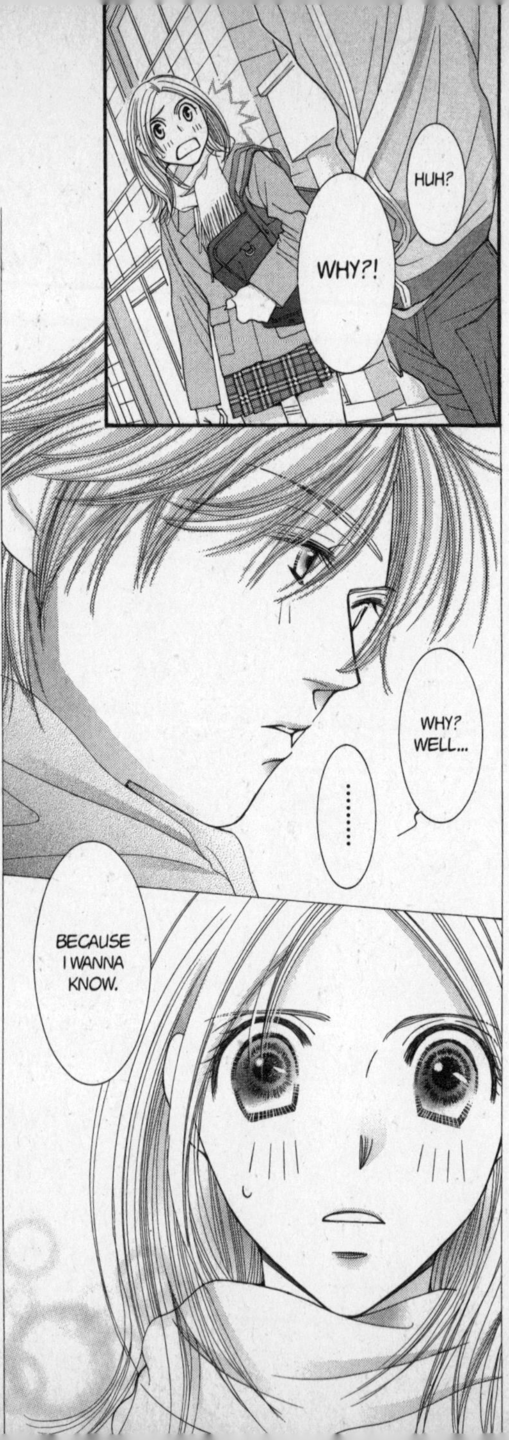
HUH?
WHY?!
WHY? WELL...
......
BECAUSE I WANNA KNOW.

notgimmick

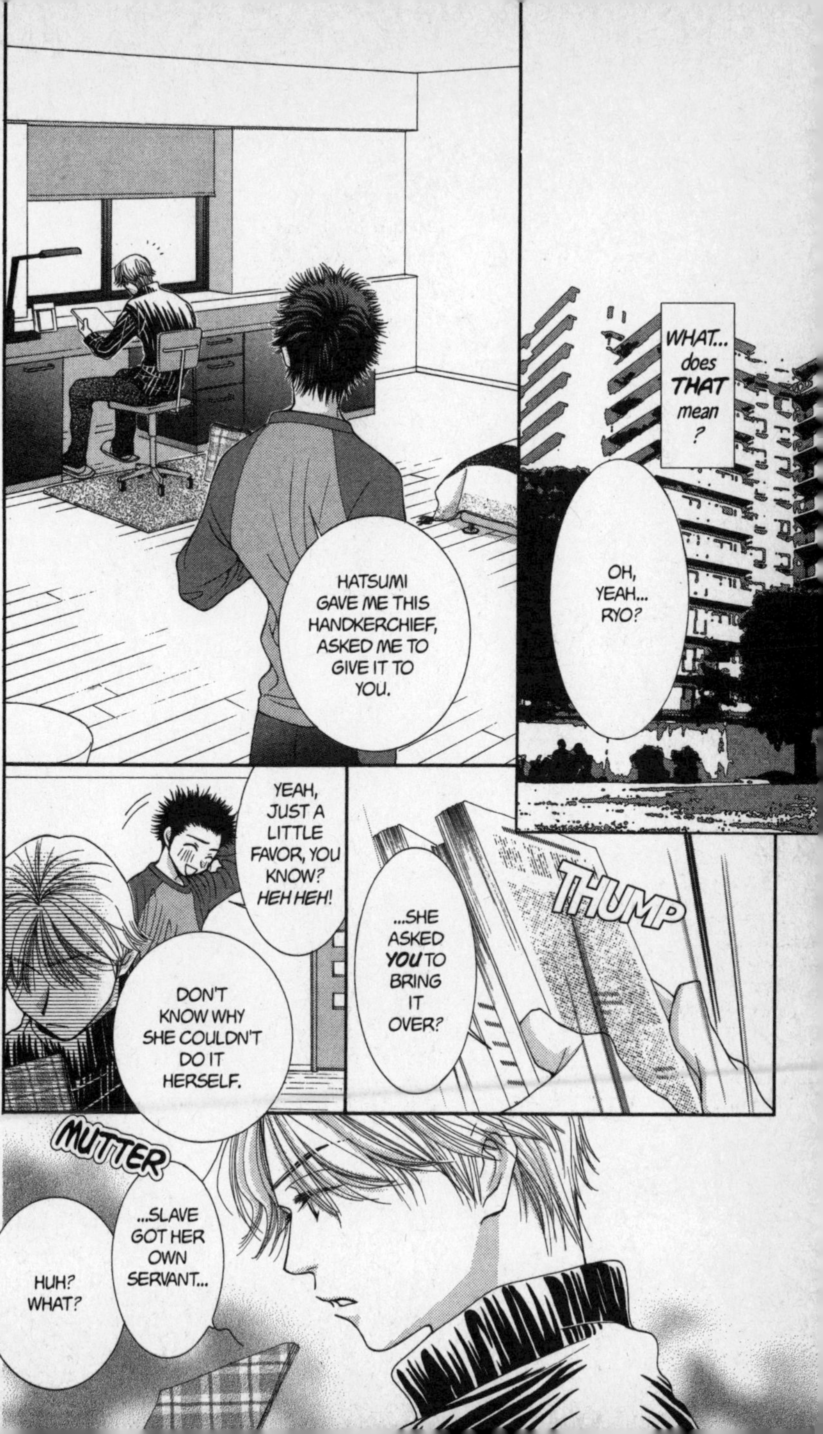
WHAT... does THAT mean?
OH, YEAH... RYO?
HATSUMI GAVE ME THIS HANDKERCHIEF, ASKED ME TO GIVE IT TO YOU.
THUMP
...SHE ASKED YOU TO BRING IT OVER?
YEAH, JUST A LITTLE FAVOR, YOU KNOW? HEH HEH!
DON'T KNOW WHY SHE COULDN'T DO IT HERSELF.
MUTTER
...SLAVE GOT HER OWN SERVANT...
HUH? WHAT?

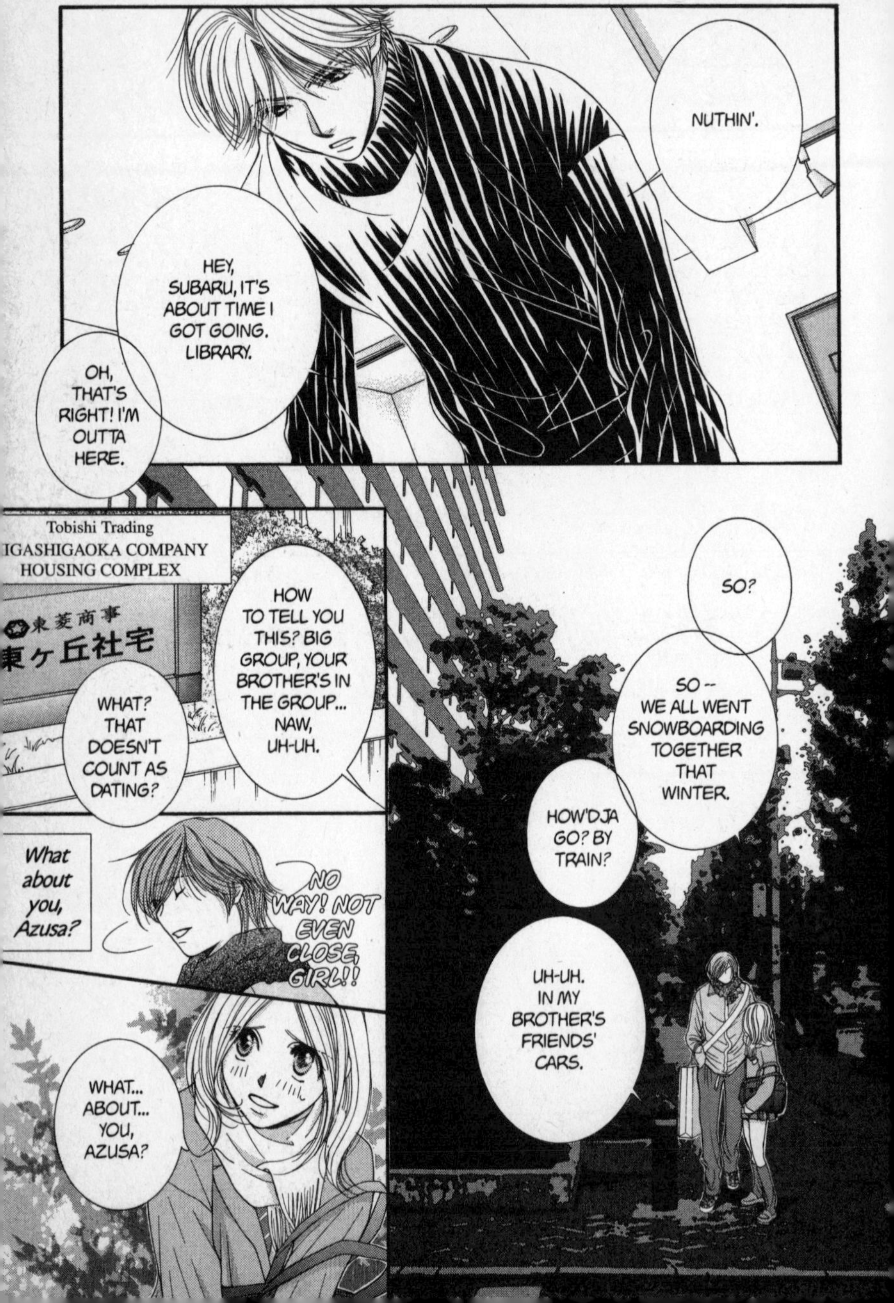
NUTHIN'.
HEY, SUBARU, IT'S ABOUT TIME I GOT GOING. LIBRARY.
OH, THAT'S RIGHT! I'M OUTTA HERE.
SO?
SO -- WE ALL WENT SNOWBOARDING TOGETHER THAT WINTER.
HOW'DJA GO? BY TRAIN?
UH-UH. IN MY BROTHER'S FRIENDS' CARS.
Tobishi Trading
IGASHIGAOKA COMPANY HOUSING COMPLEX
東菱商事
東ヶ丘社宅
HOW TO TELL YOU THIS? BIG GROUP, YOUR BROTHER'S IN THE GROUP... NAW, UH-UH.
WHAT? THAT DOESN'T COUNT AS DATING?
NO WAY! NOT EVEN CLOSE, GIRL!!
What about you, Azusa?
WHAT... ABOUT... YOU, AZUSA?

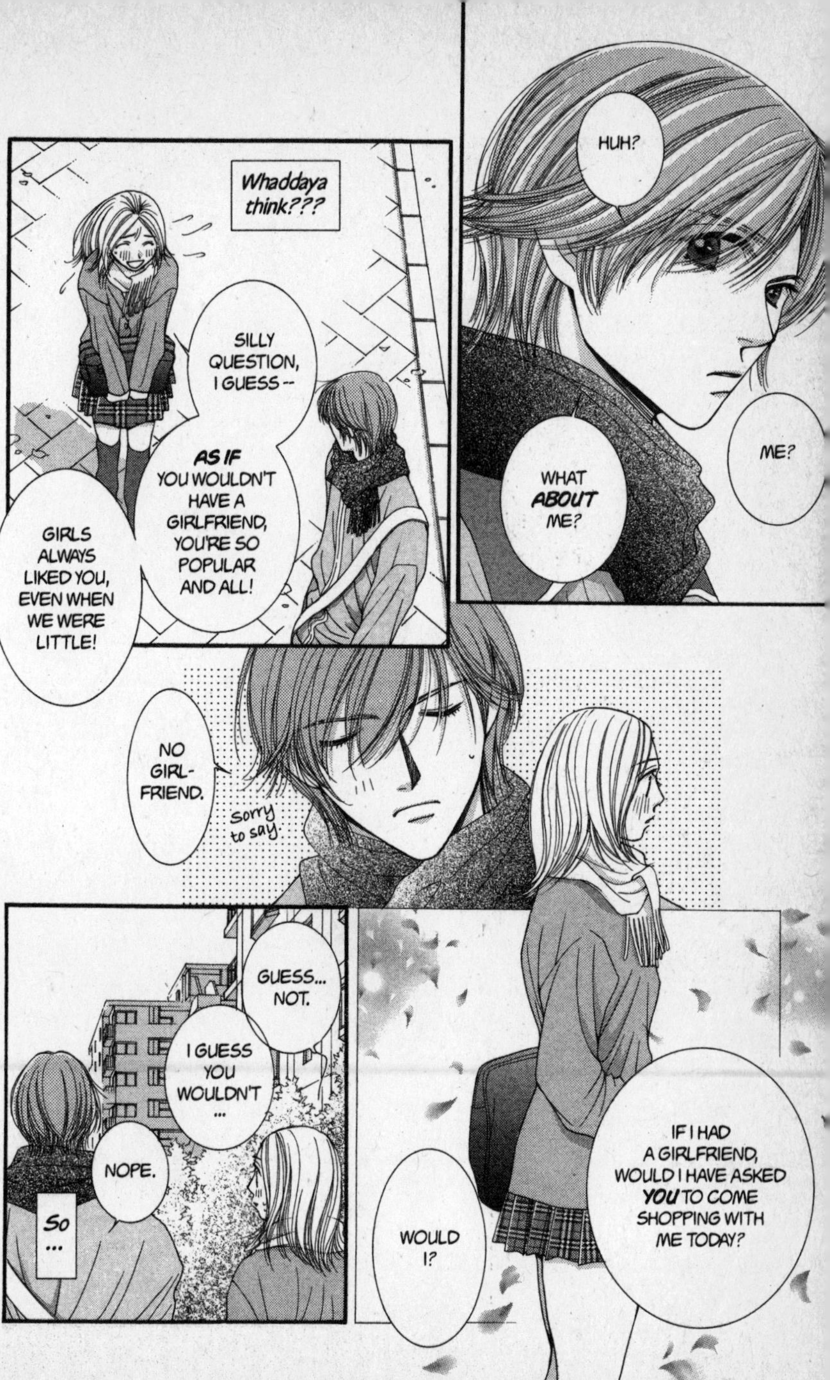
HUH?
ME?
WHAT **ABOUT** ME?
Whaddaya think???
SILLY QUESTION, I GUESS --
AS IF YOU WOULDN'T HAVE A GIRLFRIEND, YOU'RE SO POPULAR AND ALL!
GIRLS ALWAYS LIKED YOU, EVEN WHEN WE WERE LITTLE!
NO GIRL-FRIEND.
Sorry to say.
IF I HAD A GIRLFRIEND, WOULD I HAVE ASKED **YOU** TO COME SHOPPING WITH ME TODAY?
WOULD I?
GUESS... NOT.
I GUESS YOU WOULDN'T ...
NOPE.
So ...

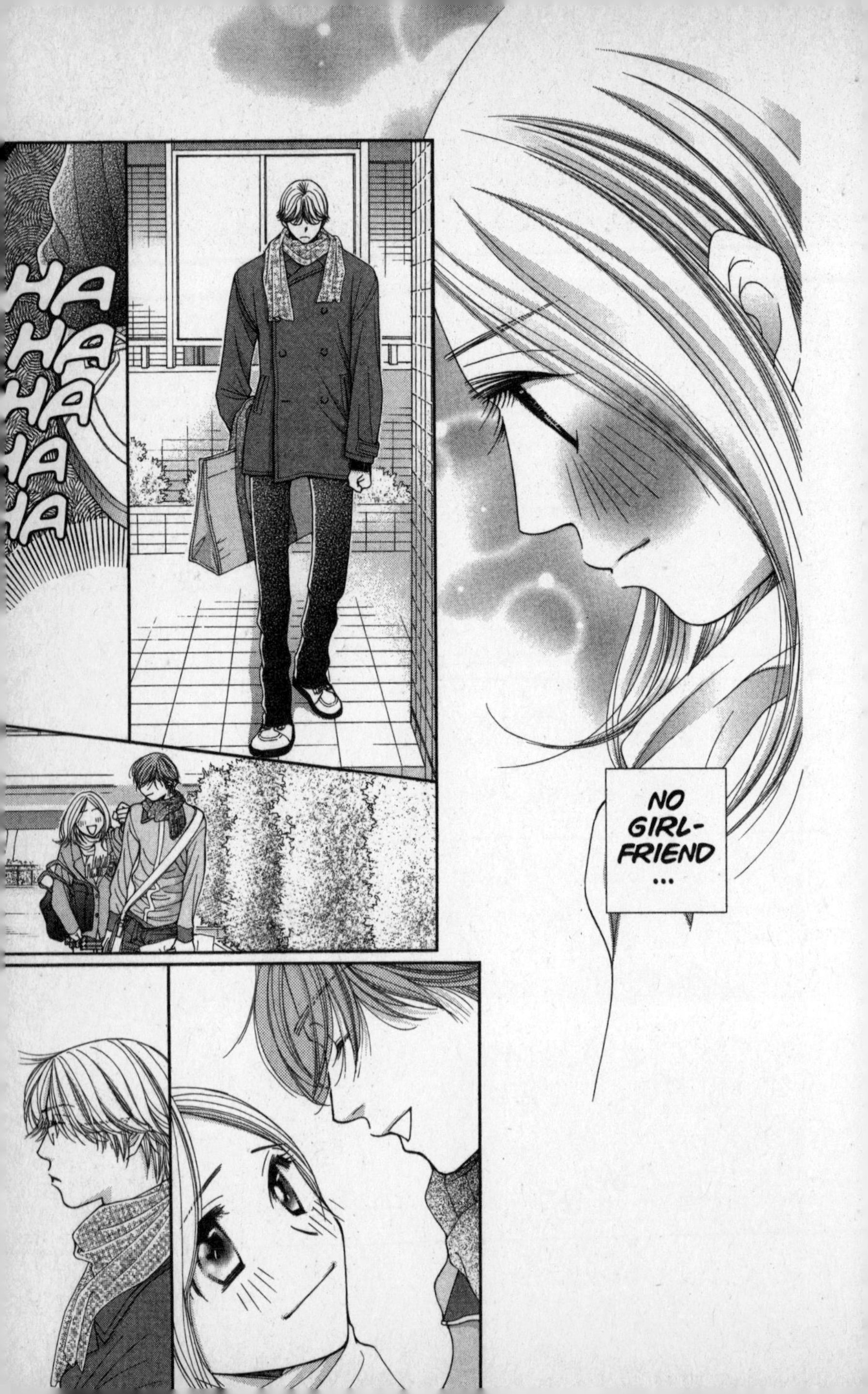
NO GIRL-FRIEND ...
HAHAHAHAHAHA

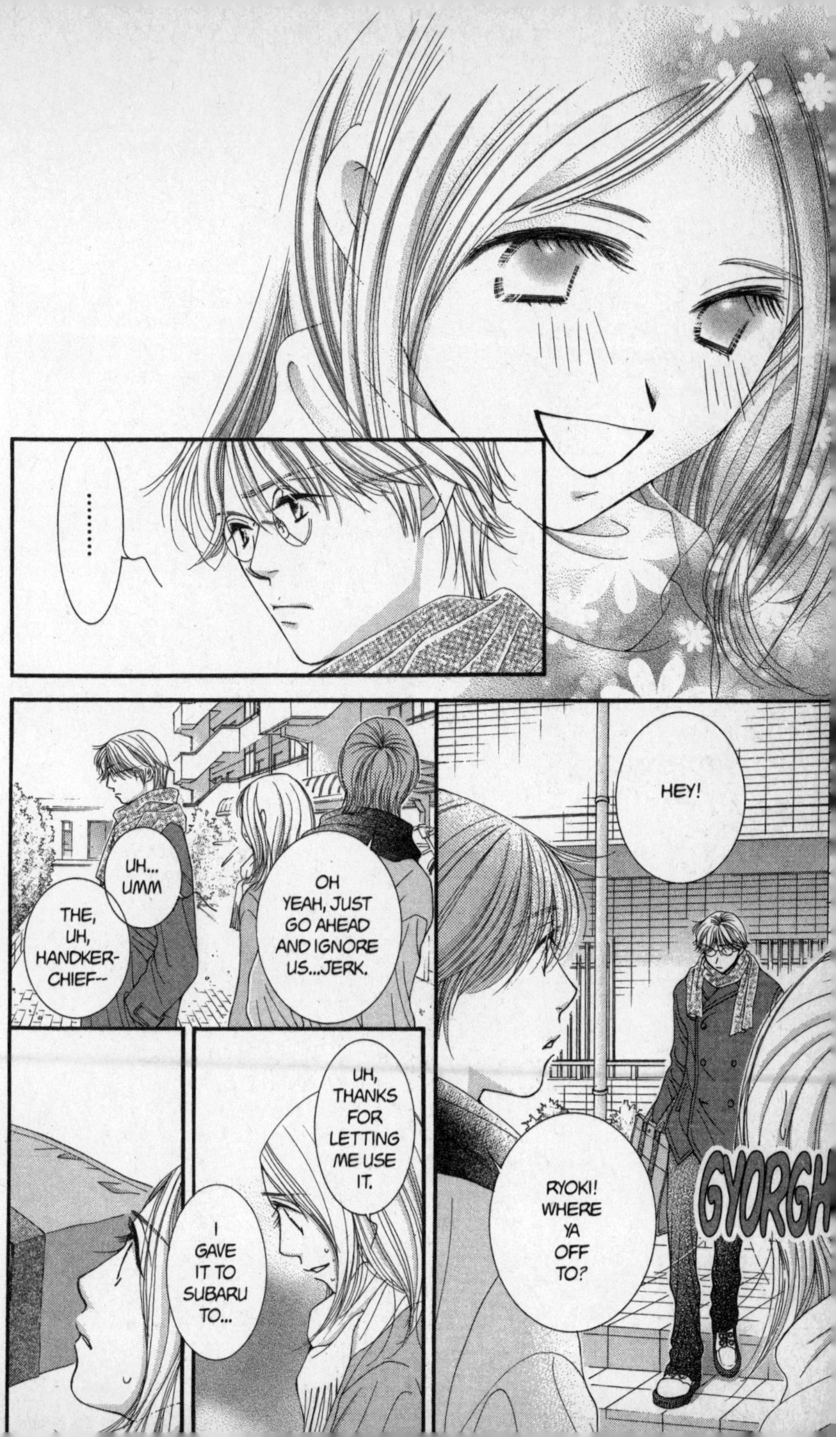
......
HEY!
RYOKI! WHERE YA OFF TO?
GYORGH
OH YEAH, JUST GO AHEAD AND IGNORE US...JERK.
UH... UMM
THE, UH, HANDKER-CHIEF--
UH, THANKS FOR LETTING ME USE IT.
I GAVE IT TO SUBARU TO...

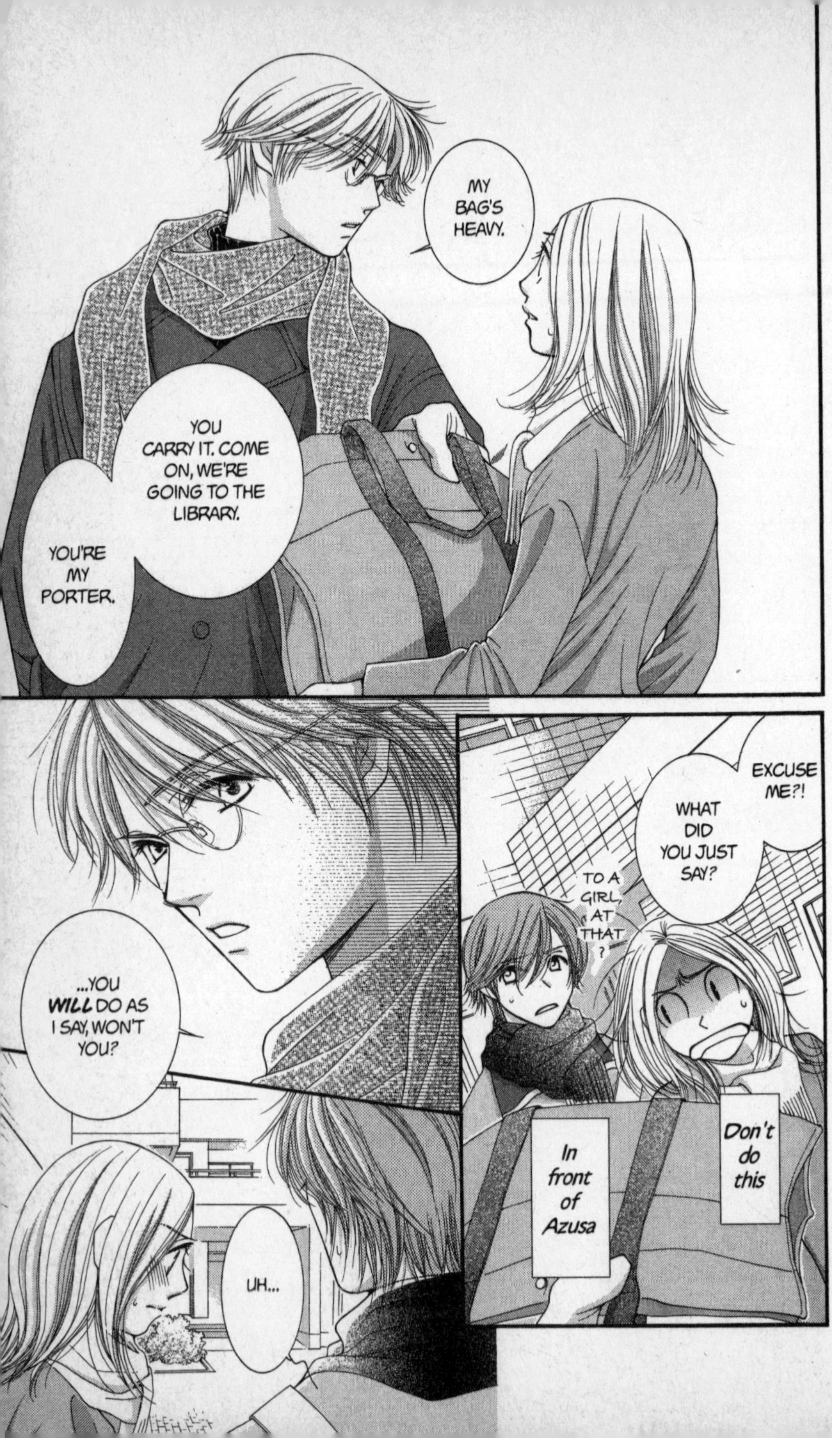

MY BAG'S HEAVY.
YOU CARRY IT. COME ON, WE'RE GOING TO THE LIBRARY.
YOU'RE MY PORTER.
EXCUSE ME?!
WHAT DID YOU JUST SAY?
TO A GIRL, AT THAT?
Don't do this
In front of Azusa
...YOU **WILL** DO AS I SAY, WON'T YOU?
UH...

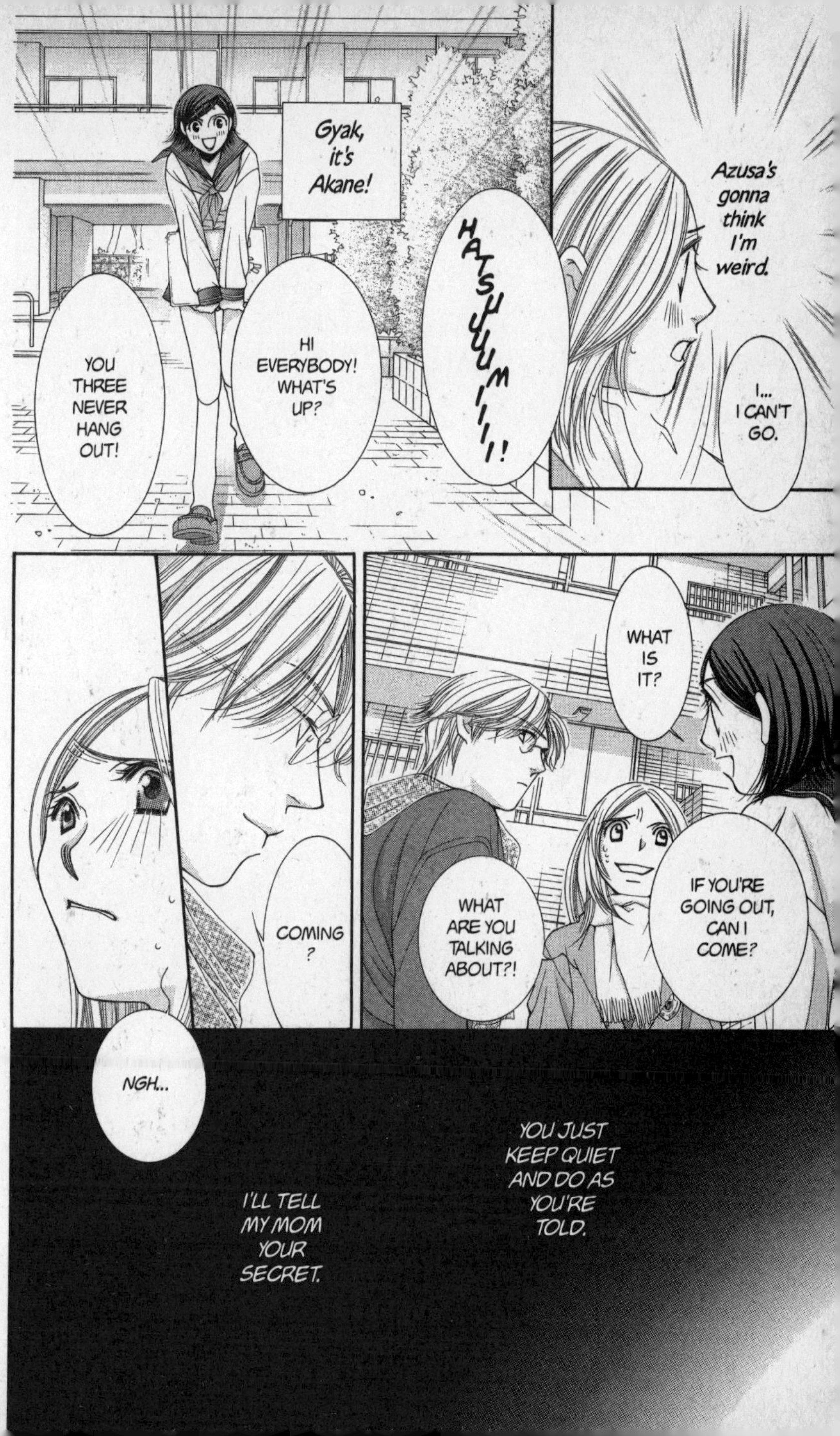
Azusa's gonna think I'm weird.
I... I CAN'T GO.
HATSUUUMIIII!
Gyak, it's Akane!
HI EVERYBODY! WHAT'S UP?
YOU THREE NEVER HANG OUT!
WHAT IS IT?
IF YOU'RE GOING OUT, CAN I COME?
WHAT ARE YOU TALKING ABOUT?!
COMING?
NGH...
YOU JUST KEEP QUIET AND DO AS YOU'RE TOLD.
I'LL TELL MY MOM YOUR SECRET.

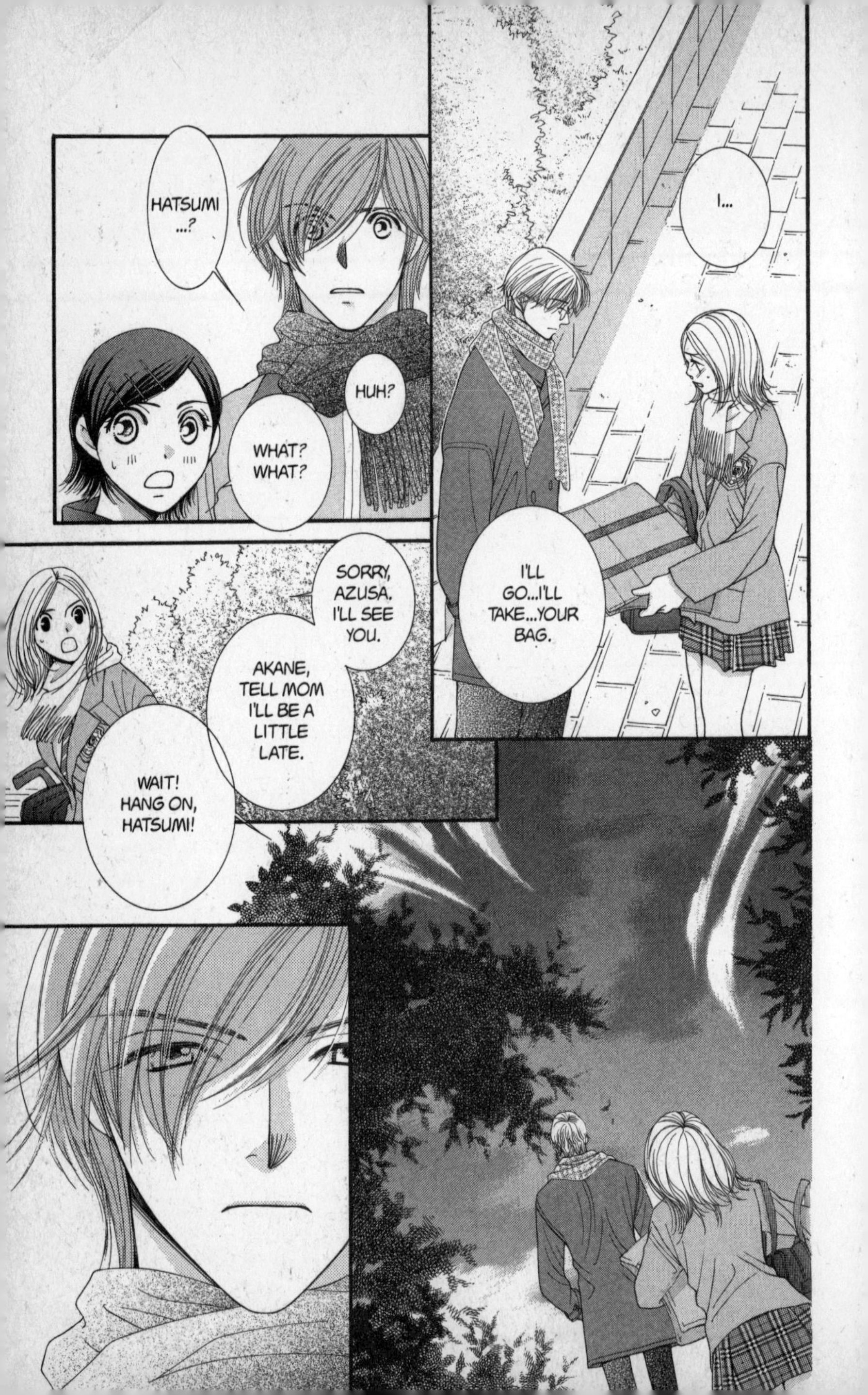
I...
I'LL GO...I'LL TAKE...YOUR BAG.
HATSUMI ...?
HUH?
WHAT? WHAT?
SORRY, AZUSA. I'LL SEE YOU.
AKANE, TELL MOM I'LL BE A LITTLE LATE.
WAIT! HANG ON, HATSUMI!

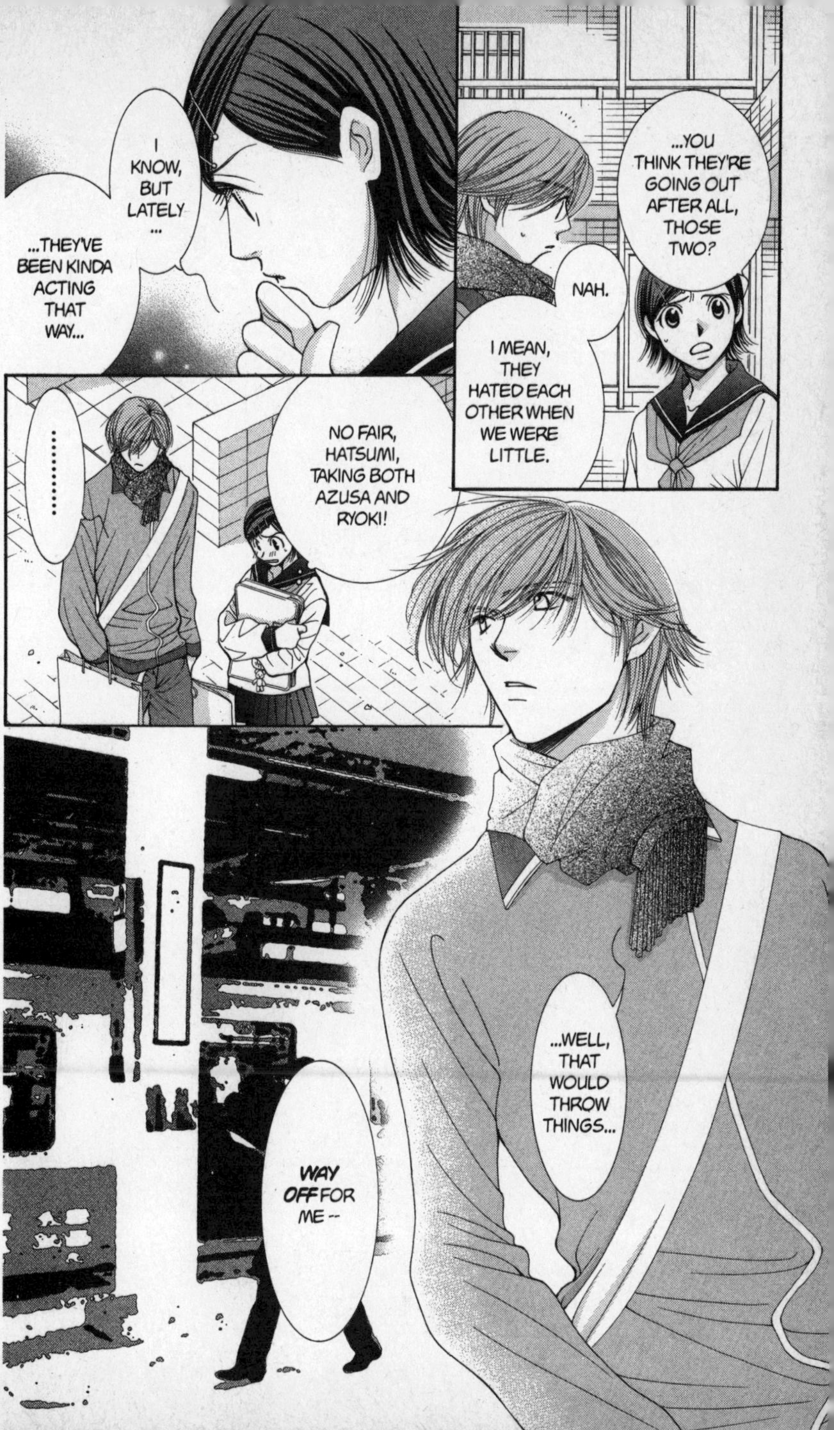
...YOU THINK THEY'RE GOING OUT AFTER ALL, THOSE TWO?
NAH.
I MEAN, THEY HATED EACH OTHER WHEN WE WERE LITTLE.
I KNOW, BUT LATELY...
...THEY'VE BEEN KINDA ACTING THAT WAY...
NO FAIR, HATSUMI, TAKING BOTH AZUSA AND RYOKI!
......
...WELL, THAT WOULD THROW THINGS...
WAY OFF FOR ME --

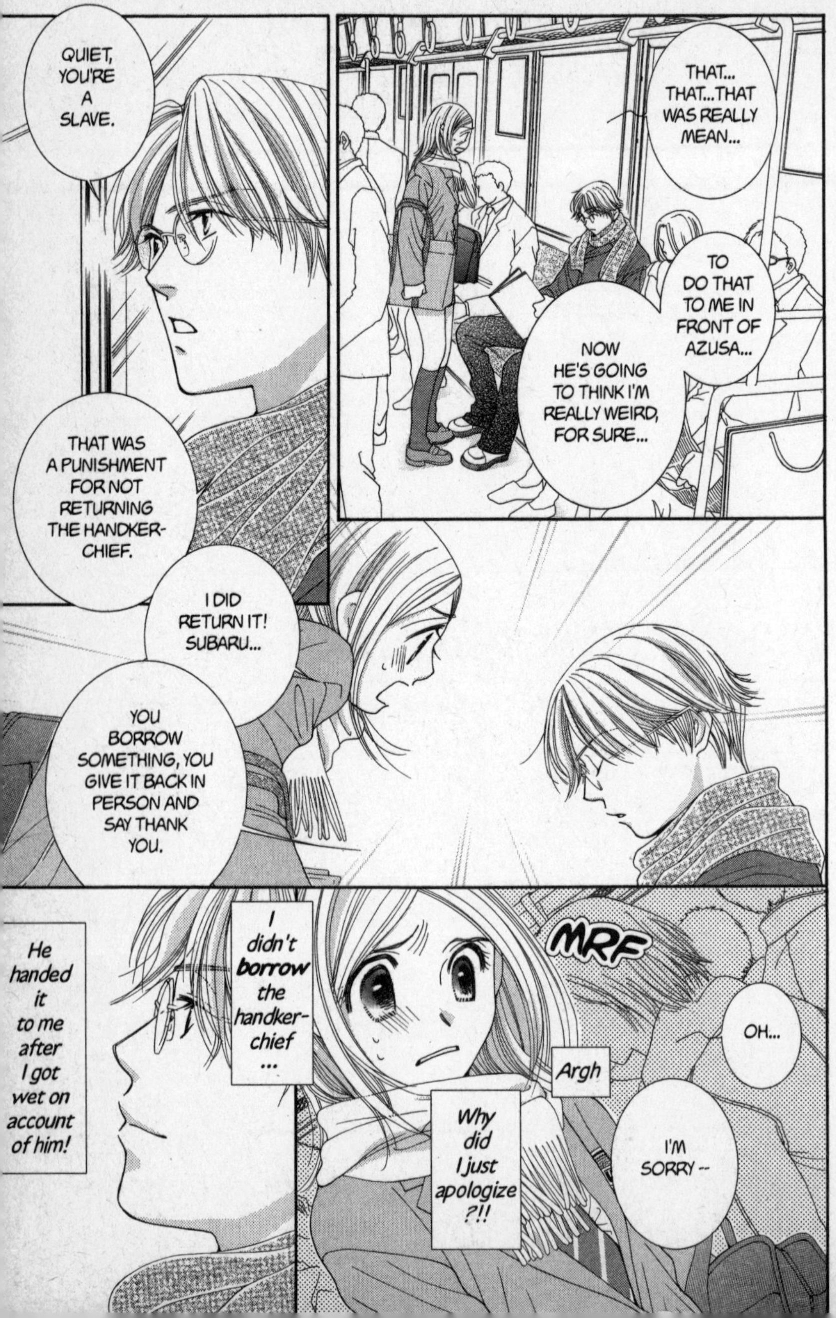
THAT... THAT...THAT WAS REALLY MEAN...
TO DO THAT TO ME IN FRONT OF AZUSA...
NOW HE'S GOING TO THINK I'M REALLY WEIRD, FOR SURE...
QUIET, YOU'RE A SLAVE.
THAT WAS A PUNISHMENT FOR NOT RETURNING THE HANDKER-CHIEF.
I DID RETURN IT! SUBARU...
YOU BORROW SOMETHING, YOU GIVE IT BACK IN PERSON AND SAY THANK YOU.
MRF
OH...
I'M SORRY --
Argh
Why did I just apologize ?!!
I didn't **borrow** the handker-chief ...
He handed it to me after I got wet on account of him!

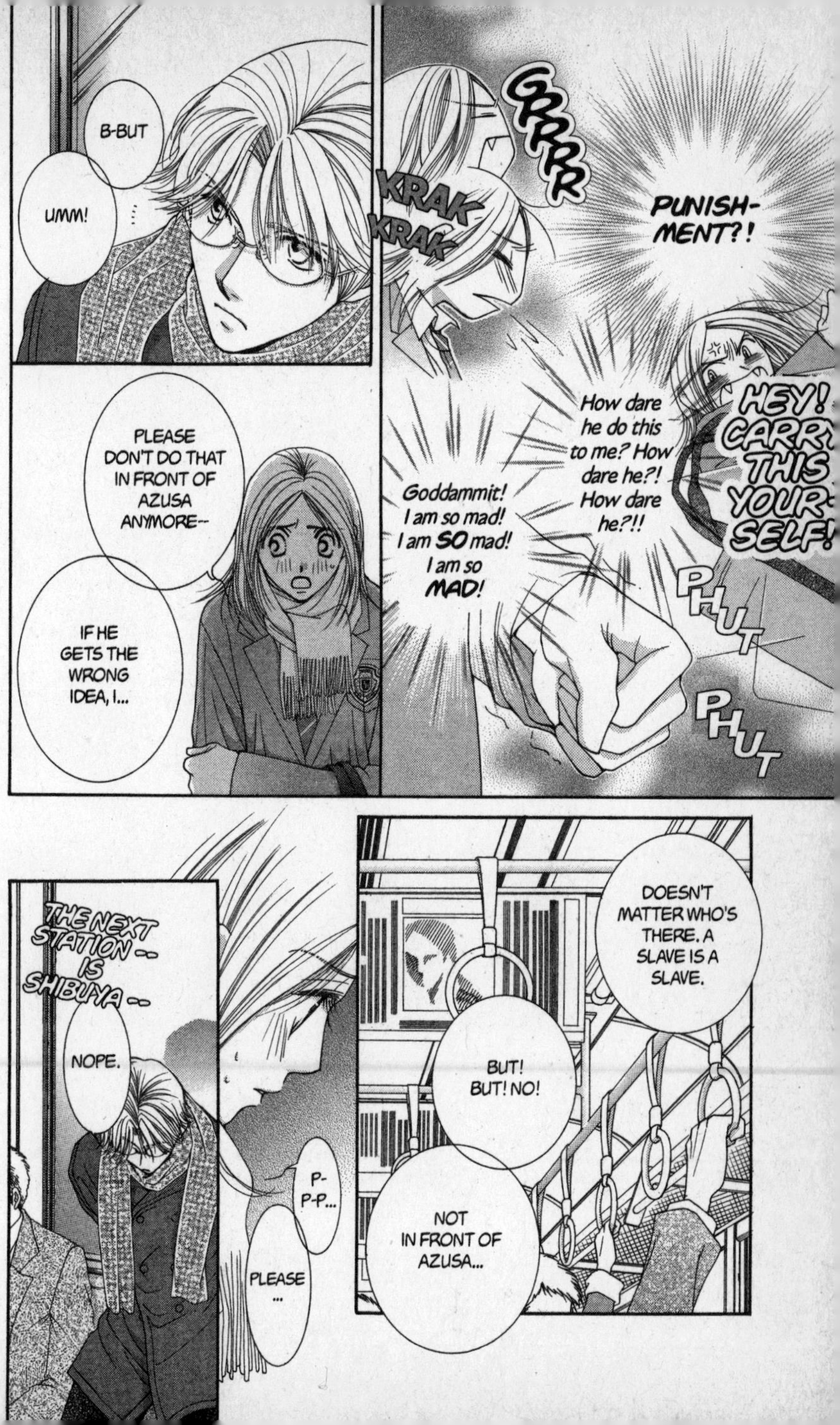
GRRRR
KRAK KRAK
PUNISH-MENT?!
HEY! CARR THIS YOUR-SELF!
How dare he do this to me? How dare he?! How dare he?!!
Goddammit! I am so mad! I am **SO** mad! I am so **MAD!**
PHUT PHUT
B-BUT
UMM!
...
PLEASE DON'T DO THAT IN FRONT OF AZUSA ANYMORE--
IF HE GETS THE WRONG IDEA, I...
DOESN'T MATTER WHO'S THERE. A SLAVE IS A SLAVE.
BUT! BUT! NO!
NOT IN FRONT OF AZUSA...
THE NEXT STATION -- IS SHIBUYA --
NOPE.
P-P-P...
PLEASE ...

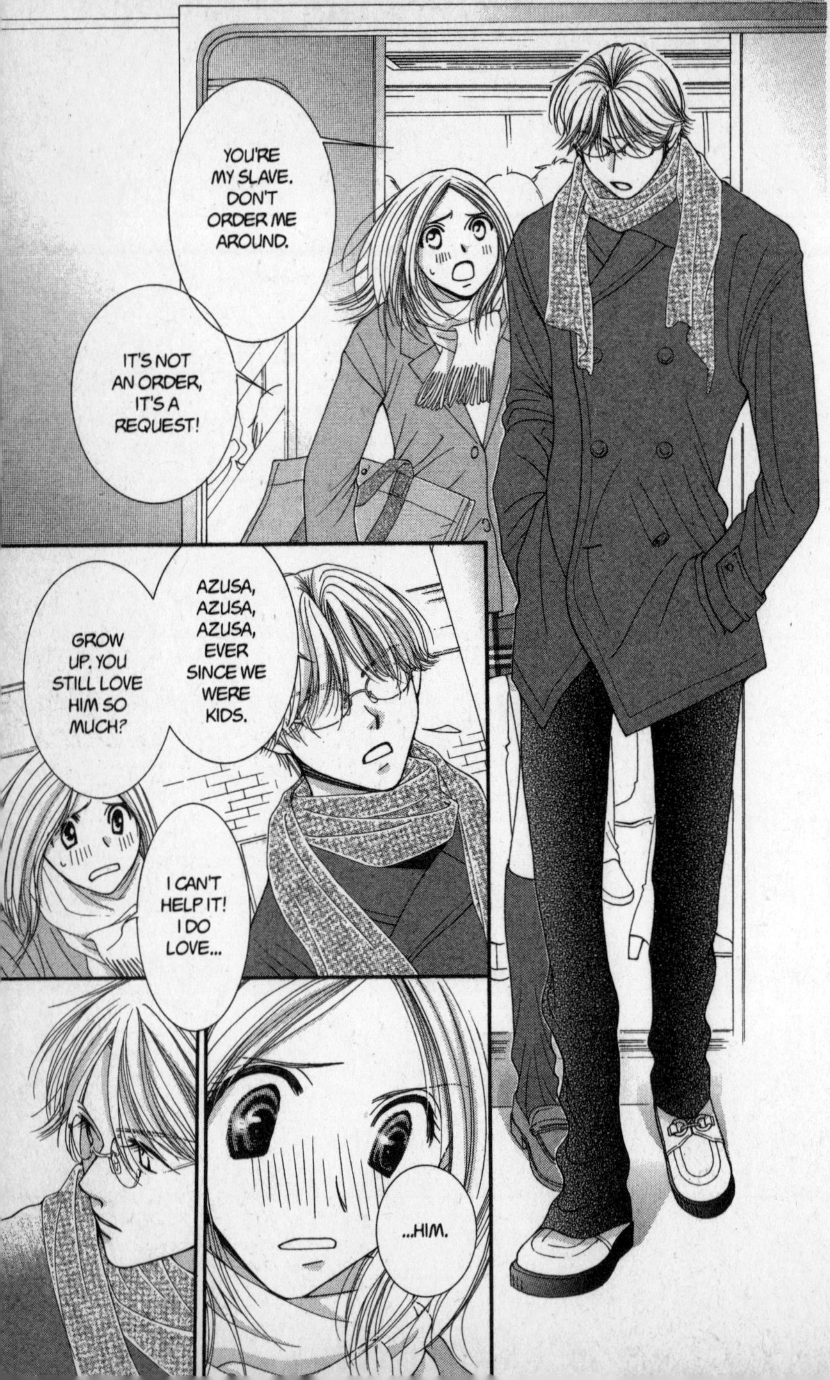
YOU'RE MY SLAVE. DON'T ORDER ME AROUND.
IT'S NOT AN ORDER, IT'S A REQUEST!
AZUSA, AZUSA, AZUSA, EVER SINCE WE WERE KIDS.
GROW UP. YOU STILL LOVE HIM SO MUCH?
I CAN'T HELP IT! I DO LOVE...
...HIM.

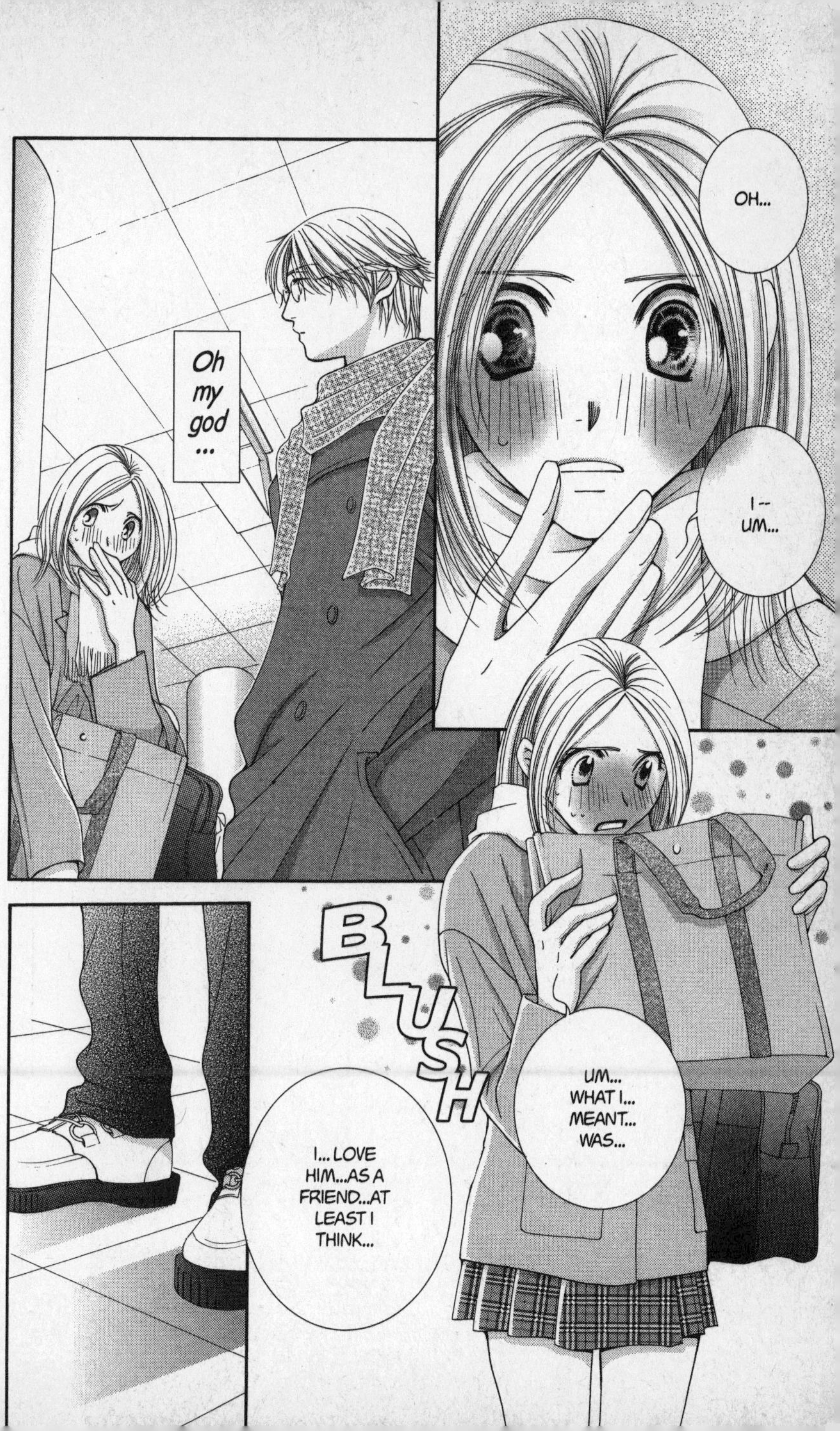
OH...
I-- UM...
Oh my god ...
BLUSH
UM... WHAT I... MEANT... WAS...
I... LOVE HIM...AS A FRIEND...AT LEAST I THINK...

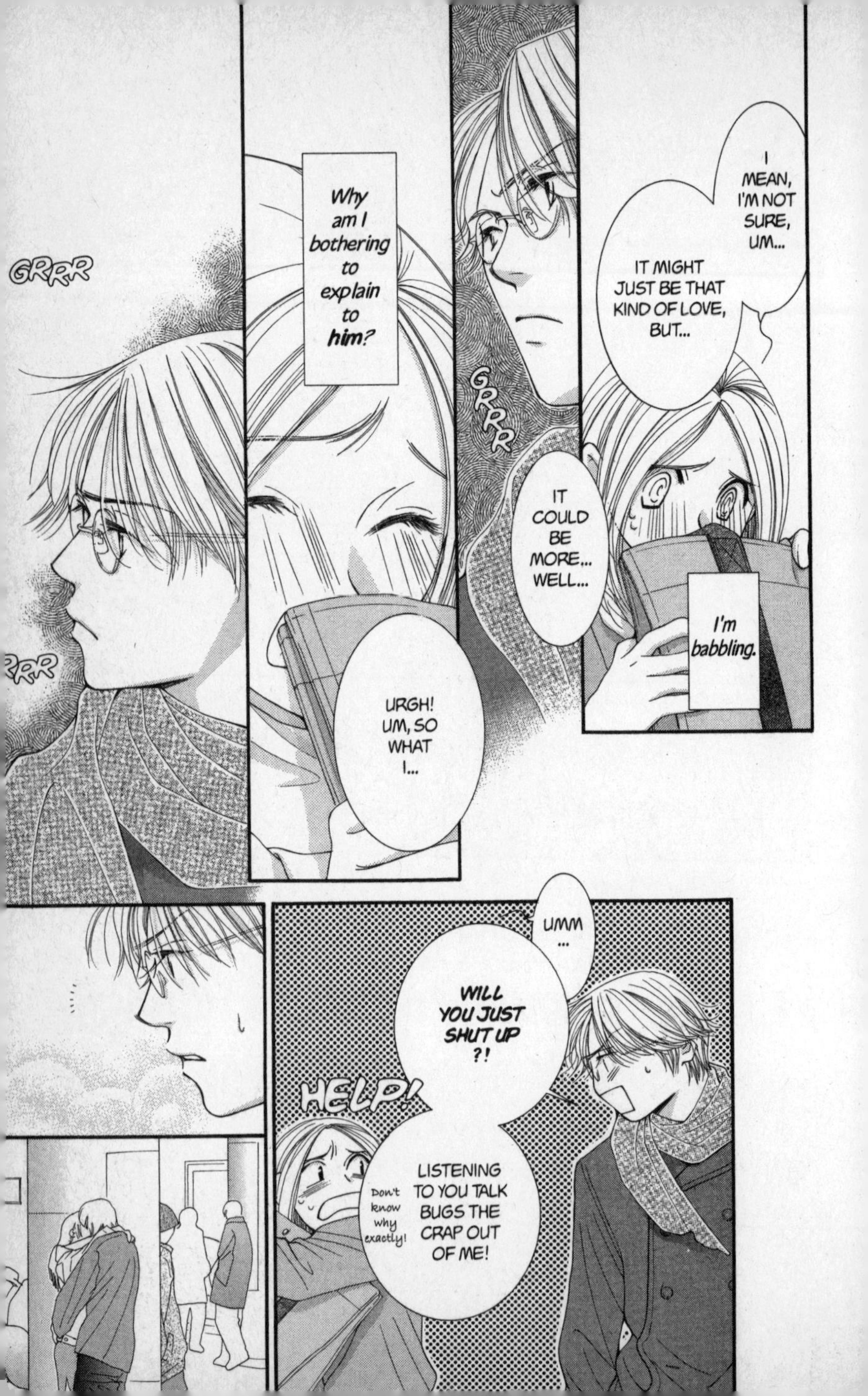
I MEAN, I'M NOT SURE, UM...
IT MIGHT JUST BE THAT KIND OF LOVE, BUT...
GRRR
IT COULD BE MORE... WELL...
I'm babbling.
Why am I bothering to explain to him?
URGH! UM, SO WHAT I...
GRRR
UMM...
WILL YOU JUST SHUT UP?!
HELP!
LISTENING TO YOU TALK BUGS THE CRAP OUT OF ME!
Don't know why exactly!

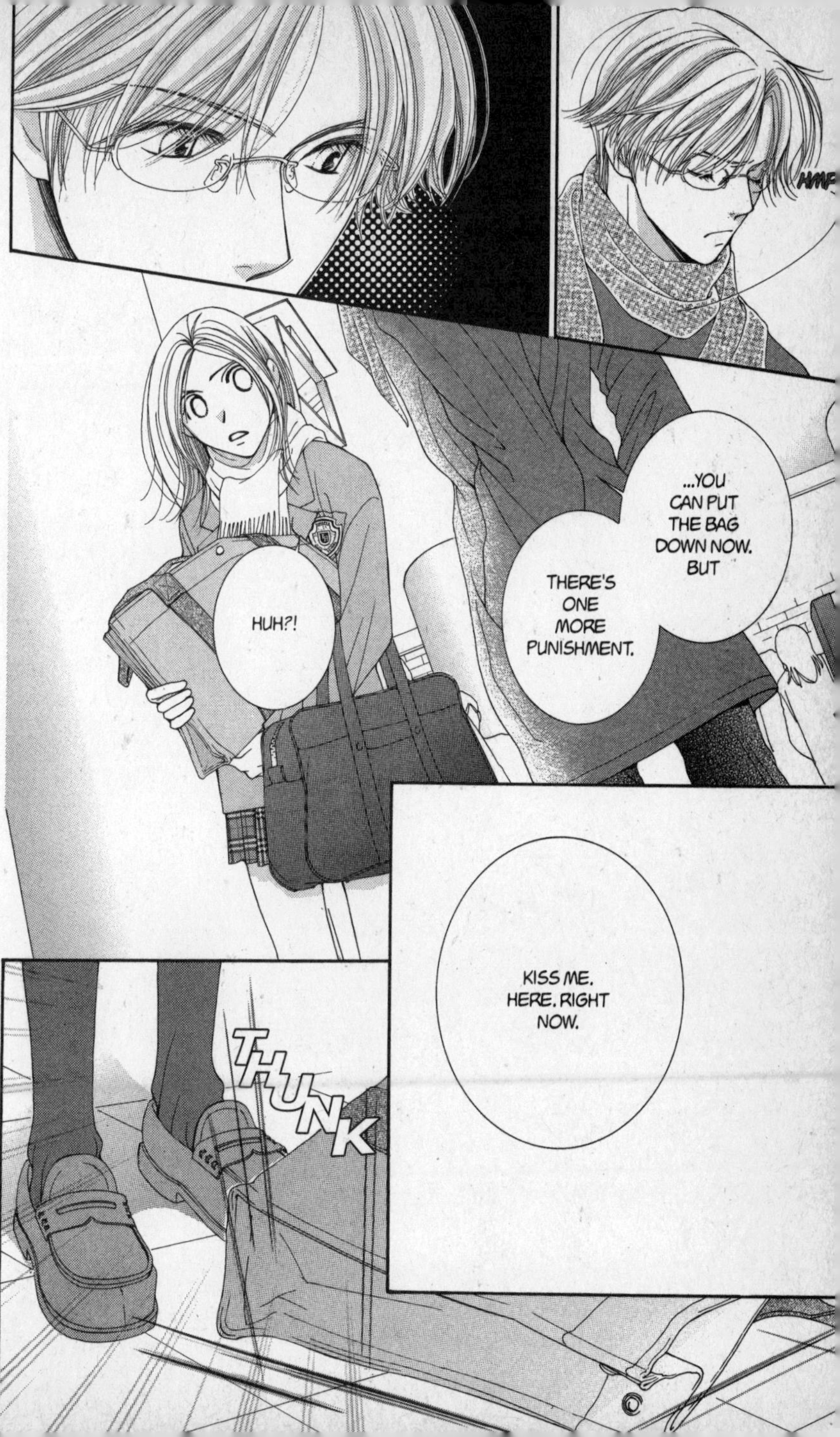
HMF
...YOU CAN PUT THE BAG DOWN NOW. BUT
THERE'S ONE MORE PUNISHMENT.
HUH?!
KISS ME. HERE. RIGHT NOW.
THUNK

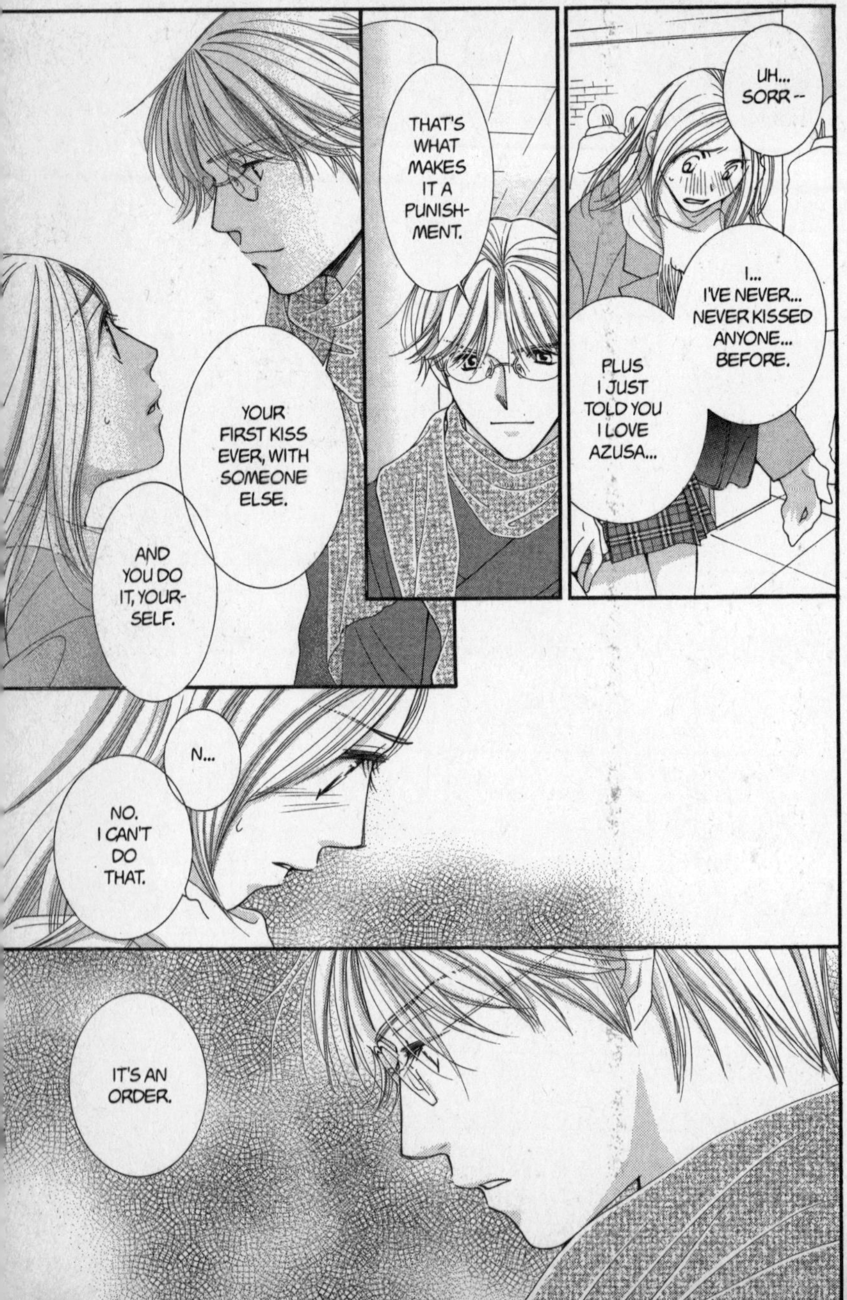
UH... SORR--
I... I'VE NEVER... NEVER KISSED ANYONE... BEFORE.
PLUS I JUST TOLD YOU I LOVE AZUSA...
THAT'S WHAT MAKES IT A PUNISH-MENT.
YOUR FIRST KISS EVER, WITH SOMEONE ELSE.
AND YOU DO IT, YOUR-SELF.
N...
NO. I CAN'T DO THAT.
IT'S AN ORDER.

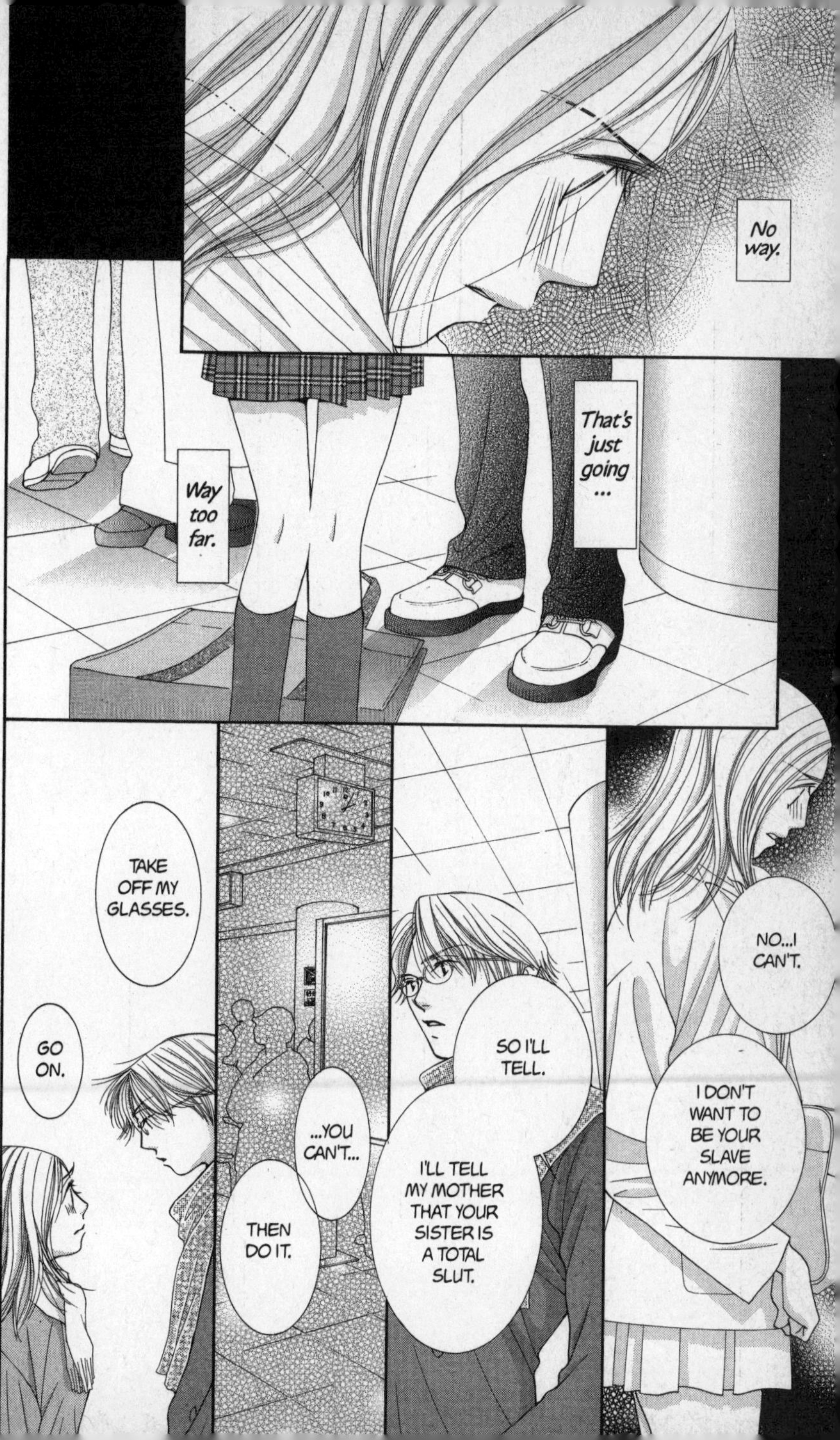
No way.
That's just going ...
Way too far.
NO...I CAN'T.
I DON'T WANT TO BE YOUR SLAVE ANYMORE.
SO I'LL TELL.
I'LL TELL MY MOTHER THAT YOUR SISTER IS A TOTAL SLUT.
...YOU CAN'T...
THEN DO IT.
TAKE OFF MY GLASSES.
GO ON.

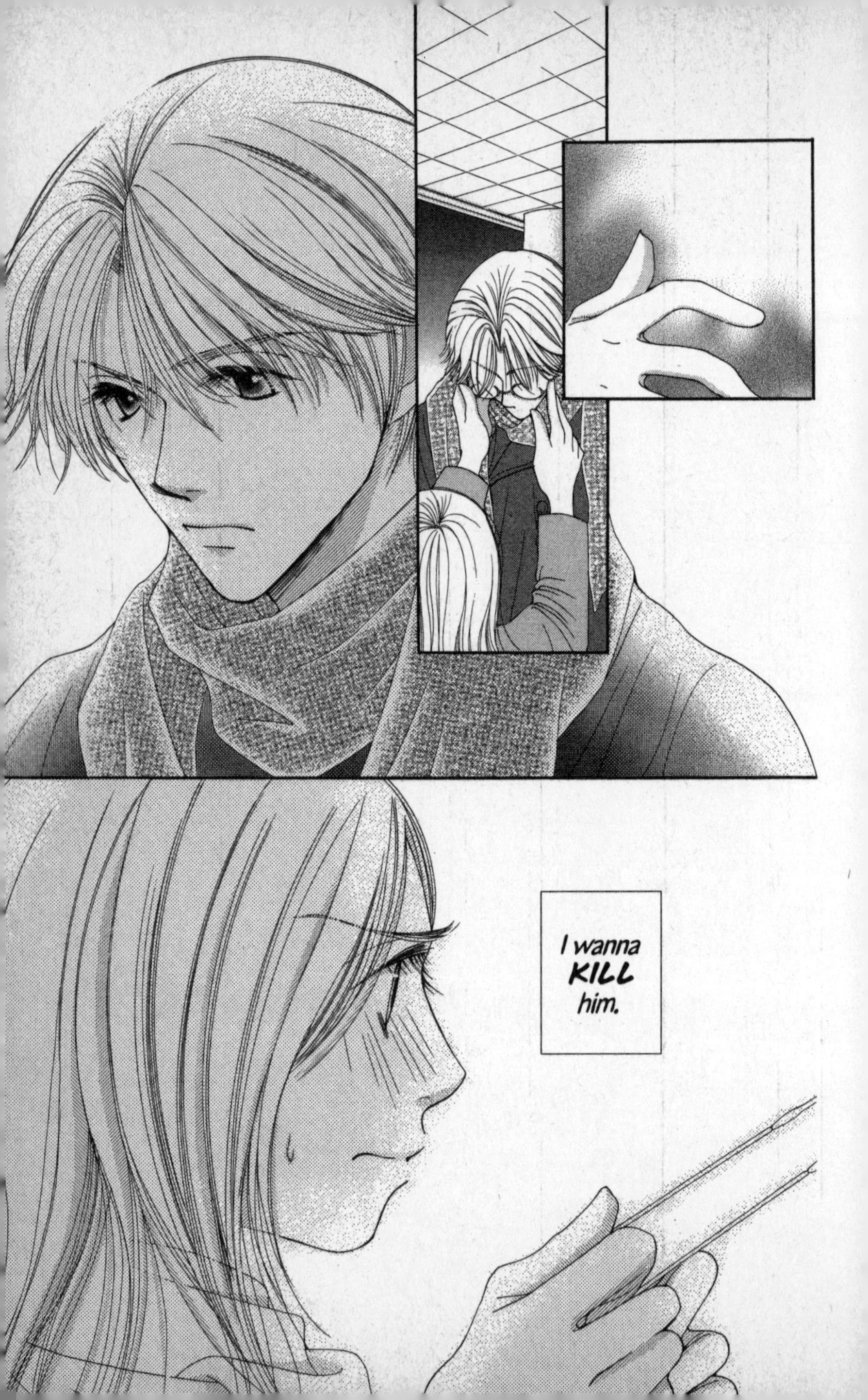
I wanna KILL him.

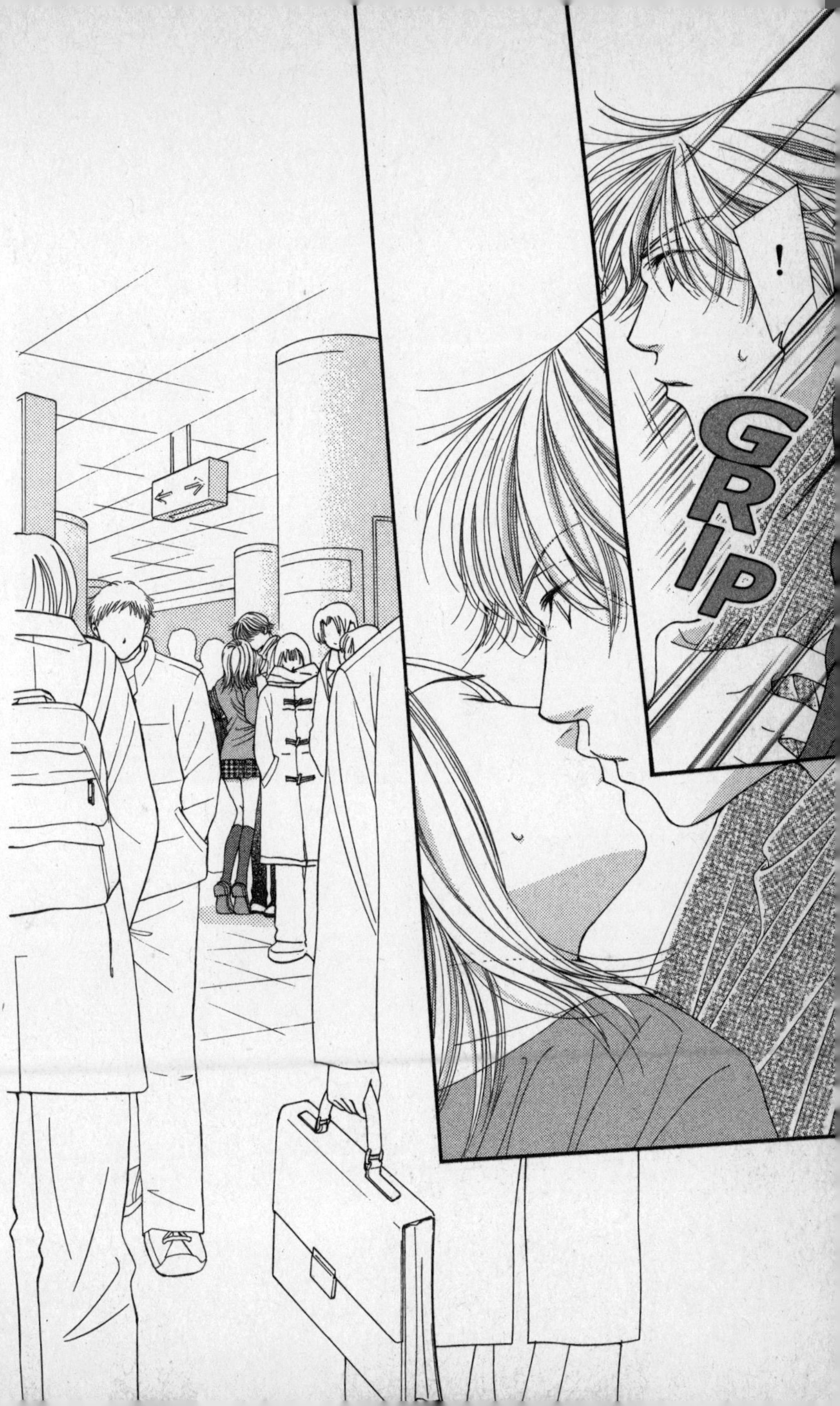
!
GRIP

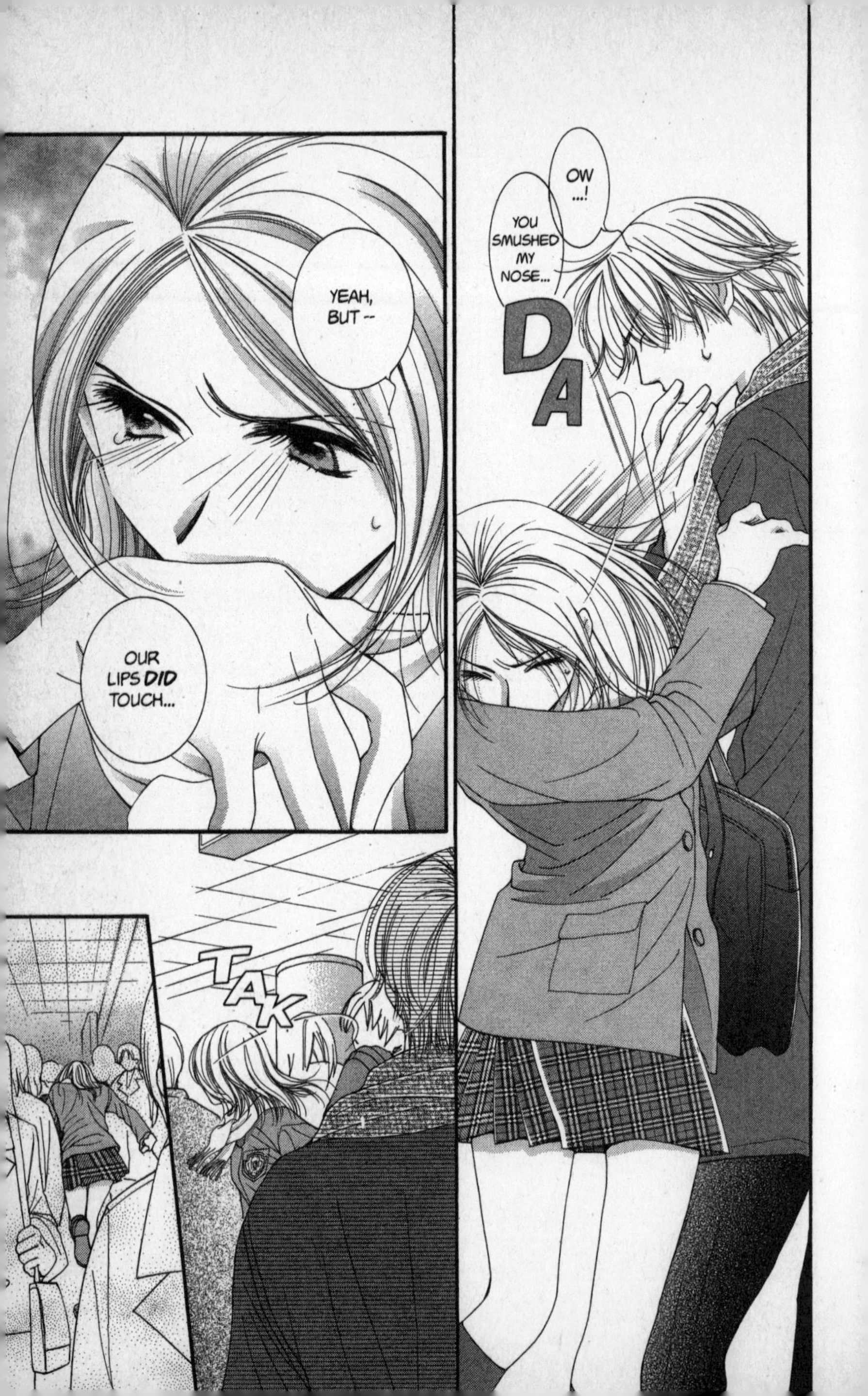
OW ...!
YOU SMUSHED MY NOSE...
DA
YEAH, BUT --
OUR LIPS DID TOUCH...
TAK

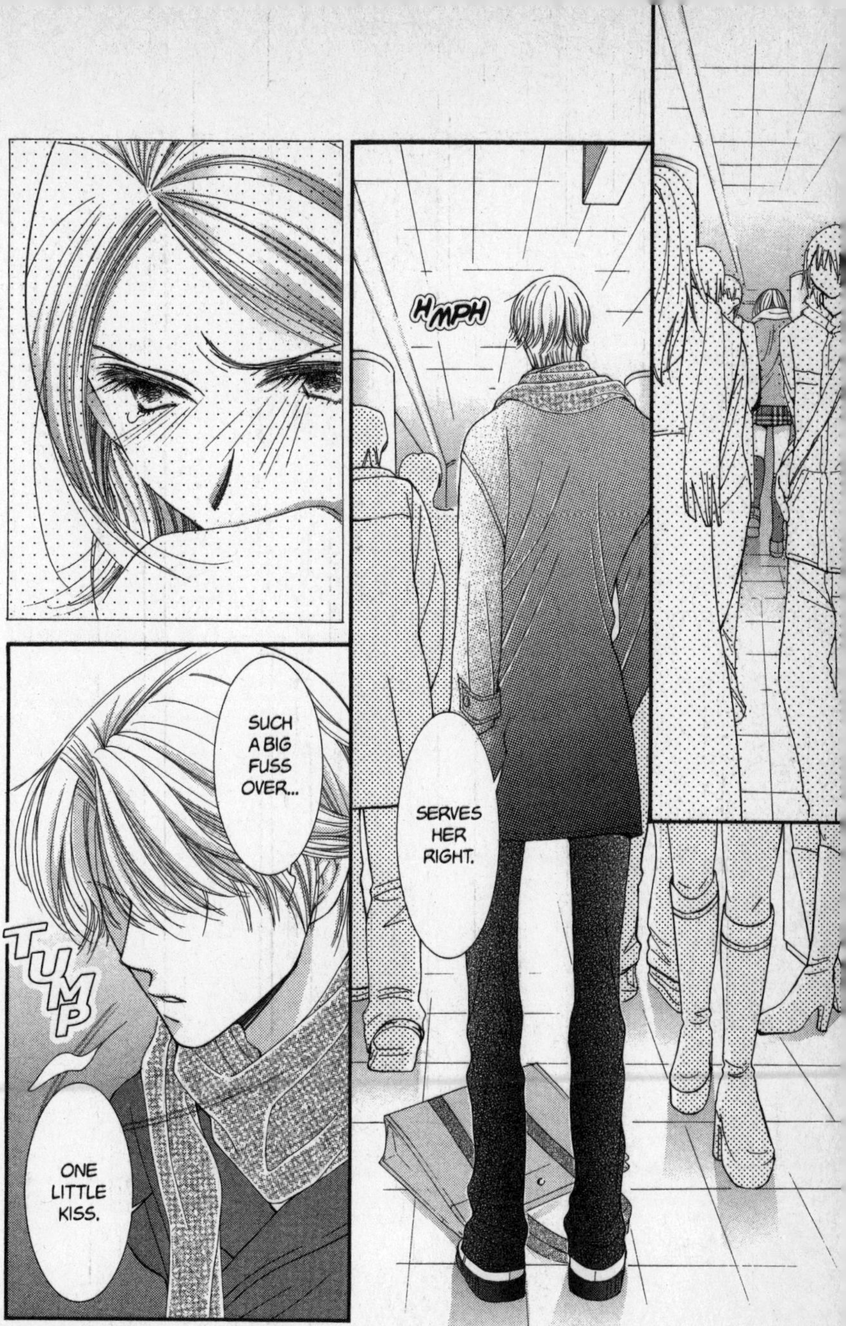
HMPH
SERVES HER RIGHT.
SUCH A BIG FUSS OVER...
TUMP
ONE LITTLE KISS.

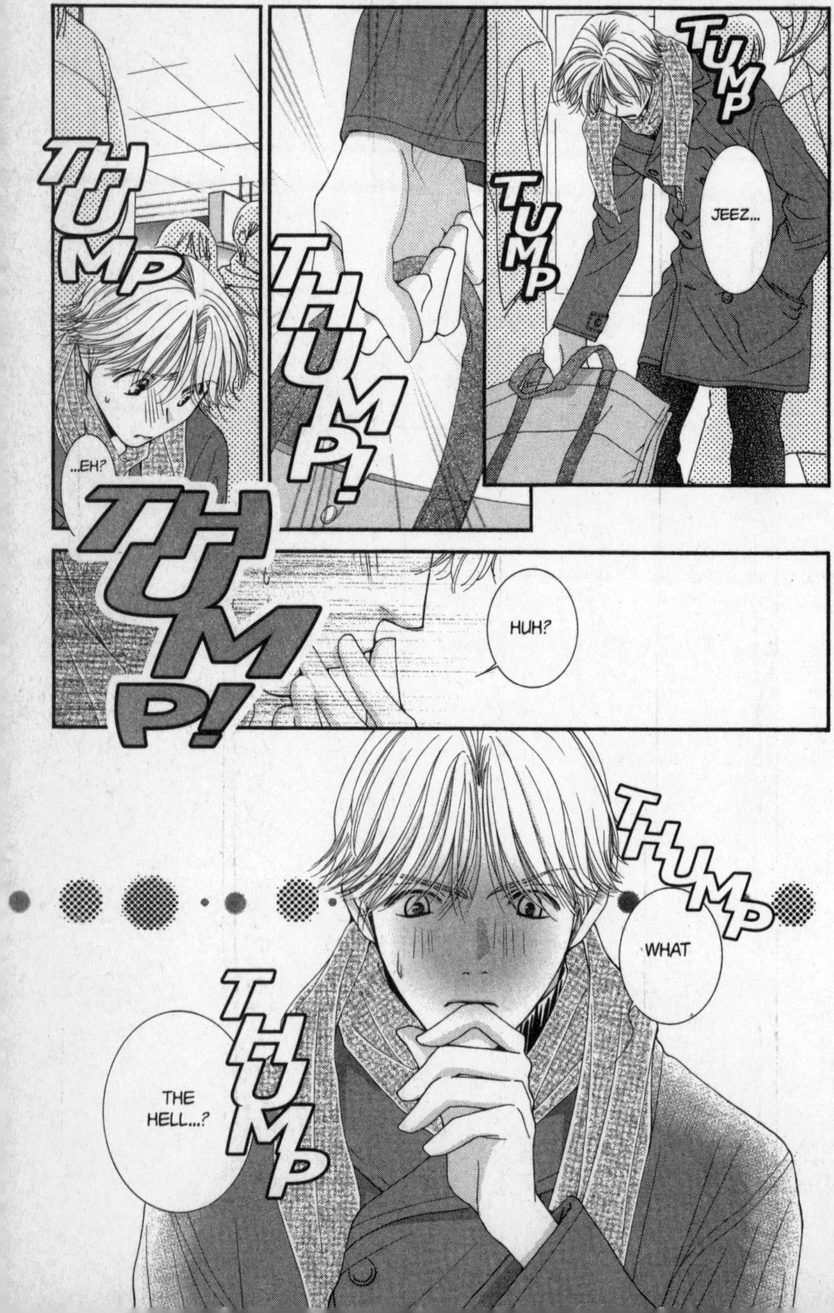
TUMP
JEEZ...
TUMP
THUMP!
THUMP
...EH?
THUMP!
HUH?
THUMP
WHAT
THUMP
THE HELL...?

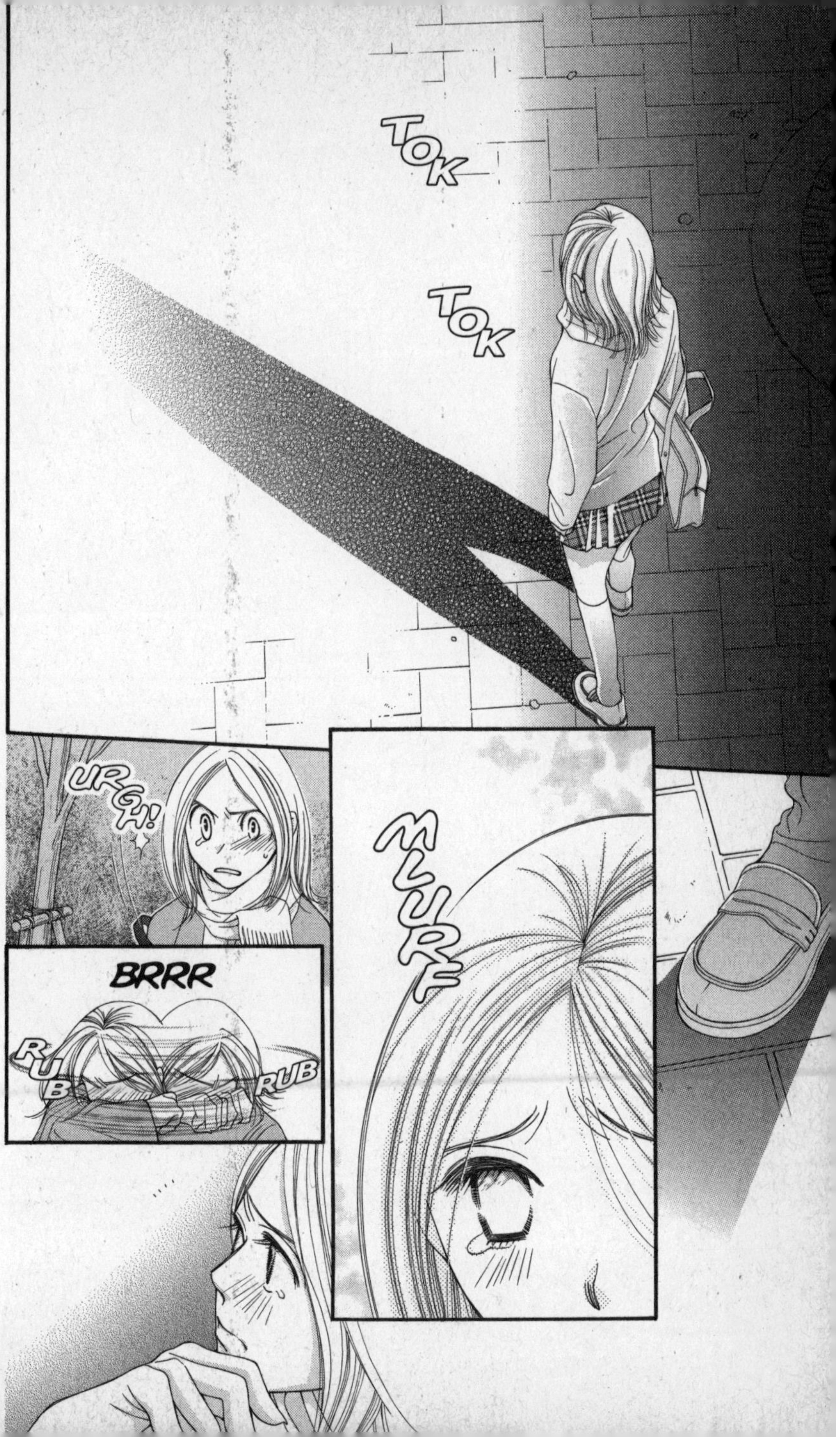
TOK
TOK
MLURF
URGH!
BRRR
RUB
RUB
....

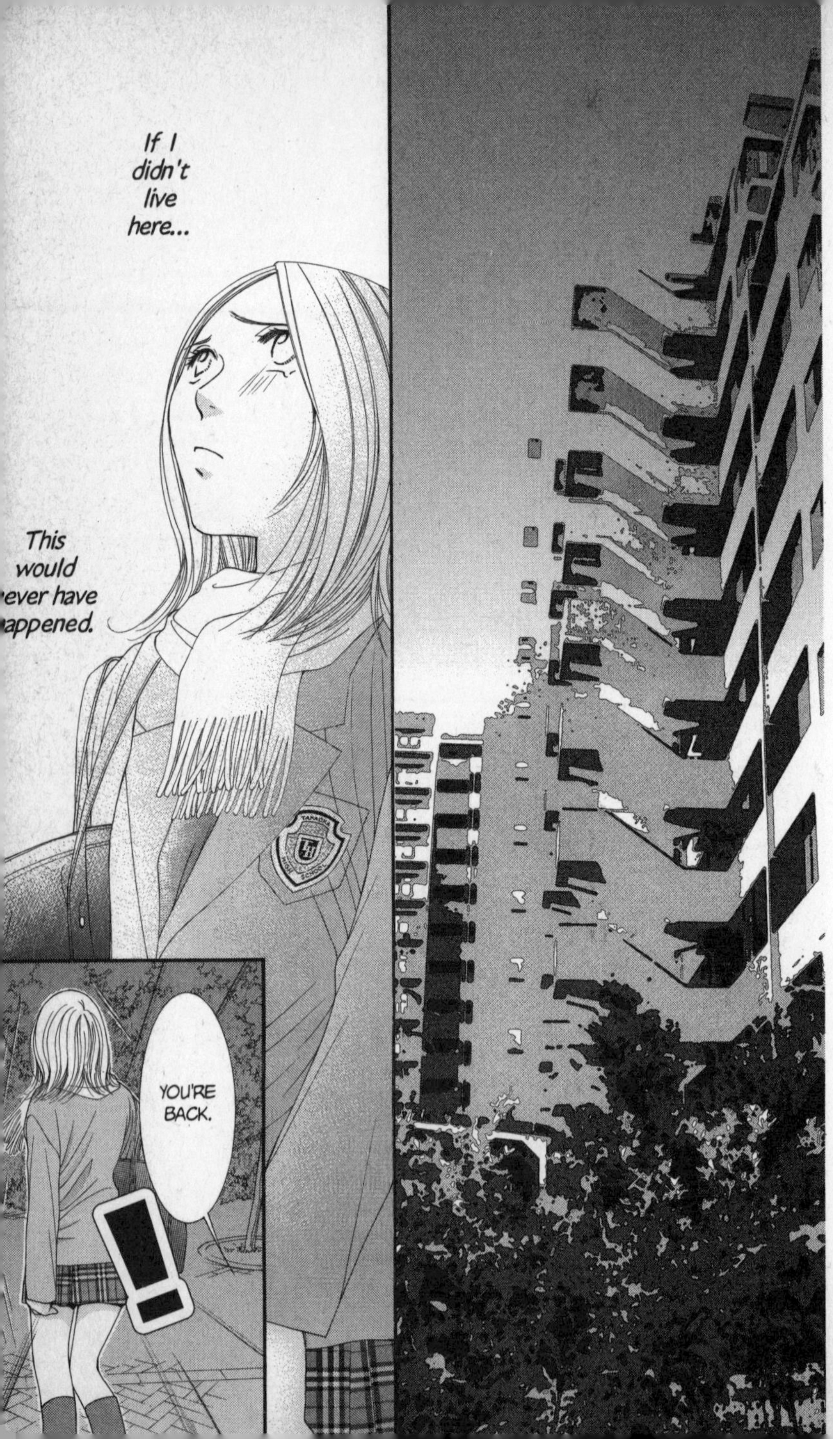
If I didn't live here...
This would ever have appened.
YOU'RE BACK.

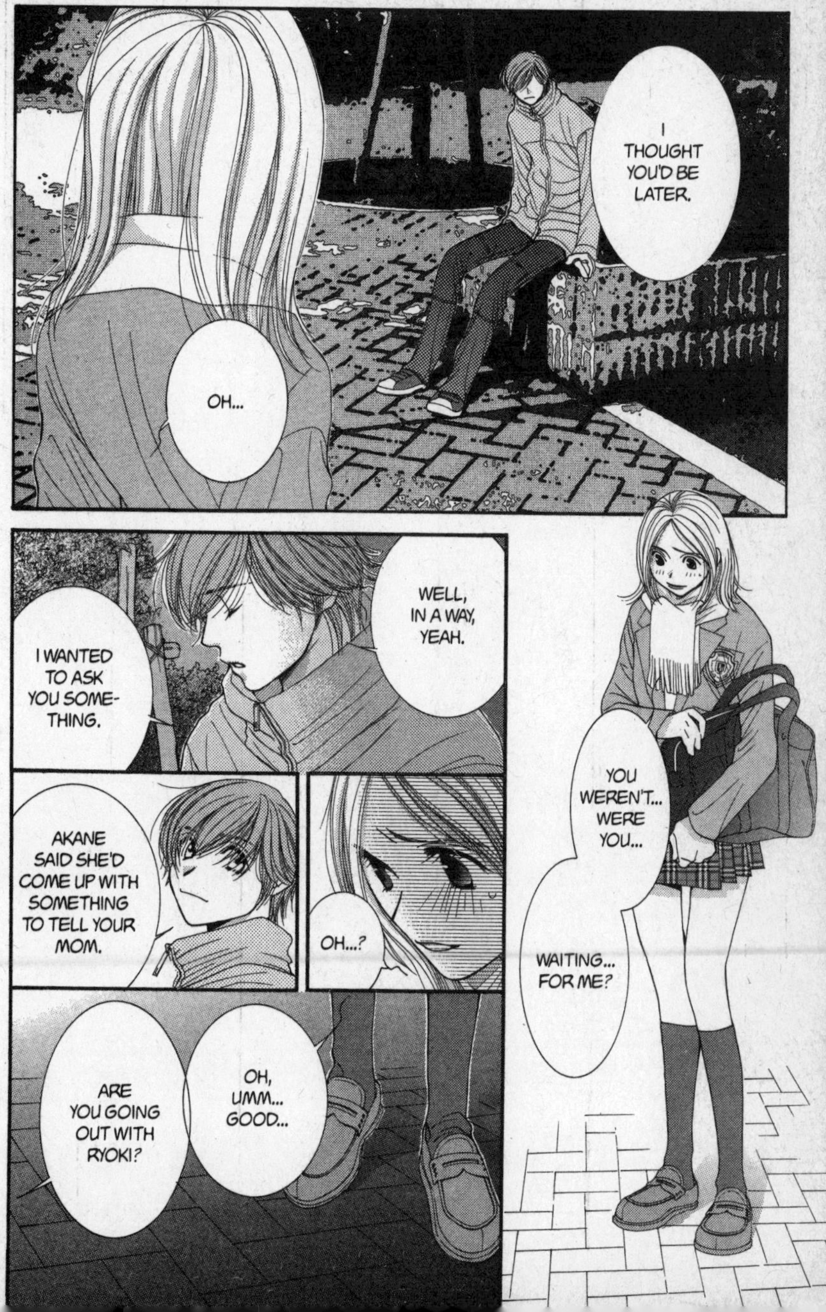
I THOUGHT YOU'D BE LATER.
OH...
YOU WEREN'T... WERE YOU...
WAITING... FOR ME?
WELL, IN A WAY, YEAH.
I WANTED TO ASK YOU SOMETHING.
OH...?
AKANE SAID SHE'D COME UP WITH SOMETHING TO TELL YOUR MOM.
OH, UMM... GOOD...
ARE YOU GOING OUT WITH RYOKI?

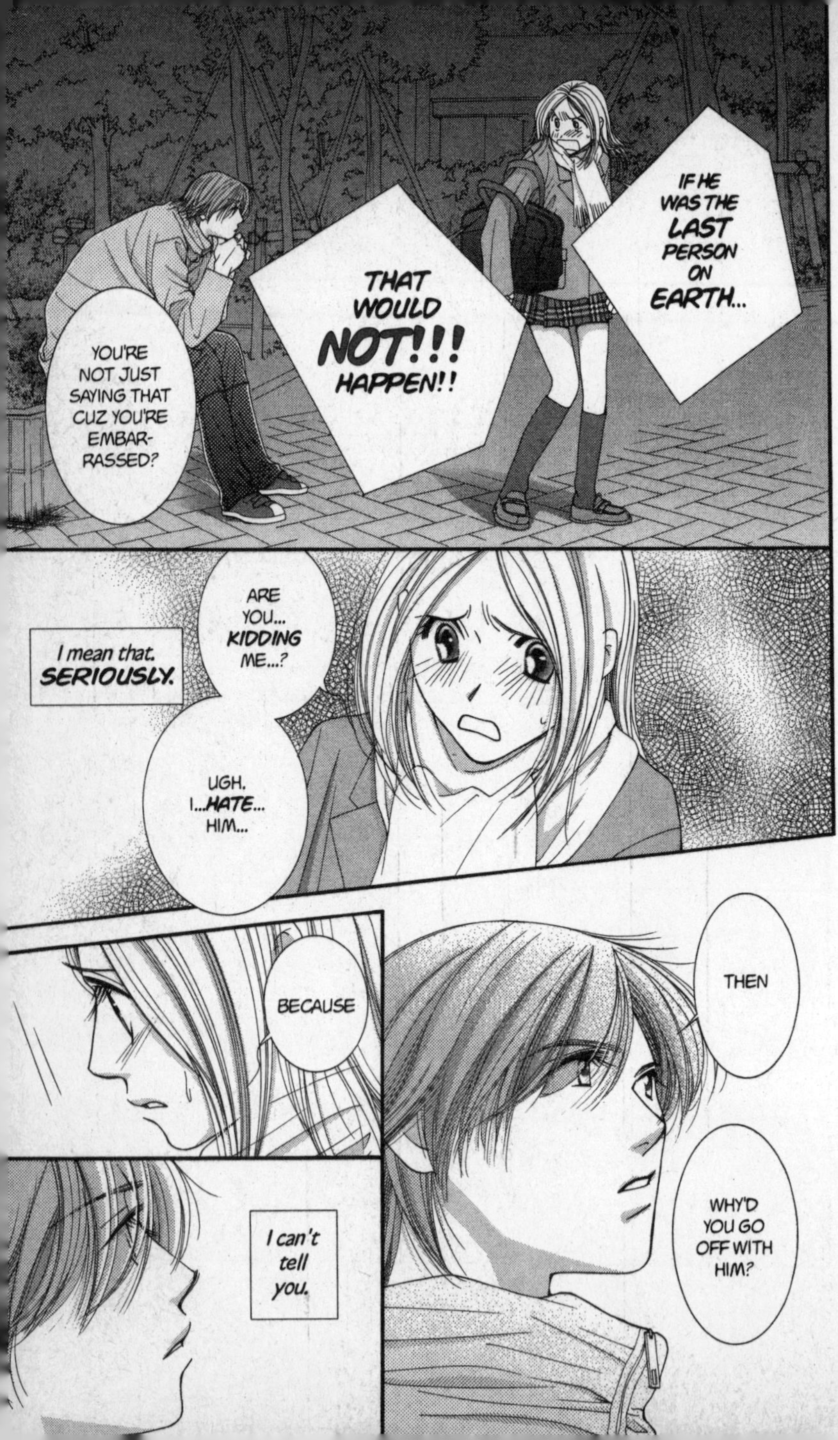
IF HE WAS THE LAST PERSON ON EARTH...
THAT WOULD NOT!!! HAPPEN!!
YOU'RE NOT JUST SAYING THAT CUZ YOU'RE EMBARRASSED?
ARE YOU... KIDDING ME...?
UGH. I...HATE... HIM...
I mean that. SERIOUSLY.
THEN
WHY'D YOU GO OFF WITH HIM?
BECAUSE
I can't tell you.

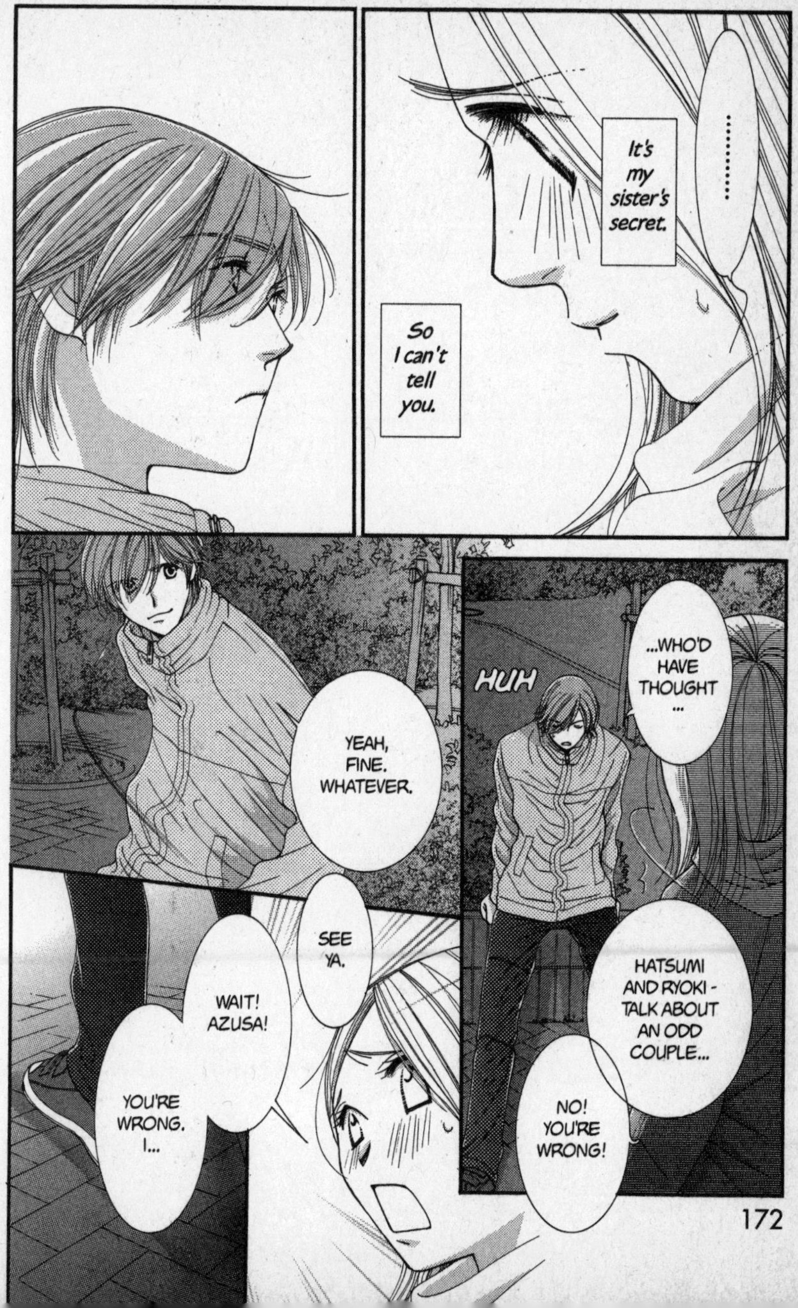

It's my sister's secret.
......
So I can't tell you.
HUH
...WHO'D HAVE THOUGHT ...
HATSUMI AND RYOKI - TALK ABOUT AN ODD COUPLE...
NO! YOU'RE WRONG!
YEAH, FINE. WHATEVER.
SEE YA.
WAIT! AZUSA!
YOU'RE WRONG. I...

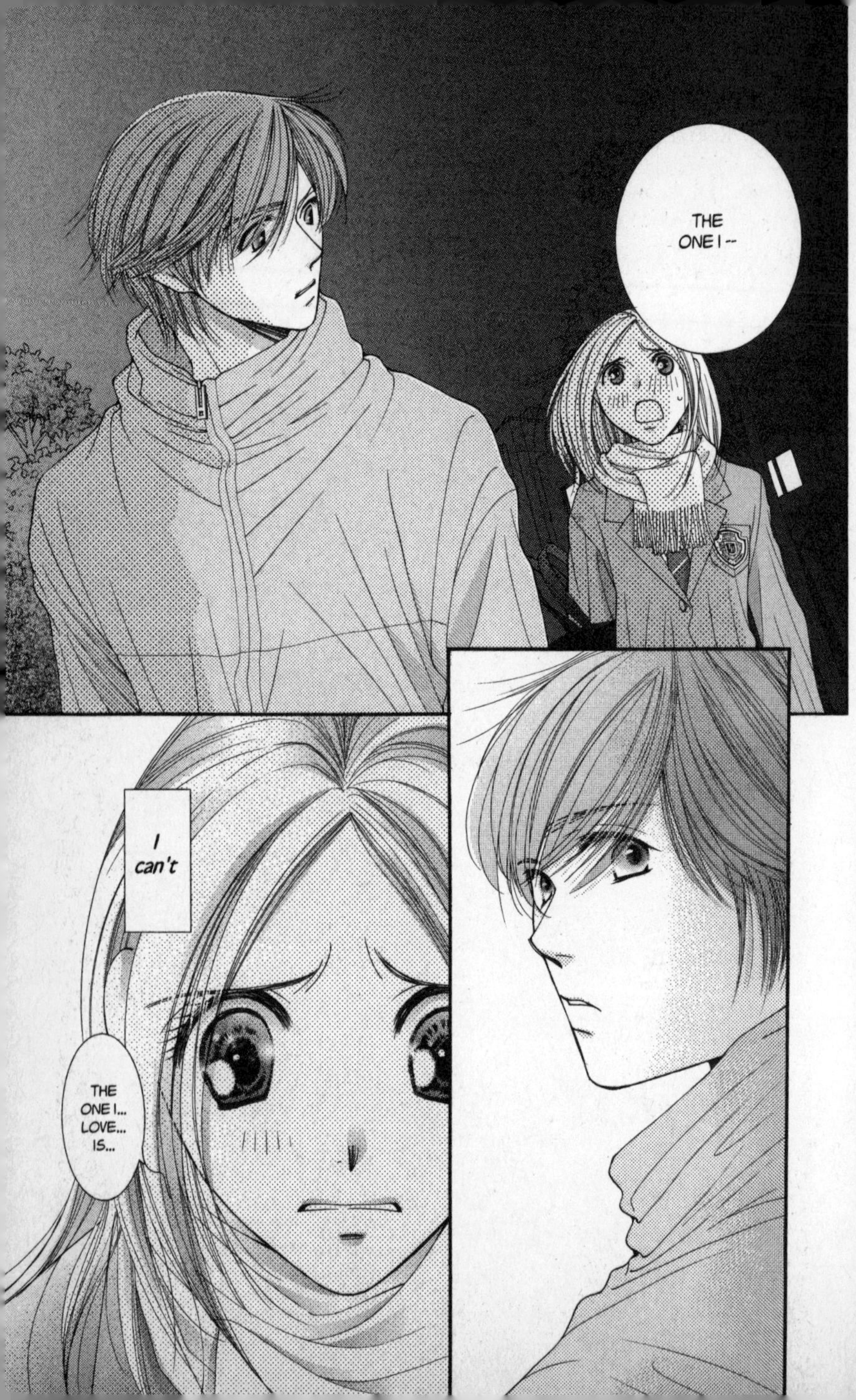
THE ONE I --
THE ONE I... LOVE... IS...
I can't

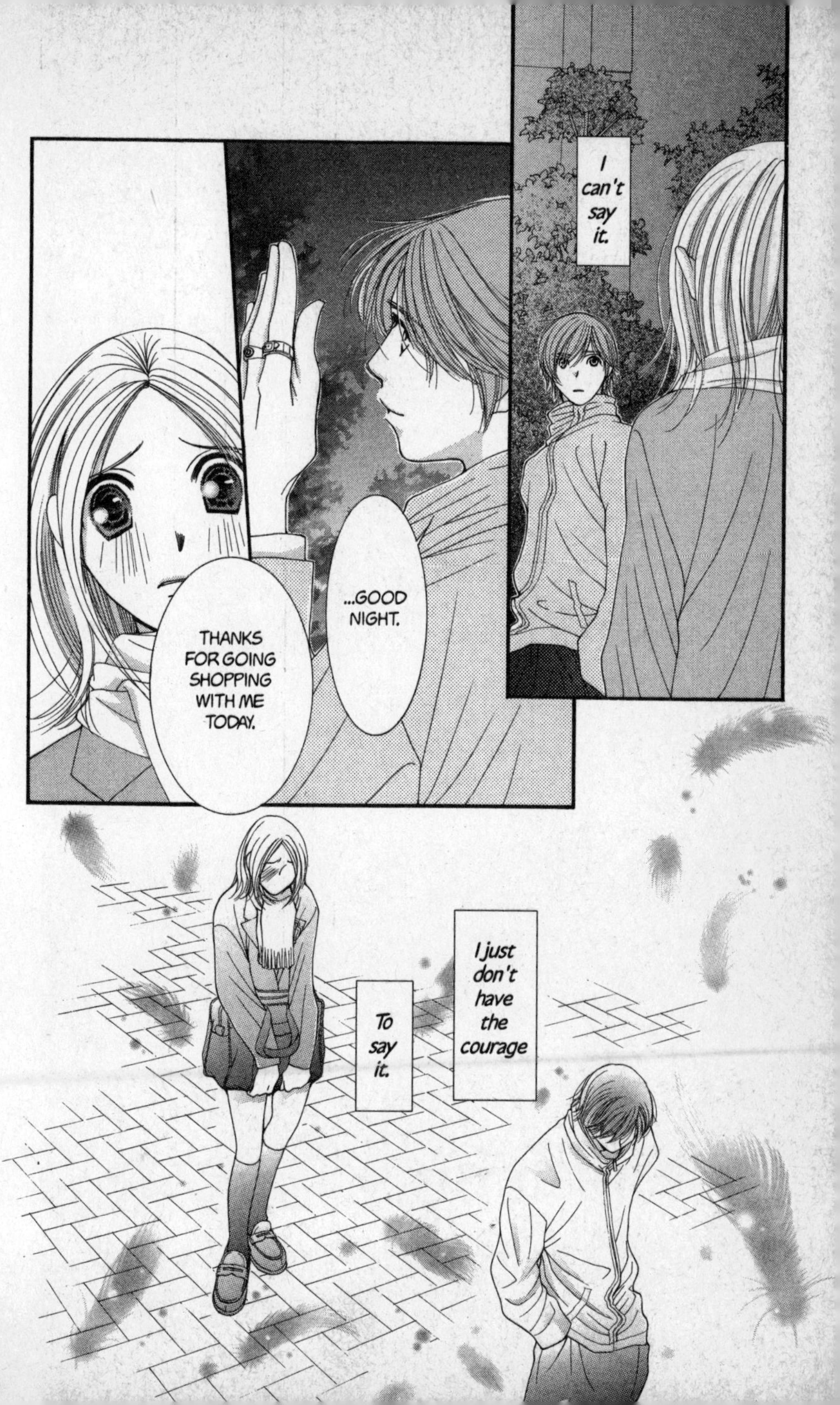
I can't say it.
...GOOD NIGHT.
THANKS FOR GOING SHOPPING WITH ME TODAY.
I just don't have the courage
To say it.

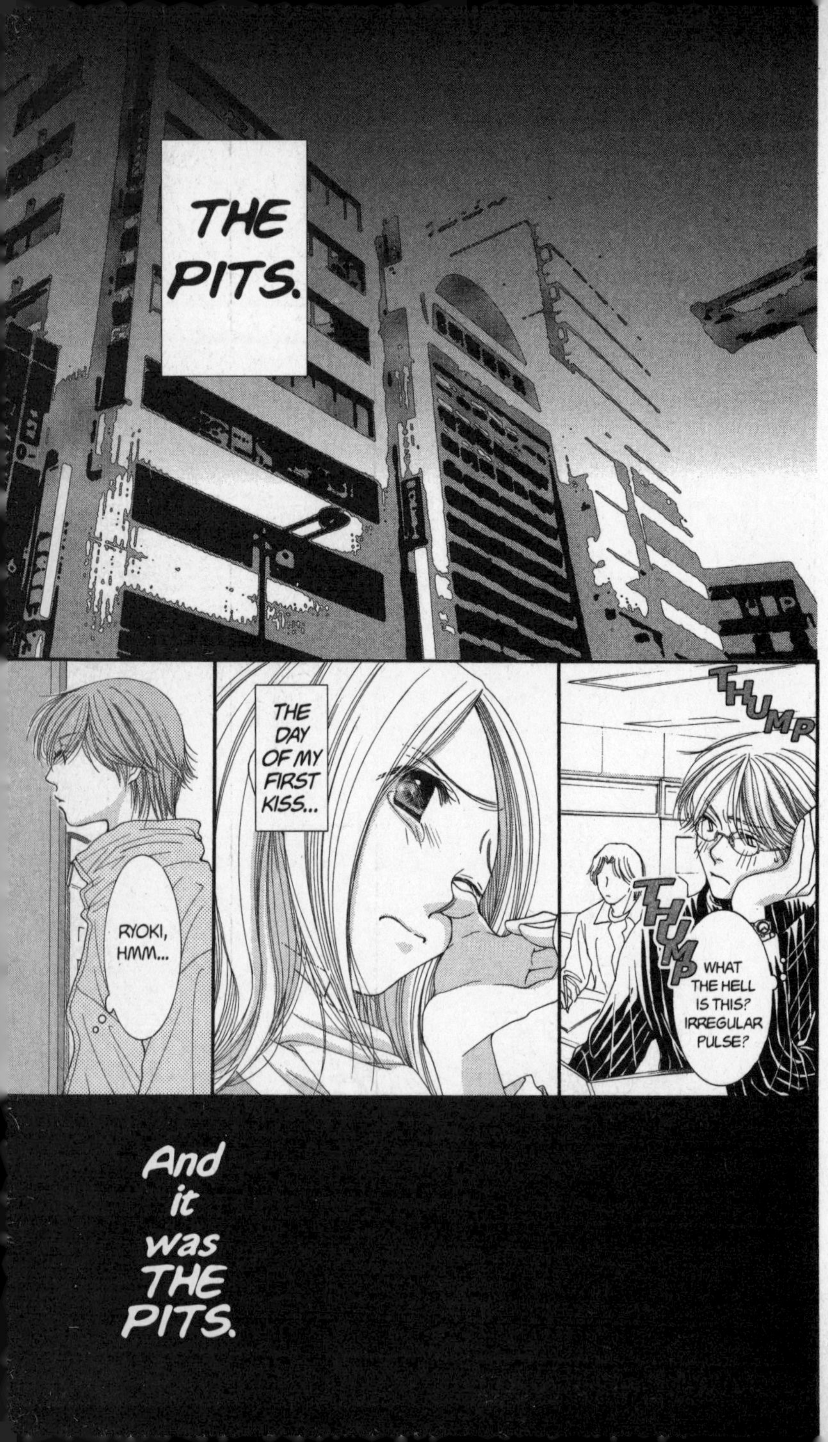
THE PITS.
THUMP
THUMP
WHAT THE HELL IS THIS? IRREGULAR PULSE?
THE DAY OF MY FIRST KISS...
RYOKI, HMM...
And it was THE PITS.

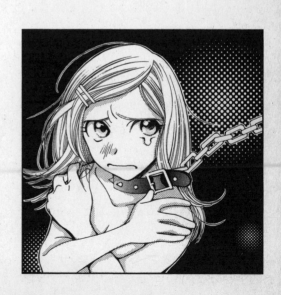

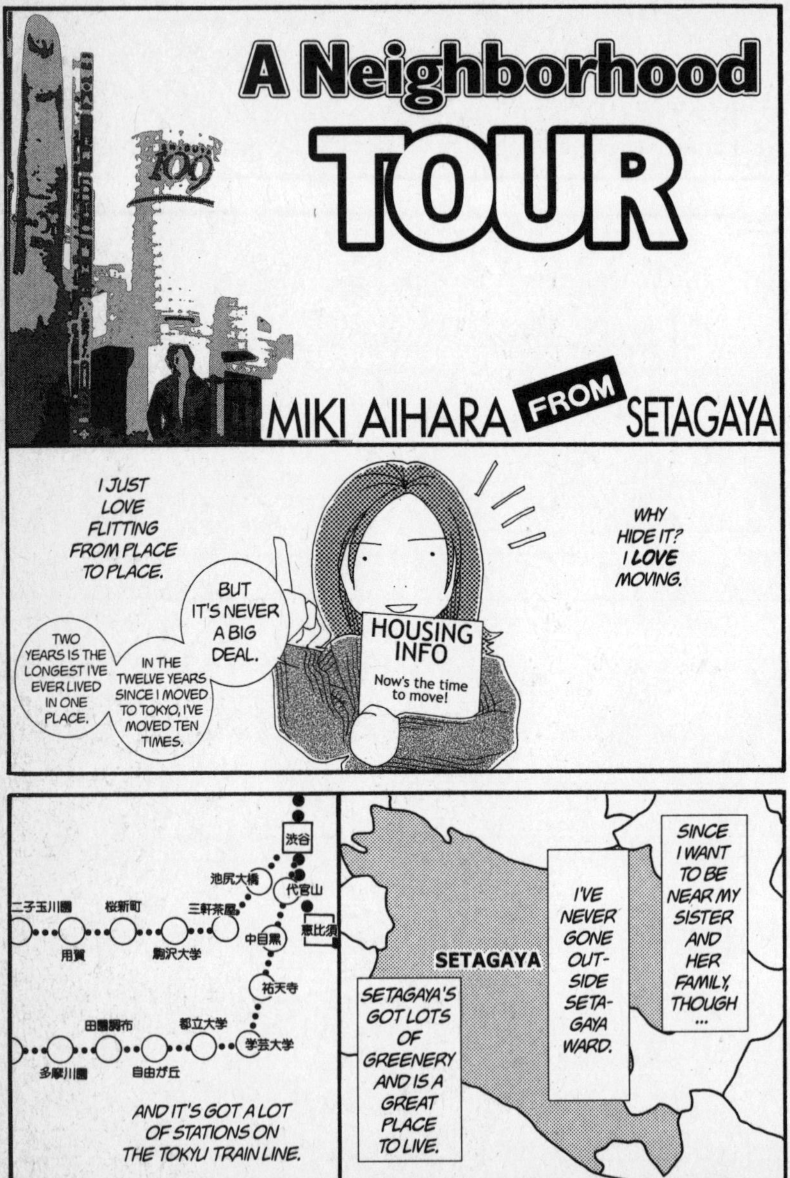
A Neighborhood TOUR
MIKI AIHARA FROM SETAGAYA
109
WHY HIDE IT? I LOVE MOVING.
I JUST LOVE FLITTING FROM PLACE TO PLACE.
HOUSING INFO
Now's the time to move!
BUT IT'S NEVER A BIG DEAL.
IN THE TWELVE YEARS SINCE I MOVED TO TOKYO, I'VE MOVED TEN TIMES.
TWO YEARS IS THE LONGEST I'VE EVER LIVED IN ONE PLACE.
SINCE I WANT TO BE NEAR MY SISTER AND HER FAMILY, THOUGH...
I'VE NEVER GONE OUTSIDE SETAGAYA WARD.
SETAGAYA
SETAGAYA'S GOT LOTS OF GREENERY AND IS A GREAT PLACE TO LIVE.
渋谷
池尻大橋
代官山
三軒茶屋
桜新町
二子玉川園
恵比須
中目黒
用賀
駒沢大学
祐天寺
都立大学
田園調布
学芸大学
多摩川園
自由が丘
AND IT'S GOT A LOT OF STATIONS ON THE TOKYU TRAIN LINE.

• SUPPORT: ASSISTANT 4 (NISSEY)

• LAYOUT HELP: ASSISTANT 3 (EMILY VOLCANO)

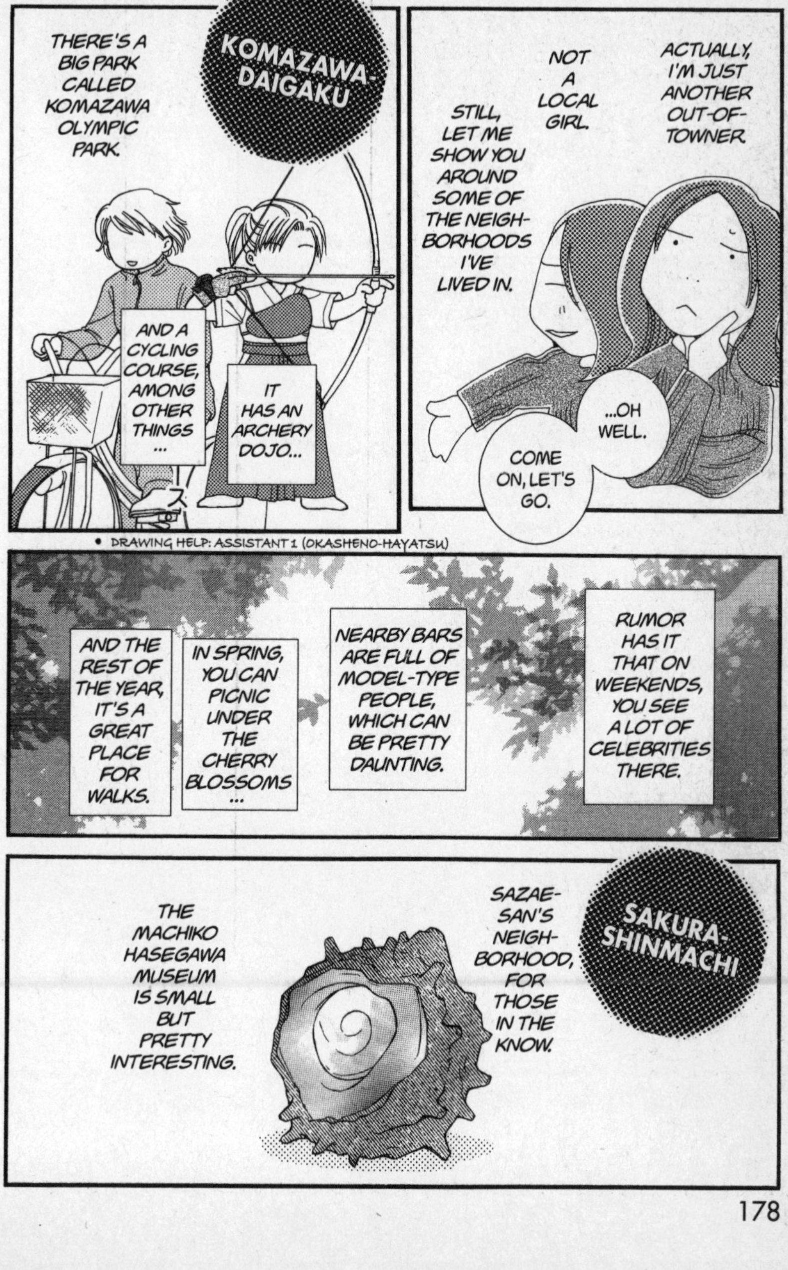
ACTUALLY, I'M JUST ANOTHER OUT-OF-TOWNER.
NOT A LOCAL GIRL.
STILL, LET ME SHOW YOU AROUND SOME OF THE NEIGHBORHOODS I'VE LIVED IN.
...OH WELL.
COME ON, LET'S GO.
KOMAZAWA-DAIGAKU
THERE'S A BIG PARK CALLED KOMAZAWA OLYMPIC PARK.
IT HAS AN ARCHERY DOJO...
AND A CYCLING COURSE, AMONG OTHER THINGS...
ス
• DRAWING HELP: ASSISTANT 1 (OKASHENO-HAYATSU)
RUMOR HAS IT THAT ON WEEKENDS, YOU SEE A LOT OF CELEBRITIES THERE.
NEARBY BARS ARE FULL OF MODEL-TYPE PEOPLE, WHICH CAN BE PRETTY DAUNTING.
IN SPRING, YOU CAN PICNIC UNDER THE CHERRY BLOSSOMS...
AND THE REST OF THE YEAR, IT'S A GREAT PLACE FOR WALKS.
SAKURA-SHINMACHI
SAZAE-SAN'S NEIGHBORHOOD, FOR THOSE IN THE KNOW.
THE MACHIKO HASEGAWA MUSEUM IS SMALL BUT PRETTY INTERESTING.

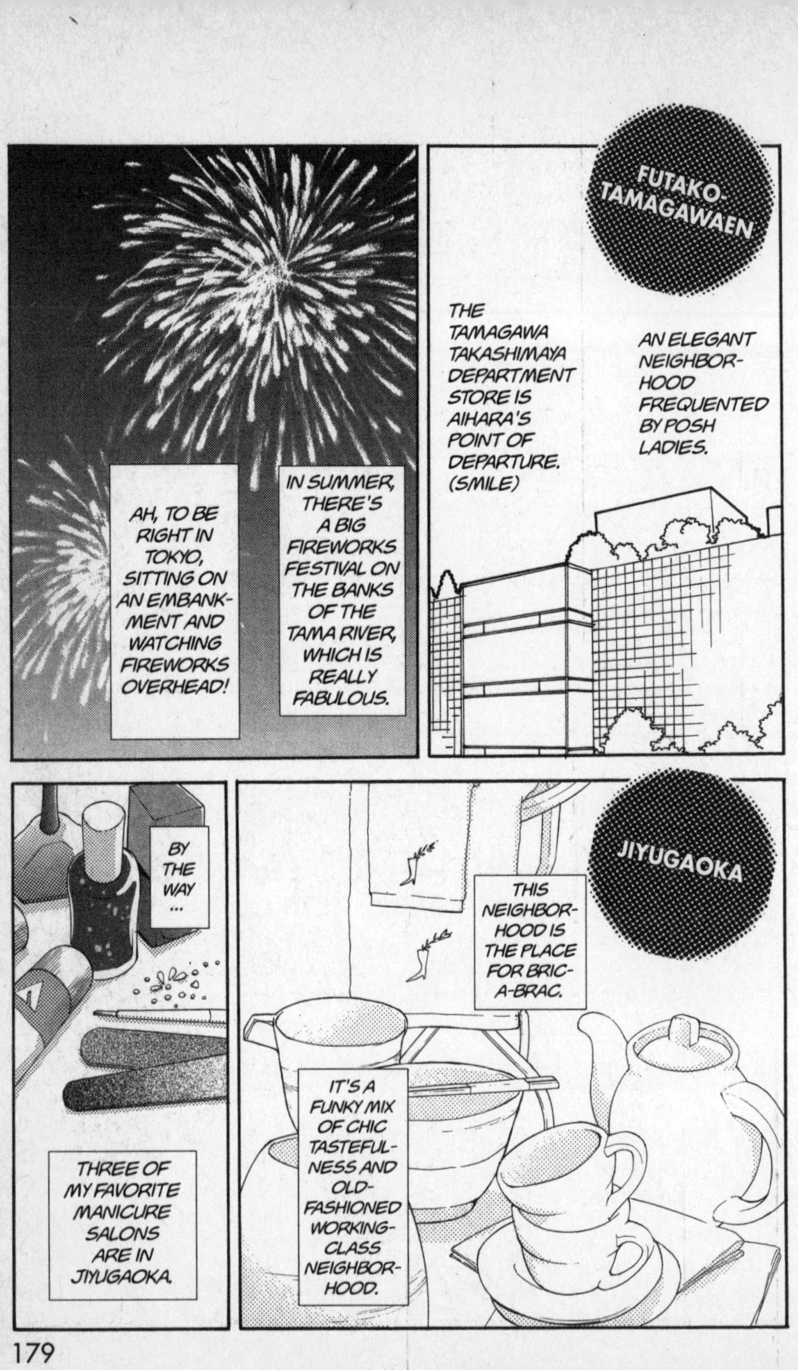
FUTAKO-TAMAGAWAEN
AN ELEGANT NEIGHBOR-HOOD FREQUENTED BY POSH LADIES.
THE TAMAGAWA TAKASHIMAYA DEPARTMENT STORE IS AIHARA'S POINT OF DEPARTURE. (SMILE)
IN SUMMER, THERE'S A BIG FIREWORKS FESTIVAL ON THE BANKS OF THE TAMA RIVER, WHICH IS REALLY FABULOUS.
AH, TO BE RIGHT IN TOKYO, SITTING ON AN EMBANK-MENT AND WATCHING FIREWORKS OVERHEAD!
JIYUGAOKA
THIS NEIGHBOR-HOOD IS THE PLACE FOR BRIC-A-BRAC.
IT'S A FUNKY MIX OF CHIC TASTEFUL-NESS AND OLD-FASHIONED WORKING-CLASS NEIGHBOR-HOOD.
BY THE WAY ...
THREE OF MY FAVORITE MANICURE SALONS ARE IN JIYUGAOKA.

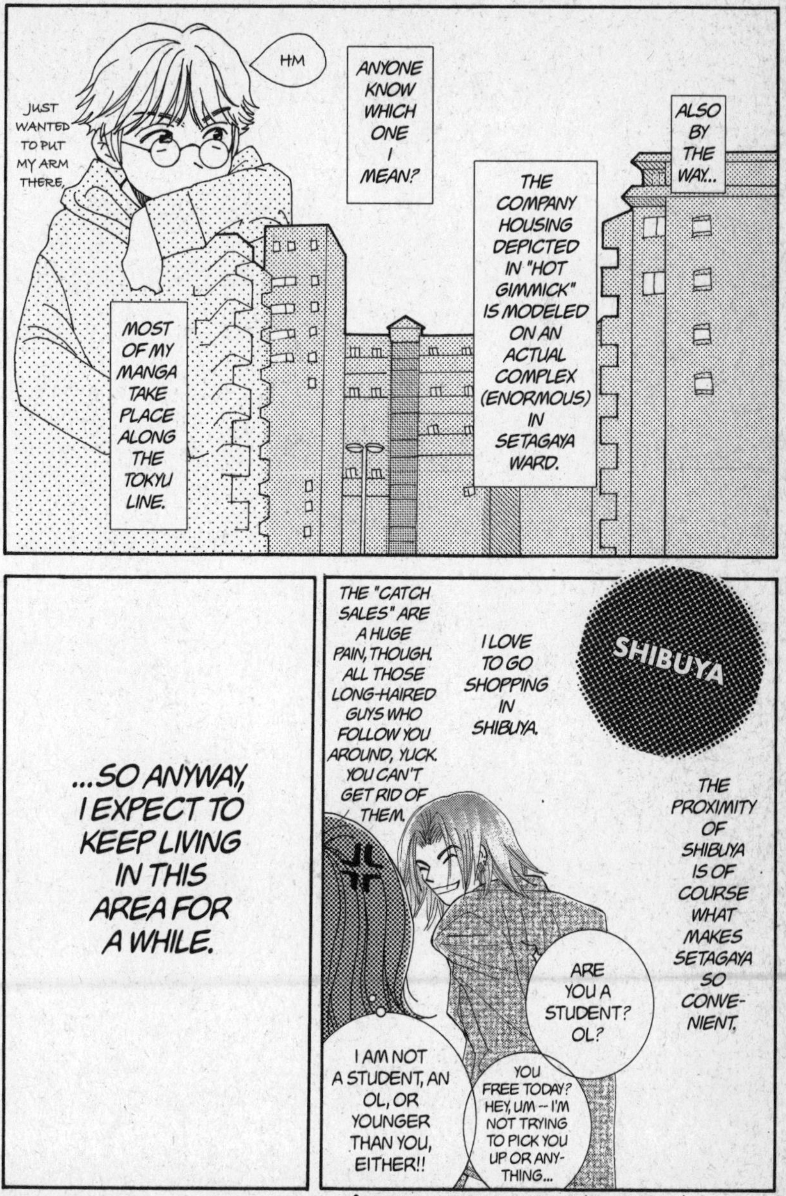
ALSO BY THE WAY...
THE COMPANY HOUSING DEPICTED IN "HOT GIMMICK" IS MODELED ON AN ACTUAL COMPLEX (ENORMOUS) IN SETAGAYA WARD.
ANYONE KNOW WHICH ONE I MEAN?
HM
JUST WANTED TO PUT MY ARM THERE.
MOST OF MY MANGA TAKE PLACE ALONG THE TOKYU LINE.
SHIBUYA
THE PROXIMITY OF SHIBUYA IS OF COURSE WHAT MAKES SETAGAYA SO CONVENIENT.
I LOVE TO GO SHOPPING IN SHIBUYA.
THE "CATCH SALES" ARE A HUGE PAIN, THOUGH. ALL THOSE LONG-HAIRED GUYS WHO FOLLOW YOU AROUND, YUCK. YOU CAN'T GET RID OF THEM.
ARE YOU A STUDENT? OL?
YOU FREE TODAY? HEY, UM -- I'M NOT TRYING TO PICK YOU UP OR ANYTHING...
I AM NOT A STUDENT, AN OL, OR YOUNGER THAN YOU, EITHER!!
...SO ANYWAY, I EXPECT TO KEEP LIVING IN THIS AREA FOR A WHILE.

• DRAWING SUPPORT: ASSISTANT 2 (LILY OKAZATO)

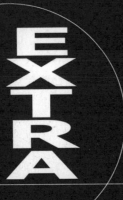

EXTRA GIMMICK

Thank you for buying Hot Gimmick Vol. 1.

My name is Miki Aihara.

Here, just for you graphic novel readers, is all
that extra information that's so hard to put into
the actual story.

Read on!

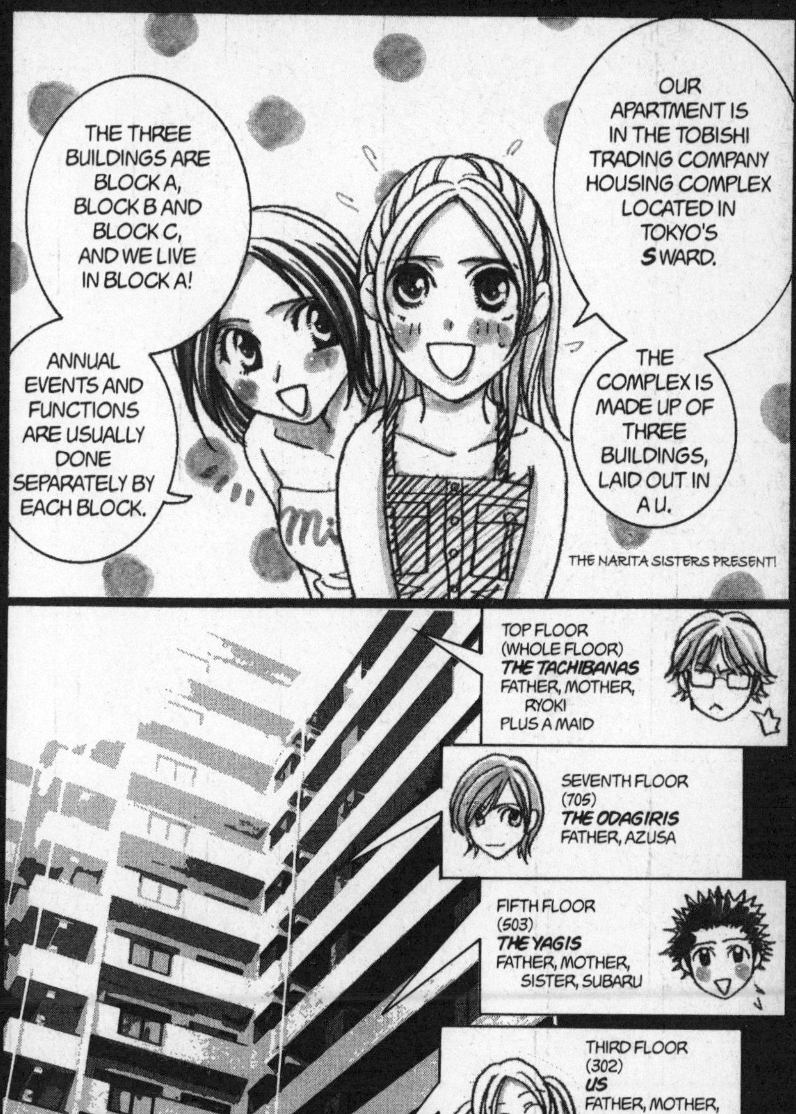
OUR APARTMENT IS IN THE TOBISHI TRADING COMPANY HOUSING COMPLEX LOCATED IN TOKYO'S S WARD.
THE COMPLEX IS MADE UP OF THREE BUILDINGS, LAID OUT IN A U.
THE THREE BUILDINGS ARE BLOCK A, BLOCK B AND BLOCK C, AND WE LIVE IN BLOCK A!
ANNUAL EVENTS AND FUNCTIONS ARE USUALLY DONE SEPARATELY BY EACH BLOCK.
THE NARITA SISTERS PRESENT!
TOP FLOOR (WHOLE FLOOR) THE TACHIBANAS FATHER, MOTHER, RYOKI PLUS A MAID
SEVENTH FLOOR (705) THE ODAGIRIS FATHER, AZUSA
FIFTH FLOOR (503) THE YAGIS FATHER, MOTHER, SISTER, SUBARU
THIRD FLOOR (302) US FATHER, MOTHER, SHINOGU, AKANE PLUS MY LITTLE BROTHER AND ME
WE'RE A BIG FAMILY (WAAH)

THE NARITA FAMILY

SHINOGU, 19 (OLDER BROTHER)

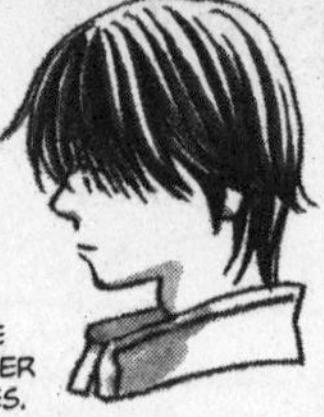

- FRESHMAN LAW STUDENT AT HITOTSUBASHI UNIVERSITY.
- 178 CM TALL, 65 g
- NOT HOME MUCH BECAUSE OF CLUB ACTIVITIES AND PART-TIME JOBS. ALSO SPENDS NIGHTS OVER AT FRIENDS' PLACES SOMETIMES.
- WORKS ***A LOT***! TUTORS ELEMENTARY AND JUNIOR HIGH STUDENTS, AND HAS A NIGHT-TIME JOB TOO.
- SAVING MONEY SO HE CAN MOVE OUT AND LIVE ALONE AS SOON AS HE CAN (SECRET)
- NO GIRLFRIEND (SPECIAL REASON)

兄

TORU (DAD)

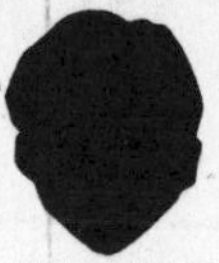

- AWAY ON SHORT-TERM TRANSFER. ONLY COMES HOME ABOUT ONCE A MONTH.

SHIHOKO (MOM)

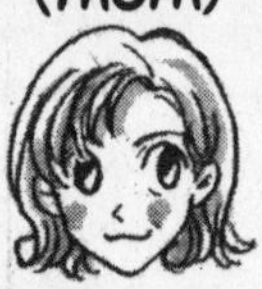

- FOR THE SAKE OF HER HUSBAND'S CAREER, FOR SELF-PROTECTION, AND FOR HER YOUNGER SON'S ENTRANCE EXAM PROSPECTS, MAKES SURE SHE DOESN'T CROSS MRS. T. HAS A PART-TIME OFFICE JOB.

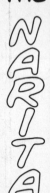

父母

HIKARU, 4 (YOUNGER BROTHER)

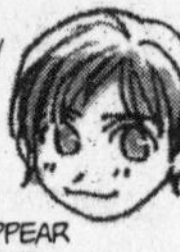

- KINDERGARTNER WITH ELEMENTARY SCHOOL ENTRANCE EXAMS COMING UP.
- NO CHANCE TO APPEAR IN THE STORY SO FAR.

WOULD BE NICE IF HE DOES LATER!

弟

AKANE, 14 (YOUNGER SISTER)

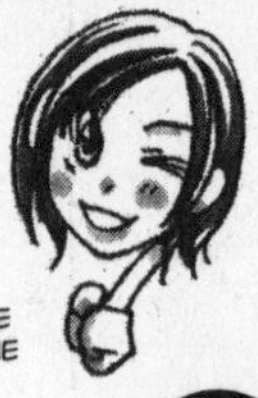

- THIRD-YEAR STUDENT AT LOCAL JUNIOR HIGH (PUBLIC).
- 154 CM TALL, 42 kg. BRA SIZE: C CUP (AND STILL GROWING!)
- TOTAL BABE, KNOWN AS THE NUMBER-ONE HOTTIE IN THE WHOLE COMPLEX. SUPER POPULAR WITH THE BOYS.
- GRADES: XXX (Ds)
- ACTUALLY HAS A CERTAIN COMPLEX TOWARDS HATSUMI, CAUSING A FULL-ON SENSE OF RIVALRY. LEADS HER TO PLAY A TRICK ON HATSUMI.

妹

HATSUMI, 16

- SECOND-YEAR STUDENT AT TAKAZONO HIGH SCHOOL (PRIVATE).
- 158 CM TALL, 46 kg (UP AND DOWN) BRA SIZE: SECRET... (WITH COMMENTS FROM RYOKI IN VOL. 2!)
- UNLUCKY IN LOVE, ONCE IN ELEMENTARY SCHOOL WHEN AZUSA MOVED AWAY, AND A COUPLE OF TIMES LATER. THINKS OF HERSELF AS UNATTRACTIVE.
- CRAZY ABOUT SHINOGU, WITH WHOM SHE'S BEEN REAL CLOSE SINCE SHE WAS LITTLE.

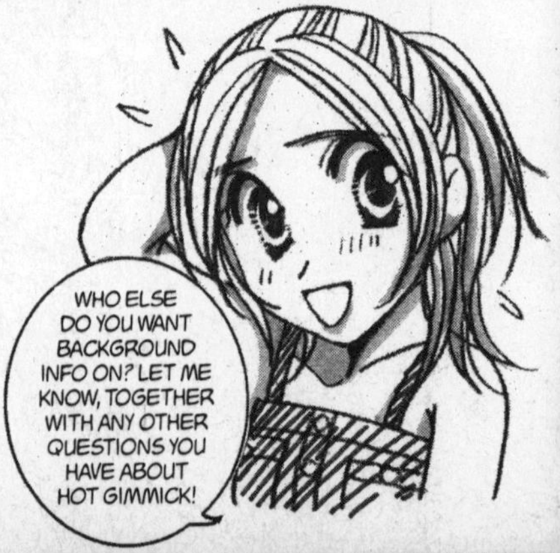
WHO ELSE DO YOU WANT BACKGROUND INFO ON? LET ME KNOW, TOGETHER WITH ANY OTHER QUESTIONS YOU HAVE ABOUT HOT GIMMICK!

And that's all the Extra!

HOT GIMMICK
Vol. 1

Shôjo Edition

STORY & ART BY MIKI AIHARA

ENGLISH ADAPTATION BY POOKIE ROLF

Touch-Up Art & Lettering/Rina Mapa
Design/Izumi Evers
Editorial Director/Alvin Lu

Managing Editor/Annette Roman
SR. Director of Licensing and Acquisitions/Rika Inouye
V.P. of Sales and Marketing/Liza Coppola
Executive V.P. of Editorial/Hyoe Narita
Publisher/Seiji Horibuchi

Printed in Canada

Published by VIZ, LLC, P.O. Box 77010, San Francisco,
CA 94107

Shôjo Edition
10 9 8 7 6 5 4 3
First printing, October 2003
Second printing, July 2004
Third printing, October 2004

EDITOR'S RECOMMENDATIONS

More manga!
More manga!

If you enjoyed this volume of

Hot Gimmick

then here's some more manga you might be interested in.

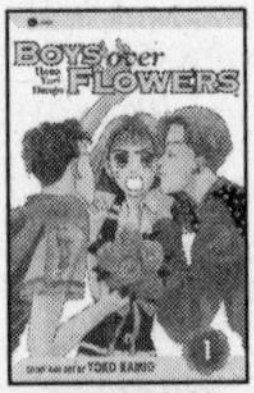

*"HANA-YORI DANGO" ©
1992 by Yoko
Kamio/SHUEISHA Inc.*

Boys over Flowers by Yoko Kamio: Meet Makino and Makiko Yuki—cute, popular high school girls whose lives take a turn for the worse when a gang of rich boys makes the whole school pick on them....

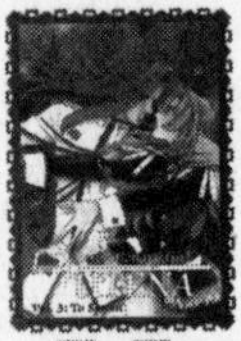

*© 1996 SAITO
CHIHO/IKUHARA KUNI-
HIKO & BE
PAPAS/SHUEISHA Inc.*

Revolutionary Girl Utena by Chiho Saito: After being saved by a prince, Utena strives to grow up strong and noble—just like him! Now she's ready to revolutionize the world, if only it will lead her to her prince!

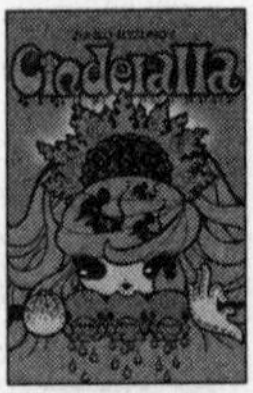

© Junko Mizuno 2000

Junko Mizuno's Cinderalla by Junko Mizuno: The classic fairy tale re-told in psychedelic colors and where Prince Charming is a... zombie?!

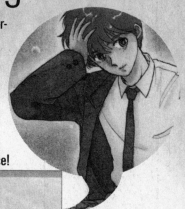

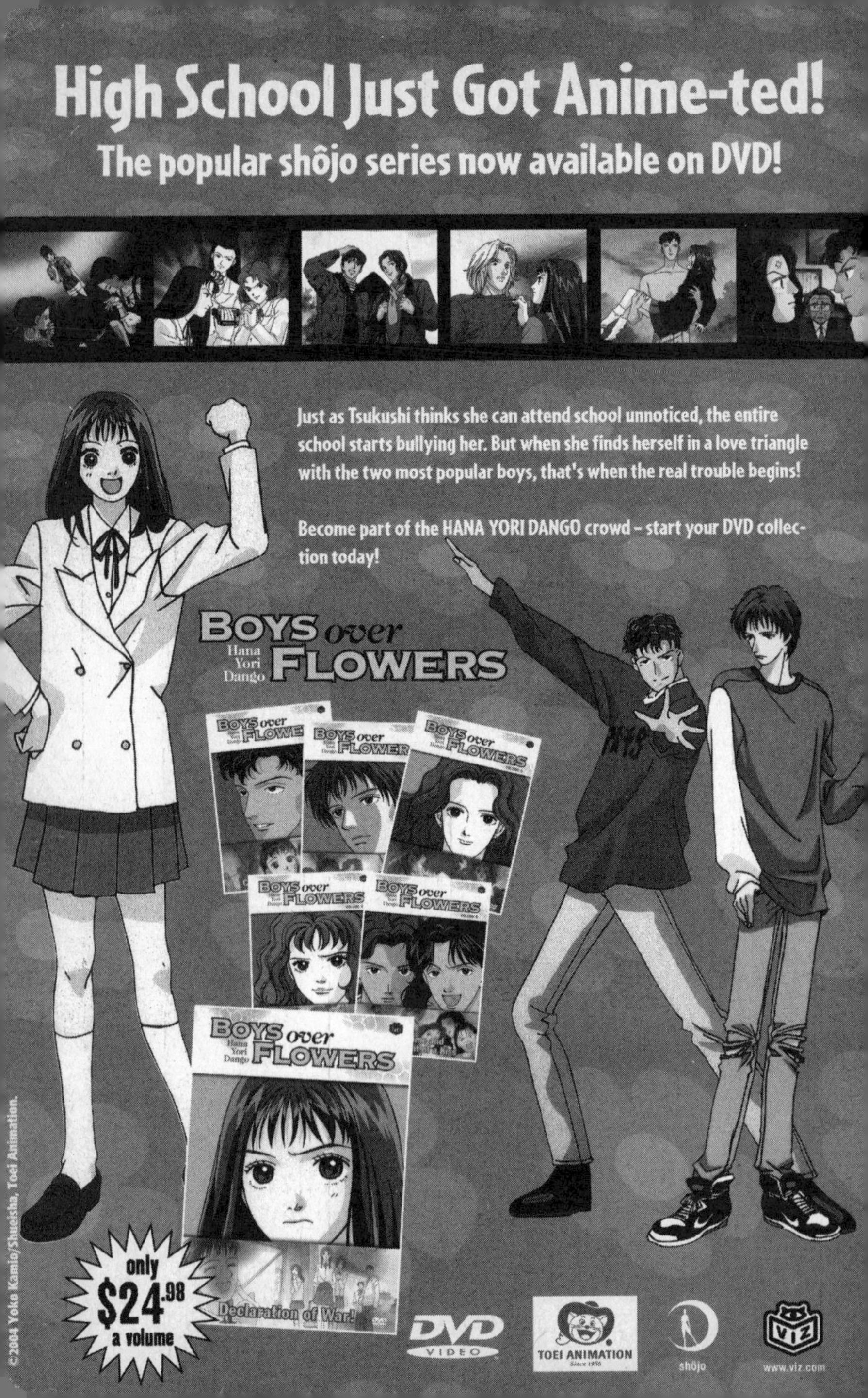
High School Just Got Anime-ted!
The popular shôjo series now available on DVD!
Just as Tsukushi thinks she can attend school unnoticed, the entire school starts bullying her. But when she finds herself in a love triangle with the two most popular boys, that's when the real trouble begins!
Become part of the HANA YORI DANGO crowd – start your DVD collection today!
BOYS over FLOWERS
Hana Yori Dango
Declaration of War!
only $24.98 a volume
DVD VIDEO
TOEI ANIMATION
shôjo
www.viz.com
©2004 Yoko Kamio/Shueisha, Toei Animation.

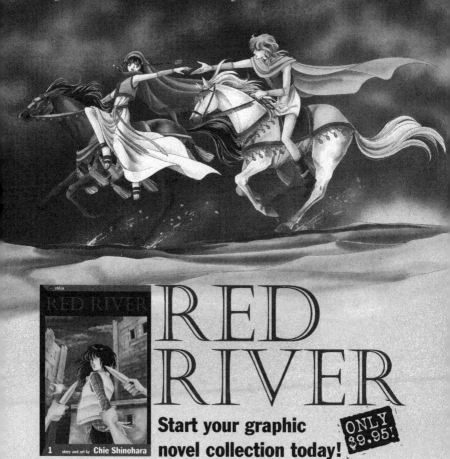

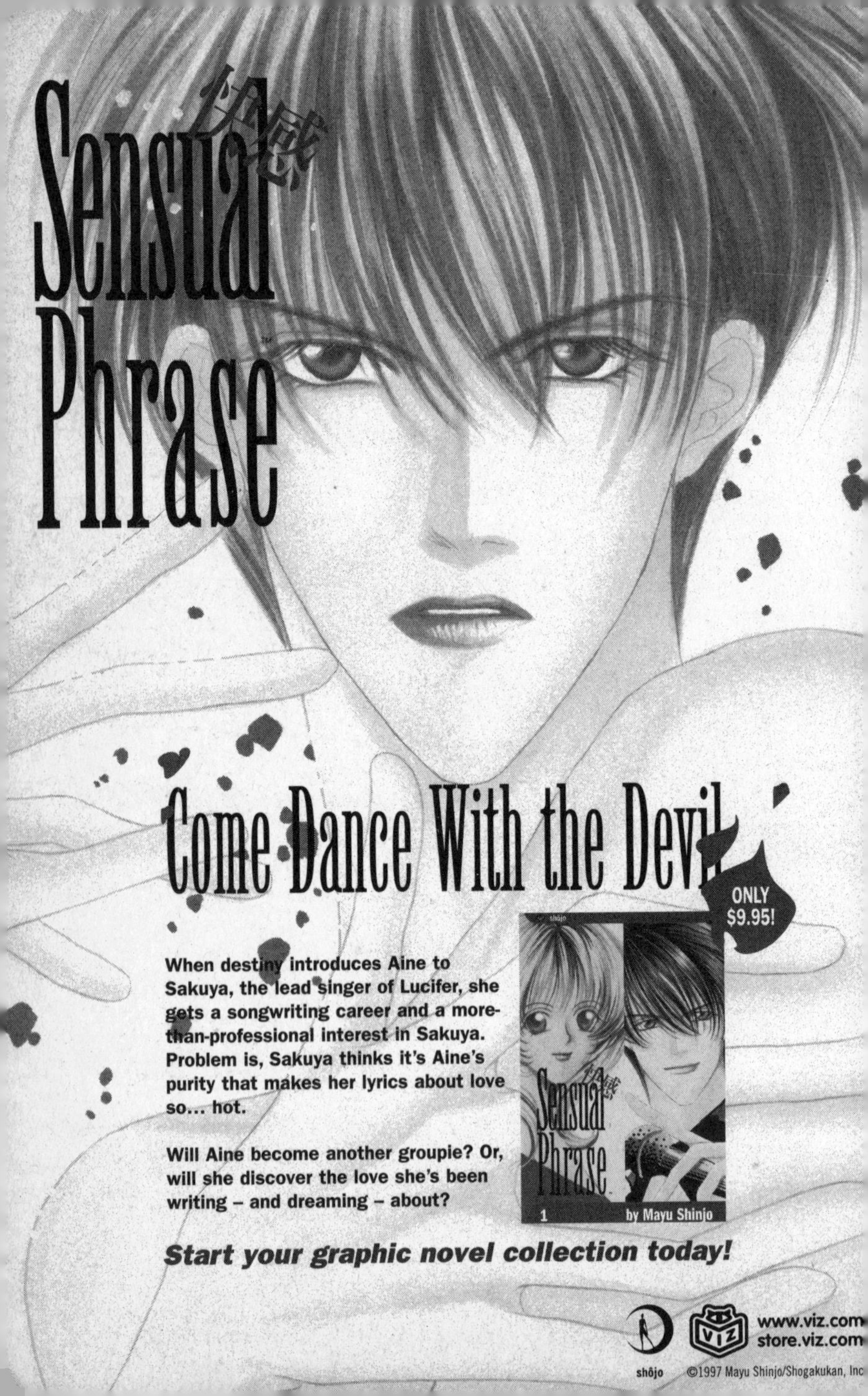

快感
Sensual Phrase™
Come Dance With the Devil
ONLY $9.95!
shōjo
快感
Sensual Phrase
1
by Mayu Shinjo
When destiny introduces Aine to Sakuya, the lead singer of Lucifer, she gets a songwriting career and a more-than-professional interest in Sakuya. Problem is, Sakuya thinks it's Aine's purity that makes her lyrics about love so... hot.
Will Aine become another groupie? Or, will she discover the love she's been writing – and dreaming – about?
Start your graphic novel collection today!
shôjo
VIZ
www.viz.com
store.viz.com
©1997 Mayu Shinjo/Shogakukan, Inc

shôjo

AT THE HEART OF THE MATTER

- Alice 19th
- Angel Sanctuary
- Banana Fish
- Basara
- B.B. Explosion
- Boys Over Flowers *
- Ceres, Celestial Legend *
- Descendants of Darkness
- Dolls
- From Far Away
- Fushigi Yûgi
- Hana-Kimi
- Here Is Greenwood
- Hot Gimmick
- Imadoki
- Kare First Love
- Please Save My Earth *
- Red River
- Revolutionary Girl Utena
- Sensual Phrase
- W Juliet
- Wedding Peach
- Wild Com.
- X/1999

Start Your Shôjo Graphic Novel Collection Today!

FRESH FROM JAPAN 日本最新

VIZ

www.viz.com

STARTING @ $9.95!

*Also available on DVD from VIZ

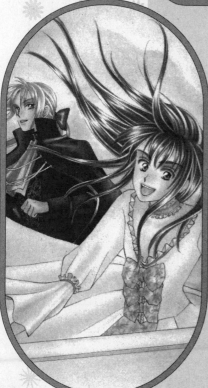

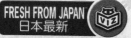